Integrating Income Maintenance Programs

**Institute for Research on Poverty
Monograph Series**

Integrating Income Maintenance Programs

Edited by

Irene Lurie

Department of Economics
Union College
Schenectady, New York
and
Institute for Research on Poverty
University of Wisconsin–Madison
Madison, Wisconsin

ACADEMIC PRESS   New York   San Francisco   London

A Subsidiary of Harcourt Brace Jovanovich, Publishers

This book is one of a series sponsored by the Institute for Research on Poverty of the University of Wisconsin pursuant to the provisions of the Economic Opportunity Act of 1964.

Academic Press, Inc.
111 Fifth Avenue, New York, New York 10003

United Kingdom Edition published by
Academic Press, Inc. (London) Ltd.
24/28 Oval Road, London NW1

Library of Congress Cataloging in Publication Data

Main entry under title:

Integrating income maintenance programs.

  (Institute for Research Poverty monograph series)
  Includes bibliographical references and index.
  1. Guaranteed annual income—United States—Congresses.   I. Lurie, Irene.   II. Series: Wisconsin. University—Madison.   Institute for Research on Poverty.   Monograph series.
HC110.15157 1975   362.5   74-30813
ISBN 0-12-460450-1

Printed in the United States of America

The Institute for Research on Poverty is a national center for research established at the University of Wisconsin in 1966 by a grant from the Office of Economic Opportunity. Its primary objective is to foster basic, multidisciplinary research into the nature and causes of poverty and means to combat it.

In addition to increasing the basic knowledge from which policies aimed at the elimination of poverty can be shaped, the Institute strives to carry analysis beyond the formulation and testing of fundamental generalizations to the development and assessment of relevant policy alternatives.

The Institute endeavors to bring together scholars of the highest caliber whose primary research efforts are focused on the problem of poverty, the distribution of income, and the analysis and evaluation of social policy, offering staff members wide opportunity for interchange of ideas, maximum freedom for research into basic questions about poverty and social policy, and dissemination of their findings.

Contents

Contents

List of Contributors and Conference Participants

Asterisks denote contributors to this volume. Numbers in parentheses indicate the pages on which the authors' contributions begin.

*Henry J. Aaron, Brookings Institution, Washington, D.C. (161)

John Akin, Department of Economics, University of North Carolina, Chapel Hill, North Carolina

Orley C. Ashenfelter, Industrial Relations Section, Princeton University, Princeton, New Jersey

D. Lee Bawden, Institute for Research on Poverty and Departments of Economics and Agricultural Economics, University of Wisconsin—Madison, Madison, Wisconsin

Adele Blong, Center on Social Welfare Policy and Law, Columbia University, New York, New York

Glen G. Cain, Institute for Research on Poverty and Department of Economics, University of Wisconsin—Madison, Madison, Wisconsin

Irene Cox, Subcommittee on Fiscal Policy, Joint Economic Committee of Congress, Washington, D.C.

Irwin Garfinkel, Institute for Research on Poverty and School of Social Work, University of Wisconsin—Madison, Madison, Wisconsin

Jon H. Goldstein, Subcommittee on Fiscal Policy, Joint Economic Committee of Congress, Washington, D.C.

Martha W. Griffiths, Representative from Michigan, Congress of the United States, Washington, D.C.

Joel F. Handler, Institute for Research on Poverty and School of Law, University of Wisconsin–Madison, Madison, Wisconsin

* *Leonard J. Hausman*, Florence Heller Graduate School for Advanced Studies in Social Welfare, Brandeis University, Waltham, Massachusetts (39)

* *Robert H. Haveman*, Institute for Research on Poverty and Department of Economics, University of Wisconsin–Madison, Madison, Wisconsin (109)

W. Joseph Heffernan, Institute for Research on Poverty and School of Social Work, University of Wisconsin–Madison, Madison, Wisconsin

Richard E. Hegner, New York State Division of the Budget, Albany, New York

Stephen J. Herzberg, School of Law, University of Wisconsin–Madison, Madison, Wisconsin

Hirschel Kasper, Department of Economics, Oberlin College, Oberlin, Ohio

* *Michael Krashinsky*, Department of Economics, Scarborough College, University of Toronto, Toronto, Ontario, Canada (289)

Robert J. Lampman, Institute for Research on Poverty and Department of Economics, University of Wisconsin–Madison, Madison, Wisconsin

Robert I. Lerman, Subcommittee on Fiscal Policy, Joint Economic Committee of Congress, Washington, D.C.

Russell Lidman, Office of Assistant Secretary for Planning and Evaluation/Income Security Policy, Department of Health, Education, and Welfare, Washington, D.C.

* *Irene Lurie*, Institute for Research on Poverty, University of Wisconsin –Madison, Madison, Wisconsin; Department of Economics, Union College, Schenectady, New York (1, 335)

James Lyday, Consultant to the Subcommittee on Fiscal Policy, Joint Economic Committee of Congress, Washington, D.C.

* *Theodore R. Marmor*, School of Social Services Administration, University of Chicago, Chicago, Illinois (271)

Nelson D. McClung, Office of Tax Analysis, Department of the Treasury, Washington, D.C.

Peter M. Mieszkowski, Department of Economics, Queen's University, Kingston, Ontario, Canada

* *Thad W. Mirer*, Institute for Research on Poverty, University of Wisconsin–Madison, Madison, Wisconsin; Department of Economics, State University of New York at Albany, Albany, New York (147)

* *Raymond Munts*, Institute for Research on Poverty and School of Social Work, University of Wisconsin–Madison, Madison, Wisconsin (241)

* *Benjamin A. Okner*, Brookings Institution, Washington, D.C. (79)

Larry L. Orr, Office of Income Security Policy/Research, Department of Health, Education, and Welfare, Washington, D.C.

William D. Popkin, School of Law, Indiana University, Bloomington, Indiana

* *Maria Schmundt*, Department of Economics, University of Wisconsin–Madison, Madison, Wisconsin (189)

Gad Shifron, Israel Institute of Technology, Haifa, Israel

Peter Sitkin, Hastings College of Law, University of California, San Francisco, California

* *Eugene Smolensky*, Institute for Research on Poverty and Department of Economics, University of Wisconsin–Madison, Madison, Wisconsin (189)

* *Leanna Stiefel*, Department of Economics, Michigan State University, East Lansing, Michigan (189)

James R. Storey, Subcommittee on Fiscal Policy, Joint Economic Committee of Congress, Washington, D.C.

* *Michael K. Taussig*, Department of Economics, Rutgers College, Rutgers–The State University, New Brunswick, New Jersey (209)

Alair A. Townsend, Subcommittee on Fiscal Policy, Joint Economic Committee of Congress, Washington, D.C.

Harold W. Watts, Institute for Research on Poverty and Department of Economics, University of Wisconsin–Madison, Madison, Wisconsin

Burton A. Weisbrod, Institute for Research on Poverty and Department of Economics, University of Wisconsin–Madison, Madison, Wisconsin

Foreword

From the very beginning of the nation's efforts to provide income support to needy citizens in the 1930s, programs have been designed for certain, well-defined categories of people. The aged, the disabled, the blind, those with dependent children, the unemployed, veterans—all of these groups have been covered by programs providing cash or services. When these programs were small in number and in size, the fact that they were categorical and uncoordinated caused few serious problems. Calls for reform that would have integrated the system were based more on a desire to include groups of needy then ineligible for support—for example, the "working poor"—than on a desire for integration per se.

During the late 1960s and early 1970s, these categorical programs grew in coverage, in benefit levels, and in number. While federal expenditures on these cash and in-kind programs totaled about $22 billion in 1960, they had risen to more than $98 billion by 1973. As a result of this growth, serious problems developed. Because some poor families became eligible for benefits from several programs, while others continued to fall through the cracks, the problem of horizontal inequity became serious. This was accentuated by the fact that the benefit levels and eligibility criteria of some programs were determined by individual states, resulting in sizable geographic differentials in levels of support. Because the benefits of many of these programs were income conditioned, participation in several programs resulted in very high implicit tax rates on earned income—a troublesome work disincentive. In addition, these programs contained serious discrepancies in fundamental definitions of eligibility, income, and accounting period. Moreover, programs were administered by many separate agencies. As a result, the set of income support programs became complex and confusing to potential participants and administratively unmanageable by the public sector. It remains that way today.

In the early 1970s, as a significant broadening of the system was debated in Congress, this integration problem came to be widely recognized by students of federal income maintenance policy. However, while the existence of the problem was recognized, little was known about either its dimensions or the alternative instruments for its solution. In conversations between staff members of the Institute for Research on Poverty and those of the Subcommittee on Fiscal Policy of the Joint Economic Committee of the Congress (which was embarking on a major study of the welfare system), it was suggested that a coordinated set of studies focusing on both the nature of the problem and the alternative approaches to its correction would serve important research and policy objectives. In response, the Institute, with Committee support, arranged a set of studies by its staff and other scholars dealing with these issues. In the summer of 1972, a conference was held in Madison to discuss these papers and the possibilities for reform that were implicit in them. About 30 people attended that conference, including the then Chairman of the Subcommittee on Fiscal Policy (Representative Martha Griffiths), members of the staff of the Institute and of the Subcommittee, members of the planning staffs of the executive branch agencies, and other students of federal income maintenance policy.

This volume is the result of that conference. The chapters it contains are revised and extended versions of papers presented at the conference. Taken together, they provide a comprehensive view of the many facets of the integration problem and of the difficulties of alternative means of resolving it. They will serve as a basic reference and guide to the nation's income support system and will be fundamental to any policy effort to reform and rationalize that system. Many of these chapters have appeared in somewhat different form in the Subcommittee's series *Studies in Public Welfare.*

Both the conference and this volume were organized by Irene Lurie, a member of the Institute staff and an Assistant Professor of Economics at Union College. She acknowledges the help of several members of the staff of the Institute for Research on Poverty in organizing the conference and commenting on drafts of these papers: Joel Handler, Robert Haveman, Joseph Heffernan, Robert Lampman, Theodore Marmor, and Raymond

Munts. Also, the contribution of the staff members of the Subcommittee who participated in the conference is appreciated. They include Alair Townsend, the Technical Director of the Subcommittee study; Irene Cox; Jon Goldstein; Robert Lerman; and James Storey. Richard Hegner was of great assistance in recording and summarizing the conference discussion, and Alice Hersh and Beverly Neupert smoothly handled the administrative details of the conference. Ann Jacobs edited the manuscript and Marjean Jondrow supervised its preparation for publication. Financial support to the Institute for Research on Poverty is provided by the Office of Economic Opportunity pursuant to the provisions of the Economic Opportunity Act of 1964.

Robert H. Haveman
DIRECTOR
Institute for Research on Poverty

1

Integrating Income Maintenance Programs: Problems and Solutions

Irene Lurie

The income maintenance system in the United States has evolved gradually, shaped over the years by perceptions both of individuals' needs for income and of the best means for satisfying these needs. As the standard of living has risen and the values of society have changed, perceptions of the amount of income people need and the circumstances under which inadequate income makes them deserving of government assistance have been altered. Parallel changes have occurred in the means used to raise incomes to more adequate levels. With changes in the perceived needs of the population, new types of programs have been developed to satisfy these needs.

Because of the varying perceptions, values, and purposes that have shaped the programs, the income maintenance system today is a crazy quilt of enormous complexity. Each program has its own eligibility rules, benefit structure, administration, and method of financing. Many programs involve more than one level of government and more than one agency at each level. Because each program was developed without careful regard to the other programs, the programs overlap in coverage, leave gaps in coverage, and often work at cross-purposes with each other

The recent growth in both the number of people receiving benefits from the income maintenance system and the cost of the system has

1

created pressures to correct these problems. Pressures to change the system also arise from new perceptions of individuals' needs and of ways to satisfy these needs. Demands are now made that the system be extended to the "working poor," that day care be provided to working mothers, that medical care be subsidized, that jobs be provided for all who want them, and that many other changes and additions be made.

If all these pressures to reform the system pointed to a single solution, to a single program or set of programs that would satisfy all the demands for changing the system, the reforms would long since have been made. But little agreement can be reached on what is "wrong" with the system, much less on what should be done to repair it. Criticisms of income maintenance programs depend as much on values as on technical analyses, and values are far from uniform in our heterogeneous society.

This wide range of opinion was no better reflected than in the congressional debate over the Nixon administration's welfare reform proposals. Known as the "Family Assistance Plan" when it was proposed in the summer of 1969, versions of it were passed by the House as H.R. 16311 of the Ninety-first Congress and as H.R. 1 of the Ninety-second. But the revisions proposed by members of the Senate were so diverse, and reflected such fundamentally different approaches toward income maintenance, that compromise was impossible.

In 1971, as the Nixon administration's welfare proposals floundered, the Subcommittee on Fiscal Policy of the Joint Economic Committee began a major study of the income maintenance system. The study was timely, given that the proposals before the Congress—embodied then as H.R. 1—were likely to fail. Failure would require a reexamination of the system and a search for new approaches to reform. Equally important was the growing recognition that, even if H.R. 1 were passed, reform of the income maintenance system would continue to be an issue. Dissatisfaction with programs untouched by H.R. 1 and pressure for the introduction of new programs, particularly day care and health insurance, meant that income maintenance legislation would be before Congress long after the success or failure of H.R. 1.

The subcommittee's study was designed to provide a picture of the operation of income maintenance programs as a single system. Rather than focus on the operation of individual programs in isolation, the study would examine how programs interact with each other in providing benefits to the low-income population. Features of programs that appear reasonable when examined in isolation often take on a different cast when examined in the light of other programs. Only by taking a broad perspective can the interdependence of the features of individual programs be understood and can the impact of the entire "nonsystem," to use the word of Subcommittee Chairman Martha Griffiths, be evaluated. This broad perspective must be the basis for reforming existing programs and developing new ones.

The subcommittee staff, in the planning stage of its study, met with the staff of the Institute for Research on Poverty to discuss its research plans and to determine if and how the institute could take an active part in the study. The wide range of expertise of the institute staff and their ability to work together as a group were well-suited to the broad perspective adopted by the subcommittee's study. This compatibility encouraged the institute to participate in the study and led it to focus its attention on an issue that requires such a group of experts working together: the problem of integrating income maintenance programs.

Integrating programs requires reforming existing programs and designing new ones so that they function together as an equitable and efficient system. Integration is the process of designing programs and the linkages among programs with a view to the impact of the system as a whole. The expected product of the institute's project was not a legislative package but an understanding of the interactions among programs and of the techniques for linking them. The ultimate objective is, of course, to help policymakers as they design programs.

A loose structure was established to organize the project and to provoke thought on the problems of program integration. Three alternative basic cash programs were postulated: H.R. 1 as passed by the House of the Ninety-second Congress, the version of H.R. 1 developed by the Senate Finance Committee, and a demogrant that would make payments to all persons regardless of income. Staff members of the institute and several experts from other institutions then designed new programs and reformed existing ones around these three alternatives, focusing attention on the interactions among the programs. Papers were presented at a conference held at the institute on July 1–7, 1972, attended also by the staff and the chairman of the Subcommittee on Fiscal Policy. The papers were then revised, some of them quite extensively, in light of the conference discussion and the other papers.

The need for integrating income maintenance programs is described in the first section of this chapter. The second section presents some of the approaches to integrating programs and the framework that was imposed to focus the conference discussion. The third section summarizes those portions of the discussion that dealt with the more technical problems encountered in designing a well-integrated system. Some of the lessons to be learned from the conference are presented in the final section.

I. The Need for Integrating Income Maintenance Programs

It is ironic that a conference on the integration of income maintenance programs should begin on the same day, July 1, 1972, that the so-called "Talmadge Amendment" (Public Law 92–223) became effective. The amendment, which requires that adult recipients of Aid to Families with Dependent Children (AFDC) register for work and training with the Department of Labor, is a manifestation of congressional dissatisfaction with the AFDC program. The dissatisfaction prompting the amendment concerned the low rate of employment among AFDC mothers. The solution was a new administrative regulation designed to require work effort, without any change in the incentives to work built into the program's benefit structure. This concern with the effect of income maintenance programs on the incentive to work also stimulated the conference. But a concern with the inequities and inadequacies of the current system was an equally important motivation. Therefore, rather than solving these problems solely by administrative regulations like the Talmadge Amendment, which are often both inequitable and punitive, the conference searched for alternative methods that would produce a more equitable system.

Each participant came to the conference with his own notion of what it means to "integrate" programs and what problems can be solved by integrating them. A list of the problems that participants felt could be ameliorated through integration constitutes almost a catalog of the ills of the income maintenance system. But a distinction can be made between inadequacies that result from low cash benefit levels and from a lack of in-kind programs with specific objectives, and between inequities and inefficiencies that result from the combined impact of the programs in the system. The focus of the conference was on the inequities and inefficiencies caused by three features of the current system: the multiplicity of programs, the high cumulative tax rate that is produced by them, and their pattern of coverage of the poor population.

The Multiplicity of Income Maintenance Programs

The sheer number of income maintenance programs is evidence of the need for some sort of integration. The process of determining families' resources and their need for transfers is duplicated by each program, resulting in a system with high administrative costs. Administrators and recipients alike are confused and hindered by voluminous rules governing eligibility and payments under the multiplicity of programs. The likelihood of inequities and adverse incentives on behavior, discussed later, greatly increases as the number of programs grows.

There is no consensus about the exact definition of an income maintenance program, as distinct from other programs that influence the distribution of income. To keep the discussion manageable, the conference was restricted to those government programs that provide cash or in-kind goods and services to families or individuals with the objective of raising their incomes or preventing their incomes from falling. This excludes "tax transfers," which increase families' disposable income by reducing their tax liability, and legal restrictions, such as the minimum wage, which affect their pre-tax earnings. Private programs such as fringe benefits and interfamily transfers also were not analyzed explicitly, although they did, of course, enter the discussion from time to time. Using this definition, it is possible to count more than 100 income maintenance programs.[1]

The greatest share of both expenditures and recipients is accounted for by the social insurance programs. These programs, such as Old Age, Survivors, Disability, and Health Insurance (OASDHI) and Unemployment Insurance (UI), are designed to prevent individuals' or families' incomes from falling following events that are accompanied by a decrease in earning power. These socially insured risks include retirement, death of the breadwinner, injury or illness, and unemployment; coverage depends on prior attachment to the labor force. The other large category of programs are those designed to raise the incomes of the poor, such as AFDC and the new Supplemental Security Income (SSI) program, Medicaid, public housing, and Food Stamps. Benefits under these programs are based on current need, not on past labor force experience. The social insurance programs, with the exception of Medicare, provide aid in the form of cash payments. Some of the needs-based programs provide cash, but many give in-kind benefits in the form of food, medical care, or housing.

Each program has its own specific objective and its own rules concerning eligibility, benefit schedules, and administrative procedures. But the objectives of many of the programs are quite similar, particularly those providing cash payments with the objective of raising the incomes of the poor. To the extent that they are similar, they could be consoli-

---

[1] The Subcommittee on Fiscal Policy identified 100 programs, without claiming to be inclusive. A list is contained in James R. Storey, Irene Cox, and Alair A. Townsend, "How Public Welfare Benefits Are Distributed in Low-Income Areas," in *Studies in Public Welfare*, Paper No. 6. U.S., Congress, Joint Economic Committee, Subcommittee on Fiscal Policy, 26 March 1973.

dated or replaced by a single program. Substituting one new program for several existing programs with similar objectives would reduce the administrative complexity and the administrative cost of the system. Perhaps even more importantly, a new comprehensive program or set of programs, if designed properly, could reduce or eliminate many of the other undesirable features of the income maintenance system. These features include the adverse effects on behavioral incentives, such as the incentives to work, save, migrate, form families, and have children; the gaps and overlaps in coverage; the wide variation in benefits given to families with the same need; and other inequities and inefficiencies that are discussed in detail later.

While virtually all conference participants agreed that reducing the number of programs was a crucial step in designing a well-integrated system, they did not agree on how many programs were necessary. Some came close to the polar position of recommending one comprehensive program that would replace all others. A negative income tax or universal demogrant, for example, could provide a floor under the incomes of all families and, if the level of benefits were high enough, bring all families' money incomes up to the poverty line. The vision of a program that would eliminate poverty simply and equitably was appealing to virtually everyone. But with the response of the public to Senator McGovern's proposal for a demogrant fresh in everyone's memory, a comprehensive and adequate program did not appear to be the most politically viable alternative.

Furthermore, although many participants favored a comprehensive program, several objections were raised to any income maintenance system that consists entirely of a cash program providing payments based solely on current money income. First, while the objectives of many of the programs are similar, the objectives of others are unique. The social insurance programs are designed both to replace the former incomes of insured workers and to guarantee a floor under their income. A health insurance program of some sort is necessary even when everyone has an adequate cash income, since the cost of a serious illness or injury can put a large strain on anyone's income. Unusual demands on income are the rationale behind not only the health insurance programs but also Workmen's Compensation, Veterans' Disability payments, and, to some extent, day care subsidies and programs giving cash to the blind and disabled. Adequate cash income may be insufficient to guarantee an adequate real income if the market fails to produce the desired goods and services. Compensating for market failure is an argument advanced for government intervention in the supply of housing, education, day care, and medical care. Such intervention, it is argued, is required to compensate for externalities in the market for housing, imperfect information in the markets for education and day care, and monopoly power in the provision of medical services. Adequate cash income will not guarantee that low-income people will choose the consumption pattern considered to be proper by the rest of society. Health programs, food programs, education, and social services are justified, at least in part, on these grounds.

These numerous objectives, which the income maintenance system is expected to serve, and the political support behind each of them made most participants recognize that a new comprehensive single cash program would not meet all the demands placed on the system. Even if there were no political constraints on reforming the system, it would probably continue to consist of many programs, although, hopefully, fewer than exist today. Devising ways to integrate them into a more rational whole therefore remains a necessary task.

High Cumulative Tax Rates

Perhaps the most serious single problem created by a multiplicity of programs is the reduction in the financial rewards from work effort which results from the high tax rate on earnings. Income maintenance programs are, by their very nature, designed to redistribute income from richer families to poorer ones. Their redistributive effects are obvious in programs such as AFDC and the SSI program, whose benefits decline in value as families' incomes increase. They are less obvious in programs where all families are eligible and all receive the same benefit, such as a universal demogrant or some types of health insurance; in these programs, the redistribution also occurs through the tax system used to finance the program. The combined effect of the benefits and the financing tax is to make net benefits received after taxes decline with income. Because the benefits of programs decline as income increases, or are "taxed" away, the incentive to obtain additional dollars of income is reduced.

The high tax rate on earnings results both from the high tax rates under individual programs, particularly AFDC and the SSI program, and from the fact that some recipients receive benefits under several programs and are subject to several tax rates simultaneously. Even when the rates under individual programs are low, the rate resulting from all programs combined often becomes very high. Leonard Hausman (see Chapter 2) measures the marginal tax rates facing AFDC recipients. (The marginal tax rate is the amount by which net benefits decline as income increases by $1.) He measures both the rates in the AFDC program itself and those in the other programs for which AFDC recipients are eligible. He finds that the cumulative marginal tax rate from all programs combined is very high over some ranges of earnings, so high that recipients obtain no net gain from increasing their earnings within these ranges.

Yet he also finds that cumulative tax rates are quite low over other ranges, lower than many critics of the system would have expected. Furthermore, he shows that new programs that would make the system more adequate and equitable would *increase* the tax rate facing many people. He measures the cumulative tax rates that would result from a negative income tax and from a demogrant, each combined with medical insurance, public housing, and a day care program. The tax rates of the cash programs are relatively low: 50 percent in the negative income tax and $33\frac{1}{3}$ percent under the demogrant. But when the in-kind programs are taken into account, the cumulative tax rate under the negative income tax would rise as high as 86 percent, and that under the demogrant would reach 62 percent.

Hausman's exercise in designing a package of programs reveals a relationship between their tax rates that has important implications for policymakers. He finds that the cumulative tax rate is not extremely sensitive to his assumptions about the tax rates of the individual programs. Raising or lowering the tax rate of the negative income tax or the demogrant would not change the cumulative tax rate by an equal number of percentage points. This occurs because the benefits of the in-kind programs depend on the benefits of the cash program, with the result that the cumulative tax rate is less than the sum of the tax rates of the individual programs. (The relationships among programs that are "sequenced" in this way are described in detail by Thad Mirer in Chapter 5.) Therefore, the relatively high tax rates that Hausman finds cannot be attributed to the precise choice of the tax rates used by each program. While very low tax rates in each program would, of course, result in lower cumulative tax rates, relatively small variations in tax rates will not change the cumulative tax rate significantly. It is here that one begins to appreciate the difficulty of designing an income maintenance system that will be a clear improvement over the existing one.

Although the cumulative tax rates resulting from a demogrant or negative income tax would be lower than those now facing many AFDC recipients, the cumulative rates could potentially have a much more negative impact on work incentives. AFDC is restricted primarily to women with children, people who are not expected to be primary breadwinners. A negative income tax or demogrant, in contrast, would be extended to the entire population. Prime-age males, the core of the labor force, would be exposed to tax rates far higher than those they now face.

A reduction in work effort by this group could result in a significant drop in the total output of the economy, as well as a change in values and life-styles. The potential increase in the tax rate facing prime-age males explains much of the resistance, by Congress and other groups, to an adequate and equitable income maintenance system.

Efforts to institute a comprehensive cash program and programs to satisfy demands for adequate health insurance, housing, day care, and so forth are therefore on a collision course with efforts to maintain the incentive to work. If these programs are enacted, the value of the benefits provided to families with no income will be quite large. If the incentive for recipients to work is to be maintained, the tax rate on earnings implicit in the benefit structure of the programs must be kept at a relatively low level, which is to say that the benefits of the programs must be reduced gradually as earnings increase. But a low tax rate implies both a large number of eligible families and high budgetary costs. The higher the budgetary costs, of course, the higher the taxes that must be raised to finance them. In short, these programs would have the advantage of being generous to recipients, at the cost of exposing a larger share of the population to the tax rates implicit in the programs and of raising the rates facing taxpayers.

One alternative is to impose high tax rates on recipients to reduce benefits rapidly as income increases, thereby sacrificing their work incentives but maintaining lower tax rates on other groups. If prime-age males are eligible, however, such a solution may not be politically viable. A second alternative is to lower both the value of the benefits provided to families with no income and the tax rates implicit in the programs, thereby maintaining work incentives without raising the budgetary cost of the programs. This means, however, that some of the demands for adequate programs will be sacrificed. Searching for a compromise between the objectives of an adequate set of programs, maintaining the work incentives of recipients, and minimizing budgetary costs absorbed a good deal of the energy of the conference. It is, in many ways, the central conflict to be resolved in designing an income maintenance system.

Gaps and Overlaps in Coverage

As was pointed out earlier, the income maintenance system evolved gradually, changing in response to changing values and perceptions concerning the needs of low-income people. The programs have been tailored to specific causes of low income: old age, unemployment, disability, illness and injury, lack of a primary breadwinner, and other specific factors that are likely to impair earning capacity. The result is a large number of categorical programs, each with its own objective and each designed to serve a well-defined population.

Viewed in historical perspective, the pattern of coverage is understandable. But when these programs are viewed solely in terms of their impact on low-income people, regardless of why their incomes are low, the pattern of coverage appears arbitrary and highly inequitable. People with certain characteristics are eligible for the benefits of many programs, while other people, with the same income and need, are ineligible for any program. Those eligible for many programs face administrative hassles, high tax rates, and restrictions that the in-kind programs impose on their expenditure patterns. Those ineligible for programs face the temptation to change their status in order to become eligible for support by having children, deserting their families, retiring, feigning disability, migrating to states with more generous programs, and so forth.

The pattern of coverage is made extremely complex by the large number of criteria that are used to determine eligibility. The age and sex of the household head, the type of family, the presence of children and whether or not they are in school, the amount and source of the household members' income, the amount and type of their assets, their employment history and current employment status, their veteran status, their health, their location, their housing arrangements, and a variety of other less important factors determine eligibility for various programs. Furthermore, the definitions of the various factors on which eligibility depends vary from one program to another. The definition of the family unit, income, assets, disability, and full- and part-time employment, to mention the most important, are unique to each program. The accounting period—the period of time over which income is measured in determining eligibility and payments—varies considerably from one program to another and is an important, although often ignored, factor in determining eligibility. The eligibility criteria of a given program vary greatly when the program is operated by the states, as does the administration of the criteria.

A MEASURE OF OVERLAPPING COVERAGE

The degree of overlapping coverage and of gaps in coverage cannot be ascertained easily. Neither the operating data of the various programs nor the data collected by the Bureau of the Census are sufficient to estimate accurately how many people satisfy these complex eligibility requirements. Due to the inadequacies of the existing data, the Subcommittee on Fiscal Policy undertook a special study to measure the extent of the overlaps in coverage.[2] Samples of households in six low-income areas of the country were taken, and the number of different income maintenance benefits received by each household was counted. Of the households sampled, 60 percent received benefits under at least one program, a result that is not surprising, considering that the samples were taken in low-income areas. What is surprising is the number of households that received benefits under more than one program. Of households receiving benefits, 66 percent received benefits from two or more programs, 43 percent received benefits from three or more programs, 29 percent benefited from four or more, and 19 percent benefited from five or more. One household, a three-generation family of five, received benefits from eleven programs, valued at a total of $691 per month.

Programs with the greatest degree of overlapping coverage are those designed for the aged and for families with children, particularly those families headed by women. Some of the overlap occurs because programs are designed with different objectives. For example, Old Age Insurance is designed to provide the aged with cash income, Medicare to finance their medical care, and housing assistance to provide an adequate level of housing. Female-headed families with children receive cash to compensate for the absence of a male breadwinner, and children in any type of family are eligible for a variety of in-kind programs to guarantee that they receive food and services that their parents might not purchase if they were given cash alone: child health services, school lunches, education programs, foster care, and so forth. Each has a unique objective, resulting in its creation as a separate program.

However, some overlap occurs because programs perform similar functions. Both Old Age Insurance and the new Supplemental Security Income program are designed to provide a floor under the income of the aged; both Medicare and Medicaid finance medical care for the aged; both Survivors Insurance and AFDC are designed to help widows with children; and both Unemployment Insurance and AFDC help unemployed fathers. Most important, many of the in-kind programs designed to guarantee that people, particularly children, receive adequate amounts of certain goods and services also serve an income support function similar to the cash programs. That is, to the extent that the in-kind programs provide goods and services that the family would have bought if it were given cash, they are equivalent to cash grants.

The large number of benefits received by households with the "right" sets of characteristics makes the gaps in coverage appear all the more inequitable. Households are least likely to be eligible for any pro-

[2] Storey, Cox, and Townsend, "Public Welfare Benefits."

gram if they are headed by a non-aged male. If the male head is unemployed, Unemployment Insurance or AFDC may be available, but full-time employment excludes men from both programs, regardless of their need. Not only are households headed by a non-aged male less likely to receive benefits but, as found by the subcommittee's study, they are less likely to receive their benefits in the form of cash. Furthermore, some of the in-kind programs for which they are eligible—public housing and manpower training programs—have waiting lists, so that eligibility does not guarantee that the programs' benefits will actually be available to them. The denial of benefits to a large segment of the "working poor" is one of the most inequitable features of the current system and a major stimulus for reform.

INTERACTIONS AMONG PROGRAMS

When a household is eligible or potentially eligible for the benefits of more than one program, the interaction among the programs becomes a crucial element in their ultimate impact. Interaction is inevitable, regardless of whether programs explicitly recognize each other or operate in nominal isolation. However, failure to consider these interactions adequately when designing the individual programs has created a wide variety of problems for the current system. These problems have become more serious and obvious as the number and size of the programs have increased.

One set of problems is that the benefit structure of one program can defeat some of the objectives of another program. For example, the tax rate on earnings in the AFDC program is kept below 100 percent for the purpose of maintaining recipients' incentive to work. The cost of keeping the tax rate below 100 percent is considerable, for it vastly increases the number of eligible families and the payments made to families that have income. However, if AFDC recipients receive benefits from other earnings-conditioned programs, as many of them do, the cumulative tax rate they face is far higher than the tax rate implicit in AFDC. As Hausman points out, the cumulative tax rate can become so high that recipients in some earnings ranges gain virtually nothing by increasing their work effort. The work incentive features of the AFDC benefit structure are thereby negated.

Much of the unearned income of AFDC and SSI recipients is taxed at 100 percent, indicating that the government is unwilling to incur budgetary costs to encourage recipients to obtain unearned income. The other income-conditioned programs, therefore, do not undermine AFDC or SSI as far as the taxation of unearned income is concerned. But the treatment by AFDC and SSI of unearned income does interfere with some of the purposes of other programs, particularly the two large insurance programs, Social Security and Unemployment Insurance. In calculating benefits under SSI, all but $20 of monthly Social Security benefits must be counted. This means that people who are eligible for both Social Security and the SSI program will have only $20 more in total income each month than people eligible for SSI alone. To some extent, this destroys the insurance component of Social Security, since the Social Security contributions that these people made during their working years do not result in significantly higher transfer incomes during retirement or when disabled than is obtained by people who did not make contributions. All Social Security benefits must be counted in determining AFDC payments; hence, a family receiving Social Security and AFDC may have exactly the same income as one receiving AFDC only.

Unemployment Insurance benefits are also taxed at 100 percent in determining AFDC benefits, so that a person eligible for both obtains no more income than someone eligible only for AFDC. While UI has no value for these people, it may have a negative value for some fathers living in states that choose to extend AFDC to unemployed fathers. Federal law prohibits the states from giving AFDC to unemployed fathers who are receiving, or are eligible to receive, UI. A male-headed family eligible for UI is denied AFDC payments even if the AFDC payments are greater than the UI. For these families, coverage by UI reduces their total income, and the objective of UI—raising the incomes of the unemployed—is to some degree defeated.

Another set of problems that results from the interaction of programs occurs when eligibility for one program is dependent on eligibility for another. For example, AFDC recipients and some SSI recipients are automatically eligible for the Medicaid program. In about half the states, recipients become ineligible for Medicaid when their income rises to the level at which they become ineligible for cash assistance. This creates a severe "notch" in the Medicaid benefit schedule: People lose many dollars worth of medical benefits when they receive the dollar of income that makes them ineligible for cash assistance. This notch is equivalent to a tax rate greater than 100 percent, and it eliminates the incentive to earn more or obtain more unearned income. The remaining states avoid the notch by extending Medicaid eligibility to the "medically needy," people who would be eligible for cash assistance if their incomes were somewhat lower. While the notch is avoided, the cost of the Medicaid program is increased.

Most AFDC recipients are also automatically eligible for Food Stamps. This creates a similar notch in the Food Stamp program in those states where the income level at which a family loses eligibility for AFDC is higher than the level at which Food Stamp benefits are phased out for non-AFDC families. In these states, the requirement that AFDC families remain eligible for stamps means that families lose the stamps as they lose eligibility for AFDC. Hence, families lose substantial amounts of in-kind income, both medical benefits and food, when they leave AFDC.

The value to welfare recipients of these in-kind benefits was demonstrated when Social Security benefits were increased in 1972. The 20 percent increase in Social Security made many people ineligible for Public Assistance, and thereby ineligible for Medicaid and Food Stamps. They complained vehemently that the loss in benefits, particularly Medicaid, was greater than the gain in Social Security, and that the Social Security increase had the paradoxical effect of making them worse off.

II. Alternative Approaches to Integrating Programs

This list of diverse problems—and it is far from exhaustive—has one common thread. All are caused by the interaction among two or more programs, interactions that are not apparent when each program is examined in isolation. The conference participants, charged with the task of "integrating" programs, were asked to focus on these interactions. Rather than prepare a brief that argues the need for a particular program, participants took the need for certain programs as given, and analyzed how they could be designed to fit together so as to avoid the inequities, inadequacies, and adverse effects on work incentives described previously. This necessarily involved examining the assumptions about which programs were needed and which could be altered or eliminated, and raised many issues beyond those relating to program interaction. But the central concern of the conference was the effect of programs in combination and the ways in which they might be designed to operate better as a consistent system.

Taxonomy of Design Alternatives

The search for ways to integrate programs leads down many paths. Some paths follow the contours of the existing programs, and lead to minor changes that result in limited improvement. Others leave the established patterns and search for the key to designing a system that is adequate and equitable and yet preserves the incentives to work. Because their ultimate destination is similar, paths often coincide and are sometimes difficult to distinguish. The range of available alternatives will be outlined here, as a sort of taxonomy of approaches to designing and integrating programs and as a perspective from which to view the approaches taken by the conference. Six approaches are described: substituting a single program for all existing programs; consolidating programs; dividing the population into categories; taxing earnings at a negative rate; insuring against certain risks; and integrating through the definition of income used to determine benefits. These approaches are not mutually exclusive, and elements of several of them could be embodied in a single program or set of programs.

The ultimate in a well-integrated income maintenance system is one that consists of a *single program*. One such program could be a universal demogrant that would make payments to all persons regardless of income, varying perhaps by some demographic characteristic such as age or family size, and that would tax all income at a single rate. All other transfer programs could be eliminated and recipients would be free to spend the payments as they wish. A negative income tax could also be designed with the objective of eliminating all other transfer programs; indeed, this was Milton Friedman's objective in proposing a negative income tax over a decade ago.[3] Little insight into integrating programs is gained by trying to distinguish between a demogrant and a negative income tax. What is important here is that each has been proposed as a substitute for all transfer programs. This would permit the total tax rate on income to remain low, and would create horizontal equity among persons in each income class. Whether or not the program would also be "adequate" would depend on the level of the income guarantee, that is, the payment made to someone with no income.

Consolidating programs with similar objectives is a second method of producing a better integrated system. Consolidation would reduce administrative costs and the inequities created when people in essentially the same situation are treated somewhat differently because they are covered by different programs. For example, health insurance for both the poor and aged could be provided through a single program; medical services programs for veterans, Indians, and low-income people could be combined; manpower and housing programs could each be consolidated, to some extent; veterans' pensions could be integrated with the SSI program; the Railroad Retirement program could be merged with Social Security; and so forth. While consolidating programs according to their objectives would reduce administrative costs and inequities, it would do relatively little to reduce the tax rate on income. Some people would still be subject to a substantial number of programs, and the tax rates under individual programs might remain high.

[3] Milton Friedman, *Capitalism and Freedom* (Chicago: University of Chicago Press, 1962).

A third approach to an integrated system that would provide adequate benefits while maintaining the incentive to work is through *categorization*. The population would be divided into various categories, each category subject to different treatment by the system. This is, of course, the approach that is used in many of the existing programs. But categorization is not necessarily synonymous with a multiplicity of programs. A single program with universal coverage could divide the population into categories and subject each category to different payment levels, tax rates, and constraints on behavior. In this way, the advantages of different treatments would be obtained, but gaps and overlaps in coverage and high administrative costs would be avoided. Several examples of this approach are discussed later.

A fourth path to a system that preserves work incentives is to provide *benefits that increase with hours worked or with earnings*. The current income-conditioned programs, and alternatives such as a demogrant or negative income tax, decrease benefits as income increases, or tax income at a positive rate. Recently, considerable attention has been focused on programs that would increase benefits as earnings increase, or tax earnings at a negative rate. The Senate Finance Committee's version of H.R. 1 provides examples of two such programs. Under the wage subsidy of the committee plan, benefits would increase in proportion to hours worked. Under the earnings bonus, benefits would increase in proportion to earnings within a certain earnings range. Henry Aaron (see Chapter 6) proposes a third type of plan with a negative tax rate that combines features of both the wage subsidy and the earnings bonus. All of these plans would therefore have the advantage of rewarding work effort by taxing the increase in earnings obtained by working longer hours at a negative rate, at least within some earnings range. However, neither the wage subsidy nor the earnings bonus provides an income guarantee for people who do not work. If an objective of an income maintenance system is to provide an adequate income for all people, then these programs must be categorical. That is, the population must be divided into those who are and are not expected to work, and a program with an income guarantee must be provided for the unemployables.

A fifth approach to providing benefits while maintaining a low tax rate on earnings is through *insurance*. Insurance benefits need not be based on current earnings and therefore need not affect the tax rate on earnings. The insurance approach is limited, however, to certain types of risks. Death, ill health, and unemployment can be insured against because they are largely beyond the control of individuals, and insurance coverage does not influence their behavior. Retirement insurance does influence behavior, but the resulting behavior is considered to be desirable. But insurance against risks such as fatherlessness, divorce, and low earning capacity would provide an incentive for behavior that is not socially desirable. Insurance programs are therefore, by their nature, categorical, in that some risks are covered while others are not, and, hence, they cannot guarantee a minimum income for all people. Furthermore, while insurance benefits need not affect the tax rate on earnings, the rate is affected by the premiums to finance the insurance. The Social Security payroll tax is now a significant share of personal taxes, and some proposed health insurance programs would require taxes of equal magnitude.

The final path to integrating programs is through the *treatment of one income maintenance program by another*. The combined impact of several programs on income and work incentives depends, in large part, on how the benefits of one program are treated as income in computing the benefits of another. Thad Mirer (see Chapter 5) describes the variety of available treatments, or "linkages" among programs, and illustrates their impact on total benefits and the cumulative tax rate. Some improvement in the income maintenance system could be made without introducing new programs, but by altering the treatment of one existing program by another. If new programs are introduced, they should be designed with an understanding of how the treatment of other programs determines their net effect.

Alternative Cash Programs Postulated for the Conference

Because of the wide range of criticisms of the current system and the numerous ways the system can be changed to meet these criticisms, the conference was given a structure that would organize and focus the papers and discussion. Three alternative cash programs were postulated, each of which would provide cash assistance in some form to all low-income people. Each of these three basic programs meets one of the major criticisms of the current system, that many poor people are ineligible for cash assistance. Yet they are sufficiently varied to raise many of the issues that have to be faced in designing any income maintenance program.

The three programs chosen were H.R. 1, as passed by the House of Representatives in June 1971; the version of H.R. 1 developed by the Senate Finance Committee in June 1972, and referred to here as the "Long plan"; and a universal demogrant. A universal demogrant was chosen because it is a polar form of a cash program; payments are made to all persons regardless of their income or any other characteristics. The Long plan is at another pole; it is highly categorical and does not guarantee a minimum income to people who are expected to work. It was chosen because it provides a strong contrast to a demogrant, and because it was under active consideration by Congress at the time of the conference. H.R. 1 was also being considered by Congress, as variants of it had been for three years, and is an example of a middle ground between a demogrant and the Long plan. It has some features of a demogrant, in that payments are made to families who have no income and their net value declines as income rises. It is categorical like the Long plan, in that eligibility is restricted to families with children and to the aged, blind, and disabled. H.R. 1 was also posited because its detailed provisions prompt questions that are rarely raised until legislative language is written. It was not chosen because it was thought to be a particularly good foundation for a well-integrated income maintenance system. In fact, the inadequacies of the program, which were discovered in its three years before Congress, were themselves a major stimulus to the conference.

The details of H.R. 1 have been analyzed at length elsewhere;[4] the section of the Ways and Means Committee Report on H.R. 1 that summarizes the Family Assistance Plan and related provisions is reprinted as the appendix to this volume. A family of four would be paid $2400 per year, with smaller families paid less and larger families paid more. Earnings of families would be taxed at $66\frac{2}{3}$ percent after an exemption of $720, and most forms of unearned income would be taxed at 100 percent. The provisions of H.R. 1 for aged, blind, and disabled individuals were enacted as the Supplementary Security Income program, which became effective in 1974. Under SSI, individuals are guaranteed $1560 per year, and couples $2340. The earnings of SSI recipients are taxed at 50 percent after an exemption of $1020; most forms of their unearned income are taxed at 100 percent.

The structure and impact of a universal demogrant plan is analyzed by Benjamin Okner (see Chapter 3). The demogrant postulated for the conference would pay all adults $1200 per year and all children $600 per year. Income other than the demogrant would be taxed at a flat rate of $33\frac{1}{3}$ percent, although no further assumptions were made about the definition of income. It was assumed that the demogrant would replace

4 U.S., Congress, House, Committee on Ways and Means, *Report of the Committee on Ways and Means on H.R. 1*, 92d Cong., 1st sess., 26 May 1971; Jodie T. Allen, *A Funny Thing Happened on the Way to Welfare Reform* (Washington, D.C.: Urban Institute, January 1972); Robert L. Lampman, "The Welfare Reform Provisions in H.R. 1," in *Proceedings*, American Home Economics Association, Consumer Economics Section, 1971.

Public Assistance, but whether or not other programs should be eliminated as well was left as a question for analysis.

The provisions of the Long plan are described and analyzed by Robert Haveman (see Chapter 4). The Long plan would establish both types of negative tax schemes just described, a wage subsidy and an earnings bonus, plus a public employment program. Up to thirty-two hours of public employment per week paying $1.50 per hour would be provided. People earning between $1.50 and $2.00 in private employment would receive a wage subsidy equal to three-quarters of the difference between their wage and $2.00, plus an earnings bonus equal to 10 percent of earnings up to $4000, declining by $.25 for each $1.00 of earnings above $4000. Families headed by mothers unable to work would continue to receive AFDC in much its current form. Payments to the aged, blind, and disabled would be the same as those under H.R. 1.

III. Issues in Integrating Programs

Participants in the conference were asked to analyze the implications of each of these three basic cash alternatives for some of the larger existing income maintenance programs and for several proposed additions to the system. They then attempted to redesign the existing and proposed programs so as to maintain their objective while preserving the objectives of the alternative cash programs. This approach was quite successful in stimulating thought on the problems of integrating programs. Only after making an attempt to design a package of programs can the issues involved be fully appreciated. Michael Taussig analyzed the implications of each of the three cash alternatives for Old Age Insurance, Raymond Munts studied their implications for Unemployment Insurance, and Irene Lurie analyzed some of the rationales for interstate differences in benefit levels under the cash programs. Michael Krashinsky examined the implications of the three alternatives for federal involvement in day care, and Theodore Marmor analyzed their implications for current and proposed health insurance programs.

Six approaches to integrating programs were described previously. Participants employed all these approaches, to a greater or lesser extent, in designing packages of programs for the conference. The conference discussion revealed many of the strengths and weaknesses of these approaches, as well as many decisions that must be made in implementing them. Some of the issues that were raised in the discussion are summarized here.

Reducing the Number of Programs

Faced with the problems created by the multiplicity of income maintenance programs, the reformer's natural impulse is to consider whether or not certain programs can be eliminated. The smaller the number of programs, the easier the task of designing a well-integrated system. In the limit, as discussed earlier, a single transfer program would eliminate all the problems resulting from overlapping programs. But whether or not a small number of programs is desirable depends on how well they can meet the wide variety of objectives that the system is expected to fulfill. Would each of the three alternative cash programs satisfy the population's needs, as they are currently perceived, or are additional programs necessary? Some of the arguments that were made for programs in addition to a basic cash program are described here, and one begins to appreciate the difficulty of designing a well-integrated system by reducing the number of programs.

PREVENTING RECIPIENTS FROM BECOMING "WORSE OFF"

One major impediment to reducing the number of programs is the likelihood that some recipients will suffer a decrease in benefits and therefore be "worse off" than they are now. While the reluctance to make people worse off is perhaps more of a political problem than a requirement for efficient or equitable program design, it is a real problem nonetheless. The drop in benefits that some AFDC recipients could suffer following the introduction of H.R. 1 was undoubtedly one of the reasons for its failure in Congress. As pointed out in Chapter 12, significant decreases in welfare benefits also would result if AFDC were replaced by the demogrant described earlier or by the Long plan. Attempts to alter the structure of the other cash programs or the in-kind programs are likely to meet similar resistance by recipients.

This resistance can be reduced if recipients receive compensation for the change. For example, opposition to the drop in benefits, which some Public Assistance recipients would have experienced with the implementation of the SSI program, led Congress to require that states supplement SSI benefits to prevent recipients from suffering a decrease in benefits. Lurie notes, however, that compensation tends to transform a new program back into the program it was designed to replace.

Adjustment to a change can be facilitated also by "grandfathering," that is, by permitting participants in a program that is changed or abolished to continue receiving benefits as they would have in the absence of the change. Grandfathering would be particularly appropriate if benefits under OASDHI or UI are reduced, since workers have contributed to these programs, either directly or indirectly, and may be considered deserving of a return on their contribution. A drawback of grandfathering is that it can effectively delay the implementation of a new program for a considerable period of time.

Some participants were less concerned than others with preventing recipients from becoming worse off. One participant argued that government policies frequently make people worse off and that a program that redistributes income must lower the income of some people if it is to raise the income of others. Another argued that we should not take the approach that some people will be worse off but, rather, proceed as if some are getting too much already! Yet many participants, regardless of their personal views concerning the equity of reducing the benefits of recipients, recognized the political pressures against changes that leave recipients worse off than they are now.

RATIONALES FOR CONTINUING EXISTING PROGRAMS

Implementation of any one of the basic cash programs posited here would clearly reduce the need for the existing income-conditioned cash programs. Some new income-conditioned cash transfer programs might be created, such as state supplementation of the federal program and assistance for emergencies and special needs, and some cash transfers for special interests groups, such as veterans, might be continued. But these programs would be relatively small and would not create a serious problem of overlapping coverage and high marginal tax rates. Implementation of an income-conditioned cash program would not, however, necessarily reduce the perceived need for many other transfer programs.

Several of the rationales for social insurance programs would remain, following the enactment of any of the three cash programs considered here. Two functions are now served by OASDI: income support and earnings replacement. An income-conditioned cash program for all the aged and disabled would provide a floor under their income and would relieve OASDI of its income support function. While the earnings replacement function could, in principle, be served by private pensions, insurance, or other forms of private saving, several arguments were made at the conference for continuing OASDI as a pure insurance program. First, the government has an incentive to force people to insure, since they will fall back on the government if they fail to do so. Second, if stigma is attached to the income-conditioned cash program, society might be reluctant to leave the "deserving poor" aged without any other source of transfer income. Third, OASDI is the nation's most popular income maintenance program, and efforts to abolish it would be met with severe political opposition.

The same arguments were made, to a greater or lesser degree, for retaining Unemployment Insurance. In addition, there are features of the three postulated cash programs that make continuation of UI desirable. First, all three plans would provide lower benefits than are now given to some UI beneficiaries, making them less effective in replacing earnings. Second, the wage subsidy and earnings bonus of the Long plan are of no help to the unemployed. Public employment could be a substitute for UI, although one participant questioned whether highly skilled workers would accept the low-grade jobs that would be offered. Nor would public employment support workers while they search for jobs, as UI does now. H.R. 1 and a demogrant would avoid some of the problems of the Long plan but would still not be a complete substitute for UI. H.R. 1 has a "quarterly carry-over" accounting period, which means that payments in each quarter of the year are determined on the basis of income in that quarter and in the three preceding quarters. The accounting period under the demogrant considered here is not specified, but the spirit of a demogrant implies a relatively long accounting period. The longer the accounting period, the less rapidly payments adjust to changes in income. Neither of these plans would respond as rapidly to changes in income as UI, which generally imposes a waiting period of only one week before unemployed people become eligible for benefits. They would therefore be less effective than UI in cushioning workers against sudden decreases in income during short periods of unemployment.

ARGUMENTS FOR NEW PROGRAMS

Recommended changes in government policies toward medical care and day care were not limited to the adjustments that would be required following the introduction of one of the postulated cash programs. Attention was focused on proposals for major extension of government involvement in the provision and financing of health and day care services. In fact, the growing sentiment for increased government action in these areas, and the likelihood that new programs will be added to a system that already suffers from overlapping coverage and high tax rates, was a prime motivation for the conference.

The arguments that were made for the need for more government involvement in these two areas illustrate a common pitfall that is encountered in designing government programs, a pitfall that produced the poorly integrated system that exists today. Many advocates of broader health insurance programs and of greater government responsibility for day care believe that these programs should cover all income groups, not just the poor. Health insurance programs are favored not only as a way to relieve the poor of medical care costs and to encourage them to seek early medical treatment, but as a way to improve the delivery of medical services to all income groups and to relieve the nonpoor from the burden of large medical expenses. Similarly, day care is favored not only as a necessary counterpart to a work requirement for mothers on welfare but as remedial education for poor children as well. It is also considered a policy to reduce discrimination against women of all classes and to aid families with only one parent. Because health insurance and day care need not be limited to the poor, some participants argued that integration with other transfer programs should not be the first consideration in designing them. Even at a conference devoted to analyzing programs as a single system, there was a desire to design programs first and integrate them with the rest of the system later. As others pointed out, it is this type of reasoning, whereby programs are designed and evaluated on their "own merits" apart from the rest of the income maintenance system, that has led to the problem we have now.

The difficulty of eliminating existing programs and the pressure for expanding the role of government suggest that integration of income maintenance plans cannot be achieved solely by reducing their number. Even a demogrant or negative income tax with a high guarantee would not be a complete substitute for social insurance and would not eliminate the pressure for the government to improve the market for medical services and provide insurance against large medical bills. Nor would many of the rationales for government involvement in day care be eliminated. The statement of one participant is an exaggeration, but it contains some truth: "We have an irreducible number of programs; this means that high tax rates are inevitable over a wide range of income."

Work Requirements

Both H.R. 1 and the Long plan make heavy use of categorization as a way to provide cash transfers while preserving the incentive to work. They categorize the population according to age, blindness, disability, presence of children in the family, and "employability." While some concern was expressed at the conference about the equity of excluding from coverage non-aged, able-bodied single persons and childless couples, attention was centered on the employable–unemployable categorization and on the work requirements for employables.

Under both plans, families with children would be divided into two groups, those with employable members and those without any members deemed to be employable. H.R. 1 would impose the work requirement administratively. Both employables and unemployables would be subject to the same benefit schedule, composed of an income guarantee and a positive tax rate. The work requirement would consist of a rule that employable family members register for training and employment; refusal to register or accept training would result in a reduction in benefits of $800 per year. The work requirement under the Long plan, where benefits are positively related to work effort, is self-enforcing; refusal to work means a complete lack of earnings and of program benefits.

ARGUMENTS FOR AND AGAINST A WORK REQUIREMENT

Debate over the desirability of a work requirement recurred throughout the conference. Many participants were ethically opposed to such a requirement, both on the grounds that all people should be guaranteed a minimum income regardless of their behavior and on the grounds that a work requirement interferes with personal freedom of choice. Others, however, felt that a work requirement is a politically necessary condition for extending assistance to male family heads. It is also a method that is efficient, in one sense, for guaranteeing that these primary workers do not reduce their work effort in response to an increase in transfer income. That is, it costs less, in terms of government expenditures, than providing work incentives through lowering the implicit tax rate on earnings. Many conference participants therefore felt that a work requirement could be an appropriate method of encouraging recipients to work if it could be administered equitably. One participant put it this way: "This whole business of trying to treat everyone equally is an error. There's nothing wrong with treating people differently if they're in different situations." If some people are more capable of working than others, a cash program that attempts to reduce poverty at minimum cost should require that those capable of working do so. One participant, who has long been a proponent of a guaranteed minimum income, stated that few people are still arguing that everyone has a right to income without work.

The difficulty is in achieving an equitable work requirement. Virtually no participant believed that an equitable work requirement could be designed or administered. Some participants were led to this conclusion by the current experience with the work requirement in AFDC. In some states, the work requirement is meaningless because it is not enforced. In areas where it is enforced, it often imposes harsh burdens on recipients. In some rural areas, the work requirement has been imposed only at harvest time when low-wage labor was needed in the fields. The lawyers at the conference doubted that it would ever be possible to draw administrative standards governing who must work that could be applied with little discretionary judgment. Once administrative judgments are required, they felt, the work test would be open to "political sabotage," as one person put it. The standards governing who must work could be interpreted harshly and be used to deny aid to people who cannot work, or they could be interpreted so loosely that the work requirement would be ineffective.

An equitable work requirement would require that recipients take only those jobs that are "suitable." But the lawyers saw little chance that this safeguard could be effectively administered. One problem is that its protection is essentially in the form of an appeals process, and there are not enough lawyers and legal rights personnel to protect recipients from the kinds of jobs they could be forced to accept. Another problem is that the agency administering the suitability safeguard may be disinclined to use it if the agency's effectiveness is measured in terms of the number of persons placed in jobs.

Whether women with children, particularly young children, should be classified as employable and subject to the work requirement is a difficult issue to resolve. Two separable issues must be faced. Should parents with children below a certain age be exempt from the work requirement? If a work requirement is imposed on the heads of families, does equity between one- and two-parent families require that a work requirement also be imposed on wives in two-parent families? H.R. 1 classifies female heads of families with children of age three or over as employable, and the Long plan classifies such women as employable if their children are age six or over. Women whose husbands are present are not required to work under either plan. Sentiment was expressed at the conference that the exemption of wives put single-parent families at a disadvantage relative to two-parent families. Either both parents should be required to work or some recognition should be taken of the home production of wives who do not work. There was no consensus on the age at which children can be expected to manage without the full-time attention of their parents. This depends on many complex factors about the quantity, quality, and effect of alternative child care arrangements, factors about which little information is available.

All agreed, however, that if a program compels beneficiaries to work, then it is obligated to guarantee that their disposable income is not lowered by virtue of having gone to work. That is, the income net of work expenses of those people classified as employable must not be lower than the income of those classified as unemployable. This has particularly important implications for the treatment of day care expenses in determining payments made by cash transfer programs. Under the provisions of H.R. 1, for example, day care expenses are deducted from earnings, up to some unspecified limit, before applying the two-thirds tax rate. This has the effect of reimbursing recipients for two-thirds of these expenses. But mothers still have to pay one-third of their day care expenses, and a low-wage worker with many children might obtain a smaller disposable income by working than by staying home. Furthermore, if a mother's productivity in the market place is less than her productivity at home, the real output of the economy may be increased if she stays home and cares for her children. This leads Krashinsky (see Chapter 11) to ask whether society is willing to pay more for mothers to work than for them not to work. Many participants felt that this should be answered in the negative and that women with day care expenses greater than their earnings should be exempt from any work requirement.

Providing Work Incentives through the Benefit Schedule

The difficulties associated with a work requirement, plus a widespread ethical opposition to regulating the behavior of the poor, makes it imperative to provide work incentives through the benefit schedules of income transfer schemes. Many of the considerations relevant in choosing a benefit schedule that provides work incentives were discussed at the conference, as well as some of the trade-offs that must be made in this choice.

All income maintenance schemes may encourage some recipients to reduce their work effort: By increasing the total income obtainable by any amount of work effort, transfer programs permit recipients to obtain a given income with fewer hours of work. But the impact on work incentives of various benefit structures is likely to vary considerably, with respect to both their magnitude and their effect on different groups in the population. The lower the income guarantee, the greater will be the incentive for people to seek work. But the desire to maintain work incentives must be balanced against the desire to provide a floor under the income of the target population. A wage or earnings subsidy, for example, scores high on grounds of providing incentives to work, but the absence of an income guarantee precludes its use for people who cannot work. Similarly, the lower the tax rate on earnings, the greater the incentive to work. But the lower the tax rate, the larger the eligible population and the budgetary cost of the program, and the greater the likelihood that benefits will accrue to income groups above the target population.

Negative tax rates, whereby benefits of a program increase with earnings, are likely to provide greater work incentives than positive rates. Benefit schedules with negative tax rates, such as the wage subsidy and the earnings bonus of the Long plan, increase the effective wage rate, thereby increasing the incentive to work. But they also increase recipients' incomes, thereby reducing the incentive to work. The net effect of these two forces is impossible to determine a priori, but it is reasonable to expect that more work effort would result under the Long plan than under a schedule with a positive tax rate. It is important to realize, however, that a benefit schedule cannot be designed that consists solely of negative tax rates. At some wage rate, number of hours worked, or level of total earnings, the tax rate must become positive. A positive rate is required in order to phase out the benefits of the program as earnings increase. Even if wages or earnings at all levels were to be taxed at negative rates, the tax required to finance the subsidy would necessitate a positive tax rate at some level of earnings (except if the subsidy is financed solely from unearned income).

The objective in designing an income maintenance system is to choose those schedules of benefits that will maximize work effort, given the other objectives of the system. The choice is not a simple one, however, as was reflected by the wide variety of schedules advocated by participants.

Some favored a schedule that provides a uniform income guarantee but applies different tax rates at different earnings levels. Lower tax rates can be imposed at earnings levels where work decisions are more sensitive to the tax rate, and higher rates can be imposed elsewhere. This is, in effect, a method of having "categories without categorization," as one participant put it. One example of this, a regressive rate schedule with tax rates declining as earnings increase, was discussed at some length. A regressive schedule would target work incentives on primary workers. They are likely to be committed to the labor force and have relatively large amounts of earnings, and would be encouraged to maintain their work effort by a regressive rate structure. However, a regressive rate structure discourages part-time work, thereby interfering with the process by which many people enter the labor market. A regressive rate structure therefore protects against a marginal reduction in work effort by full-time workers, at the cost of discouraging the basic work decision. A progressive rate structure, such as that embodied in H.R. 1, has the opposite effect, fostering the basic decision to work but discouraging full-time workers. Which rate structure is best depends on the numbers and types of people who would be encouraged to enter the labor force if they faced a low tax rate on their initial earnings as compared to those full-time workers who would be adversely affected by a high tax rate. The decision also depends on value judgments concerning the importance of ensuring that each of these groups of people work.

Categorizing the population according to some criterion and applying a different benefit schedule to each category is another approach to encouraging work effort. If the population were divided into categories according to their employability, employable persons could be subject to a low income guarantee and a low tax rate, while unemployables would face a high guarantee and high tax rate. The advantage of this approach is that it would be possible to pursue two simultaneous goals at a given budgetary cost. First, the incomes of most people could be raised to an adequate level, the unemployables by a high income guarantee and most of the employables by their earnings supplemented by the program's benefits. Second, because the employables would face a lower income guarantee and a lower tax rate, they would have a greater incentive to work than under a payment schedule designed also for people who were not expected to work. The drawbacks of this approach would be the administrative cost of dividing the population into employables and unemployables and the inequity that would result if people were incorrectly classified. A further inequity would be created if no jobs were available for people who were correctly classified as employable.

Interestingly, a few participants proposed a schedule of rates that was almost the opposite of this one. Their position was based on the findings of the Graduated Work Incentive experiment in New Jersey and Pennsylvania. The experiment has shown that the labor force behavior of prime-age men is not strongly affected by a negative income tax with tax rates between 30 and 70 percent, but that their wives were more likely to reduce their work effort. These findings indicate that prime-age men can be taxed at a higher rate than married women to achieve any given amount of work effort. They suggest the general principle that people with a stronger attachment to the labor force can be taxed at a higher rate than those with a weaker attachment. However, this conclusion was criticized on several grounds. First, if society believes that some people with a weak labor force attachment, such as women with young children, should not be encouraged to work, it might want to subject them to a fairly high tax rate. Second, as one participant argued, even if the experiment were to show that tax rates have no effect whatsoever on the labor force behavior of men, it might be politically necessary to have work incentive provisions built into a plan. "Even if the provisions are unnecessary or ineffective, Congress might require work incentives for men which are at least logically persuasive."

We usually assume, when we speculate about the effect of various benefit schedules on the incentive to work, that recipients are well-informed about the tax rates they face. In fact, however, recipients may have little idea what tax rates are in effect. Under AFDC, for example, the discretion vested in caseworkers produces a tax rate that is highly variable and that recipients cannot be expected to predict. Whether ignorance of the true tax rate causes recipients to underestimate or over-estimate it, and to work more or less than they otherwise would, is not known. Under a less discretionary system, the tax rate would be more predictable but the recipient might still be ignorant as to what it is. Both Taussig and Munts (see Chapters 8 and 9, respectively) question whether recipients would be able to respond rationally to a composite schedule of benefits created by two or more overlapping programs. Unless a certain amount of effort is devoted to informing recipients of the cumulative tax rate produced by overlapping programs, lowering the tax rate may prove futile in increasing work effort.

Definition of Income

Income maintenance programs are most commonly described in terms of the payments made to a defined group of recipients with various amounts of income, either current income or income earned during some previous period. Less often described, but equally important, is the defini-tion of income on which payments are based. The way in which income is defined can mean the difference between a generous program and a niggardly one. The definition of income under each program in an income maintenance system is also the key determinant of how the programs are related to each other. Integrating programs to achieve a given set of objectives amounts, in large part, to choosing the definition of income to be used in determining payments under each program.

Three issues that arise in defining income are particularly crucial in designing a well-integrated set of programs. One concerns the deductions from earnings that will yield the proper concept of net income, given the overall objectives of the system. The second concerns the treatment of unearned income, which includes the benefits from other income maintenance programs, private transfers, and income from property. A third issue is the treatment of income in kind, particularly the benefits of in-kind transfer programs.

TREATMENT OF WORK EXPENSES

A good deal of attention at the conference was focused on one type of deduction from earnings, deductions of work expenses. Deductions of work expenses from earnings can have a very significant effect on the size of transfer payments and, therefore, deserve careful consideration when designing a new program. The importance of such deductions is seen in the operation of the AFDC program where, several participants argued, they have been abused. Federal statutes give the states authority to determine what can be deducted as work expenses in determining the net income of AFDC recipients, and many states in turn give wide discretion to the caseworkers in charge of calculating payments. As a result, deductions vary considerably, being far below actual work expenses in some states and including items that are not clearly expenses of working (lunch, for example) in others. In 1971, the average work expense claimed by AFDC families with work expenses was $65 per month, excluding day care expenses, and averaged over $100 in at least one state. Further, work expenses are effectively reimbursed at 100 percent, which means that $1 of work expense deductions results in an additional $1 of benefits. As a result of the large deductions in some states, some families can continue to receive AFDC until their earnings reach fairly high levels, more than $6000 for a family of four in about thirty states. In order to curb what many congressmen consider to be an abuse of the deduction for work expenses, it was eliminated under H.R. 1 and replaced by a flat deduction of $720 per year.

Whether H.R. 1 is an improvement over the existing treatment of work expenses, or a retrogression, was debated at great length. In the process of analyzing the merits and drawbacks of each approach, four alternative methods of treating work expenses were identified: (1) All work expenses are itemized and deducted from earnings; (2) a flat amount is deducted from the earnings of each worker; (3) a constant percentage of the earnings of each worker is deducted, perhaps up to some maximum; and (4) no deductions for work expenses are permitted. There was widespread agreement that itemizing all work expenses and deducting them from earnings would yield the best measure of net income on which to base payments under programs like H.R. 1. But, as the experience of AFDC indicates, it is extremely difficult to distinguish between work expenses and pure consumption. Many goods, such as clothing and automobiles, clearly can serve both functions, and the ability of consumers to substitute among goods makes it difficult to identify any single item as an expense of working. For example, higher expenditures on housing near work can often be substituted for commuting expenses, so that viewing commuting but not housing as an expense of working will give some families an advantage over others. Furthermore, inequities inevitably result if administrators are given the discretion to determine what should be counted as a work expense. Most participants were therefore willing to sacrifice the theoretically ideal definition of net income, for basically the same reason it has been sacrificed in the individual income tax.

A flat deduction or a deduction equal to some fraction of earnings would be only a crude approximation of true work expenses, but the ease of administering these deductions made them the favored alternative of many participants. The $720 disregard of H.R. 1 was therefore considered to be a fairly satisfactory method of accounting for work expenses. The primary objection was that it applies to the earnings of the entire family, not the individual worker, thereby treating one-earner families more generously than families with several earners.

The choice between a flat deduction and a percentage-of-earnings deduction depends on whether most work expenses are fixed or vary according to the number of hours worked and the wage rate. The choice of a limit to a percentage-of-earnings deduction would similarly depend on an empirical judgment. A combination of these two alternatives is also possible, with a flat initial amount of earnings deducted and a percentage deduction applied to the remainder. Of course, both these types of deductions amount to changing the tax rate on earnings; a flat deduction of a given amount of earnings is equivalent to a zero tax rate on those earnings, and a deduction of x percent of earnings is equivalent to lowering the tax rate on earnings by x percent. These deductions must therefore be considered as part of the earnings tax structure and chosen to conform to a program's objectives concerning work incentives and budgetary cost.

The realization that deductions for work expenses are equivalent to lowering the tax rate on earnings led at least one participant to argue that work expenses should be ignored. One of the main purposes of such deductions is to provide recipients with an incentive to work. If, however, provisions for work incentives are provided elsewhere in the program, through a work requirement or a low tax rate on earnings, then there is no need to make special provisions for the deduction of work expenses. A second argument for permitting no deductions for work expenses was made on equity grounds: Transfer recipients should not be treated differently from taxpayers, who are permitted quite limited deductions for work expenses. Finally, if wages rise to compensate for work expenses, the expenses are actually borne by the employer and should not be deducted in computing employees' net income.

If earnings are taxed at a negative rate, as under an earnings bonus or a wage subsidy, deductions for work expenses are actually counterproductive. Every dollar deducted as a work expense means a dollar less of earnings on which to base the payments. Deductions thereby lower, rather than raise, the payments that are made. Deductions for day care expenses have a similar effect, which implies that day care cannot be financed by deductions under a program with a negative tax rate. Direct subsidies, in the form of cash or services, must be used.

TREATMENT OF TRANSFER INCOME

Designing a well-integrated set of transfer programs revolves, in large part, about choosing the appropriate definition of unearned income for each program. Unearned income can be narrowly defined under each program to include only income from property or can be broadly defined to include the benefits of all transfer programs except the program in question. Thad Mirer (see Chapter 5) illustrates various methods of treating the benefits of one transfer program in calculating the benefits of another. These methods range from ignoring the benefits of other programs, to taxing them at 100 percent, to making people ineligible for one program if they receive benefits from another. Mirer shows that these methods can have a tremendous impact on the amount and distribution of benefits of the programs.

The definition of unearned income that is appropriate for each program depends on the objectives of the program. Therefore, it is appropriate that the definition vary from one program to another. (Indeed, it is necessary that the definition vary if transfer payments are counted as unearned income; the benefits of one program cannot be counted as unearned income in determining the benefits of a second program if the benefits of the second are counted in determining the benefits of the first.) Generalizing somewhat, it is possible to distinguish three groups of programs according to how they treat the benefits of other transfer programs. The insurance and retirement programs designed to replace earnings—OASDI, UI, Workmen's Compensation, Veterans' Compensation, and government retirement programs—ignore all unearned income, both property income and other government transfers. The income-conditioned cash programs—AFDC, SSI, and veterans' pensions—count the cash benefits from the insurance and retirement programs as unearned income. The third group of programs are income-conditioned, in-kind programs, such as Food Stamps, Medicaid, and public housing, which count as income the cash benefits of *both* groups of transfer programs. Some of the reasons for this order of programs are clear. The first group of programs ignores unearned income because they are designed to replace earnings and have no objective concerning a household's total income. The second group is designed to provide a floor under income and therefore takes account of all sources of cash income. In-kind programs are last in the sequence, in part because of the difficulty of determining their value to recipients and therefore counting them as income.

The definition of unearned income under the existing programs is responsible for much of the criticism claiming that the current system is poorly integrated. One major criticism is the 100 percent taxation of the benefits from social insurance and retirement programs by the income-conditioned programs. To a certain extent, this treatment is justified. Social insurance is not pure insurance, with benefits related directly to contributions, but has an income support function by providing benefits in excess of contributions to people who are presumed to be most needy. To the extent that social insurance benefits are greater than contributions, the income-conditioned programs duplicate their function and should tax them at 100 percent. But taxing payments based on contributions at 100 percent results in an inequity: People who have made contributions may end up with the same total income as noncontributors. Under the SSI program, for example, an aged person eligible for Social Security will receive only $240 per year more than someone with no Social Security entitlement, in spite of the contributions made during his working years.

The "dual system" proposed here by Taussig would eliminate this problem. It would consist of a pure insurance program, with benefits based on past contributions, and an income-conditioned program with benefits based solely on current income. Because the insurance program would not have any income support function, there would be less pressure to tax its benefits at 100 percent under the income-conditioned program. If benefits are not taxed at 100 percent, people who made contributions would always have a higher total income than those who did not.

TREATMENT OF ALIMONY AND CHILD SUPPORT

Alimony and child support are currently taxed at 100 percent under the AFDC program. Because a father's payments do not raise his family's total income, there is no financial incentive for him to make such payments. This places the burden for enforcing alimony and child support obligations on the legal system. The legal system, however, has not been very successful in this task; one participant noted that about 85 percent of absent fathers are not making support payments in his state, California. One explanation is that about 30 percent of the fathers have no income. But another factor is the reluctance of local district attorneys to become "bogged down" in support payment litigation. The local officials identify with the welfare recipient's interest, which is not served by such litigation when alimony and child support are taxed at 100 percent. A high tax rate might be thought to have the counterbalancing effect of encouraging government litigation, since every dollar of alimony and child support payments is a dollar saved in welfare costs. But because local governments finance only a small share of welfare expenditures, this incentive is not very powerful.

This suggests two alternative policies for encouraging fathers to fulfill their financial obligations to their families. Alimony and child support can be taxed at a rate significantly below 100 percent, thereby providing an incentive for fathers to make these payments voluntarily. This is the approach taken under H.R. 1, which taxes alimony at 66⅔ percent. Alternatively, these payments could continue to be taxed at a high rate, but responsibility for enforcing these obligations could be given to the federal government, which bears the greatest responsibility for financing the program and which has more legal, financial, and administrative resources at its command.

TREATMENT OF PROPERTY INCOME AND ASSETS

Income from property is also taxed at 100 percent by many, but not all, of the income-conditioned programs. This treatment creates the same inequity as is caused by the 100 percent taxation of social insurance benefits: Persons who save may be no better off than those who do not. It also reduces the incentive to save among people who expect to be eligible for these programs in the future. However, at least one participant argued that it is appropriate for an income-conditioned program to tax property income at 100 percent. According to his view, earnings should be taxed at less than 100 percent only because it is politically necessary to preserve the incentive to work, not for reasons of equity. Equity under an income-conditioned program only requires that all families be guaranteed a minimum income. It does not require that families with relatively high pretransfer incomes continue to have *higher* posttransfer incomes than families with relatively low pretransfer incomes.

Although current income is the base of the nation's largest taxes, it has not gained acceptance as the sole measure of need under transfer programs designed to reduce poverty. AFDC, SSI, Medicaid, Food Stamps, and the housing programs for low-income families also take assets into account in determining eligibility. The difficulties of accounting for assets in computing benefits under income-conditioned programs were not discussed at great length, probably because low-income households tend to have small amounts of assets. Perhaps the major inequity results from the wide discretion caseworkers are given in administering asset tests. Some applicants can pass the test while others, with the same amount of assets but a different caseworker, cannot. One participant familiar with the operation of income-conditioned programs at the local level argued that caseworker discretion is at its highest in asset testing, even higher than in determining work expenses. A second inequity is caused by the different treatment of liquid and nonliquid assets. Assets such as a home, car, personal belongings, and property used to produce income are generally exempt, at least up to some amount. Families who can convert cash and other liquid assets into these forms are thereby treated more favorably than those who cannot.

The disincentive to accumulate assets is inherent in any asset test, regardless of how equitably it is imposed. One method to reduce this disincentive, and yet to satisfy society's apparent desire to deny income-conditioned transfers to people with large amounts of assets, would be to impute income from assets and count it as unearned income. An approximation that would have a similar effect but be easier to administer would be to count a specified fraction of assets as income. These approaches were favored by a large number of participants. However, many agreed that certain nonliquid assets might still have to be treated more generously than liquid ones. A family with resources that can be used to produce income should not be forced to divest itself of these resources, which might occur if income were imputed to them.

TREATMENT OF IN-KIND TRANSFERS

Economists generally consider in-kind transfer programs to be inefficient, and their arguments were reiterated at the conference. Participants argued that beneficiaries of in-kind programs usually value the goods and services provided at less than their market value and would be better off if they were given cash instead. Moreover, much of the benefit of the programs accrues not to the poor beneficiary but to the taxpayer or to the nonpoor supplier of the good or service: Housing programs benefit builders, medical programs help physicians, and food programs benefit farmers. Further, the administrative cost of the numerous in-kind programs could be saved if they were replaced by cash.

Given the strength of these arguments, it is interesting that a fair amount of attention was devoted to arguing about why in-kind programs might be desirable. First, it was argued that in-kind programs may be more politically popular than cash programs. "Taxpayers generally empathize with people who are hungry, suffering from ill health, or out in the cold, but they turn a deaf ear if you tell them that people simply lack money." Nor do taxpayers generally trust the poor to spend cash on the "right" items. Taxpayers therefore prefer to give goods and services rather than cash. Second, encouraging the poor to consume certain goods and services may reduce poverty in the future, thereby reducing the cost of income maintenance over the long run. Preventive health programs, for example, can both increase earning capacity and reduce the risk of large medical expenses. Finally, in-kind programs may be appropriate if the private market is imperfect and does not provide an adequate supply of a particular commodity. The arguments for direct government provision of medical care and day care rest heavily on the existence of market imperfections.

Maria Schmundt, Eugene Smolensky, and Leanna Stiefel (see Chapter 7) critically examine the argument that beneficiaries would be better off if the government gave them cash rather than goods and services. They find several situations in which goods and services are as valuable to recipients, or more valuable, than cash. These situations are not unusual, and their analysis suggests several policies the government could follow to increase the value to recipients of in-kind transfers. However, at least one of the policies poses a dilemma for policymakers. In-kind benefits will be as valuable as cash if the government provides commodities that the recipient would have purchased if he were given cash instead. But this conflicts with one of the primary rationales for giving benefits in kind, namely encouraging the poor to consume more of certain commodities. This means that policies designed to maximize the welfare of the recipients are those that minimize the satisfaction received by the taxpayer in altering the consumption patterns of the poor.

Because of the difficulty of determining the value to recipients of in-kind transfers, the benefits from in-kind transfer programs are currently ignored in determining the income of the poor and in calculating their need for additional transfer income. Schmundt, Smolensky, and Stiefel outline a procedure for estimating their value. A good measure of the value of in-kind transfers could significantly improve the equity and efficiency of the income maintenance system. Currently, all households that are eligible for certain in-kind programs may not actually receive benefits. For example, the number of households eligible for public housing far exceeds the number of available housing units, and food programs do not operate in all areas of the country. Hence, households that actually receive benefits obtain a higher total income than eligible households that do not. If an accurate dollar value could be given to these benefits, an income-conditioned cash program could compensate those households that cannot obtain in-kind benefits. This could be done by counting the value of the in-kind benefits as income in determining payments under the income-conditioned program. The cash program would, in effect, be the last in a sequence of programs, and would fill any gaps in coverage and adjust for any differences in payment levels produced by the preceding programs.

IV. Conclusion

The conference did not attempt to reach a consensus concerning the choice among the three alternative cash programs or the design of other individual programs. It became clear early in the conference that there is no "right" answer to many of the questions raised in designing an income maintenance system, but that the design of programs requires the value judgments of policymakers. Furthermore, consensus on a set of integrated programs was hindered by the failure of any one of the three basic cash programs to emerge as the clear favorite of the majority of participants. None appeared to provide an adequate income for the poor while preserving an effective and equitable incentive to work. H.R. 1 provides a floor under the income of many poor individuals but taxes income at a high rate, particularly in combination with other income-conditioned programs. Work incentives are provided through an administratively imposed work requirement that is likely to be ineffective or unfair, or both. The Long plan provides strong incentives to work, and its negative tax rates reduce the potential for high tax rates in combination with other programs, but it does not provide a floor under the income of people who are expected to work. A demogrant provides a floor under income, taxes income at a relatively low rate, and leaves recipients freedom to decide whether or not to work. However, a demogrant does not meet all the objectives that are thrust upon the income maintenance system, and other programs would coexist with it. The tax rates from all programs combined could become quite high, leaving a system that provides little incentive to work.

The dissatisfaction with each of the programs points to one of the major lessons of the conference: All desired goals cannot be achieved simultaneously and trade-offs among them must be made in designing a system of programs. At least four broad goals were emphasized repeatedly: (1) guaranteeing all people adequate levels of cash income and of certain goods and services; (2) maintaining incentives for desirable behavior on the part of both recipients and taxpayers; (3) promoting equity among people in similar circumstances; and (4) minimizing the administrative costs of the system. Yet it became clear during the discussion that attainment of some goals requires sacrifice of others. If an adequate cash income is provided and recipients are guaranteed the goods and services that are frequently proposed, for example, work incentives must be provided either through an administratively imposed work requirement or through a low tax rate in the programs' benefit structures. A work requirement entails administrative costs, costs that are likely to vary directly with the equity with which the requirement is administered. If a strong work incentive is provided through the benefit structure of the system, the system will be costly and taxpayers will be exposed to high tax rates. Alternatively, work incentives can be provided by providing greater benefits to people who cannot or should not work than to those who are expected to work. This approach, which is the one used in the existing system, maintains work incentives by sacrificing equity and the goal of guaranteeing all persons an adequate income. Other approaches are also available, all involving some sort of trade-off among desired goals.

A second lesson is that there is a practical limit to the number of income-conditioned transfer programs that can be enacted. The number of such programs has grown rapidly in recent years as programs providing food, housing, medical care, and education have been passed, and the trend is toward more programs and further growth in the number of families receiving benefits. This raises the prospect of a large share of the employed population being subject to the high tax rates on earnings that are now imposed on the poor, a situation which could have serious effects on morale as well as on the output of the economy. Policymakers should therefore design programs carefully, income conditioning only those whose objectives cannot be achieved in another way.

Finally, it became clear that an integrated system cannot be achieved through the design of a single program, but that all programs must be designed with a view toward their combined effect. However, a single cash program that provides a minimum income for all people is perhaps a first step toward a well-designed system. It would provide the nucleus around which to design other programs, it would close some of the more serious gaps in coverage, and it would permit some of the other programs to operate more efficiently by freeing them from the income support function. Attention should therefore be devoted to designing a form of such a program that will provide a politically acceptable compromise among the many goals of the income maintenance system.

2

Cumulative Tax Rates in Alternative Income Maintenance Systems

Leonard J. Hausman

I. Introduction

On some widely accepted criteria, much welfare reform has been effected in the past decade. In the AFDC program, income guarantees[1] have been raised, coverage has been extended, and implicit tax rates[2] on earnings have been reduced. In housing and food assistance programs for low-income families, income conditioning of benefits has been rationalized and a partial integration of these programs with AFDC has been achieved. Yet, in each of these and in other respects, the process of welfare reform is incomplete.

From the point of view of many, the most urgently needed reform is the extension of coverage under a cash transfer program to low-income

[1] This term refers to the payments made to families who have no nonassistance income. Since the application of AFDC eligibility rules is alleged to be inequitable in many states, some may find questionable the use of the word "guarantees."
[2] This term refers to the reduction in cash payments that results from a $1 change in earnings. In the chapter, the term is used interchangeably with the terms "tax rate" and "benefit reduction rate."

39

families headed by working males. This chapter demonstrates the difficulty of retaining income guarantees and tax rates at their present levels while extending cash transfers to families headed by working males. Since guarantees are quite high in many instances for current AFDC families while implicit tax rates are quite low, extending the system so as to treat similarly male- and female-headed families of the same income level would be very expensive. In a large number of states, families of four would receive partial benefits until their incomes were $7000 or more.

This chapter focuses on the problem of attaining a low "cumulative tax rate" in a system of tax and transfer programs. A cumulative marginal tax rate measures the change in all regular taxes paid, plus the change in all transfer payments received by a family unit as its income changes by $1. For example, a family receiving AFDC in Chicago will have its monthly payment reduced as its monthly earnings rise from $200 to $201. Because it is simultaneously receiving Food Stamps and living in public housing, it may lose a fraction of its Food Stamp bonus and be required to pay a slightly higher rent; and, of course, it also must pay additional Social Security and income taxes. The sum of the lost benefits and the additional taxes associated with the $1 increase in earnings measures the cumulative marginal tax rate that this family faces.

A cumulative tax rate, like any individual benefit reduction or tax rate, is a matter of concern because it helps determine the cost of a system of programs. The cumulative tax rate may influence work behavior and thereby affect the cost of a system. More directly, the cumulative tax rate will affect the amount of benefits a household receives at any given level of private income; and it also will affect the number of families eligible for the benefits received from component programs in the transfer system. The conflicts faced in setting a cumulative tax rate are similar to those faced in setting a single implicit tax rate in one program. For example, a high cumulative rate may affect work effort negatively and thereby raise costs; but a high cumulative rate will either limit program coverage or reduce net benefits at every level of earnings. The exact trade-offs depend on the techniques of program integration that are used in setting the cumulative tax rate.

This chapter illustrates cumulative tax rates in the current transfer system as well as in alternative schemes and stresses the difficulty of maintaining cumulative tax rates at their present low levels, since it is impossible, under any scheme, to maintain low cumulative tax rates while extending substantial cash and in-kind transfers to the working poor without also extending the coverage of these programs to middle-income brackets.

II. Cumulative Tax Rates in the Current Transfer System for Low-Income Families

Since the 1962 and 1967 amendments to the Social Security Act have been applied in state AFDC programs, there no longer is a 100 percent tax rate on earnings, for two reasons. In 1967, the "30 and $\frac{1}{3}$ rule" was adopted; it provides that the first $30 of monthly earnings and one-third of all earnings above $30 are retained by the recipient and do not result in a reduction of benefits. A provision in 1962 allowed for the deduction from earnings of broadly defined work-related expenses; this deduction is now made *after* the "30 and $\frac{1}{3}$ rule" is applied to earnings, and serves as an additional reduction on the amount of earnings used as an offset to benefits. These two major modifications in the AFDC tax structure will be illustrated with examples from three states that are representative of the three major varieties of tax structures that exist in the AFDC program.

The AFDC tax structure in Illinois is representative of what was in effect in thirty-five states (including the District of Columbia) in December 1971.[3] The procedure for adjusting benefits to earnings is as follows: From gross monthly earnings, $30 and one-third of earnings above $30 are deducted; then work-related expenses, as defined by each state, are deducted from earnings net of the "30 and $\frac{1}{3}$." Earnings net of all these deductions are then subtracted from the payment made to the family at zero earnings.[4] The result is that AFDC payments are reduced

---

[3] The group of thirty-five states subdivides into groups of twelve and twenty-three, with the twelve paying 100 percent of the state cost standard and the twenty-three paying some amount below their cost standards to families with no other income. In the group of twenty-three, payments are reduced when earnings rise in the same manner as they are reduced in the group of twelve. (The states are divided here based on information available from U.S., Department of Health, Education, and Welfare, Social and Rehabilitation Services, "State's Methods for Determination of Amount of Grant for an AFDC Family Size of Four [I Adult and 3 Children] as of December 1971," unpublished table, 31 March 1972.)

[4] This procedure can be expressed by the equation

(1) $$B = G - [E - (S + [1 - t][E - S] + F)],$$

where

B = the net benefit received by a family,
G = the payment made to a family when its nonassistance income is zero,
E = gross earnings,
S = the monthly set-aside of $30,
t = the benefit reduction rate of two-thirds,
F = work-related expenses.

Other income is assumed to be zero throughout this chapter.

by under $.67 for each dollar of earnings above $30. The deduction of work-related expenses from earnings after the "30 and $\frac{1}{3}$" deduction means that earnings equal to such expenses do not affect AFDC payments.[5] If such expenses are $.25 per dollar of earnings, then each dollar of earnings reduces the AFDC payment by $.42 ($= \$1.00 - \$.33 - \$.25$).[6] This $.42 reduction in the AFDC benefit per dollar of earnings is the implicit AFDC tax or benefit reduction rate.[7]

Note, though, that although a recipient in Illinois loses only $.42 of AFDC benefits for every dollar earned above $30, his net gain in spendable income always is less than $.58 ($=\$1.00 - \$.42$). This is because he does incur actual expenses in producing his income. Thus, we may distinguish between total tax rates resulting from the reimbursement of work-related expenses that are relevant for AFDC administrators and those facing AFDC recipients.[8] In Illinois, for example, the 42 percent benefit reduction rate is what concerns administrators because it affects actual AFDC payments and thus government costs. For AFDC recipients, the reimbursement of work-related expenses never reduces the cumulative tax rate to 42 percent. Lerman points out that an employed recipient pays Social Security taxes and may consider actual work expenses as taxes in the sense that they reduce spendable income. The total tax rate facing an AFDC recipient falls below 67 percent only to the extent that an employed recipient is reimbursed for consumption expenditures that are defined by welfare departments as work-related expenses. In view of this

[5] A regulation issued by HEW in early 1969 specified that work-related expenses were to be deducted from earnings net of the "$30 and $\frac{1}{3}$" rather than before the $30 and one-third deductions were made. Gary L. Appel, *Effects of a Financial Incentive on AFDC Employment: Michigan's Experience between July 1969 and July 1970* (Minneapolis: Institute for Interdisciplinary Studies, March 1972), pp. 19–22.

[6] This can be demonstrated by rearranging terms in equation (1) of Footnote 4:

(1a) $$B = G + F - t(E - S)$$

Equation (1a) indicates that benefits are raised by the full amount of work-related expenses; or, alternatively, the net reduction in benefits associated with an increase in earnings is decreased by the full amount of work-related expenses.

[7] The *net* change in benefits per dollar of earnings above $30 per month where $F = .25E$, $t = \frac{1}{3}$, and $S = \$30$ is

(1b) $$B = G + .25E - \tfrac{1}{3}(E - \$30)$$
(1c) $$\partial B / \partial E = -.42.$$

[8] For an emphasis on the net gain in spendable income resulting from a rise in earnings see Robert I. Lerman, "Incentive Effects in Public Income Transfer Programs," in U.S., Congress, Joint Economic Committee, Subcommittee on Fiscal Policy, *Income Transfer Programs: How They Tax the Poor*, 92d Cong., 2d sess., 22 Dec. 1972.

argument, the reader should be careful, when viewing the tax rates in Tables 2.1–2.3, not to overstate the financial incentive to work that is afforded recipients by the current system. (Of course, the 42 percent rate always retains some relevance for the recipient: It determines the level of earnings at which his AFDC benefit is reduced to zero—his break-even point—and at which, consequently, he loses his eligibility for Medicaid.)

Table 2.1 contains information on the tax rates faced by a female-headed AFDC family of four in Chicago. An important observation to make is that a family receiving AFDC, Food Stamps, and Medicaid faces relatively low tax rates, both in the AFDC program alone and from these three programs combined. This holds true over a broad range of earnings for families not in public housing (or in some other type of federally subsidized housing unit).[9] Between $576 and $4300 of annual earnings,[10] the family head faces a 42 percent tax rate in AFDC, a 5.2 percent Social Security tax rate, and a 2.5 percent state income tax rate on the last $300 of this amount of earnings.[11] These yield a cumulative tax rate ($CMTR_1$) in column F of 50 percent.[12] Above $4300 of earnings, the individual also begins to pay federal income taxes, which add roughly fourteen points to the cumulative tax rate. Including the tax rate built into the public housing program, the average cumulative tax rate over the range of earnings between $576 and $8600 is roughly 70 percent. Given the number

[9] An estimate provided by James R. Storey is that 13 percent of all AFDC recipients live in public housing. In Chicago, with its extensive public housing program, this figure probably is higher. U.S., Congress, Joint Economic Committee, Subcommittee on Fiscal Policy, *Public Income Transfer Programs: The Incidence of Multiple Benefits and the Issues Raised by Their Receipt*, 92d Cong., 2d sess., 10 April 1972, Table 8.

[10] Note that, although the accounting period in AFDC is one month, the tables are drawn as if it and the ones in the housing, Food Stamp, and Medicaid programs are annual. The use of annual data in this context implies that earnings are assumed to be fairly stable throughout the year.

[11] This is somewhat below the cumulative rate in other states of this first group. The Illinois welfare department puts a ceiling on the amount of money that an AFDC family can spend on Food Stamps at $1008 per year. This ceiling is reached before gross money income—the sum of gross earnings and AFDC benefits—reaches $3960 (in Table 2.1). Thus, above $576 of earnings, the Food Stamp bonus is constant until AFDC benefits are zero.

[12] Cumulative tax rates were computed, in general, over ranges of earnings in which marginal tax rates—which are changes in benefits and/or taxes per *single* dollar of a change in earnings—are constant. That is, except to illustrate notches, as in the fourth line of Table 2.1, the amounts of earnings selected in column A of Tables 2.1–2.11 are those at which new taxes take effect or the benefits of a transfer program are reduced to zero.

Table 2.1 Earnings, Taxes, and Transfers for a Female-Headed AFDC Family with Three Children in Chicago, 1971

A	B	C	D	E	F	G	H	I	J	K	L	M
Gross earnings ($)	Take-home pay^a ($)	Work-related expenses^b ($)	AFDC benefits^c ($)	Net income_1 (B+D) ($)	Cumulative marginal tax rate_1 $(1-\frac{\Delta E}{\Delta A})$ (%)	Food Stamp bonus^d ($)	Net income_2 (E+G) ($)	Cumulative marginal tax rate_2 $(1-\frac{\Delta H}{\Delta A})$ (%)	Average Medicaid benefit^e ($)	Public housing subsidy^f ($)	Net income_3 (H+I+K) ($)	Cumulative marginal tax rate_3 $(1-\frac{\Delta L}{\Delta A})$ (%)
0	0	0	3384	3384	5	408	3792	30	888	1341	6021	52
576	546	144	3384	3930	50	264	4194	50	888	1214	6296	64
4300	3968	1075	1832	5800	61	264	6064	61	888	689	7641	76
8600	7414	2150	42	7456	120	264	7720	notch	888	92	8700	notch
8698	7436	2175	0	7436		0	7436		0	79	7515	

Note—The "Δ" symbol in parentheses means the "change in." For example, "ΔL" means the change in net income in column L between $6021 and $6296, and between $6296 and $7641, and so on.

^a Entries in this column are computed by subtracting the Social Security tax, federal income tax, and state income tax from "Gross Earnings," column A. The Social Security tax is determined by multiplying gross earnings under $9000 by .052. The federal income tax payment is computed in the following manner. Under the 1971 income tax law, a family of four that claimed four exemptions at $750 per exemption and the minimum standard deduction of $1300 would not pay any income tax on the first $4300 of annual income. Above $4300, the following schedule was in effect:

Income (dollars)	Tax rate (percent)
4301–5300	14
5301–6300	15
6301–7300	16
7301–8300	17
8301–12,300	18

of exemptions for a four-person family. Income above $4000 is taxed at a 2.5 percent rate. *Source*—State of Illinois, Department of Revenue, Form IL–1040.

[b] After $360 and $\frac{1}{3}$ of earnings above $360 are deducted from earnings in the process of computing the AFDC benefit, the Illinois Department of Public Aid allows the deduction of all mandatory payroll deductions, like taxes and health insurance premiums. Child care expenses are added to the benefit rather than deducted from earnings. Both these procedures involve the complete reimbursement of all work-related expenses. Gary Appel has estimated the relationship between payroll deductions, work-related expenses, and recipient earnings for the state of Michigan in fiscal year 1970. Relying on his findings and on the comparability of the definitions of payroll deductions and work-related expenses in Illinois and Michigan, I assumed that, on the average, they totaled 25 percent of gross earnings. *Sources*—U.S., Department of Health, Education, and Welfare, Assistance Payments Administration, "Summary of State Agency Policy on Expenses Reasonably Attributable to the Earning of Income—AFDC," mimeographed chart, 1971; and Gary L. Appel, *Effects of a Financial Incentive on AFDC Employment: Michigan's Experience between July 1969 and July 1970* (Minneapolis: Institute for Interdisciplinary Studies, March 1972), pp. 21–22.

[c] The annual AFDC benefit is determined by the following equation:

$$B = \$3384 - \{E - [\$360 + \tfrac{1}{3}(E - \$360) + .25E]\},$$

where the notation is the same as that given in footnote 4 in the text.

[d] The value of the Food Stamp bonus at zero income is $1272. Money income reduces the bonus at a rate of 25 percent, until the family is paying $1008 for its stamps—or receiving a bonus of $264. Then the bonus is not reduced any further until the AFDC benefit is zero. This procedure may be summarized in the following equations:

if

$0 < Y \le \$3960$,	$X = \$1272 - .25Y$	
$\$3960 < Y \le \$8698$,	$X = \$264$	
$Y > \$8698$,	$X = 0$	

where

$Y =$ gross money income, and is the sum of gross earnings and AFDC benefits, and
$X =$ Food Stamp bonus.

[e] The average Medicaid expenditure per person per month for AFDC recipients in Illinois was $19.54 in October, $18.33 in November, and $16.09 in December of 1971. From these data, I assumed that the average monthly expenditure was $18.50 throughout 1971. For a four-person family, the average Medicaid expenditure would be $888. The family receives Medicaid until its welfare benefit is reduced to zero. *Source*—Correspondence from Harold Nudelman, Illinois Department of Public Aid, 20 July 1972.

[f] The estimated market value of a two-bedroom public housing unit in Chicago in 1971 was $1920. The subsidy is equal to $1920 less the rent paid by the family. Rents in public housing units in Chicago are determined according to Secs. 212 and 213 of the Housing and Urban Development Act of 1969 (the Brooke amendment). From gross money income, a family deducts 5 percent of income, child care expenses, and $300 for each dependent. We assumed that child care expenses are zero. Then rent is set equal to 25 percent of net income. At $3384 of gross money income, the rent is $579 per year and the subsidy is $1341 (= $1920 − $579). *Source*—U.S., Congress, Senate, Committee on Finance, *Hearings on H.R. 1*, 92d Cong, 1st sess, 27 and 29 July, and 2 and 3 August 1971, p. 56; and U.S., Department of Housing and Urban Development, Housing Program Management Branch, Transmittal Notice 15, HM 7465.10, 4 April 1972.

45

of transfer programs considered, the cumulative tax rate is kept this low by a substantial "notch" at the break-even level of earnings in AFDC. At $8698 of annual earnings, the family loses its free medical care[13] and its remaining Food Stamp benefits, both of which were conditioned on AFDC eligibility.

In the AFDC–UF program,[14] the tax structure is the same as that in AFDC, except for one rule, that an AFDC–UF father forgoes the family's monthly benefit if he works 100 or more hours in the month, without regard to his earnings at that point. For example, if a man in Chicago worked exactly 100 hours in every month of the year at a wage of $1.00 per hour or $1200 per year, his AFDC–UF benefit would be zero.[15] His loss of AFDC–UF benefits would be cushioned by the fact that Food Stamp and public housing subsidies are income-conditioned, which means that those benefits would rise as his gross money income falls. In Illinois, he would also be eligible for Medicaid benefits until his income rose to four-thirds of the state cost standard, or $4504.[16] By contrast, if he worked exactly ninety-nine hours in every month at a wage of $7.23 per hour and earned $8600 per year, his earnings would be treated according to the "30 and $\frac{1}{3}$" and work-related expense rules, and he would receive an AFDC–UF benefit of $42 per year (see Table 2.1, line 4).[17]

The AFDC tax structure in Missouri is representative of that of a group of states (nine in December 1971) that impose a maximum on the size of their AFDC payments. Their procedure for adjusting benefits to earnings is the following: From gross earnings, $30 and one-third of the remainder are deducted; then work-related expenses, as defined by each state, are deducted from earnings net of the $30 and one-third. Next, earnings net of these deductions are compared to the difference between the state's "cost standard" and its maximum payment at zero income.

[13] Under the Medicaid "spend-down" rule, this family can begin receiving Medicaid benefits if its income remains above the AFDC break-even level, only if its medical costs exceed $4194 (=$8698 − $4504) per year; $4504 is ⁴⁄₃ of G, and is the level of income below which non-AFDC families may receive full Medicaid benefits.

[14] The AFDC–UF program is a segment of the AFDC program in which families with unemployed male heads receive federally aided Public Assistance. The program operates, with varying degrees of coverage, in just over 40 percent of the states.

[15] This would not be the case if he could establish eligibility for general assistance. His chances of doing so would vary by locality and state, and might be rather good in Chicago.

[16] At that point, he would not lose all of his Medicaid benefit. Rather, he would be subject to the Medicaid "spend-down" described in footnote 13.

[17] It would have been preferable to use data for California, since it had over one-third of the 138,000 AFDC–UF cases in early 1972. Illinois had the second largest AFDC–UF caseload, amounting to roughly one-seventh of the national caseload. U.S., Department of Health, Education, and Welfare, Social and Rehabilitation Service, *Public Assistance Statistics, January 1972*, Table 8.

Where net earnings are less than this difference, the earnings remained "untaxed" in the sense that the AFDC benefit is not reduced on their account; where earnings are larger than the difference, the family retains earnings equal to the difference, with earnings in excess of that difference reducing payments on a dollar-for-dollar basis. Families therefore receive the maximum payment if their net earnings are zero, and continue to receive the maximum until net earnings equal the difference between the cost standard and the maximum. The maximum has the effect of reducing the tax rate to zero on net earnings up to the difference between the cost standard and the maximum.[18]

The result of this procedure is that AFDC payments are reduced by less than $.67 for each dollar of earnings above $30. As in the first group of states, the deduction of work-related expenses from earnings after the "30 and $\frac{1}{3}$" rule has been applied means that earnings equal to such expenses do not affect AFDC payments. Here, too, a dollar of earnings eventually reduces the AFDC payments by $.42. In addition, though, in the instance of a family of four whose cost standard is $338 and whose maximum payment is $130, earnings net of the standard deductions less than or equal to $208 (=$338 − $130) do not reduce the welfare payment. Therefore, in this case, not until gross monthly earnings reach $547 do they begin to affect the welfare payment. Below $547 of monthly earnings, the AFDC benefit of $130 is not reduced at all; all earnings are absorbed by the various deductions, including the special one of this group of states, which is less than or equal to the cost standard minus the maximum payment. This special deduction varies by state and family size within the nine states.

The consequence of these deductions, apparent in Table 2.2, is that the combined tax rate from taxes and AFDC benefit reductions, $CMTR_1$

---

[18] Using the same notation as that used in footnote 4, the procedure can be described by the following equations:

(2a)		$B = C - [t(E - S) - F]$
when		$[t(E - S) - F] > C - G$
and		$B = G$
when		$[t(E - S) - F] \leqslant C - G,$

where C is the monthly state cost standard and G is the maximum payment. For a family of four in Missouri, C equals $338 and G equals $130, so $C - G$ equals $208. On the assumption that S equals $30, t equals $\frac{1}{3}$, and F equals $.25E$, net earnings equal $208 when gross earnings equal $547. For a family of four with gross earnings over $547,

(2b) $$B = C - \tfrac{1}{3}(E - \$30) + .25E.$$

The marginal tax rate on earnings for such a family is

(2c) $$\partial B / \partial E = -.42.$$

Table 2.2 Earnings, Taxes, and Transfers for a Female-Headed AFDC Family with Three Children in St. Louis, 1971

A	B	C	D	E	F	G	H	I	J	K	L	M
Gross earnings ($)	Take-home pay[a] ($)	Work-related expenses[b] ($)	AFDC benefits[c] ($)	Net income$_1$ (B+D) ($)	Cumulative marginal tax rate$_1$ $(1 - \frac{\Delta E}{\Delta A})$ (%)	Food Stamps bonus[a] ($)	Net income$_2$ (E+G) ($)	Cumulative marginal tax rate$_2$ $(1 - \frac{\Delta H}{\Delta A})$ (%)	Average Medicaid benefit ($)	Public housing subsidy[f] ($)	Net income$_3$ (H+J+K) ($)	Cumulative marginal tax rate$_3$ $(1 - \frac{\Delta L}{\Delta A})$ (%)
0	0	0	1560	1560		1116	2676		450	1600	4726	
					6 ∧			20 ∧				43 ∧
4300	4069	1075	1560	5629		794	6108		450	632	7190	
					48 ∧			42 ∧				56 ∧
6565	5248	1641	1559	6817		624	7441		450	308	8199	
					38 ∧			41 ∧				57 ∧
8550	7326	2137	739	8065		557	8622		450	0	9072	
					68 ∧			71 ∧				71 ∧
10,300	8627	2575	5	8632		499	9131		450	0	9581	
					43 ∧			notch ∧				notch ∧
10,326	8647	2581	0	8647		0	8647		0	0	8647	

[a] See Table 2.1, footnote a, but substitute the following in computing the state income tax. A female-headed family with three children may claim $3200 of personal exemption. Beyond that, it may deduct 5 percent of income and federal income taxes from income. Starting at 1 percent on the first $1000 of taxable income, the tax rate rises by ¼ of a percentage point for each $1000 of taxable income. *Source*—Missouri Department of Revenue, Form 28–19.

[b] Missouri has a schedule for relating the expenses of producing earned income to earnings. The average proportion of earnings spent producing them is roughly .25. *Source*—Missouri Division of Welfare *Caseworker's Manual*, Sec. VI, Appendixes A and D.

[c] See footnote 18 in the text. The numbers in that footnote should be converted to annual figures to compute annual AFDC benefits in the table.

[a] We were unable to obtain the formula used by the St. Louis Welfare Department in computing Food Stamp bonuses. Although we knew that the technique used is similar to that described in Table 2.1, footnote *d*, we assumed for convenience that Food Stamp benefits declined gradually as income rose. The equation used here was $X = \$1272 - .10(E + B - F)$, where X = Food Stamp bonus, and the rest of the notation follows footnote 4.

[e] Source—Correspondence from Bruce E. Smith, Missouri Department of Public Health and Welfare, 7 August 1972.

[f] The St. Louis Housing Authority determines rents by setting rents, R, at $R = .25 \ (.75E + .80B - \$600)$, where the notation follows footnote 4. The family's subsidy in this instance would be equal to the difference between the estimated market rental of its apartment (\$1600) and its rent. Source—St. Louis Housing Authority, "Rental Policy, Definition of Aggregate Gross Family Income and Definition of Adjusted Gross Income for Eligibility and for Rent."

Table 2.3 Earnings, Taxes, and Transfers for a Female-Headed AFDC Family with Three Children in Wilmington, 1971

A	B	C	D	E	F	G	H	I	J	K
Gross earnings ($)	Take-home pay[a] ($)	Work expenses[b] ($)	AFDC benefits[c] ($)	Net income_1 (B+D) ($)	Cumulative marginal tax rate_1 $(1-\frac{\Delta E}{\Delta A})$ (%)	Value of surplus commodities[d] ($)	Medicaid benefit[e] ($)	Public housing subsidy[f] ($)	Net income_2 (E+G+H+I) ($)	Cumulative marginal tax rate_2 $(1-\frac{\Delta J}{\Delta A})$ (%)
0	0	0	2066	2066		661	695	854	4276	
					> 7					> 54
420	392	0	2066	2458		661	695	656	4470	
					> 35					> 53
4172	3845	840	1069	4914		661	695	0	6270	
					> 86					> 86
6840	5295	840	2	5297		661	695	0	6653	
					> 60					> notch
6845	5299	840	0	5299		0	0	0	5299	

[a] See Table 2.1, footnote a, but substitute the following in computing the state income tax: The Delaware tax law allows a $600 exemption for each member of the family, a standard deduction of 10 percent of income, and the deduction of federal income taxes. The tax schedule for taxable income is

Taxable income (dollars)	Tax rate in bracket (percent)
0–1000	1½
1000–2000	2
2000–3000	3
3000–4000	4
4000–5000	5

Source—Delaware Division of Revenue, Form 200.

[b] The Delaware Welfare Department allows the deduction from earnings of $50 per month for work-related expenses and up to $20 per month for day care costs. We assumed that the maximum deduction was applied to earnings above $133 per month.

[c] The welfare benefit, B, is determined by the following formulas:

where

$$E \leq \$420, \quad B = \$2066,$$

where

$$E > \$420, \quad B = .60(\$3444 - \{E - [\$420 + \tfrac{1}{3}(E - \$420) + F]\}).$$

[d] The estimated market value of surplus foods for a family of four in 1971 was $661. The total package of foods is not reduced as E increases. *Source*—U.S., Congress, Senate, Committee on Finance, *Hearings on H.R. 1*, 92d Cong., 1st sess., 27 and 29 July and 2 and 3 August 1971, p. 53.

[e] The average expenditure per month on a family of four under the Medicaid program was $57.90 in 1971. *Source*—Correspondence from Harriet W. Duff, Delaware Division of Social Service Payments, 28 July 1972.

[f] The estimated market rental of a two-bedroom apartment in Wilmington in 1971 was $1020. Rents in public housing in that city are determined according to the Brooke amendment, described in footnote *f* of Table 2.1.

(column F), is 5.2 percent for the first $4300 of annual earnings and then barely exceeds 20 percent over the next $3000 of annual earnings. Even $CMTR_3$ (column M), the cumulative rate faced by recipients of AFDC, Food Stamps, and public housing, is kept around 50 percent up to $6568 of annual earnings. This implies that the current transfer system in this group of states affords recipients substantial financial incentive to work. Again, though, there is a sizable notch at $10,300 of annual earnings.

The AFDC tax structure of Delaware is representative of a third group of states (seven in December 1971). This procedure is the same as that used in the other two groups of states for the first two steps. But after earnings net of "30 and ⅓" and work expense deductions are subtracted from the state cost standard, the family receives an AFDC payment equal to a percentage of this difference.[19] The result of this procedure is that AFDC payments are reduced by less than $.67 for each dollar of earnings above $30. Again, the deduction of work-related expenses from earnings after the "30 and ⅓" rule has been applied means that earnings equal to such expenses do not affect AFDC payments. But now the marginal tax rate on earnings net of these deductions works out to be the product of multiplying 67 percent by the percentage applied to the cost standard minus net earnings. In the case of Delaware, the percentage is .60. So .60 times .667 is .40, which is the marginal tax or benefit reduction rate.

The tax rates for states in this third group are suggested by the numbers in Table 2.3, in which earnings, taxes, and benefits are computed again on an annual basis. Note that, for a family receiving food, housing, and medical subsidies, $CMTR_2$ is about 50 percent over the first $4200 of annual earnings. Again, though, there is a severe notch at the AFDC break-even level, where the rules of the surplus commodities and Medicaid programs dictate that families suddenly lose their benefits from these programs. Having such a notch, of course, makes it easier to retain low cumulative tax rates without raising break-even levels of income.

[19] Using p for some percentage of the difference between the cost standard and net earnings (countable income), and otherwise using the same notation employed in footnotes 4 and 18, their procedure can be expressed in this manner:

(3) $$B = p(C - \{E - [S + (1 - t)(E - S) + F]\}).$$

In Delaware, S equals 35 and F is fixed at $70, which divides into $20 for child care and $50 for other work-related expenses; p equals .60; thus,

(3a) $$B = .60[\$287 - \tfrac{2}{3}E + \$105].$$

Therefore, the marginal tax rate in the AFDC program is

(3b) $$\partial B/\partial E = -.40.$$

For families receiving AFDC, tax rates under AFDC alone and cumulatively are surprisingly low. Tables 2.1 through 2.3 also show that benefits to families receiving in-kind transfers raise total benefits at zero earnings to substantial levels. Even in Missouri, where the AFDC guarantee is $1560 per year, total benefits can be raised to over $4600 by the receipt of Food Stamps, Medicaid, and public housing.[20] In states with high AFDC guarantees, the low AFDC tax rate raises break-even levels of income for female-headed families to over $7000 to $8000. In states with low AFDC guarantees, even lower tax rates can raise break-even income levels to those reached in the high-payment states. Cumulative tax rates are kept below 80 or 90 percent by the fact that Food Stamp and public housing benefits are conditioned on total income—including AFDC payments adjusted for earnings. (To understand this last point well, the closing part of Section IV must be read carefully.) Cumulative tax rates are also kept down by the notches in the benefit schedules.

In actuality, average effective cumulative tax rates may be lower than those suggested in Tables 2.1–2.3. First, some earnings may go unreported by recipients or be ignored by caseworkers.[21] Second, the one-month accounting period in AFDC allows for a family to receive no earnings and full benefit in month 1; substantial earnings and no benefit in month 2 as the family is removed from AFDC; and no earnings and full benefit again in month 3, if the earnings of month 2 were spent and the family reestablished eligibility. This allows the family to receive higher total benefits than if the accounting period were one year. Third, there are lags in accounting in the Food Stamp, Medicaid, and housing programs; and one suspects that, if the lags exist, they are more likely to exist when earnings rise than when they fall. That is, the Food Stamp, Medicaid, and housing authorities either are too busy to adjust bonuses, eligibility, and rents to increases in earnings or simply are not informed of such increases. On the other hand, as earnings decline, beneficiaries are more likely to demand upward adjustments in benefits.

III. Cumulative Tax Rates under the House-Passed Welfare Reform Plan (H.R. 1, 92d Cong.) and in the BritishWelfare Reform Programs

The previous section indicated that the current transfer system contains high cumulative benefits, surprisingly low cumulative tax rates, and,

[20] The benefits are valued at this cost to the government, not by the recipients.
[21] Joel F. Handler and Ellen Jane Hollingsworth, *"The Deserving Poor": A Study of Welfare Administration* (Chicago: Markham, 1971), pp. 143–146.

consequently, high break-even levels of earnings and large notches. Given these characteristics, this system is sustainable at an acceptable cost for two reasons. One is that families do not qualify for AFDC until their incomes fall below the AFDC cost standards;[22] or, for Medicaid, until their incomes are either less than four-thirds of the AFDC standards or less than the AFDC standards, depending upon the state. A second reason is that three-fourths of all poor families headed by males are excluded from the AFDC and AFDC–UF program because the males are neither incapacitated nor unemployed or because the states in which they reside do not have an AFDC–UF program. A program of welfare reform that seeks to remove the horizontal inequities that arise from these exclusions must either lower benefits or raise tax rates, unless it is to be substantially more expensive than the current system. The version of welfare reform proposed by the Nixon administration, and passed by the House in 1972 as H.R. 1, sought to eliminate those inequities by raising benefits for families with the lowest AFDC payments, raising tax rates substantially, tightening the income accounting system, and raising total costs by roughly $5 billion. The tax rates in H.R. 1 and related programs are discussed here.

A major modification in the AFDC tax structure contained in H.R. 1 is the replacement of the full reimbursement of broadly defined work-related expenses by an increase in the monthly disregard from $30 to $60 per month, or to $720 on an annual basis; and by making child care expenses, up to a limit of $2000 per year, deductible from earnings. Two-thirds of earnings net of these deductions are deducted from the payment made to the family at zero income. The benefit reduction rate that results from this procedure is 67 percent above the earnings disregard, for families that incur no child care expenses. If a family were to incur such expenses equal, say (very generously), to 20 percent of gross earnings, then benefits would be reduced at a 53 percent rate as earnings increase.[23] The tax rates that prevail in the current AFDC program are lower than these for two reasons. One is that, under AFDC, work-related expenses are defined to

---

[22] This does not contradict the material in Section II, which shows that women with earnings above AFDC guarantees can receive AFDC benefits. One cannot qualify initially for AFDC until his income falls below the cost standard, however.

[23] Algebraically, the procedure for determining the net benefit can be expressed as follows:

$$(4) \qquad B = G - [(E - F - S) - (1 - t)(E - F - S)]$$

where F equals child care costs and the other notation is the same as that employed above. From (4), the marginal tax rate can be derived:

$$(4a) \qquad B = G - t(E - F - S)$$
$$(4b) \qquad \partial B / \partial E = -t.$$

include more than child care costs, and are more likely to include expenditures that are not purely work-related. A second is that, under AFDC, such expenses are deducted after the "30 and $\frac{1}{3}$" deductions are made from gross earnings. Thus, in AFDC, a dollar of earnings adds more to the real net income of a family than it would under H.R. 1.

In some states, the payment level would be $2400 for a family of four. In others, it would exceed $2400, if it currently is above $2400 in the AFDC program and if the state decides to continue to support families at current levels with state supplementary payments. Table 2.4 shows how the payment varies with earnings in a state that makes supplementary payments. Note that the H.R. 1 proposal specifies that the federal portion of the payment is reduced by increases in earnings before the state portion of the payment. With the same payment level as that used in Table 2.1, the new H.R. 1 tax structure reduces the break-even level of earnings from $8698 to $6000. Table 2.5 shows how the payment varies with earnings in a state that does not make supplementary payments. In Delaware, although the guarantee level was $2066 under AFDC and would rise from there to $2400 under H.R. 1, the new tax structure would mean that the break-even level of earnings would fall from $6850 per year to $4320. Thus, even with an increase in the initial disregard, the elimination of both the reimbursement of all work-related expenses and of the special deductions for families in the second and third groups of states described in Section II means a large increase in average tax rates and thus a fall in break-even levels of income in all three groups of states. If work-related expenses were considered as taxes by recipients, then one-third of such expenses should be added to taxes. In this case, the tax rates are higher than those given in Tables 2.4–2.6.

Tables 2.4 and 2.5 were constructed on the assumption that the female head of the family would place one of her children in a federally financed full-time day care center under the fee schedule included in the Mondale day care bill (S. 3617). It proposed that a family would pay no fee for this day care if its earnings were less than $4320 per year. Above $4320, it would be charged fees based on the schedule given in footnote *b* of Table 2.4. What appears in column C of Tables 2.4 and 2.5 is the *net* day care subsidy that would be received by the H.R. 1 family. From the dollar value of the day care subsidy, from the point of view of the government paying for it, the day care fee paid by the family is deducted.

Where F is some constant proportion of E, say F equals .20E, and t equals .67, the marginal tax rate is

(4c)
$$B = G - \tfrac{2}{3}(E - .20E - S)$$
$$\partial B / \partial E = -.533.$$

Table 2.4 Earnings, Taxes, and Transfers for a Female-Headed H.R. 1 Family with Three Children in Chicago

A	B	C	D	E	F	G	H	I	J	K	L	M
Gross earnings ($)	Take-home pay[a] ($)	Net day care subsidy[b] ($)	H.R. 1 benefit[c] ($)	State supplement[d] ($)	Net income$_1$ $(B+C+D+E)$ ($)	Cumulative marginal tax rate$_1$ $(1-\frac{\Delta F}{\Delta A})$ (%)	Medicaid benefit[e] ($)	Net income$_2$ $(F+H)$ ($)	Cumulative marginal tax rate$_2$ $(1-\frac{\Delta I}{\Delta A})$ (%)	Public housing subsidy[f] ($)	Net income$_3$ $(I+K)$ ($)	Cumulative marginal tax rate$_3$ $(1-\frac{\Delta L}{\Delta A})$ (%)
0	0	2052	2400	984	5436		691	6127		1329	7456	
						5			25			50
720	683	2052	2400	984	6119		547	6666		1149	7815	
						72			79			87
4320	4084	2052	0	984	7120		307	7427		849	8276	
						91			99			107
6000	5392	1884	0	0	7276		168	7444		675	8119	
						36			56			81
6840	6037	1778	0	0	7815		0	7815		465	8280	
						40			40			65
8700	7438	1500	0	0	8938		0	8938		0	8938	

[a] See Table 2.1, footnote a.

[b] Note that we assumed that women placed their children in day care centers on a full-time basis, no matter how many hours they worked. Had we assumed that their use of day care varied directly with hours worked, the net day care subsidy also would have risen with hours worked. Thus, net income in column F would have increased more rapidly with earnings and hours worked—and the cumulative marginal tax rate would have been lowered substantially. Unless the day care subsidy is viewed by recipients as an increase in spendable income, as opposed to an offset to an expense that otherwise would be incurred, the lowered tax rate then would have overstated the financial incentive to increase work effort. If some part of the day care subsidy is viewed by recipients as a consumption good, then the tax rates in the table should be somewhat lower. The day care fee schedule is taken from the Mondale day care bill (S. 3617, 92d Cong., 2d sess.). That bill set upper limits on the fees that

DHEW can charge for day care centers. For families with one child in a day care center, no fee is charged on the first $4320 of annual income; a fee of no more than 10 percent of income above $4320 and below 85 percent of the local BLS lower level of living budget can be charged over that range of income; and, between 85 and 100 percent of the BLS budget, a ceiling of 15 percent of the income is placed on day care fees. The bill is not clear about its definition of family income, but we assumed it to exclude transfer payments.

In Chicago in the fall of 1971, the lower level of living budget for a four-person family was $7536, 85 percent of which is $6406. Thus, we set the fees at 0 between 0 and $4320, at 10 percent of income between $4321 and $6406, and at 15 percent of income between $6407 and $7536, and at the same 15 percent above $7536. The day care subsidy is the difference between the market value of day care, estimated by Krashinsky to be $2052 for developmental day care in 1972, and the paid fees. Source—Michael Krashinsky, "Day Care and Welfare," this volume.

[c] The H.R. 1 formula for computing benefits is $B = G - t(E - F - S)$. The notation is the same as that given in footnote 4.

In Illinois, where state supplementary payments would equal $984 at zero income if current benefits are maintained, $G = \$3384$; $S = \$720$ annually nationwide and t is assumed to equal $\frac{2}{3}$ until state supplements are reduced to zero. In this instance, F is not positive until E exceeds $4320.

[d] Under H.R. 1, the state supplement is not reduced until the federal portion of G is reduced to 0. The tax rate is allowed to be something other than $\frac{2}{3}$ when the federal benefit reaches 0. In this illustration, t is always $\frac{2}{3}$.

[e] Under a proposed change in the Medicaid program passed by the Senate Finance Committee in mid-1972, eligible families would have to pay a deductible equal to 20 percent of income in excess of $2400 before they could receive free Medicaid benefits. Although this formula was designed to accompany the Finance Committee's work and assistance program, it was used here on the assumption that it was likely to be attached to H.R. 1. The subsidy recorded in this column is the average value of Medicaid benefits in Illinois, $885, less the deductible. Income is equal to take-home pay plus assistance benefit.

[f] See Table 2.1, footnote f.

Table 2.5 Earnings, Taxes, and Transfers for a Female-Headed H.R. 1 Family with Three Children in Wilmington

A	B	C	D	E	F	G	H	I	J	K	L	M
Gross earnings [a] ($)	Take-home pay [a] ($)	Net day care subsidy [b] ($)	H.R.1 benefit [c] ($)	State supplement [d] ($)	Net income$_1$ (B+C+D+E) ($)	Cumulative marginal tax rate$_1$ $(1-\frac{\Delta F}{\Delta A})$ (%)	Medicaid benefit [e] ($)	Net income$_2$ (F+H) ($)	Cumulative marginal tax rate$_2$ $(1-\frac{\Delta I}{\Delta A})$ (%)	Public housing subsidy [f] ($)	Net income$_3$ (I+K) ($)	Cumulative marginal tax rate$_3$ $(1-\frac{\Delta L}{\Delta A})$ (%)
0	0	1952	2400	0	4352		695	5047		675	5722	
720	683	1952	2400	0	5035	5	551	5586	25	495	6081	50
4320	4067	1952	0	0	6019	73	311	6330	79	195	6525	88
5100	4686	1874	0	0	6560	31	155	6715	51	0	6715	76
5875	5261	1796	0	0	7057	36	0	7057	56	0	7057	56

[a] See Table 2.1, footnote a.
[b] We arbitrarily assume that a given quality day care cost $100 less in Wilmington than in Chicago. The BLS budget in the area closest to Wilmington, Philadelphia, costs out at $7406, 85 percent of which is $6295. See Table 2.4, footnote b.
[c] See Table 2.4, footnote c, for the H.R. 1 benefit formula. In it, G = $2400 for Wilmington.
[d] We assumed that Delaware would not supplement the basic federal benefit.
[e] See Table 2.4, footnote e, for the Medicaid deductible formula and Table 2.3, footnote e, for the value of Medicaid in Delaware.
[f] See Table 2.1, footnote f, for the Brooke amendment formula and Table 2.3, footnote f, for the value of public housing apartments in Wilmington.

Thus, net income in column F of Tables 2.4 and 2.5 includes the gross day care subsidy as income and the day care fee as a tax on income.[24]

In a state where the guarantee level is $2400 and the break-even level is $4320, the deductibility of the day care fee cannot affect the break-even level—simply because no fee is charged until the break-even level is reached. In a state where the guarantee exceeds $2400, the deductibility of the day care fee reduces further the burden of day care and does affect the break-even level. Thus, in Illinois, the break-even level without deducting the day care fee would be $5796, not the $6000 that it would become when a deduction is allowed.

Table 2.6 illustrates a case where a family would finance completely its own day care. The deductibility of the day care fee, which here is below the $2000 limit in H.R. 1 on the day care deduction, has the effect of reimbursing the recipient for two-thirds of her day care expenses, and thus of keeping the sum of reduced benefits and nonreimbursed day care costs to two-thirds of earnings above the disregard. The deduction also raises the break-even level by the amount of gross day care costs. This means that the break-even level of earnings in Illinois would be raised from the $5796 level that it would be without the deduction of the day care fee to $6440.

Besides the major changes made by H.R. 1 in the deductibility of work-related expenses, the second modification in the welfare tax structure is the elimination of the "100-hour notch" for male heads of AFDC–UF families. Male-headed families would face the same tax rates under H.R. 1 as female-headed families. Differences in cumulative tax rates would result, however, because male-headed households would probably not receive state supplements and, typically, would not avail themselves of day care and the deduction for associated expenditures.

Now it is necessary to compare the cumulative tax rates under the current transfer system with those that would obtain were H.R. 1 to be passed. H.R. 1 has generated a number of proposals concerning the Food Stamp and Medicaid programs. The Food Stamp program would be ended for all H.R. 1 families. The public housing rent formula would be that embodied in the Brooke amendment to the Housing and Development Act of 1969. When H.R. 1 passed the House in 1971, it contained a provision for a Medicaid deductible to eliminate the notch in the current program. In essence, H.R. 1 families would have had to pay for those medical costs that equaled the one-third of earnings above the $720 dis-

---

[24] The income figures in Tables 2.4 and 2.5, as well as others including a net day care subsidy, appear high. They reflect what the government is spending on families receiving the particular configuration of benefits, not necessarily the family's dollar value of the combination of commodities it receives.

Table 2.6 Earnings, Taxes, and Transfers for a Female-Headed H.R. 1 Family with Three Children in Chicago, Where Day Care Is Paid Initially by Recipient

A	B	C	D	E	F	G	H	I	J	K	L	M	N
Gross earnings ($)	Take-home pay[a] ($)	Day care fee[b] ($)	Implicit day care subsidy[b] ($)	H.R. 1 benefit[c] ($)	State supplement[d] ($)	Net income$_1$ $[B+(D-C)+E+F]$[f] ($)	Cumulative marginal tax rate$_1$ $(1 - \frac{\Delta G}{\Delta A})$ (%)	Medicaid benefit[e] ($)	Net income$_2$ $(G+I)$ ($)	Cumulative marginal tax rate$_2$ $(1 - \frac{\Delta J}{\Delta A})$ (%)	Public housing subsidy[f] ($)	Net income$_3$ $(J+L)$ ($)	Cumulative marginal tax rate$_3$ $(1 - \frac{\Delta M}{\Delta A})$ (%)
0	0	0	0	2400	984	3384		691	4075		1329	5404	
800	758	80	53	2400	984	4169	2	531	4700	22	1166	5866	43
4800	4460	480	320	0	984	5604	65	211	5815	73	854	6669	80
6440	5731	644	430	0	0	5945	80	80	6025	88	789	6814	92
6840	6040	684	456	0	0	6268	20	0	6268	40	725	6993	56

[a] See Table 2.1, footnote a.

[b] H.R. 1 permits the deduction of expenditures on day care from income before the benefit is computed. The assumption here is that a mother pays the full cost of day care, which is assumed to equal 10 percent of earnings. Allowing the deduction when the implicit tax rate on earnings is 66⅔ percent means that the family is reimbursed for two-thirds of its day care expenditures. That is the subsidy listed in column D.

[c] See Table 2.4, footnote c.

[d] See Table 2.4, footnote d.

[e] See Table 2.4, footnote e.

[f] See Table 2.1, footnote f.

regard that would be retained under the earnings deduction in H.R. 1.[25] In mid-1972, the Senate Finance Committee developed an alternative Medicaid deductible in connection with its Guaranteed Job Opportunity program. This deductible would equal 20 percent of cash income in excess of $2400. This would lower the potential Medicaid tax rate from the level initially proposed by H.R. 1, because the deductible is based on changes in money income, inclusive of H.R. 1 benefits, rather than changes in gross earnings, as well as because it is set at 20 percent rather than $33\frac{1}{3}$ percent.

A comparison of the figures in Tables 2.4, 2.5, and 2.6 with those in 2.1, 2.2, and 2.3 shows a marked increase in cumulative tax rates under the H.R. 1 system over those in the AFDC system. For families receiving only H.R. 1 and Medicaid benefits, cumulative tax rates generally would be higher because of the elimination of the full reimbursement of work-related expenses and the types of deductions available in the second and third groups of states discussed in Section I. For families using either income-conditioned, publicly financed day care or privately financed day care, marginal tax rates would rise, although the day care deduction would reduce that increase. For H.R. 1 families using day care, it is appropriate to compare $CMTR_2$ in Tables 2.4, 2.5, and 2.6 with $CMTR_1$ in Tables 2.1, 2.2, and 2.3, remembering that all ought to be equally higher to the extent that work expenses are treated as taxes. Families in public housing that also use income-conditioned day care facilities generally would face marginal cumulative tax rates in excess of 80 percent under H.R. 1. These higher cumulative tax rates would mean that, in most AFDC families where the head currently is employed, the implementation of H.R. 1 would reduce net income. The one great advantage of H.R. 1 with regard to tax rates would be its elimination of notches and most horizontal inequities among low-income families.

At this point, a digression is in order, to observe how the recently instituted reforms in British income maintenance programs compare with H.R. 1 as regards cumulative tax rates.[26] In 1971, the British government established the family income supplements (FIS) program, an income-conditioned transfer program for households headed by employed men

[25] This Medicaid deductible would have taken effect at different levels of earnings in the fifty states. Where states provide Medicaid to the "medically indigent," for those with incomes between G and $\frac{4}{3}G$, the deductible was to be paid when earnings exceeded $720 by $\frac{4}{3}G - G$. U.S., Congress, Senate, Committee on Finance, *Medicare and Medicaid Amendments: Material Related to H.R. 1*, 92d Cong., 1st sess., 16 July 1971, pp. 20–25.

[26] I obtained the material on welfare reform in Great Britain as well as ideas about its characteristics from Martin Rein and Hugh Heclo, both of whom I wish to thank.

Table 2.7 Weekly Earnings, Transfers, Taxes, and Marginal Tax Rates after British Welfare Reform for a Male-Headed Family with Two School-Age Children in Oxford City, 1972

A	B	C	D	E	F	G	H	I	J	K	L	M	N	O
Weekly earnings	National insurance tax[a]	Family allowance	Total taxable income (A+C)	Income tax[b]	Family income supplement[c]	Total income for housing benefits (A+C+F)	Rent rebate[d]	Property tax rebate[e]	Free school meals[f]	Free prescriptions[g]	Optical-dental benefits	Net cash and in-kind income $(G-(B+E)+H+I+J+K+L)$	Change in net income (ΔM)	Marginal tax rate $1-\left(\frac{\Delta N}{\Delta A}\right)$
(£)	(£)	(£)	(£)	(£)	(£)	(£)	(£)	(£)	(£)	(£)	(£)	(£)	(£)	(%)
12.00	1.03	0.90	12.90	0	5.00	17.90	3.51	0.80	0.92	0.50	0.75	23.35		
													0.32	68
13.00	1.08	.90	13.90	0	4.50	18.40	3.38	.80	.92	.50	.75	23.67		
													.36	64
14.00	1.13	.90	14.90	0	4.00	18.90	3.29	.80	.92	.50	.75	24.03		
													.36	64
15.00	1.18	.90	15.90	0	3.50	19.40	3.20	.80	.92	.50	.75	24.39		
													.34	66
16.00	1.23	.90	16.90	0	3.00	19.90	3.12	.77	.92	.50	.75	24.73		
													.24	76
17.00	1.28	.90	17.90	0	2.50	20.40	3.03	.65	.92	.50	.75	24.97		
													.25	75
18.00	1.32	.90	18.90	0	2.00	20.90	2.95	.52	.92	.50	.75	25.22		
													.25	75
19.00	1.36	.90	19.90	0	1.50	21.40	2.86	.40	.92	.50	.75	25.47		
													.25	75
20.00	1.40	.90	20.90	0	1.00	21.90	2.78	.27	.92	.50	.75	25.72		
													.16	84

20.60	1.42	.90	21.50	0	.70	22.20	2.73	.20	.92	.50	.75	25.88	>	−.02	102
21.00	1.44	.90	21.90	.12	.50	22.40	2.70	.15	.92	.50	.75	25.86	>	−1.31	231
22.00	1.48	.90	22.90	.42	0	22.90	2.61	.02	.92	0	0	24.55	>	.47	53
23.00	1.52	.90	23.90	.72	0	23.90	2.44	0	.92	0	0	25.02	>	.49	51
24.00	1.56	.90	24.90	1.02	0	24.90	2.27	0	.92	0	0	25.51	>	.49	51
25.00	1.60	.90	25.90	1.32	0	25.90	2.10	0	.92	0	0	26.00	>	.49	51
26.00	1.64	.90	26.90	1.62	0	26.90	1.93	0	.46	0	0	26.49	>	.49	51
27.00	1.68	.90	27.90	1.92	0	27.90	1.76	0	0	0	0	26.06	>	−.43	143

[a] The national insurance tax rate is 5 percent of earnings up to £17 per week, above which it is 4 percent of each increment in earnings.

[b] The income tax rate is 30 percent of earnings in excess of £21.50.

[c] The FIS benefit equals 50 percent of the difference between £22 and gross weekly earnings.

[d] Families in public housing are charged rents according to a national rent rebate and allowance scheme. Under this scheme, income is defined to include all money income less specified exemptions (which are not relevant in this illustration). A family is then assigned a needs allowance, A, of £13.50 for a couple plus £2.50 per child per week. (A British pound is now worth roughly $2.40.) If the family's gross rent, R_g, is £5.60 per week and if its nonexempt income, Y_n, is below an A of £18.50, its net rent payment, R_n, is .40 R_g − .25($A − Y_n$). Its rent rebate, S, then, is $R_g − R_n$. Where $Y_n > A$, S declines by 17 percent of the change in Y_n. The rent assumption is taken from Tony Lynes, "How to Pay Surtax While Living on the Breadline" (unpublished, Center for Environmental Studies, London, March 1971). The rent rebate rules are given in Social Services Department, *A Guide to Welfare Benefits in Oxfordshire*, April 1972, p. 6c.

[e] In a two-parent two-children family, the property tax rebate is set at ½ of the tax up to an income of £19.75 per week. Above that income level, the rebate is reduced at a 25 percent rate. The gross property tax is assumed to be £1.60 per week. *Sources*—Lynes, "How to Pay Surtax"; Social Services Department, *Guide*, p. 7a.

Table 2.7 (cont.)

f Over the entire calendar year, the average value of school meals is 46p per child per week. From the sum of earnings and family allowances, but not family income supplements, a family deducts its net rent, net property taxes, and work-related expenses. For a family with two children, free school meals are provided to both children until net income reaches £15.75 per week; from that point up to the point where net income reaches £16.75 per week, only one child remains eligible for free school meals. Beyond £16.75 per week, both children are ineligible.
Sources–Lynes, "How to Pay Surtax"; Social Services Department, *Guide*, pp. 8a–b.

g Having no data, I arbitrarily assigned an average weekly value to the pharmaceutical prescriptions and optical and dental benefits that the average family might receive. A family loses its eligibility for these benefits when its income reduces its family income supplement to zero.
Source–Social Services Department, *Guide*, pp. 2a, 3.

or women who must be employed for thirty or more hours per week to be eligible for benefits; FIS contains a 50 percent tax rate on earnings. Along with FIS, an income-conditioned national rent rebate and allowance program was passed for families in public housing. The British also have an income-conditioned property tax rebate system that varies by locality but covers a substantial proportion of all families. As seen in Table 2.7, certain food and medical programs are also income-conditioned, albeit on an eligible versus ineligible basis.

Given this great variety of income-conditioned cash and in-kind transfer programs, cumulative tax rates are quite high, roughly up to the mean production worker's wage of £26 ($62 in 1972) per week. The British also have a Social Security tax (column B) and an income tax that has but a small overlap with the FIS system. The combination of tax and transfer programs produces cumulative tax rates that do not fall below 64 percent up to £23 ($55) weekly earnings, and then not below 51 percent up to the mean wage, in spite of the definitions of income used in the housing, food, and medical programs. Notch problems persist in these programs, as is evident in column O. Given the thirty-hour work rule, the high tax rates are likely to affect workers who can control their hours of work above thirty per week, as well as full-time workers who consider moving to higher-wage jobs.

Apparently, when the electorate demands a variety of transfer programs, it is quite difficult to keep cumulative tax rates down without extending coverage too far. The tables on H.R. 1 and the British income transfer system tend to validate that point.

IV. Cumulative Tax Rates in Alternatives to H.R. 1

Thus far, we have demonstrated that, while the current AFDC program and related transfer mechanisms have surprisingly low cumulative tax rates, efforts to eliminate inequities and notches in the existing system under H.R. 1 would result in exceedingly high and sometimes confiscatory cumulative rates. Consequently, the search for alternatives to H.R. 1 continues. This section explores the cumulative rates in various negative income tax, demogrant, and earnings subsidy plans.

In analyzing these three types of cash transfer plans, the same formulas, contained in the notes to Table 2.8, are used to compute work-related, medical, housing, and day care expenditures and, thus, subsidies. The benefit formulas have been carefully developed by other persons, and are held constant in all the transfer systems discussed here to allow comparison among the various cash transfer proposals working in con-

Table 2.8 Earnings, Taxes, and Transfers for a Family of Four under a Negative Income Tax Program with a Constant Tax Rate

A	B	C	D	E	F	G	H	I	J	K	L	M	N
Gross earnings ($)	Work-related expenses[a] ($)	Negative income tax benefit[b] ($)	Net income_1[c] ($)	Cumulative marginal tax rate_1 $\left(1-\frac{\Delta D}{\Delta A}\right)$ (%)	Medical insurance subsidy[a] ($)	Net income_2 $(D+F)$ ($)	Cumulative marginal tax rate_2 $\left(1-\frac{\Delta G}{\Delta A}\right)$ (%)	Housing subsidy[e] ($)	Net income_3 $(G+I)$ ($)	Cumulative marginal tax rate_3 $\left(1-\frac{\Delta J}{\Delta A}\right)$ (%)	Day care subsidy[f] ($)	Net income_4 $(J+L)$ ($)	Cumulative marginal tax rate_4 $\left(1-\frac{\Delta M}{\Delta A}\right)$ (%)
0	0	3600	3600		463	4063		490	4553		2052	6605	
				> 50			> 55			> 59			> 59
2800	280	2340	4993		329	5322		386	5708		2052	7760	
				> 51			> 56			> 62			> 65
4780	478	1449	5960		237	6197		254	6451		2009	8460	
				> 66			> 69			> 73			> 86
8000	800	0	7050		131	7181		145	7326		1569	8895	
				> 26			> 31			> 38			> 58
9800	980	0	8429		0	8429		7	8436		1208	9644	
				> 22			> 22			> 29			> 49
9900	990	0	8507		0	8507		0	8507		1188	9695	

[a] Work-related expenses are assumed to be proportional to earnings. For some interesting thoughts on the issue of work-related expenses, see Michael K. Taussig, "Notes on Work Expenses and Related Issues for Personal Income Taxation" (unpublished memorandum, Rutgers University, New Brunswick, N.J., July 1972).

[b] The benefit, B, is determined by the following formula: $B = \$3600 - .50(E - D)$ where the notation follows that given in footnote 27 of the text.

[c] Entries in this column are computed by adding earnings to the negative income tax benefit and then subtracting the Social Security tax payment, federal income tax payment, and the state income tax payment. The Social Security tax payment is determined by multiplying earnings by .052. Work-related expenses are deducted from gross earnings before the federal tax is computed. Except for this modification, the regular federal tax schedule is assumed here. The state tax schedule that is used is that of Illinois for 1971. See Table 2.1, footnote a.

[d] The value of the medical insurance provided to a family with zero income is assumed to incur medical costs of $800 per year. It pays for a part of these costs (and thereby has its medical insurance subsidy reduced) according to a formula offered by Feldstein, Friedman, and Luft: It must pay a premium for health insurance equal to $50 plus 1 percent of income in excess of $3000 but less than $12,000 per year; it also must pay a deductible of $50 per adult plus $25 per child, plus 5 percent of income in excess of $3000 but less than $12,000 per year; it must also pay a portion of medical costs above the deductible and up to a maximum of $1400 per year equal to 8 percent of those costs plus 4 percent of the costs for every $1000 of family income above $3000 but below $12,000. The subsidy shown is $750 less medical payments at the given level of income and with annual medical costs of $800. The assumption that medical costs do not vary with income may be weak. If medical costs rise with income, the medical "tax rate" would be higher than that shown here. For the medical insurance formula and program, see Martin Feldstein, Bernard Friedman, and Harold Luft, "Distributional Aspects of National Health Insurance Benefits and Finance" (unpublished paper, Harvard University, 1972), p. 18.

[e] The housing allowance is equal to $500 − .10(net income$_1$ − $3500). This is obtained from Henry J. Aaron, "Alternative Ways to Increase Work Effort under Income Maintenance Systems," this volume.

[f] See Table 2.4, footnote b.

junction with a particular set of in-kind components. The medical, housing, and day care programs use a comprehensive definition of income, one that includes cash transfer benefits adjusted for earnings. When the benefits of a program depend on earnings plus the net benefits from other programs that are calculated first, the programs are said to be "sequenced." The programs here are sequenced to the extent that the medical, housing, and day care programs base their benefits on earnings plus cash benefits. A fully sequenced system would, for example, also count the value of Medicaid benefits in computing housing benefits and the value of both these in-kind programs in computing the day care subsidy.

Table 2.8 shows a negative income tax plan that has a constant implicit tax or benefit reduction rate of 50 percent. Using the notation employed in footnote 4, the net benefit, B, under this program can be computed from the following equation: $B =$ the family guarantee minus the tax rate on income (or the benefit reduction rate) times the quantity family income minus allowable deductions.[27] As an example, with a tax rate of 50 percent if the family guarantee is $3600, family earnings are $3000, and work expenses of $300 can be deducted, a family of four would have the following benefit:

$$B = \$3600 - 0.50(\$3000 - \$300)$$
$$= \$3600 - \$1350$$
$$= \$2250.$$

In Table 2.8, where the guarantee is $3600, the tax rate is 50 percent, and work-related expenses are 10 percent of earnings, the cumulative tax rate on earnings for a family receiving only negative income tax (NIT) benefits never falls below 50 percent until earnings reach $8000. The effect of allowing a deduction of 10 percent of earnings for work-related expenses is to reduce by five percentage points the effective benefit reduction rate and to increase the break-even level of income from $7200 to $8000. On the assumption that all NIT families also would receive income-conditioned medical and housing subsidies, but no food subsidies,

---

[27] Algebraically expressed, the equation is

$$B = G - t(E - D)$$

where B, G, and E are defined in footnote 4 and

  $t =$ the tax rate on income or benefit reduction rate,
  $D =$ deductions from income, assumed throughout to be composed solely of work-related expenses.

If E and D are related positively, the marginal tax rate is less than t.

$CMTR_3$ would never be below roughly 60 percent up to $8000; and over the broad $4780 to $8000 range of earnings, in which blue-collar and clerical workers would be concentrated, $CMTR_3$ would be 73 percent. While $CMTR_3$ might become the cumulative rate facing male heads of household, for female-headed families, among whom use of subsidized day care would be concentrated, $CMTR_4$ in column N would be the relevant cumulative rate. It would be yet higher than $CMTR_3$, rising to 86 percent over the same important range of earnings.

The cash transfer program contained in Table 2.9 is a demogrant, a program in which each person in the population is *nominally* eligible for a payment that typically is offset against whatever income tax is owed. The same formula used to compute benefits under the NIT program can be used in the case of a demogrant. In principle, what differentiates the NIT from the demogrant are administrative aspects of the program, not the benefit formulas. For example, one administrative difference is that, under an NIT, the tax rate actually serves to reduce the size of the benefit check that a family receives as earnings rise. In a demogrant, the tax rate applies directly to earnings, with the paycheck and not the benefit check being reduced as earnings increase; the benefit check always is constant for individuals with given demographic character-istics.[28] The demogrant program illustrated in Table 2.9 provides $1200 per year to adults and $600 to children. The tax rate arbitrarily is set at $33\frac{1}{3}$ percent so as to be lower than the tax rate in Table 2.8[29] The lower tax rate necessitates higher tax rates on nonbeneficiaries, of course.

While the demogrant starts with a low tax rate on earnings, the cumulative tax rate again depends on the number of in-kind transfer programs in operation and the tax rates (and tax bases) in each of them. $CMTR_3$ and $CMTR_4$ for from $2800 to $8000 of earnings are much lower in Table 2.9 than in Table 2.8. Note, though, that above $9800 of earnings, the reverse is the case, because $8000 is the break-even earnings level in the NIT and $12,000 is the break-even level under the demogrant. For a society concerned with the impact of cumulative tax rates on work effort, it is important to establish how work effort would respond to the various tax rates and how many workers would be affected in these ranges

[28] Of course, it is possible to make the demogrant and federal income tax calculations one transaction, so that demogrants are received net of income taxes or taxes are paid net of demogrant credits. This type of transfer program often is called a "credit income tax."
[29] The tax rates could have been $33\frac{1}{3}$ percent in the NIT and 50 percent in the demogrant programs, with the same labels being affixed to the respective programs.

Table 2.9 Earnings, Taxes, and Transfers for a Family of Four under a Demogrant Program

A Gross earnings ($)	B Work-related expenses[a] ($)	C Demo-grant[b] ($)	D Net income[c] $_1$ ($)	E Cumulative marginal tax rate$_1$ $(1-\frac{\Delta D}{\Delta A})$ (%)	F Medical insurance subsidy[a] ($)	G Net income$_2$ $(D+F)$ ($)	H Cumulative marginal tax rate$_2$ $(1-\frac{\Delta G}{\Delta A})$ (%)	I Housing subsidy[e] ($)	J Net income$_3$ $(G+I)$ ($)	K Cumulative marginal tax rate$_3$ $(1-\frac{\Delta J}{\Delta A})$ (%)	L Day care subsidy[f] ($)	M Net income$_4$ $(J+L)$ ($)	N Cumulative marginal tax rate$_4$ $(1-\frac{\Delta M}{\Delta A})$ (%)
0	0	3600	3600		463	4063		490	4553		2052	6605	
				35			41			48			48
2800	280	3600	5421		281	5702		308	6010		2052	8062	
				36			42			48			50
4780	478	3600	6691		167	6858		181	7039		2009	9048	
				37			43			48			62
8000	800	3600	8708		0	8708		0	8708		1569	10,277	
				37			37			37			57
9800	980	3600	9834		0	9834		0	9834		1208	11,042	
				37			37			37			57
9900	990	3600	9897		0	9897		0	9897		1188	11,085	

[a] See Table 2.8, footnote a.
[b] The demogrant benefit does not vary with income.
[c] See Table 2.8, footnote c, but substitute the following method of computing the federal income tax payment: Federal income taxes equal ⅓ of earnings net of work-related expenses.
[d] See Table 2.8, footnote d.
[e] See Table 2.8, footnote e.
[f] See Table 2.4, footnote b.

of earnings. The same questions arise with respect to those who have to pay increased net taxes under the two programs. Since this particular NIT plan contains higher tax rates for beneficiaries with earnings under $9800 than does the demogrant, the former plan is more likely to cause reductions in work effort up to that level of earnings. But since the demogrant contains the same guarantee and lower tax rates than does the first NIT plan, it extends benefits to more people. At first blush, therefore, the demogrant would be likely to cost more than the NIT. This implies that the demogrant would necessitate a larger tax increase among net taxpayers. Thus, the income tax increase might affect work effort among net taxpayers. In order to determine the relative costs of the two programs, then, one must look at their work effort effects among all income classes. If the total work effort response to the two programs does not differ greatly, this demogrant would be more costly but would offer the benefit of redistributing more income.

Also noteworthy in comparing Tables 2.8 and 2.9 is the convergence in cumulative tax rates observed as one proceeds from the cash transfer programs to each $CMTR_4$. For example, $CMTR_1$ in Table 2.9 is 37 percent over the range of earnings $4780 to $8000, or twenty-nine percentage points less than $CMTR_1$ in Table 2.8. Over the same range of earnings, the respective $CMTR_4$s differ by only twenty-four percentage points, five points less. As one adds identical in-kind programs to two cash transfer programs with different implicit tax rates, one narrows the gap in cumulative tax rates in the two systems.[30] This convergence is due to the sequencing of programs described previously.

[30] This can be demonstrated in the following manner:

Let

$$T_{11} = t_{11}Y_{11}$$
$$T_{21} = t_{11}Y_{11} + t_{21}Y_{21}$$
$$T_{12} = t_{12}Y_{12}$$
$$T_{22} = t_{12}Y_{12} + t_{22}Y_{22}$$
$$Y_{21} = Y_{11} - t_{11}Y_{11} = (1 - t_{11})Y_{11}$$
$$Y_{22} = Y_{12} - t_{12}Y_{12} = (1 - t_{12})Y_{12}$$

then

$$T_{21} = [t_{11} + t_{21}(1 - t_{11})]Y_{11}$$
$$T_{22} = [t_{12} + t_{22}(1 - t_{12})]Y_{12},$$

where the Ts represent the total taxes paid (or, actually, benefit reductions) after each of two transfer *programs* as a result of applying particular tax rates, represented by t's, to identical amounts of income, Y_{11} and Y_{12}; and the first subscripts refer to the first and second of two linked programs within given transfer *systems*, which are represented by the second subscripts. The point is that, if $t_{11} > t_{12}$ and $t_{21} = t_{22}$, then $t_{11} - t_{12} > [t_{11} + t_{21}(1 - t_{11})] - [t_{12} + t_{22}(1 - t_{12})]$, where the expressions in brackets are the cumulative tax rates in the first and second systems, respectively, after benefits have been adjusted to income in the second program of each system. Although the stated tax rate in the second program of each of the two

To make clear the point about convergence, we can ignore Social Security taxes and all but one other program and we can simplify from what is presented in the tables. If recipients of both types of cash transfers were to receive a housing subsidy, in which the tax rate is specified as being 25 percent of income inclusive of cash transfers, then the difference between cumulative marginal tax rates would be less than seventeen percentage points, that is, less than 50 percent minus 33 percent. If his earnings increased by $1.00, an NIT recipient would lose $.50 from his benefit. The housing authorities then would reduce his subsidy by 25 percent of his change in net income, which is $.50; and 25 percent of $.50 is $.12. For having earned an additional dollar, the NIT recipient would have lost $.62 in cash and housing benefits. The demogrant recipient would initially lose $.33 when his earnings rise by $1.00. If the housing program reduced his subsidy by 25 percent of the change in his net income, $.67, he would lose another $.17. Thus, the cumulative tax rate facing the NIT recipient would be 62 percent, while that facing the demogrant recipient would be 50 percent. This is a difference of twelve percentage points, or five less than the difference after the first program. This is how the convergence of tax rates observed in Tables 2.8 and 2.9 is explained. And this means that the advantage of having a cash transfer program with a low tax rate is destroyed, in part, when additional programs are added to it, even if they use changes in net income and not changes in gross earnings as the tax base.

Income maintenance plans whose essential characteristics can be expressed in the form of the equation presented at the outset of this section must choose between high tax rates with substantial work disincentives or low tax rates with costly extensive coverage. Negative income tax, credit income tax, demogrant, and H.R. 1 welfare reform plans all face this trade-off, as well as the tax problems resulting from related in-kind transfer programs. Recognizing this conflict, some policymakers have rejected this universal approach to income maintenance and have proposed a categorical program under which "employables" and "unemployables" would be distinguished and subject to different plans.

---

transfer systems is the same, they differ in effect when they are part of a system of transfer programs and when they are both measured against the original income base. Against the original income base, the tax rate in the second program of the first system is t_{21} $(1 - t_{11})$ and the tax rate in the second program of the second system is $t_{22}(1 - t_{12})$. Since $t_{11} > t_{12}$, the latter product is larger than the former. More is added to the tax bill by the *same* second program in the second system than in the first. The advantage of the lower tax rate in the first program of the second system over that in the first system is reduced as identical second or subsequent transfer programs are combined with the original programs in this particular manner.

The first of these categorical programs, represented in Table 2.10, is the Guaranteed Job Opportunity program (GJO) reported out of the Senate Finance Committee in the fall of 1972.[31] It offers traditional welfare assistance with high tax rates for women with children under age six and other "unemployables," and either subsidized regular jobs or specially created public jobs for "employables," who are able-bodied female and male heads of low-income families. The subsidies of regular jobs are of two types: (*1*) a wage subsidy, to people earning less than the minimum wage, equal to three-fourths of the difference between their wage and the minimum; and (*2*) an earnings subsidy of 10 percent of earnings up to an earnings level of $4000, which declines at a 25 percent rate (from $400) as earnings rise above $4000. The earnings subsidy break-even level is $5600 for families of all sizes. Families with employable heads are denied welfare payments apart from state supplements. States must assume, in determining these supplements, that an employable family head earns at least $200 per month and must not reduce the supplement for earnings between $200 and $300 per month. We chose to avoid complicating Table 2.10 with the wage rate subsidy and to concentrate on the earnings subsidy given to an able-bodied female or male head who obtains a regular job at a wage of $3 per hour. The program is shown in Table 2.10 with the same modifications of medical, housing, and day care benefits as were assumed in the NIT and demogrant examples.

The GJO would create confiscatory tax rates for persons receiving state supplements and earning between $4000 and $5600 per year. Up to $4000 of annual earnings, the marginal tax under GJO would be negative and the cumulative tax rate would be minimal, even if the family received medical, housing, and day care subsidies. Following the committee's rules, a city like Chicago could provide a $984 supplement to up to $4000 of earnings, if it used tax rates like those in the current or H.R. 1 programs (see column H of Table 2.4 and column G of Table 2.1). Above $4000, the earnings subsidy would decline at a 25 percent rate and the state supplement would decline at a 67 percent rate, less an adjustment for work-related expenses. With income and Social Security taxes, $CMTR_1$ would exceed 95 percent up to $5600 of earnings and $CMTR_4$ would exceed 100 percent. Of course, $CMTR_1$ would be much lower where state supplements are not provided to either female- or male-headed families or both. Thus, GJO substantially increases financial incentives to work up to $4000 and then reduces them to nil until $5640. Beyond the latter point

---

[31] U.S., Congress, Senate, Committee on Finance, *Guaranteed Job Opportunity: Welfare Reform*, 92d Cong., 2d sess., 28 April 1972.

Table 2.10 Earnings, Taxes, and Transfers for a Family of Four under the Senate Finance Committee Plan

A	B	C	D	E	F	G	H	I	J	K	L	M	N	O
Gross earnings ($)	Earnings subsidy[a] ($)	Work-related expenses[b] ($)	State supplement[c] ($)	Net income$_1$ ($)	Cumulative marginal tax rate$_1$ $(1-\frac{\Delta E}{\Delta A})$ (%)	Medical benefit[e] ($)	Net income$_2$ (E+G) ($)	Cumulative marginal tax rate$_2$ $(1-\frac{\Delta H}{\Delta A})$ (%)	Housing subsidy[f] ($)	Net income$_3$ (H+J) ($)	Cumulative marginal tax rate$_3$ $(1-\frac{\Delta K}{\Delta A})$ (%)	Day care subsidy[g] ($)	Net income$_4$ (K+M) ($)	Cumulative marginal tax rate$_4$ $(1-\frac{\Delta N}{\Delta A})$ (%)
0	0	0	984	984		750	1734		500	2234		2052	4286	
					> −5			> 7			> 7			> 7
2400	240	240	984	3499		473	3972		500	4472		2052	6524	
					> −5			> 5			> 16			> 16
4000	400	400	984	5176		313	5489		332	5821		2052	7873	
					> 93			> 94			> 95			> 101
4800	200	480	504	5231		307	5538		327	5865		2004	7869	
					> 105			> 105			> 104			> 114
5600	0	560	24	5190		311	5501		331	5832		1924	7756	
					> 82			> 82			> 85			> 95
5640	0	564	0	5197		311	5508		330	5838		1920	7758	
					> 22			> 30			> 38			> 55
9800	0	980	0	8429		0	8429		7	8436		1208	9644	
					> 22			> 22			> 29			> 49
9900	0	990	0	8507		0	8507		0	8507		1188	9695	

[a] The earnings subsidy is equal to 10 percent of gross earnings up to $4000. The earnings subsidy of $400 at $4000 is reduced at a 25 percent rate for earnings above $4000 per year. See U.S. Congress, Senate, Committee on Finance, *Guaranteed Job Opportunity: Welfare Reform, Explanation of Committee Decisions* (Washington, D.C.: 92d Cong., 2d sess., 28 April 1972), pp. 5, 6.

[b] See Table 2.8, footnote *a*.

[c] The state supplement is $984 at zero earnings, which is what it would be in Illinois if that state maintained benefits at current levels. The supplement is reduced at 66⅔ percent rate for earnings, net of incremental work-related expenses, in excess of $4000.

[d] See Table 2.8, footnote *c*.

[e] See Table 2.8, footnote *d*.

[f] See Table 2.8, footnote *e*.

74

Table 2.11 Earnings, Taxes, and Transfers for a Family of Four under an Earnings Subsidy Plan

A	B	C	D	E	F	G	H	I	J	K	L	M	N	O
Gross earnings ($)	Earnings subsidy[a] ($)	Work-related expenses[b] ($)	State supplement[c] ($)	Net income$_1$[d] ($)	Cumulative marginal tax rate$_1$ $(1-\frac{\Delta E}{\Delta A})$ (%)	Medical benefit[e] ($)	Net income$_2$ (E+G) ($)	Cumulative marginal tax rate$_2$ $(1-\frac{\Delta H}{\Delta A})$ (%)	Housing subsidy[f] ($)	Net income$_3$ (H+J) ($)	Cumulative marginal tax rate$_3$ $(1-\frac{\Delta K}{\Delta A})$ (%)	Day care subsidy[g] ($)	Net income$_4$ (K+M) ($)	Cumulative marginal tax rate$_4$ $(1-\frac{\Delta N}{\Delta A})$ (%)
0	0	0	984	984		750	1734		500	2234		2052	4286	
					−90			−74			−71			−71
1500	1500	150	984	3906		435	4341		459	4800		2052	6852	
					55			59			64			64
3000	750	300	984	4578		371	4949		392	5341		2052	7393	
					55			60			64			64
4000	250	400	984	5026		326	5353		347	5699		2052	7751	
					118			116			114			117
4500	0	450	684	4937		337	5274		356	5630		2034	7664	
					77			79			82			92
5640	0	564	0	5197		311	5508		330	5838		1920	7758	
					22			30			38			55
9800	0	980	0	8429		0	8429		7	8436		1208	9644	
					22			22			29			49
9900	0	990	0	8507		0	8507		0	8507		1188	9695	

[a] The earnings subsidy rises dollar for dollar with earnings up to $4500 of annual earnings. Thereafter, the subsidy is decreased at a 50 percent rate, falling to zero at $4500 of annual earnings. *Source*—Robert H. Haveman, see Chapter 4.
[b] See Table 2.8, footnote *a*.
[c] See Table 2.10, footnote *c*.
[d] See Table 2.8, footnote *c*.
[e] See Table 2.8, footnote *d*.
[f] See Table 2.8, footnote *e*.
[g] See Table 2.4, footnote *b*.

and up to $8000, the plan again provides incentives superior to the NIT plan but roughly equivalent to those of the demogrant plan. Above $8000 of earnings, $CMTR_4$ is roughly the same for all the programs discussed here. Even if its own break-even level is relatively low, GJO cannot overcome the effects on cumulative tax rates of related transfer programs, because of the convergence problem discussed earlier.

A more carefully structured version of the plan passed by the Senate Finance Committee has been proposed by Robert Haveman.[32] While the Haveman plan differs in many details from the one just discussed, a major distinguishing characteristic is that it contains only an earnings subsidy and no wage rate subsidy. The earnings subsidy is equal to 100 percent of earnings up to $1500 per year, declining at a 50 percent rate above that point. Table 2.11 indicates that, unless it eliminates state supplements and related in-kind transfer programs, the Haveman plan will result in con-fiscatory tax rates over the same range of earnings in which they appear under GJO and is not superior to the demogrant plan in keeping $CMTR_4$ well below 50 percent on earnings above $8000. For the relatively small number of workers at the very bottom of the earnings distribution, it pro-vides extraordinary financial incentives to increase earnings by getting a higher-paying job or by working more hours.

V. The Dilemmas of Income Maintenance Programs

The selection of a guarantee, a tax rate, and a break-even level of income is usually the first task of creating a new cash transfer scheme. Political pressures weigh heavily in specifying the first and third charac-teristics: Segments of the electorate have strong notions of minimum in-comes at which families can survive; and political leaders are anxious to not have to defend a program that allows people to still be on welfare at high levels of income. Given these pressures, it is difficult to keep the tax rate at low levels. Even if the objective of a low tax rate is met by the cash transfer program, however, keeping the cumulative tax rate at tolerably low levels is exceedingly difficult because other political pres-sures generate other income-conditioned transfers in-kind—in health, food, housing, and, of late, day care and higher education. The existence of these other transfer programs, as well as income taxes, makes it especially difficult, in any income maintenance system, to maintain financial incen-tives to work.

There are alternative ways to relate in-kind transfers and positive

[32] Robert H. Haveman, see Chapter 4 of this volume.

income taxes to each other and to a cash transfer program to produce various cumulative tax rates. Thad Mirer has articulated these alternatives very well, and they all cannot be explained here.[33] But the same basic problem of influencing the cumulative tax rate arises when a set of programs are linked to each other as when a tax rate is set in a cash transfer program. When designing a cash transfer program, policymakers seek high guarantees, low tax rates, and low break-even income levels. But attaining any two of these objectives conflicts with the third. Likewise, in integrating a group of transfer programs, reducing the cumulative tax rate while maintaining cumulative benefits must raise break-even levels of income for some of the programs in the group. Alternatively, reducing the cumulative tax rate while keeping the break-even income levels down necessitates lowering the cumulative level of benefits. In sum, policymakers face the same difficult choices in integrating transfer programs into an overall scheme that they face in designing a simple cash transfer program. No system of transfers can escape the dilemmas of income maintenance programs. The high cumulative tax rates under the various "reforms" discussed here should come as no surprise.

Acknowledgments

I would like to thank Professor Barry Friedman for his suggestions; and Mitchell Jacobson, Thomas P. Glynn III, and Bryna Sanger for their assistance in the preparation of the tables. Some of the research effort involved in writing this chapter was financed by a research contract with the Manpower Administration of the Department of Labor. Points of view or opinions stated in this document do not necessarily represent the official position or policy of the Department of Labor.

[33] Thad W. Mirer, see Chapter 5 of this volume.

3

The Role of Demogrants
as an Income Maintenance
Alternative

Benjamin A. Okner[1]

I. Introduction

In recent years, national attention has been directed toward the idea of instituting a universal demogrant or credit income tax in the United States. While the idea is not a new one, a great deal of interest and controversy was generated by the discussion of a $1000-per-person demogrant during the 1972 presidential campaign. At about the time its importance as a campaign issue diminished, a Green Paper was issued recommending adoption of a credit income tax in Great Britain.[2] Although the British Green Paper has not yet been widely discussed in this country, there is little doubt that various proposals for using demogrants and tax credits as an income maintenance alternative will be with us for many years.

The purpose of this chapter is to examine the nature and magnitude of the income redistribution that would be effected by alternative demogrant plans and the income tax changes needed to finance them. While certain assumptions are made about the degree of income tax reform and

[1] The views expressed are the author's and are not necessarily those of the officers, trustees, or other staff members of the Brookings Institution.
[2] Great Britain, Parliamentary Papers, "Proposals for a Tax-Credit System," Cmnd. 5116 (London: H.M. Stationery Office, October 1972).

welfare reform that could accompany these demogrant plans, an in-depth critique of political, administrative, or other problems associated with such reform is beyond the scope of this study. Also, the chapter does not deal with the pros and cons of a demogrant as compared with existing welfare programs or with other approaches to welfare reform, such as a negative income tax plan or a wage subsidy plan, and no attempt is made to examine the variety of ways in which a demogrant could be administered.

Basically, a demogrant is simply a per capita benefit paid to persons regardless of the amount or sources of their other income.[3] The grant amount can be structured in a number of different ways. For example, if paid only to children, the demogrant would be a children's allowance. Alternatively, the benefit could be paid to all persons but with a different amount paid to persons of different ages. Still further modifications could be introduced so that the first two children in a family receive higher benefits than do additional children. Regardless of what criteria are chosen, the essential feature of a demogrant program remains unchanged: Benefits are paid solely on the basis of some demographic features of persons, and once these features are established, payments are made to qualified individuals as a matter of right and without any demonstration of need.

Although the demogrant may seem new and radical to some people, tax provisions that serve in lieu of a demogrant program have existed in the United States since 1913, when the present federal individual income tax was adopted.[4] Under 1974 law, there was a $750 per capita exemption and a $1300–$2000 standard deduction permitted when computing one's federal individual income tax liability. For an individual with $3000 of income, the $2050 exemption plus deduction reduced his tax liability by $287. Since after-tax income was increased by this amount, the personal exemption and standard deduction were equivalent to an annual $287 demogrant. These substitute "demogrants" in the federal income tax work in a rather curious manner. For those with no income subject to tax, we now provide no "demogrant." The grant size then increases as income rises because of the progressive tax rate structure. For an individual in the 50 percent tax bracket, the personal exemption and standard deduction re-

[3] "Demogrant" and "tax credit" are used interchangeably and are considered synonymous. A demogrant or tax credit program might be administered in different ways, but the net effect of either on the after-tax and benefit distribution of income can always be made identical.

[4] Actually, the implicit "demogrant" in the individual income tax has an even longer history, since it was also a feature of the 1861 income tax imposed to finance the Civil War.

duce his tax liability by $1375; hence, the implicit "demogrant" is $1375. For a very wealthy individual subject to the 70 percent marginal tax rate, the implicit "demogrant" rises to $1925.[5]

A universal demogrant–tax credit can be thought of as a means to rationalize and correct the regressive system of grants that is now implicit in the income tax. This could be accomplished by replacing the personal income tax exemptions (and possibly deductions) with a payment that does not vary with the size of income. However, it would have an additional feature not now in the income tax law: It would provide payments or rebatable tax credits to everyone, even those persons with incomes too low to be liable for federal income taxes.

A universal demogrant would probably involve taxes and transfers of very large magnitudes. For this reason, most demogrant proposals are accompanied by financing proposals that involve broadening the individual income tax base.[6] Such base-broadening along with a single proportional rate on taxable income could simultaneously provide a minimum income guarantee for the poor, a progressive effective tax on income,[7] and a simpler and more equitable income tax system.

Although it is not imperative that reform and simplification of the income tax and of welfare programs accompany institution of a demogrant–tax credit program, many people (including the author) would consider this approach to be highly desirable. The most logical alternative for raising the revenue needed to finance the grants would be a surtax on tax liabilities under existing law. The size of the surtax needed would depend upon the demogrant plan adopted; under plans with fairly generous benefits, the surtax could produce extremely high marginal tax rates. Because tax reform and welfare reform both seem to be desirable goals, in our analyses we have followed the practice of others in proposing that the benefits be financed by tax reform rather than by simply raising tax rates on the existing income tax base.

---

[5] These last two examples are admittedly unrealistic since they assume that such wealthy individuals are still using the maximum standard deduction of $2000.

[6] For example, see Earl R. Rolph, "The Case for a Negative Income Tax Device," *Industrial Relations* 6 (February 1967):155-165.

[7] A fixed-dollar demogrant–tax credit and a proportional tax rate *does* produce a mildly progressive effective tax rate. For example, assume that the grant amount is $1000 and the tax rate is 30.0 percent. At the $4000 income level, gross tax liability would be $1200 (30.0 percent of $4000), net liability would be $200 ($1200 less $1000 grant), and the effective tax rate would be 5.0 percent ($200/$4000). At the $10,000 income level, gross tax liability would be $3000 (30.0 percent of $10,000), net liability would be $2000 ($3000 less $1000 grant), and the effective tax would be 20.0 percent ($2000/$10,000). At the $15,000 income level, the effective tax rate would be 23.3 percent and, at $20,000, the effective rate would be 25.0 percent. The effective rate continues to rise with income and will approach a maximum of 30.0 percent.

In the remainder of the chapter, we examine the distributional effects of four different demogrant systems, accompanied by partial or comprehensive tax reform for calendar 1970.[8] For each of the plans, we present estimates of the gross "costs" of the program, the amounts of income redistributed by income level and family size, the resulting effective tax rates, the number of families with increases and decreases in after-tax or benefit income, and the effect of the grants on the poverty population.

II. The Demogrant and Tax Reform Structures

In an integrated tax and demogrant system, each family's net tax liability is equal to the algebraic sum of its gross tax liability less the amount of its demogrant. Thus, if the gross tax liability for a four-person family were $2000 and its demogrant were equal to $3500, it would have a negative net liability and receive a payment of $1500 ($2000 less $3500). With the same grant amount, a higher-income family whose gross tax liability was $7500 would pay a net tax of $4000 ($7500 less $3500). Thus, the gross tax liability on income other than the demogrant would continue to increase as income rises; the demogrant is nontaxable and remains constant regardless of income.[9]

---

[8] The analysis is for calendar 1970 because that is a recent year for which we have reliable data on population, income, and taxes. All calculations are based on the Brookings MERGE file of 72,000 family units for the year 1966 with incomes and population projected to the 1970 level. The MERGE data file was created by combining financial and demographic data from the 1967 Survey of Economic Opportunity (SEO) with income and tax information from the 1966 Internal Revenue tax file. For a more detailed description of the file and how it was constructed, see Benjamin A. Okner, "Constructing a New Data Base from Existing Microdata Sets: The 1966 MERGE File," *Annals of Economic and Social Measurement* 1 (July 1972) (Brookings Reprint No. 251).

[9] In this chapter, all the calculations assume a nontaxable demogrant. While it is possible to tax the demogrant along with other income, we do not do so since this usually involves an unnecessary complication. Under a proportional rate schedule, it is always possible to achieve identical results under a taxable or nontaxable demogrant simply by changing the tax rate (this is not necessarily true under a progressive rate schedule). However, there is one advantage to making the demogrant taxable if one wishes to concentrate the net benefits more heavily among low-income families. This would involve a recoupment surtax levied on the grant above some chosen income level. Such a proposal is discussed by Harvey E. Brazer in "Tax Policy and Children's Allowances," in *Children's Allowances and the Economic Welfare of Children, a Conference Report*, ed. Eveline M. Burns (New York: Citizens Committee for Children of New York, Inc., 1968), p. 140. While Brazer's discussion has to do with concentrating the benefits of children's allowances among the poor, exactly the same scheme could be employed with respect to any other type of demogrant.

Benefit Levels

In our analysis, we use four different demogrant schedules. Under Schedule A, benefits of $1500 are paid only to adults (persons age eighteen or over) and no allowances are paid to children. Schedule B provides allowances of $1500 for each adult and $300 for each person under age eighteen in the family. Schedule C provides differential benefits based on the person's age: Each person age sixty-five or over receives $1500; each person age fifty-five to sixty-four receives $1200; all other adults (age eighteen to fifty-four) receive $1000; children age fourteen to seventeen each receive $400, and children under age fourteen receive $200. Finally, Schedule D provides $1250 benefits for the first two family members and variable benefits for additional members (regardless of age); the next two persons receive $750 each; the fifth and sixth, $500 each; and all persons after the sixth each receive $250.

The total benefits for selected families of different size and type are shown in Table 3.1. Aged individuals and couples fare equally well under Schedules A, B, and C but receive somewhat reduced amounts under Schedule D. The amounts paid to non-aged families vary considerably under the different schedules. Thus, for a four-person family (married couple with two young children) headed by a person under age fifty-five, total benefits range from $2400 under Schedule C to $4000 under Schedule D. Of course, total payments do not vary with the number of children under Schedule A; for the six-person family, this results in a $2000 difference between the $3000 benefit under Schedule A and the $5000 payment under Schedule D.

When measured against their poverty-income thresholds, most types of families fare extremely well under the various demogrant schedules. Aged couples with no children receive payments in excess of their poverty-income level under all schedules. Aged, single persons receive about 80 percent of their poverty-income level under all schedules except D.

For the typical non-aged four-person family, payments are equal to 90 percent or more of the poverty-income threshold under Schedules B and D. Only under Schedule D do benefits stay close to the poverty line as family size increases (payments to non-aged single persons are equal to only about 60 percent of their poverty-income level, however). On the other hand, under Schedule A, payments decline relative to the poverty-level income as family size increases, because there are no benefits paid for children.

It should be noted that the benefits under A, B, and C possess several administrative advantages over the Schedule D benefit schedule. Under the former schedules, where the amount of payment depends solely on

Table 3.1 Illustrative Benefit Levels for Selected Types of Families under Various Demogrant Schedules

Family type	Amount of benefit: Schedule—				Benefit as percentage of poverty level:[a] Schedule—			
	A	B	C	D	A	B	C	D
Non-aged family head:[b]								
Single person	$1500	$1500	$1000	$1250	74.6	74.6	49.8	62.2
Married couple:								
No children	3000	3000	2000	2500	114.6	114.6	76.4	95.5
One child under fourteen	3000	3300	2200	3250	96.4	106.0	70.7	104.4
Two children under fourteen	3000	3600	2400	4000	75.6	90.7	60.5	100.8
Three children: two under fourteen and one age fifteen to eighteen	3000	3900	2800	4500	64.1	83.3	59.8	96.1
Four children: two under fourteen and two age fifteen to eighteen	3000	4200	3200	5000	57.0	79.8	60.8	95.0
Aged family head:[b]								
Single person	1500	1500	1500	1250	80.6	80.6	80.6	67.2
Married couple, no children	3000	3000	3000	2500	127.7	127.7	127.7	106.4

[a] Computation based on 1970 poverty-income levels for nonfarm families with male head. See U.S., Bureau of the Census, *Current Population Reports, Consumer Income*, Ser. P–60, No. 77 (Washington, D.C.: U.S. Government Printing Office, 7 May 1971), p. 20.
[b] For non-aged families, adults are assumed to be age eighteen to fifty-four; for aged families, adults are assumed to be sixty-five years and over.

the person's age, there are no incentives for either forming or dissolving existing family units in order to receive larger payments. While it is impossible to assess its importance, there is the possibility of such changes taking place under a schedule, such as D, where benefits are related to the family size. For example, it is possible that a six-person family consisting of husband, wife, and four children might decide to call itself two three-person units, each containing one of the spouses and two children. As a single unit, it would receive total payments of $5000 under Schedule D. As two units, each "family" would receive $2750, and together the six persons would get $5500—$500 more than if they filed as a single unit. This possibility is probably more important theoretically than it would be in practice, but the investigation and enforcement procedures that would undoubtedly accompany such a program would be costly and could be avoided under the age-related benefit schedules.

In addition to avoiding possible family-splitting problems, a constant per capita grant eliminates any advantages that could exist with respect to splitting of income among family members or manipulations to affect the timing of income when the program is financed with a single proportional tax rate. A proportional rate also would aid in the administration of a demogrant since tax on all income at its source could be easily withheld. This is essentially the approach outlined for the tax credit proposed for Great Britain in the recent Green Paper.

How Much Do the Demogrant Programs Cost?

In 1970, gross outlays under Schedule A would have been about $194 billion; under Schedule B, they would have been about $215 billion; under C, about $158 billion; and under D, about $201 billion. However, it is incorrect to call these sums the cost of the programs; rather, they are simply the total amount of the various grants or credits.

Since the programs only transfer income from one group to another, at least in the first stage, they do not use or reallocate economic resources.[10] However, the relevant cost of these programs is the amount by which after-tax income is reduced for "loser families" who will pay more in taxes to finance the grants than they will receive from the grants. This amount is equal to the increase in the after-benefit incomes of the "gainer families." In other words, the cost of a program is the amount of in-

---

[10] There may be real economic costs in subsequent stages if the programs cause people to change their work and leisure patterns or if the programs have other real effects on the quantity or quality of economic resources. Since there is no way to estimate such effects, they are omitted in this analysis.

creased taxes that will have to be paid by some families in order to finance the net grants or credits received by the gainer families.[11]

Financing the Grants and Tax Reform

It is certain that a large number of people of diverse political persuasions and in very different economic circumstances feel that tax reform is long overdue. The federal individual income tax is not the only levy toward which the so-called "tax revolt" is directed, but it certainly is a major item on the reform agenda.

For the integrated tax reform and demogrant analysis presented here, we have chosen two different levels or kinds of tax reform.[12] The first is a "comprehensive reform" of the individual income tax structure, which would eliminate virtually all tax preferences, nonessential deductions, and personal exemptions. This would result in increasing the taxable income base by more than 70 percent. Under the comprehensive reform, the tax base would be increased primarily by fully taxing realized capital gains and gains on assets transferred by gift or bequest; by eliminating homeowners' preferences by taxing net imputed rent on owner-occupied dwellings and eliminating all itemized deductions for property taxes and mortgage interest; by taxing transfer payment receipts; by disallowing itemized personal deductions for medical expenses that are less than 5 percent of income and for charitable contributions that do not exceed 3 percent of income; and by removing the percentage standard deduction allowed under current law. This is the tax base suggested by Pechman and Okner in their study for the Joint Economic Committee.[13] In addition, the taxable income base would be increased by the amount of the personal exemptions for taxpayers, spouses, and dependents, which would be unnecessary under a demogrant–tax credit system. The "comprehensive reform" taxable income base would have been $690 billion in 1970.

The second tax reform plan is less comprehensive but probably more realistic politically; this is called "partial reform." Under partial reform, the tax base would include realized capital gains in full, capital gains transferred at death or by gift (beginning with enactment of the legisla-

---

[11] We assume that the demogrant plans are to be self-financing through the individual income tax and that federal expenditures on other programs (with the exception of spending reductions noted later) remain unchanged. Of course, it is possible to finance the grants through increases in other taxes and reductions in other expenditures. However, because the inclusion of such alternatives would greatly complicate the analysis, the self-financing assumption is retained in this chapter.

[12] A detailed description of the tax changes and resulting taxable income levels under the reforms is given in the appendix to this chapter.

[13] See "Individual Income Tax Erosion by Income Classes," in *The Economics of Federal Subsidy Programs*, U.S., Congress, Joint Economic Committee, 92d Cong., 2d sess., 1972.

tion), as well as all the income items now taxable. Itemized personal deductions would be retained for state–local income and property taxes, interest up to the amount of property income reported on the tax return, medical expenses and charitable contributions to the extent that they exceed 3 percent of income, and miscellaneous deductions (child care, alimony, and so forth). Tax credits would replace the present per capita exemptions, and the standard deduction would be reduced to 8 percent of income, up to a maximum of $800 for taxpayers who do not itemize their deductions. The rate advantages of income splitting would be eliminated under both reform programs. The "partial reform" tax base would have been $633 billion in 1970.

While the second package contains much less reform than the comprehensive program, it features a substantial reduction in the standard deduction, complete elimination of the deduction for gasoline taxes, and a large reduction in deductions for small charitable contributions.

Redistribution Cost of a Tax-Credit— Demogrant System

The calculation of the distribution cost of a tax-credit–demogrant program starts with the necessity for sufficient revenue to cover the total grant outlays under the program. To this must be added the 1970 yield of the individual income tax (on the assumption that other government services are maintained). From this can be subtracted the 1970 federal outlays on cash Public Assistance, Food Stamp and other nutrition programs, and the housing assistance programs, on the assumption that these programs would be eliminated if a demogrant were introduced. The resulting amount is the gross revenue needed to finance the demogrant plus other government programs remaining after institution of the grants. As shown in Table 3.2, under Schedule A, gross tax collections required

Table 3.2 Gross Tax Collections Required to Finance Various Demogrants and Other Government Programs

	Schedules			
	A	B	C	D
Tax credit outlays	194.3	215.4	158.4	200.7
1970 income tax yield	83.8	83.8	83.8	83.8
Less expenditures on:				
Cash public assistance	−4.7	−4.7	−4.7	−4.7
Food Stamps and other nutrition	−2.2	−2.2	−2.2	−2.2
Housing assistance	− .6	− .6	− .6	− .6
Gross tax collections required	270.6	291.7	234.7	277.0

Note—In billions of dollars.

would be about $271 billion while, under Schedules B, C, and D, the totals required would be about $292 billion, $235 billion, and $277 billion, respectively.[14] This compares with $83.8 billion actually collected in 1970.

Before proceeding with the cost calculation, it is worth considering how Social Security, Unemployment Insurance, and other transfer payments would be treated under a demogrant program. The proper treatment of such receipts presents difficult problems, to which there are no simple answers. In our analysis, we do not want people to end up worse off financially than they were before the program's inception. Thus, we assume people are given the option of either (*1*) taking their existing transfers tax free as they now do or (*2*) participating in the program but counting the existing transfers as income subject to tax. The simulation model makes the choice for each household so that its disposable income is maximized.[15]

Returning to the redistributional cost calculation: Once the amount of gross tax collections required is determined, it is not difficult to compute the average rate on taxable income required under a given tax program. For example, Schedule A, requiring gross collections of $271 billion, could be financed with the comprehensive tax base of $690 billion and an average tax rate of 39.2 percent. The various combinations of schedules, tax bases, and average rates required are shown in Table 3.3. For comparison purposes, it should be noted that the actual effective rate on taxable income in 1970 (including the 2.5 percent surcharge) was 20.9 percent.

An alternative method for determining the redistributional effect of a demogrant–tax credit program would require first setting the desired tax rate to be used and then calculating the level of benefits that could be paid under the program. For example, one might set 35 or 40 percent as the desired tax rate. This would then generate a given amount of

[14] The calculation implies that the new demogrant–tax credit program would totally supplant the existing federal categorical Public Assistance programs, the Food Stamp program, and housing assistance programs. No saving from the state–local government expenditures on existing Public Assistance programs is taken into account since, in many jurisdictions, the demogrants would be less than existing welfare payments and the states would need a substantial portion of the revenue newly available to them to supplement benefits paid under a federal demogrant program. If state–local Public Assistance savings are also counted as cost offsets, the gross tax collections under each of the schedules would be reduced by about $4 billion.

[15] An alternative treatment might be to eliminate the welfare-type transfer programs (such as veterans' pensions) and restructure the social insurance programs (such as Social Security) so that they become strictly contributions-related programs with no welfare elements. This approach should lower the budgetary cost of these programs relative to the assumptions used in this study.

Table 3.3 Effective Tax Rates and Redistributional Cost of Various Demogrants under a Proportional Tax Schedule, 1970

Item	Schedule A		Schedule B		Schedule C		Schedule D	
	Comprehensive reform tax base	Partial reform tax base	Comprehensive reform tax base	Partial reform tax base	Comprehensive reform tax base	Partial reform tax base	Comprehensive reform tax base	Partial reform tax base
Gross tax collections	$270.6	$270.6	$291.7	$291.7	$234.7	$234.7	$277.0	$277.0
Taxable income	$689.6	$632.6	$689.6	$632.6	$689.6	$632.6	$689.6	$632.6
Average effective rate on taxable income (percent)[a]	39.2	42.8	42.2	46.1	34.0	37.1	40.2	43.8
Net redistributional cost (tax increases)[b]	$42.4	$39.4	$47.0	$44.2	$33.5	$30.9	$45.3	$43.3

Note—Dollar amounts in billions.
[a] These are the tax rates applied to taxable income that would be required to finance general government expenditures and the demogrants.
[b] Computed using proportional effective tax rate shown above.

revenue that could be distributed through a grant program, and the benefits would then be scaled to exhaust the sum available. Under the self-financing assumption adopted for this analysis, it is obvious that, once a decision is made concerning the benefit levels, the required tax rate is also determined, and vice versa. Since there is no analytically "correct" way to proceed, we started with a given structure and level of benefits that were of interest and allowed the needed tax rates to vary. Obviously, for many purposes, it might be more interesting to examine the distributional effects of different benefit structures all of which are financed by the same rate on taxable income.

In the bottom half of Table 3.3, we show the total redistributional costs of the four demogrant plans as measured by the total increase in taxes for those families who will pay more tax (net of grants received) under the new program. They are all calculated using the proportional tax rate on taxable income shown in the table. Schedule B benefits of $1500 for adults and $300 for children are clearly the "most expensive." Benefits under Schedule A ($1500 per person only for adults) and Schedule D payments ($1250 for adults and variable amounts for children) cost roughly the same. The least costly program uses Schedule C benefits (variable amounts depending on the person's age). As can be seen, even in a "cheap program," redistributional costs will be in excess of $30 billion, while an expensive one would have cost $44–$47 billion in 1970.

While the concept of cost associated with a purely redistributive program is elusive, even when it is defined as we have done here, the amount of the redistribution is influenced greatly by which tax base is used to finance the program. As can be seen in Table 3.3, the cost varies depending on whether a comprehensive or partial tax reform base is used. The costs would be still different from those shown if the programs were financed by progressive rate schedules rather than the proportional ones used in our analysis.

III. Effect of Demogrants on the Distribution of Income

It is useful to compare the after-tax–after-grant distributions of income under each of the proposed plans with that resulting under the existing tax and transfer system. The distributions by income class of 1970 income, taxes, transfers, and income after existing taxes and transfers are shown in Table 3.4. Not surprisingly, we find that transfer payments are concentrated among families at the low end of the income scale, while individual income taxes primarily affect those in the middle and at the high end of the scale.

Table 3.4 Distribution of Income, Taxes, Transfers, and Income after
Taxes and Transfers under the Existing System, 1970

Income class[a]	Number of families	Aggregate income before taxes and transfers[a]	Aggregate transfer payments	1970 income tax	Income after taxes and transfers
Under $3	18,017	$16,343	$30,051	$450	$45,945
$3 to $5	6,485	25,918	5,336	1,773	29,481
$5 to $10	16,753	123,844	8,914	11,954	120,805
$10 to $15	11,091	136,612	4,395	15,095	125,912
$15 to $20	6,369	109,833	2,786	12,905	99,714
$20 to $25	3,449	76,602	1,258	9,662	68,198
$25 to $50	3,680	119,883	1,239	17,202	103,920
$50 to $100	547	35,118	99	7,269	27,948
$100 to $500	126	20,366	—	5,429	14,937
$500 to $1,000	4	2,541	—	738	1,804
$1,000 and over	2	3,714	—	1,118	2,596
All classes[b]	67,133	664,419	54,363	83,833	634,949
		Percentage distribution			
Under $3	26.8	2.5	55.3	.5	7.2
$3 to $5	9.7	3.9	9.8	2.1	4.6
$5 to $10	24.9	18.6	16.4	14.3	19.0
$10 to $15	16.5	20.6	8.1	18.0	19.8
$15 to $20	9.5	16.5	5.1	15.4	15.7
$20 to $25	5.1	11.5	2.3	11.5	10.7
$25 to $50	5.5	18.0	2.3	20.5	16.4
$50 to $100	.8	5.3	.2	8.7	4.4
$100 to $500	.2	3.1	—	6.5	2.4
$500 to $1,000	[c]	.4	—	.9	.3
$1,000 and over	[c]	.6	—	1.3	.4
All classes[b]	100.0	100.0	100.0	100.0	100.0

Note—Income classes and families in thousands; money amounts in millions.
[a] Money receipts exclusive of transfers and taxes; receipts include total amount of realized capital gains and total gain on assets transferred by gift or bequest.
[b] Includes negative income class not shown separately.
[c] Less than one-half of .1 percent.

Our figures indicate that 36.5 percent of families had pre-tax and pre-transfer incomes under $5000 and received 6.4 percent of total income before taxes and transfers. These families received 65.1 percent of all transfer payments, paid 2.6 percent of federal income taxes, and wound up with 11.8 percent of total income after taxes and transfers.

At the other end of the income scale, 6.5 percent of families had pre-tax and pre-transfer income of $25,000 and above and received 27.4 percent of aggregate income before taxes and transfers. This group received 2.5 percent of all transfer payments, paid 37.9 percent of total income taxes, and retained 23.9 percent of the total after-tax–after-transfer income.

The existing tax and transfer system does redistribute income from the rich to the poor. However, the degree of redistribution is far less than most people probably believe.

A comparison of the 1970 distribution of income after taxes and transfers with those under the various demogrant schedules, financed by comprehensive tax reform, is shown in Tables 3.5 and 3.6. Table 3.5 compares the distribution by income classes, and Table 3.6 presents the same information for families grouped by before-tax–before-transfer income quintiles. As can be seen in the latter table, Schedule B provides the largest degree of income redistribution in favor of families in the lowest quintile of before-tax–before-transfer income; their share of income after taxes and transfers increases from 5.3 percent under the present system to 7.0 percent under the credits provided by Schedule B. The smallest amount of redistribution in favor of those at the bottom of the income scale is provided by Schedule D benefits.

Under each of the schedules, we find that after-tax–after-grant income increases most for families in the lowest three quintiles; in terms of absolute income, this corresponds roughly to those with less than $10,000. The share received by those in the fourth quintile is reduced only slightly from the 1970 level, while after-tax–after-transfer income of families in the highest quintile (before-tax incomes of about $15,000 and over) falls substantially. However, the share of total income received by those at the very top of the income distribution is not very much changed under any of the demogrant schedules examined. Under the most redistributive structure, Schedule B, the share of income received by the top 1.0 percent of families drops from 7.3 to 6.5 percent—.8 percentage point. This is the greatest proportionate reduction under any of the demogrant programs.

Effective Tax (Benefit) Rates

Another way to view the effect of the demogrants is to examine the effective rates of tax or transfer (that is, net tax or transfer divided by total income) at different income levels. As compared with the 1970 tax and transfer system, all the demogrant schedules result in larger average amounts of transfer income for families with incomes below $5000, and, on the average, change families from net taxpayers to net grant recipients in the $5000–$10,000 income class (Table 3.7). For those with higher incomes, the various demogrant schedules have different effects on the

Table 3.5 Distribution of Before-Tax and After-Tax Income under Various Demogrant Schedules, by Income Classes, 1970

Income class[a]	Number of families	Aggregate income before taxes and transfers	1970 income after taxes and transfers	Income after taxes and transfers under demogrant schedules[b]			
				A	B	C	D
Under $3	18,017	$16,343	$45,945	$59,836	$60,676	$58,425	$57,974
$3 to $5	6,485	25,918	29,481	35,601	36,232	33,921	35,579
$5 to $10	16,743	123,844	120,805	130,122	131,923	126,947	132,276
$10 to $15	11,091	136,612	125,912	123,660	124,248	123,376	125,193
$15 to $20	6,369	109,833	99,714	92,655	92,140	93,586	92,731
$20 to $25	3,449	76,602	68,198	61,786	61,168	62,923	61,465
$25 to $50	3,680	119,883	103,920	91,890	90,181	94,402	90,642
$50 to $100	547	35,118	27,948	25,208	24,596	26,437	25,098
$100 to $500	126	20,366	14,937	14,094	13,650	14,924	13,999
$500 to $1,000	4	2,541	1,804	1,690	1,625	1,803	1,671
$1,000 and over	2	3,714	2,596	2,403	2,301	2,578	2,373
All classes[c]	67,133	664,419	634,949	633,541	633,483	633,755	633,632

Table 3.5 (cont.)

			Percentage distribution				
Under $3	26.8	2.5	7.2	9.4	9.6	9.2	9.1
$3 to $5	9.7	3.9	4.6	5.6	5.7	5.4	5.6
$5 to $10	24.9	18.6	19.0	20.5	20.8	20.0	20.9
$10 to $15	16.5	20.6	19.8	19.5	19.6	19.5	19.8
$15 to $20	9.5	16.5	15.7	14.6	14.5	14.8	14.6
$20 to $25	5.1	11.5	10.7	9.8	9.7	9.9	9.7
$25 to $50	5.5	18.0	16.4	14.5	14.2	14.9	14.3
$50 to $100	.8	5.3	4.4	4.0	3.9	4.2	4.0
$100 to $500	.2	3.1	2.4	2.2	2.2	2.4	2.2
$500 to $1,000	a	.4	.3	.3	.3	.3	.3
$1,000 and over	a	.6	.4	.4	.4	.4	.4
All classes[c]	100.0	100.0	100.0	100.0	100.0	100.0	100.0

Note–Income classes and families in thousands; dollar amounts in millions. Figures are rounded and will not necessarily add to totals.
[a] Money receipts exclusive of transfers and taxes; receipts include total amount of realized capital gains and total gain on assets transferred by gift or bequest.
[b] Taxes computed using a proportional tax rate on the comprehensive tax base. See Table 3.3 for taxable income and tax rates.
[c] Includes negative income class not shown separately.
[d] Less than one-half of .1 percent.

94

Table 3.6   Percentage Distribution of Before-Tax Income and Income after Taxes and Transfers, under Present Law and under Various Demogrants, by Population Quintiles, 1970

Population quintile	Aggregate income before taxes and transfers[a]	1970 income after taxes and transfers	Income after taxes and transfers under demogrant schedules[b]			
			A	B	C	D
Lowest fifth	1.80	5.29	6.91	7.01	6.75	6.70
Second fifth	6.82	8.84	10.58	10.76	10.19	10.54
Third fifth	14.67	14.97	16.18	16.41	15.77	16.45
Fourth fifth	24.09	23.27	22.98	23.08	22.90	23.24
Highest fifth	52.62	47.63	43.35	42.74	44.39	43.07
Top 5 percent	22.06	19.03	17.13	16.76	17.77	16.95
Top 1 percent	9.07	7.27	6.69	6.51	7.05	6.65
Total	100.00	100.00	100.00	100.00	100.00	100.00

[a] Total money receipts exclusive of taxes and transfers; receipts include total amount of realized capital gains and total gain on assets transferred by gift or bequest.
[b] Taxes computed using a proportional tax rate on the comprehensive tax base. See Table 3.3 for taxable income and tax rates.

average dollar amount of tax paid and the effective tax rates. Average taxes for families with incomes of $10,000–$15,000 are increased least under Schedule D, while those in this income class experience the largest tax increases under the Schedule C program. For all families with incomes of $15,000 or above, the largest tax increases occur under the Schedule B structure while the smallest tax hikes take place under the Schedule C program.

Distribution of Benefits by Family Size and Income

Because of the way the various demogrant schedules are structured, the differences in net taxes paid or benefits received by families of different size is of even greater interest than those found in comparisons displayed only by income class. Table 3.8 shows the number of families who will lose from the program by experiencing net tax increases and the amount of the increase. Table 3.9 presents similar information for gainer families whose after-tax–after-benefit income rises under the various demogrant schedules. In these tables, families are classified by broad income classes within the small, medium, and large size-categories in order to summarize the large amount of data involved.

The number of families that experience net tax increases ranges between 26.1 million under Schedule A and 28.2 million under Schedule D.

Table 3.7 Effective Tax or Benefit Rates and Average Net Tax Payments or Benefit Receipts under Various Demogrant Schedules, by Income Classes, 1970

| Income class[a] | 1970 tax (+) or transfer (−) | | Taxes (+) or benefit payments (−) | | | | | | | |
| | | | Schedule A | | Schedule B | | Schedule C | | Schedule D | |
	Effective rate	Average amount	Effective rate	Average amount	Effective rate	Average amount	Effective rate	Average amount	Effective rate	Average amount
Under $3	−181.1[c]	−$1,643[d]	−266.1[c]	−$2,414[d]	−271.3[c]	−$2,461[d]	−257.5[c]	−$2,336[d]	−254.7[c]	−$2,311[d]
$3 to $5	−13.8	−549	−37.4	−1,493	−39.8	−1,590	−30.9	−1,234	−37.3	−1,490
$5 to $10	2.4	182	−5.1	−375	−6.5	−482	−2.5	−185	−6.8	−504
$10 to $15	7.8	965	9.5	1,168	9.1	1,115	9.7	1,193	8.4	1,030
$15 to $20	9.2	1,589	15.6	2,697	16.1	2,778	14.8	2,551	15.6	2,685
$20 to $25	11.0	2,437	19.3	4,296	20.1	4,475	17.9	3,996	19.8	4,389
$25 to $50	13.3	4,337	23.4	7,606	24.8	8,070	21.3	6,923	24.4	7,945
$50 to $100	20.4	13,114	28.2	18,124	30.0	19,243	24.7	15,877	28.5	18,326
$100 to $500	26.7	42,949	30.8	49,619	33.0	53,130	26.7	43,048	31.3	50,370
$500 to $1,000	29.0	195,709	33.5	225,915	36.1	243,214	29.0	195,837	34.3	230,956
$1,000 and over	30.1	671,366	35.3	787,371	38.0	848,362	30.6	682,402	36.1	805,526
All classes[b]	4.4	439	4.7	460	4.7	460	4.7	460	4.7	460

Note—Income classes in thousands.

[a] Money receipts exclusive of transfers and taxes; receipts include total amount of realized capital gains and total gain on assets transferred by gift or bequest.

[b] Includes negative income class not shown separately.

[c] This minus amount indicates that incomes in this class were raised by the percentage amount shown through transfer payments net of taxes. That is, under the column "1970 tax (+) or transfer (−)," the −181.1 shown indicates that transfer payments raised the income of this class by 181.1 percent.

[d] This minus amount is the average amount by which incomes in this class were raised by income transfer payments.

96

Summary of After-Tax Increases for Lower Families under Various Demogrant Schedules, by Family Size and Income Classes, 1970

Family size and income class[a]	Schedule A		Schedule B		Schedule C		Schedule D	
	Number of families	Tax increase	Number of families	Tax increase	Number of families	Tax increase	Number of families	Tax Increase
Small families[b]	10,881	$12,374	13,103	$17,087	11,422	$9,859	15,361	$18,720
Under $5	2,725	1,847	3,363	2,472	2,325	1,361	4,277	3,156
$5 to $10	2,770	1,694	3,597	2,524	3,230	1,518	4,378	3,092
$10 to $15	2,174	1,931	2,833	2,895	2,719	1,789	3,367	3,367
$15 to $20	1,598	2,036	1,665	2,867	1,597	1,751	1,694	3,036
$20 to $25	792	1,395	792	1,893	768	1,111	803	1,900
$25 and over	822	3,471	853	4,436	783	2,329	842	4,169
Medium-size families[b]	11,851	21,976	11,358	23,740	12,760	18,320	10,824	21,570
Under $5	372	745	344	727	407	666	428	673
$5 to $10	831	867	604	739	978	777	541	669
$10 to $15	3,332	2,471	2,790	2,066	3,677	2,166	1,999	1,643
$15 to $20	2,962	4,498	3,143	4,611	3,260	3,880	3,258	3,850
$20 to $25	1,799	3,742	1,870	4,182	1,897	3,249	1,984	4,024
$25 and over	2,555	9,653	2,607	11,415	2,541	7,582	2,614	10,711
Large families[b]	3,383	8,008	2,418	6,191	2,874	5,276	2,023	4,963
Under $5	103	242	58	159	74	162	42	100
$5 to $10	313	299	72	159	137	171	63	129
$10 to $15	995	987	423	290	694	456	129	119
$15 to $20	710	1,396	639	904	706	935	507	567
$20 to $25	548	1,514	519	1,141	554	1,026	562	865
$25 and over	714	3,570	707	3,538	709	2,526	719	3,183
All groups	26,116	42,360	26,880	47,016	27,057	33,455	28,205	45,253

Note—Income classes and number of families in thousands; dollar amounts in millions. Details may not add to totals because of rounding. All taxes and benefits calculated using a proportional rate on the comprehensive tax base.
[a] Total money receipts exclusive of taxes and transfers; receipts include amount of realized capital gains and total gain on assets transferred by gift or bequest.
[b] One- and two-person families are classified as small; three-, four-, and five-person families as medium size; and six-person or larger families as large.

Table 3.9 Summary of Grant Payments and Tax Relief for Gainer Families, by Family Size and Income Classes, 1970

Family size and income class[a]	Schedule A		Schedule B		Schedule C		Schedule D	
	Number of families	Income increase	Number of families	Income increase	Number of families	Income increase	Number of families	Income Increase
Small families[b]	23,336	$24,632	21,113	$22,212	22,794	$20,666	18,857	$16,904
Under $5	16,538	19,595	15,900	18,649	16,938	17,273	14,987	14,631
$5 to $10	5,051	4,025	4,225	3,082	4,591	2,440	3,444	1,911
$10 to $15	1,523	605	863	235	978	260	330	75
$15 to $20	127	62	60	35	128	30	31	19
$20 to $25	21	14	20	9	44	20	9	4
$25 and over	76	331	45	202	115	643	56	264
Medium-size families[b]	14,676	19,697	15,168	22,791	13,765	14,654	15,702	24,877
Under $5	4,372	9,062	4,399	10,664	4,336	7,336	4,315	11,193
$5 to $10	6,540	7,459	6,766	9,164	6,392	5,228	6,829	10,410
$10 to $15	2,627	2,071	3,169	2,205	2,282	1,172	3,960	2,755
$15 to $20	782	612	601	464	483	272	486	241
$20 to $25	228	174	157	99	130	78	43	34
$25 and over	127	319	76	195	142	568	69	244
Large families[b]	3,008	5,063	3,971	8,990	3,518	5,382	4,368	10,594
Under $5	1,013	2,404	1,058	3,889	1,042	2,555	1,074	4,484
$5 to $10	1,238	1,515	1,479	3,118	1,414	1,763	1,488	3,863
$10 to $15	439	679	1,011	1,364	741	660	1,305	1,796
$15 to $20	191	246	261	356	195	183	393	259
$20 to $25	62	73	90	100	56	33	48	39
$25 and over	65	146	72	163	70	188	60	153
All groups	41,017	49,395	40,253	53,992	40,076	40,704	38,928	52,377

Note—Income classes and number of families in thousands; dollar amounts in millions. Details may not add to totals because of rounding. All taxes and benefits calculated using a proportional rate on the comprehensive tax base.

a Total money receipts exclusive of taxes and transfers; receipts include total amount of realized capital gains and total gain on assets transferred by gift or bequest.

b One- and two-person families are classified as small; three-, four-, and five-person families as medium size; and six-person or larger families as large.

These loser families represent 38.9 and 42.0 percent of all families in the population, respectively. Thus, regardless of the benefit schedule used, approximately 40 percent of all families experience net tax increases to finance the benefits paid to the gainer families.

Despite the considerable difference in total costs among the various programs—for example, $33 billion under Schedule C versus $47 billion under Schedule B—there is not a great deal of variation in the distribution of the net tax increases among families of different size under the various schedules. Under each program, roughly 50 percent of the total net tax increase would be paid by medium-size families containing three to five persons. The largest difference in the distribution of total cost by family size occurs under Schedules A and D, that is, between the $1500 adult-only grant and the schedule providing near-poverty-level benefits to families with declining amounts for the third and subsequent children. Only about 32 percent of all small families would pay increased net taxes under Schedule A, while 45 percent of such families would have tax hikes under Schedule D. The situation for large families under the two schedules is just the reverse: Of all six-person or larger families, 53 percent would pay increased net taxes under Schedule A while only 32 percent of such families would pay higher taxes under Schedule D. This difference is particularly interesting since the total cost of these two plans is fairly close.

As shown in Table 3.9, after-tax–after-grant income for about 40 million families would increase under the demogrant–tax credit schedules. About 60 percent of the total population would therefore be gainers under the program. Since tax increases and tax relief roughly balance one another, the patterns and amounts of relief are pretty much the complement of the amounts and patterns of tax increases shown in Table 3.8. Small families receive about 50 percent of the total grant and tax relief amount under Schedules A and C; under Schedule B, they receive 41 percent; and, under Schedule D, they get only 32 percent of the total benefit. In terms of the number of families receiving relief, small families fare best under Schedules A and C where about two-thirds of all such units receive increases in their after-credit income. Large families fare best under Schedule D benefit levels where about 68 percent of these units receive grants or tax relief.

There is about $7 billion more in grants and tax relief than in tax increases because of the assumed reduction of federal expenditures for Public Assistance, Food Stamps, and housing assistance. Thus, the gains shown in the previously mentioned tables are overstated for households benefiting from present welfare programs.

The proportions of the gainers who are currently taxable and will pay lower net taxes under a demogrant (those with tax relief) and those who are not now subject to tax but will experience an increase in transfer income under the new program are also similar under all four benefit structures. Regardless of the benefit structure, about 24 million families or 60 percent of all gainer families receive tax relief, and the remaining 40 percent are currently nontaxable families whose after-credit income rises under the demogrant program.

IV. The Effect of Demogrants on the Size of the Poverty Population

In the United States, poverty status is now measured by comparing a family's total census money income (which includes all transfer payments but excludes income from capital gains) with the official poverty-income level for families of a given size, composition, and (farm/nonfarm) place of residence. Under this procedure, there is no allowance made for income tax or any other tax payments for which the family is liable.

Using the conventional method, there were an estimated 25.5 million poor persons and 10.2 million poor families in 1970.[16] Our estimate of the 1970 poverty population based on the MERGE file projection is 22.8 million persons and 9.0 million families with Census incomes below the poverty-income level.[17] While our estimates are somewhat lower than the official figures, we feel that they are sufficiently close to Census Bureau figures to be used in the remainder of this section.

In order to measure the poverty population after institution of a demogrant program, two changes in the conventional procedure must be made. Since it is assumed that the demogrant will replace the current federal Public Assistance programs, these payments are subtracted from the amount of census income received by a family when comparing its income to the appropriate poverty-income level.[18] In lieu of Public Assistance, the amount of gross demogrant received by each family is included in income for determining its poverty status. No account was taken of

---

[16] U.S., Bureau of the Census, *Current Population Reports, Consumer Income*, Ser. P-60, No. 77 (Washington, D.C.: U.S. Government Printing Office, 7 May 1971).

[17] Our estimate is lower than the official one because, as discussed in footnote 8, it is based on a projection from 1966, after correction for income underreporting in that year.

[18] We recognize that this procedure is not consistent with the earlier assumption that the states would continue to supplement demogrant benefits in many jurisdictions where the new benefits are not as generous as the existing welfare payments. However, it was impossible to adjust for this, using our data base. As a result, our poverty estimates are higher than is likely to be true under a demogrant–tax credit program.

tax payments that would offset the amount of net benefit to be received in order to keep the data comparable with the present before-tax measure.

As can be seen from Table 3.10, which shows the number of poor families under current law and under each of the demogrant schedules, all demogrants examined would virtually wipe out poverty in this country —as it is currently defined. The extent to which the poverty population is reduced is perfectly correlated with the total outlays under a demogrant–tax credit. Gross outlays are lowest under Schedule C, $158 billion, and the poverty population would be reduced by the smallest amount, to 7.7 million persons living in 2.7 million families. Under Schedule B, which requires the largest gross outlays, $215 billion, poverty would be reduced the most, to 4.8 million persons living in 1.8 million families. The poverty-income deficit would be quite small under all schedules. Table 3.10 also classifies families by age of head and by size.

Because of the way benefits are structured, it is not surprising that poverty among the aged is, for all intents and purposes, eliminated under

Table 3.10 Comparison of the Number of Poor Families under Current Law and under Various Demogrant Schedules, by Age of Family Head and Family Size, 1970

Age of head and family size	Current law	Schedule			
		A	B	C	D
Non-aged head:[a]					
Single	2226	737	733	1068	897
Two persons	962	286	255	386	247
Three to five persons	1732	580	439	681	164
Six or more persons	962	414	223	384	154
Subtotal	5881	2007	1650	2520	1461
Aged head:[a]					
Single	2109	123	123	123	382
Two persons	821	11	5	5	—
Three to five persons	187	12	2	4	—
Six or more persons	43	9	4	9	—
Subtotal	3159	156	135	141	382
All ages:					
Single	4334	861	856	1192	1279
Two persons	1782	298	260	391	247
Three to five persons	1919	592	441	685	164
Six or more persons	1005	424	228	393	154
Total	9041	2174	1785	2661	1844

Note—Number of families in thousands. Details may not add to totals because of rounding.

[a] "Non-aged" refers to families headed by a person age sixty-four or under; "aged" refers to families headed by a person age sixty-five or above.

all schedules. The only families headed by an aged person who remain poor after any of the demogrant programs are the small number of such families with virtually no income or with negative income (for example, from farm or business losses).

There are also impressive cuts in the number of poor families headed by a person under age 65 under all the benefit schedules. The largest drop occurs under Schedule D, where the number of poor families drops by 4.4 million. This is closely followed by the reduction under Schedule B: 4.2 million families. The number of poor non-aged families under Schedule C drops by the smallest number: "only" 3.4 million.

The 2.7 million poor non-aged families with three or more persons comprise almost half of the 1970 non-aged total. And the 13.9 million persons in these families account for about three-fourths of the non-aged poverty population. These large families fare best under Schedule D benefit levels, and, under this program, the number of these families in poverty is cut to 318,000, or by about 88 percent. The number of persons living in such families is reduced to 1.7 million under Schedule D benefits. As we have seen before, the Schedule A payments are least beneficial to large families. Under this program, the number of non-aged poor families with three or more members is reduced to about 994,000, containing a total of about 5.4 million persons. Stated differently, Schedule A payment levels will leave about 3.6 million more non-aged persons in large families in the poverty population than would be the case under the Schedule D payment schedule.

Non-aged single persons fare best under Schedules A and B, and do worst under the low Schedule C benefits, where most of them will receive only $1000. There are very small differences in the numbers of two-person families removed from poverty under all programs other than Schedule C; there, again, smaller families fare considerably worse than they do under the other schedules.

V. Conclusions

There is no question that universal demogrants or tax credits combined with tax reform can significantly redistribute income in the United States. The amount of redistribution actually achieved is a function of how the benefit levels are structured and the degree to which the income tax is altered in order to finance the grants.

Using a proportional rate and comprehensive tax reform, it is possible to raise the share of total after-tax–after-grant income going to the lowest 20 percent of the population from 5.3 percent under the existing tax and transfer system to 7.0 percent under Schedule B benefit levels. In terms of the degree of redistribution achieved, Schedule D benefit levels were least effective; under that schedule, the share of income received by the lowest one-fifth of all families was raised to 6.7 percent.

Of course, income redistribution of such magnitudes cannot be achieved without cost. In our analysis, the relevant cost was considered to be the redistributional cost of a program: namely, the amount by which taxes would have to be increased (or future tax cuts forgone) by loser families. Under Schedule B, which redistributed the greatest amount of income, we estimate that 26.9 million families (of the 67.1 million total in 1970) would have to pay net increased taxes of about $47 billion. For the "cheapest" schedule of benefits, the distributional cost would be about $34 billion in additional taxes paid by 27.1 million families.

All programs examined had a sizable impact on the size of the poverty population as it is currently measured. Poverty among the aged is virtually eliminated, regardless of which benefit schedule is adopted. For non-aged families, schedules that continue to pay generous benefits to large families remove the greatest number from poverty.

While it is clear that any of the programs discussed are economically feasible, they have not yet been tested politically. Put most concisely, the real question is, Do the American people want the degree of income redistribution that would be achieved under a demogrant program, and are the loser families willing to accept the tax increases they would be obliged to pay in order to obtain the amount of tax and welfare reform suggested in this chapter?

Acknowledgments

The author is grateful for many helpful comments received, on an earlier draft of this chapter, from Russell Lidman of the Institute for Research on Poverty, University of Wisconsin. The computer work involved in our examination of distributional effects of demogrant systems was performed at the Brookings Social Science Computer Center, with the major share of the programming done by Ralph W. Tryon and Andrew D. Pike. Marjorie P. Odle and Stephen W. Kidd were also responsible for part of the computer programming. I gratefully acknowledge the efforts of all these persons.

Appendix

Comprehensive and Partial Tax Reform Bases

In 1970, adjusted gross income (AGI) of all family units in the United States amounted to $637 billion. Under the comprehensive income tax base, AGI would have risen to $730 billion, or by 14.5 percent. Taxable income would have risen from $401 billion to $690 billion, an increase of $289 billion or 72.1 percent. Under the partial tax reform, AGI would have amounted to $703 billion, an increase of 10.3 percent, and taxable income would have risen $232 billion, or 57.9 percent.

Comprehensive reform attempts to make the income tax base correspond as closely as practical to an economic concept of income, that is, consumption plus tax payments plus (or minus) the net increase (or decrease) in the value of assets during the year. However, some modifications are made on the grounds of historical precedent or to take account of administrative considerations. Thus, capital gains would be taxed only when actually realized or constructively realized when transferred to others through gift or bequest rather than on an accrual basis; gifts and inheritances would be excluded from income; all dividends would be included in income, but not undistributed profits; and employer contributions to private health and pension plans would not be considered current taxable income.

Such a tax base would differ greatly from that which now exists in the United States. To achieve the comprehensive reform base, the following changes from present tax law would have to be made: Treat as ordinary income all realized gains (and losses) and gains on property transferred by gift or bequest; eliminate the tax exemption for interest on state and local government bonds; limit depletion allowances to cost depletion; limit depreciation to amounts computed under the straight-line method; tax interest on the current-year increment to the cash surrender value of life insurance policies; include net imputed rent in taxable income and eliminate the personal deductions for real property taxes and mortgage interest; tax transfer payments as ordinary income; eliminate most itemized deductions;[19] eliminate the minimum standard deduction (but not the low-income allowance); eliminate the special exemptions for the aged and blind and the retirement income tax credit; and eliminate the dividend exclusion. In addition, the rate advantages (but not the mechanics) of income splitting for married couples and the maximum tax on earned income are eliminated under the comprehensive income tax reform. For purposes of this chapter, taxpayer and dependents' exemptions would also be eliminated, as they would be replaced by the demogrants.

The partial reform tax base excludes certain features of the comprehensive tax base, which, on political grounds, we feel would be extremely difficult to implement. Under the partial tax reform, the following changes from the comprehensive tax were made: State and local government bond interest remains nontaxable; interest earned on life insurance policies is not taxed; and homeowners' preferences, in the form of mortgage interest and real estate taxes paid, continue to be allowed as itemized personal deductions.[20] In addition, only the first 3 percent of medical expenses are nondeductible (as opposed to the first 5 percent under the comprehensive law).

Under both the comprehensive and partial tax reforms, the increases in AGI, taxable income, and tax liability are considerable (see Tables 3A.1 and 3A.2). In

[19] The following itemized deductions would be eliminated or modified: medical expenses up to 5 percent of income, charitable contributions up to 3 percent of income, gasoline, and personal property taxes paid. In addition, interest payments would be deductible only up to the level of income received from property.

[20] This is subject to the qualification that all interest expenses are deductible only up to the level of income earned from property. This qualification applies to all interest expenses, not just those on home mortgages, and therefore does not affect only homeowners.

both cases, the greatest increases in taxable income and tax liability result from changes in the treatment of exemptions and personal deductions. Under the comprehensive law, the elimination of homeowners' preferences, the various other itemized deductions, and the inclusion of transfers as taxable income each add $30–$40 billion to taxable income. Since transfers are largely received by the poor, the revenue effect of taxing transfers is less than that of the other two changes, the benefits of which accrue mainly to the more well-to-do. Thus, the taxation of capital gains adds $19.0 billion to taxable income and more than $9.0 billion to revenue, while taxation of transfers increases taxable income by $32.0 billion, but results in only $7.5 billion additional revenue.

Table 3A.1 Comparison between Adjusted Gross Income, Taxable Income, and Tax Liability under Present Law and the Comprehensive Reform Income Tax, 1970 Income Levels

Item	Adjusted gross income[a]	Taxable income[a]	Tax liability
Present law	$636,915	$400,614	$83,833
Elimination of rate advantages of income splitting[b]	–	–	15,613
Plus:			
½ realized capital gains	10,487	9,709	5,381
Constructive realization of gain on gifts and bequests	10,097	9,362	4,207
Tax-exempt state and local bond interest	1,647	1,616	1,019
Other preference income[c]	633	555	194
Dividend exclusion	1,492	1,342	451
Interest on life insurance policies	10,461	9,900	2,871
Homeowners' preferences[d]	15,257	39,132	12,525
Transfer payments	43,210	31,694	7,543
Personal exemptions[e]	–	147,466	42,669
Personal deductions[f]	–	38,230	14,808
Equals: Comprehensive reform income tax	730,199	689,620	191,114

Note—In millions of dollars. Details may not add to totals because of rounding.
[a] The increase in taxable income is greater than the change in adjusted gross income because the elimination of certain exemptions and deductions increases taxable income but does not affect adjusted gross income.
[b] Includes revenue effect of eliminating the 50 percent maximum tax on earned income.
[c] Excess of percentage over cost depletion and accelerated over straight-line depreciation.
[d] Includes effects of adding net imputed rent and disallowing itemized deductions for mortgage interest and real estate taxes.
[e] Includes effect of eliminating retirement income credit.
[f] The following itemized deductions have been eliminated or modified: charitable contributions up to 3 percent of income, gasoline and personal property taxes paid. In addition, interest payments are deductible only up to the level of income received from property.

Table 3A.2 Comparison between Adjusted Gross Income, Taxable Income, and Tax Liability under Present Law and the Partial Reform Income Tax, 1970 Income Levels

Item	Adjusted gross income[a]	Taxable income[a]	Tax liability
Present law	$636,915	$400,614	$83,833
Elimination of rate advantage of income splitting[b]	–	–	15,613
Plus:			
½ realized capital gains	10,487	9,709	5,381
Constructive realization of gain on gifts and bequests	10,097	9,362	4,207
Other preference income[c]	633	547	185
Dividend exclusion	1,492	1,342	436
Transfer payments	43,210	30,051	6,856
Personal exemptions[d]	–	145,820	37,521
Personal deductions[e]	–	35,185	12,698
Equals: Partial reform income tax	702,834	632,630	166,730

Note—In millions of dollars. Details may not add to totals because of rounding.

[a] The increase in taxable income is greater than the change in adjusted gross income because the elimination of certain exemptions and deductions increases taxable income but does not affect adjusted gross income.'

[b] Includes revenue effect of eliminating the 50 percent maximum tax on earned income.

[c] Excess of percentage over cost depletion and accelerated over straight-line depreciation.

[d] Includes effect of eliminating retirement income credit.

[e] The following itemized deductions have been eliminated or modified: charitable contributions up to 3 percent of income, gasoline and personal property taxes paid. In addition interest payments are deductible only up to the level of income received from property.

If taxed at 1970 rates, the total of all the additions to the base under the comprehensive tax law plus the elimination of the rate advantages of income splitting would increase tax collections by more than $107 billion. Close to 40 percent of this increase is due to the elimination of personal exemptions and deductions. Elimination of income splitting, taxation of capital gains, and elimination of the homeowners' preferences each account for between 9 and 15 percent of the increase in tax liability. The total of all the other features accounts for roughly one-quarter of the $107 billion revenue increase.

Under the partial tax reform, more than three-fifths of the increase in taxable income is due to the elimination of the exemption and personal deductions, roughly 15 percent is due to the elimination of the itemized deductions, another 13 percent reflects the inclusion of transfers in the tax base. The combined effect of the other provisions accounts for about 9 percent of the increase in taxable income.

Again using the 1970 tax rates, the elimination of exemptions and personal deductions accounts for more than 45 percent of the $83 billion increase in tax revenue under the partial tax reform. Elimination of the advantages of income splitting accounts for another 19 percent. The inclusion of transfers and capital gains in the tax base accounts for 8 and 12 percent, respectively. And the elimination of the other itemized deductions accounts for almost 15 percent of the increased tax liability.

4

Earnings Supplementation as an Income Maintenance Strategy: Issues of Program Structure and Integration

Robert H. Haveman

I. Introduction

During the early 1970s, the income maintenance system in the United States came under increased public scrutiny. Viewed as a whole, it had many characteristics that gave it the appearance of unwise—indeed, unproductive—social policy. Because of eligibility standards and benefit levels, some families on welfare had higher total incomes than similar families in which the head worked full time. Because of the benefit schedule and the lack of integration among the many programs, little if any income improvement could be obtained by increased effort to earn income. Because of the restriction of eligibility in the AFDC program to female-headed families[1] together with the increasing number of apparently "able-bodied" women receiving support, the program was viewed by many as unfair to male-headed poor families, as "sexist" in its discouragement of labor force participation by women, and as conducive to family breakup and family instability. Because of the variance in eligibility

[1] Some families with an unemployed or incapacitated male head also receive benefits from AFDC.

and benefit levels by state, interstate inequities persist and artificial inducements to mobility are feared. Moreover, even though the system has grown rapidly, poverty has not been eliminated.[2]

In response to these concerns, many reform proposals have been made—negative income tax plans, demogrant schemes, and children's allowances. In all cases, these proposals were aimed at alleviating many of the problems of the existing system. To be seriously considered, a proposed plan had to demonstrate an increase in work incentives, an increase in equity between able-bodied male and female heads (often stated as extending coverage from the deserving to the working poor), the establishment of an acceptable need-related income floor for all families, and administrative feasibility—all of this without any major expansion in roles or costs. Because of the conflicting nature of some of these objectives, proposals traded gains in achieving one objective with costs in achieving the others.

The proposal that has received the most widespread attention is the Family Assistance Plan—later known as H.R. 1—of the Nixon administration. The latest version of this program called for a national minimum income guarantee of $2400 for a family of four persons, both male- and female-headed. As the earnings of a family increased above $720 per year, the level of the guarantee would have decreased by $.67 per $1.00 of earnings—a 66.7 percent tax rate. However, because recipients of cash transfers often receive other income-conditioned benefits—for example, Medicaid and public housing—and pay other positive taxes on their earnings, the effective tax rate would have been substantially in excess of 67 percent. For some recipients and over some income ranges, the effective rate would have been more than 100 percent. To counteract these offsets to the work incentive implied by the basic tax rate of 67 percent, the proposal incorporated a work requirement for adult benefit recipients who were not ill, incapacitated, needed in the home because of illness, elderly, mothers with children under six, or youths between sixteen and twenty-two who are attending school.

To assist those required to register for work and training, H.R. 1 would have provided financing for 200,000 public service jobs, and support for some job training and day care. If an "employable" adult refused employment or training, a penalty of $800 would have been subtracted from family annual benefits.

In addition to these provisions, H.R. 1 would have eliminated the Food Stamp program, altered the eligibility requirements of Medicaid and

[2] For an analysis of the nature and evolution of the Public Assistance system, see Sar A. Levitan, Martin Rein, and David Marwick, *Work and Welfare Go Together* (Baltimore: Johns Hopkins Press, 1972).

public housing to eliminate the "notch," encouraged states to supplement federal benefits so as to minimize the adverse effect of the program on current recipients, and established federal government administration of the program. The effect of these changes would have increased the number of recipients from 15 million in 1973 to about 25 million, at a total additional federal cost of about $2 billion.

While the House of Representatives passed H.R. 1 on two separate occasions, it was not supported by the Senate Finance Committee. In its place, the committee put forth an income maintenance plan of its own. By comparing the provisions of this plan with H.R. 1, the failure of H.R. 1 to gain committee approval appears to be attributable to the lack of effective work incentives implicit in the high, cumulative, marginal tax rate on earned income, the likely ineffectiveness (in employing able-bodied family heads) of a work test that is not accompanied by sufficient employment and training opportunities and day care support, and the high income guarantee available to an able-bodied family head—male or female —who manages to elude the work test.

The keystone of the strategy developed by the Senate Finance Committee was the proposition that both male and female family heads without severe impediments to work should rely on earned income as their primary means of support. There are four corollaries to this proposition. First, a criterion must be established to distinguish employable family heads from those with severe impediments to work. Second, positive work-related incentives—as opposed to work disincentives in the form of implicit tax rates—are important both to induce work effort by employable family heads and to supplement their earned income. Third, a program of guaranteed public jobs is essential to offset the destructive effect of a loose labor market on such an employment-related program. Finally, for those family heads who cannot be expected to work, a more traditional income support system with little concern for work incentives should be made available.

While such a work-conditioned, income maintenance strategy has some familiar components, it represents a policy approach rather different from either the current welfare system or H.R. 1. As such, the committee plan leaves many unanswered questions and unresolved problems. In succeeding sections of this chapter, many of these will be raised and analyzed. In the second section, the specifics of the Senate Finance Committee strategy will be described and its impact on various categories of low-income families analyzed. In the third section, the committee proposal will be criticized and compared with H.R. 1. This critique will focus on considerations of efficiency, equity, effect on the national wage structure, and administrative feasibility. The fourth section presents an alternative work-conditioned, income maintenance scheme that corrects a number of the structural problems of the Senate Finance Committee proposals. The integration of this plan with other income transfer programs is also discussed in this section, and some of its advantages and disadvantages are evaluated.

II. Work-Conditioned Income Supplementation, Senate Finance Committee Style

In June 1972, when the Senate Finance Committee announced their version of a welfare reform bill, it was denounced by the administration, Senate liberals, and the media as "slavefare," as "barbaric," and as "a $9 billion step backward." The proposal that drew this response is not a simple and straightforward scheme. While it would reduce the size of the current AFDC program, it would not eliminate it. It would require some current welfare recipients to be employed in order to qualify for income supplementation, and it would guarantee success to their efforts to find employment. Moreover, it would provide substantial assistance for child care services to heads of single-parent families who are declared to be "employable." While it would be a less attractive program to some current welfare recipients than the current AFDC program, it would funnel substantial income support to working poor and near-poor families who are now effectively excluded from the nation's income maintenance system. In describing their strategy, the committee stated:

> Paying an employable person a benefit based on need, the essence of the welfare approach, has not worked. It has not decreased dependency—it has increased it. It has not encouraged work—it has discouraged it. It has not added to the dignity in the lives of recipients, and it has aroused the indignation of the taxpayers who must pay for it. . . . The only way to meet the economic needs of poor persons while at the same time decreasing rather than increasing their dependency is to reward work directly by increasing its value.

The Structure of the Senate Bill

The primary provisions of the Senate Finance Committee proposal are described by focusing first on the program of assistance to families without an employable head and then on those with such a head. The program, it should be noted, provides no assistance to single individuals or childless couples.

ASSISTANCE TO FAMILIES WITHOUT AN EMPLOYABLE HEAD

Under the current welfare system, income support through AFDC is provided for families that are headed by females or by incapacitated fathers and stepfathers and that meet the income and asset tests of state welfare systems—about 3 million families. In addition, in about twenty-five states, families headed by long-term unemployed fathers receive support through AFDC–UF.[3] The committee bill would continue these cash transfer programs only for those single-parent (primarily female-headed) families in which the parent has a child under age six or is ill, incapacitated, attending school full time, or residing in a geographically remote region. About 1.8 million families fall into this category, approximately 60 percent of the current AFDC population.

For this residual AFDC population, the Senate bill would require that states with high benefit levels not reduce payment levels below $2400 for a family of four. States with payment levels below this amount could not reduce them at all. In addition, a block grant would be provided states to enable them to raise benefits to this level with no additional cost to them.[4] After disregarding $240 of earnings plus earnings to cover another $240 of child support costs, earned income would be taxed at a 100 percent rate.[5]

The committee proposal, like H.R. 1, would not provide federal matching of the state supplemental payments. Also, like the administration proposal, the Food Stamp program would be eliminated for families who are eligible for welfare benefits. However, states could choose to supplement the basic federal program by the amount of the implicit cash value of Food Stamps to a family (an average of about $800) without incurring additional cost. However, unlike H.R. 1, the Senate proposal does not encourage states to cede administration of the welfare program to the federal government.

ASSISTANCE TO FAMILIES WITH AN EMPLOYABLE HEAD

Under the committee proposal, families with heads who are classified as employable would not be eligible for direct cash transfers unrelated to work. For some of these families—employable female- and male-headed families who are now receiving AFDC or AFDC–UF benefits—this would

[3] About 20 percent of all AFDC families are male-headed.
[4] The block grant, however, does not cover costs for benefit levels beyond $2400 even though the family has more than four members. It should be noted that some states may well not increase benefit levels, even though such an increase would be costless.
[5] The 100 percent tax rate provision goes into effect only after the employment program (described later) is in operation.

114 / *Robert H. Haveman*

significantly change their status. Such family heads, however, are guaranteed a minimum income of $2400 per year (unrelated to family size) provided they participate in the employment program.[6]

The employment program would be administered by a Work Administration (WA), which would be created by the bill. Any eligible family head would be guaranteed a job by the WA. In dealing with registrants in the program, the WA would have three options available. First, the participant could be placed by the WA in a regular public or private sector job paying $2 per hour or more. Full-time work for a year in a job provided by the WA would yield the worker an income of at least $4000 per year.

A second option for the WA would be to place the participant in a regular private or public sector job that pays less than the national minimum wage[7] but more than three-fourths of it. In this case, the WA would subsidize the applicant's wage rate by three-fourths of the difference between his wage rate and the national minimum wage rate.[8]

For applicants who find themselves in either of these circumstances, there is a supplemental subsidy that would be administered by the WA—an earnings bonus. For every dollar earned by the family head and his wife in employment covered by the Social Security program,[9] an additional 10 percent bonus would be paid, up to an earnings level of $4000. Beyond $4000 of husband's plus wife's earnings, the bonus (which reaches a maximum of $400 at an earnings level of $4000) would be decreased by $.25 for each additional dollar of earnings, hence falling to zero at an earnings level of $5600. The schedule of work-conditioned subsidies related to the earnings of a family head in full-time employment (without a working wife) is shown in Figure 4.1. Total income for such a family is shown in Table 4.1. It should be noted that both the wage rate subsidy and the earnings bonus would also be payable to low-income family heads

[6] Eligibility for the employment program is limited to the heads of families with less than $300 per month of unearned income or $5600 of total family income per year.
[7] Except where noted, the discussion of the proposal will assume that the minimum wage is $2 per hour.
[8] The formula for this form of wage rate subsidy is $S = .75(X - W)$, where S is the per-hour subsidy, W is the actual wage rate, and X is the national minimum or target wage rate. To be eligible for the subsidy, $.75X < W < X$. For example, if the national minimum wage rate is $2.00 per hour and if the applicant is placed in a position paying $1.50 ($1.80) per hour, the WA would subsidize the wage rate by $.375 ($.15) per hour. From the employee's point of view, his wage rate would be $1.875 ($1.95) per hour, which, for full-time work, implies an income of $3750 ($3900) per year.
[9] A part of the rationale for the earnings bonus is to eliminate the Social Security payroll tax for low-income workers. The earnings bonus would be administered by the Internal Revenue Service.

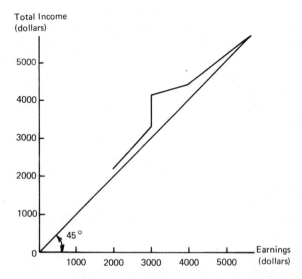

Figure 4.1. Earnings supplements to a family head in regular employment under the Senate Finance Committee bill. Increased earnings from $3000 to $4000 assumed to come from full-time work but at increasing wage *rates*.

who secured regular public or private employment on their own, without the help of the WA.

The third option available to the WA would be exercised if it failed to place the applicant in regular private or public sector employment. In this case, the applicant would be employed in one of the public service activities to be either arranged or operated by the WA. For such employment, the applicant would be paid three-fourths of the national minimum wage and would be guaranteed thirty-two hours of work per week. Presuming a $2 minimum wage and thirty-two hours of work per week,

Table 4.1 Earnings, Subsidies, Bonuses, and Total Income for Participants in Employment Program Working Full Time in Regular Employment

Wage rate	Annual earnings from employer	Wage rate subsidy	Earnings bonus	Total income
1.00	2000	—	200	2200
1.50	3000	750	300	4050
1.75	3500	375	350	4225
2.00	4000	—	400	4400
2.50	5000	—	150	5150
2.80	5600	—	—	5600

Note—All amounts in dollars.

this would imply an annual income of $2400.[10] Neither the wage rate subsidy nor the earnings bonus would be paid for such employment.

A special arrangement is provided for the low-income family head who is able to secure only part-time regular public or private employment. In such a situation, the employee would receive his wage rate from the regular private or public sector job, the wage rate subsidy (if his wage rate was less than the minimum wage but more than three-fourths of it), and the earnings bonus on the sum of husband's and wife's earnings. In addition, the part-time worker would be eligible for additional employment from the WA to result in a combined total of forty hours per week. The amount of income (and, hence, employment) that the WA would provide the applicant through some regular part-time employment is shown in Table 4.2.[11]

Of concern is the matter of state income supplementation programs and their relationship to the work-conditioned subsidies embodied in the committee bill. To eliminate the chance that state supplementation would reduce the work incentives of the plan, the bill requires states that choose to supplement the incomes of participating families to assume that the annual earnings of the family are at least $2400—implying thirty-two hours of work at the guaranteed wage rate of $1.50. Moreover, states would be required to disregard annual earnings between $2400 and $4500 in computing state supplemental payments. This implies a constant additional cash benefit that is not eroded by incremental earnings until earnings equal more than $4500. As the Finance Committee report states:

> The effect of this requirement would be to give a participant in the work program a strong incentive to work full-time . . . , and it would not interfere with the strong incentives he would have to seek regular employment rather than working for the Government.

In addition to this basic structure of the cash transfer, work-conditioned subsidy, and public service employment programs, there are other

[10] The limitation of work to thirty-two hours appears to be based on a desire to keep the guarantee at the $2400 level, hence making the public service alternative less desirable than full-time private employment. An alternative would be to guarantee full-time employment, which, at $1.50 per hour, implies an annual income of $3000. In the remainder of this chapter, both alternatives are analyzed.

[11] An interesting question affecting this package of employment options concerns the availability of public service employment to a family head currently holding full-time regular employment at, say, the minimum wage. With a minimum wage of $2, the annual earnings of the worker would be $4000, to which would be added the earnings bonus of $400. Could this person become eligible for additional public service employment through the WA? The committee has answered this affirmatively, stating that the WA *may* provide the worker up to twenty additional hours of work per week if such employment is available.

Table 4.2 Public Service Income and Employment Provided by Work Administration to Low-Income Family Head with Part-Time Regular Employment

Number of hours of work and wage rate	Annual income from employer	Income from wage rate subsidy	Income from earnings bonus	Total income from part-time employment	Additional income and hours per week guaranteed by Work Administration	Total income
10 hours/week:						
$1.20/hour	$600	–	$60	$660	$2250(30)	$2810
1.60/hour	800	$150	80	1030	2250(30)	3280
2.00/hour	1000	–	100	1100	2250(30)	3350
2.40/hour	1200	–	120	1320	2250(30)	3575
20 hours/week:						
1.20/hour	1200	–	120	1320	1500(20)	2820
1.60/hour	1600	300	160	2060	1500(20)	3560
2.00/hour	2000	–	200	2200	1500(20)	3700
2.40/hour	2400	–	240	2640	1500(20)	4140
30 hours/week:						
1.20/hour	1800	–	180	1980	750(10)	2730
1.60/hour	2400	450	240	3090	750(10)	3840
2.00/hour	3000	–	300	3300	750(10)	4050
2.40/hour	3600	–	360	3960	750(10)	4710

Note—Assumes employee is head of house and that there are no secondary workers in family. Numbers in parentheses after dollar income entitlement is number of hours per week the Work Administration would have to provide in public service employment.

important provisions. One such provision concerns the subsidization of child care services for participants in the employment program. Perhaps more than other proposals for welfare reform, a work-conditioned, income support program has implications for the public sector provision or subsidization of day care services. Because the committee bill would lead to essentially full-time employment for over 1 million mothers of school-age children who are currently receiving AFDC benefits, a major increase in the supply of after-school and full-time summer day care services is required.

The Senate bill would establish within the WA a Bureau of Child Care that would have as its central function the provision of child care services to single-parent family heads participating in the employment program. The bureau would train persons to provide family day care, contract with existing day care providers, give technical assistance to organizations wishing to establish facilities, and provide day care services in its own, to-be-developed facilities, making maximum use of mothers who are participants in the employment program.[12] While mothers employed in special public service jobs would apparently receive free day care services—valued at $800 per child per year—the day care benefit would be diminished for employable mothers who earn in excess of $2400. The committee has not specified the rate at which this subsidy is to be reduced as earnings increase above $2400.

A second important provision enables participants in the employment program to volunteer for training programs to be administered by the WA. However, during the training, participants would be paid $1.30 per hour rather than the $1.50 in the special public service jobs. The cumulated difference between the two wage rates would be paid as a lump sum to those trainees who complete the program.

III. The Senate Finance Committee Proposal: A Policy Evaluation

The Finance Committee proposal represents a major alternative to other proposed welfare reform strategies such as negative income taxation, the credit income tax (demogrant), and H.R. 1. As such, its efficiency and equity characteristics require evaluation, as do the likely effects of its implementation on the national wage structure and the behavioral patterns of recipients. In this section, several of these probable impacts will be analyzed.

Equity Effects

The Finance Committee proposal is likely to cost $12–$15 billion over and above the cost of the existing AFDC, AFDC–UF, and Food Stamp programs. About 40 percent of this cost is attributable to the public employment program, with the work-conditioned subsidies and the direct transfer components accounting for 20 percent each. Each of these components has equity effects that must be considered.

First, the public employment program: The participants in this program will be those current AFDC and AFDC–UF recipients declared to be employable and those persons who find the public service option superior to their current job. It is apparent that the overwhelming majority of these people are below the poverty line and most of them are substantially below. Government expenditures providing income for these

---

[12] The committee would authorize $800 million for the provision of such services.

people have a high "target efficiency"—a high proportion of the dollars spent would be received by the poor with little of the cost spilling over to nonpoor recipients.

A second component of this strategy is the work-conditioned subsidy.[13] This subsidy would be paid to workers who are household heads and who are earning a wage rate below the national minimum wage but above three-fourths of it. Because of the low level of this standard, most of these workers would have incomes below the poverty line. However, it should be noted that some of the family heads holding such low-paying jobs may not be poor. Examples would include individuals with substantial unearned income, family heads holding second jobs, families with two or more full-time earners, and the heads of small families. While evidence for the extent to which this subsidy would spill over to nonpoor recipients is not firm, there is some indication that it would not be trivial.

In a recent study, Michael Barth analyzed the distribution of the benefits of a universal wage rate subsidy among poor and nonpoor.[14] Because this study displayed the population subgroups that would be recipients of such a universal program, it is possible to estimate the distributional effect of a program limited to family heads (as the Senate bill is). Table 4.3 displays such results for two wage rate subsidy plans—a $1.60 minimum wage and a $2.00 minimum wage, with the subsidy equal to 50 percent of the differential between the actual wage and the national minimum.

The table shows that, for the smaller plan, nearly 65 percent of total recipients are poor and that well over one-half of the benefits go to poor recipients. Comparable figures for the larger plan are 41 and 40 percent. The same study shows that, for the smaller plan, 65 percent of poor family heads who work for wages would receive some subsidy while 75 percent of such workers would be subsidized under the larger plan.[15]

[13] Because the wage rate form of a work subsidy has been most extensively studied, it will be used in this subsection as the basis of the analysis.

[14] Michael C. Barth, "Cost, Coverage, and Antipoverty Effect of a Per Hour Wage Subsidy" (Ph.D. diss., City University of New York, 1971). Barth estimated that a *universal* wage rate subsidy plan would target only about 20 percent of its benefits on recipients below the poverty line. See also Michael C. Barth, "Universal Wage Rate Subsidy: Benefits and Effects," in *The Economics of Federal Subsidy Programs*, Part 4, U.S., Congress, Joint Economic Committee, 92d Cong., 2d sess., August 1972, pp. 497–540.

[15] A number of things should be emphasized regarding the implication of these results for estimating the target efficiency of a work-conditioned, income supplementation strategy. First, because of the change in wage rate level between 1966 and 1973, work subsidy based on a $2.00 wage standard is closer in real terms to the $1.60 plan described in the study. Second, because the plans discussed in the study subsidize 50 percent of the wage rate differential, they would concentrate a smaller share of the

Table 4.3 Distribution of Recipients and Benefits of Wage Subsidy Plans among Poor and Nonpoor

| | Poor | | | | Nonpoor | | | |
| | Recipients | | Benefits | | Recipients | | Benefits | |
	Millions	Percent of the total	Millions of dollars	Percent of the total	Millions	Percent of the total	Millions of dollars	Percent of the total
$1.60 plan	2.5	62.5	1.0	52.6	1.5	37.5	0.9	47.5
$2.00 plan	2.9	41.4	1.7	39.5	4.1	58.6	2.6	60.5

Note—Based on the 1967 Survey of Economic Opportunity.

While there would be some leakage of benefits to those families who are not classified as being in poverty, it seems safe to claim that three-fourths of the benefits from the work subsidy component of the strategy would accrue to poor or near-poor families. Moreover, to the extent that a program objective is to insure that work effort by the primary earner is rewarded at some "reasonable" level, the provision of some subsidy to the nonpoor would be warranted.

Finally, the additional public expenditures required to support a $2400 benefit level for all families of four in the non-work-related cash transfer program would have a 100 percent target efficiency. All of the beneficiaries would be single-parent families without an employable head with current benefits below such a national standard.

Although this evaluation is a crude one, it seems clear that the target efficiency of the Finance Committee strategy is very high. For example, it is not unreasonable to assert that at least 75–80 percent of the subsidy provided will be received by families below the poverty line with much of the remainder accruing to the near-poor. This level of target efficiency, it should be emphasized, is higher than that of an equally costly negative income tax type plan. The reason for this is the relatively high break-even earnings level for moderately large negative tax plans with "reasonable" tax rates. The work-conditioned, income supplementation strategy is able to avoid some of this leakage of support to the nonpoor by tying subsidies

subsidy on those with actual wage rates at the lower end of the wage distribution than would a plan with a higher percentage subsidy. Such plans, however, would concentrate a larger share of the subsidy on very low-wage-rate earners than would a plan that subsidized only wage rates above some level, as in the Senate Finance Committee bill. Finally, to the extent that there is nontrivial leakage of benefits, it seems highly likely that the bulk of the leaked benefits would accrue to near-poor family heads.

to labor market performance, hence eliminating the tax rate of negative income tax plans required to erode the guarantee.[16]

Would the committee bill establish a minimum income below which no family would fall? In considering the existence of an income floor in the bill, several categories of low-income families must be distinguished. One primary category consists of the head who would continue to be eligible for cash transfers unrelated to work. The committee bill would enable states to establish an income floor of $2400 for families of four persons in this category at no additional state cost, plus enabling states to supplement the federal benefit by "cashing out" Food Stamps—worth $800 to a family with no income—at no additional cost. It seems likely then that the minimum income guarantee would be at least three-fourths of the poverty line for most families in this category.[17]

A second category consists of those families whose head is declared to be employable. For these families, there is also a guarantee. However, access to it requires work effort. In addition to subsidized regular employment, employable family heads would always have the guarantee of public service employment on which to fall back. Even if this program paid but three-fourths of a national minimum wage of $2 per hour, full-time work would yield an annual income of $3000. Consistent with such a strategy, single-parent family heads who are employable would be guaranteed after-school and summer day care subsidies (valued at about $800 per year) for each child. For the group of employables, then, an income floor also would be established.[18]

This is not to say, however, that all of these families would be as well off in terms of spendable income (cash benefits less net child care and other work expenses) in this program as they would be under the current welfare system or H.R. 1. Some clearly would not be. In particular, those mothers now receiving AFDC who are declared employable and who reside in current high-benefit states are likely to find themselves with less spendable income under the Finance Committee strategy than under either the current system or H.R. 1. This is especially true if the

---

[16] It should, in addition, be noted that nearly 30 percent of the costs of H.R. 1 is earmarked for state and local government savings—a not very "target effective" expenditure if the target is low-income families. See Jodie T. Allen, *A Funny Thing Happened on the Way to Welfare Reform* (Washington, D.C.: Urban Institute, 1972).

[17] However, some of these women both work and draw AFDC benefits. Because the Senate Finance Committee bill erodes benefits in response to earnings at a very high rate, some of these women would be made worse off because of the bill, and existing work effort would tend to be eliminated.

[18] An apparently unresolved question, however, concerns the support provided children in case the family head *refuses* to work.

high-benefit states—in the absence of a federal mandate—reduce their current benefit levels or fail to provide supplemental benefits to public service employees. Moreover, for some family heads currently receiving AFDC, the welfare loss induced by requiring work outside the home in lieu of "home work" may be substantial.

However, because of the work subsidy, most of the current working poor would find themselves with substantially more net spendable income than they currently have. Moreover, those families whose heads earn a very low market wage rate, even though they would get a work subsidy, might not have income above that guaranteed by public service employment provided by the WA. The heads of these families would have every incentive to shift from regular employment to the WA program to take advantage of its guaranteed employment and income.[19] With this option available, no family headed by an employable person who is willing to work should find itself with less spendable income than that guaranteed by special public service employment programs.

While the Finance Committee strategy appears both to target its support on the poverty population rather effectively and to establish a minimum income floor for all families, it has some additional equity effects which are not so attractive. One of these structural problems is that the subsidies provided through the Work Administration depend only on the wage rate received and the number of hours worked. As a consequence, large-size families will be substantially less well off if the head is declared to be employable than under the current welfare system (if eligible) or H.R. 1. However, although not included in the legislation, the committee anticipates that state supplementation plans will reinstate family-size-conditioned benefits.[20]

A second provision generating horizontal inequities is a fundamental one. The only way in which a participant who is directly employed by the WA in a public service job can be distinguished from one placed in

[19] While the wage rate paid to public service employees—being below the national minimum wage rate—would seem to be in conflict with the notion of a minimum standard, it should be noted that 2.3 million workers in the United States earn less than $1.50—three-fourths of the minimum wage (from surveys conducted in 1970 and 1971 by the Employment Standards Administration of the U.S. Department of Labor). From a special tabulation of the SEO tape (1967), it was estimated that 4 million family heads earned less than $1.60 per hour and 7 million family heads earned less than $2.00 per hour. Similar figures for *male* heads are 3 million and 6 million.

[20] An earlier version of the bill did provide for a children's allowance to be paid to all low-income families with more than four members. For the fifth, sixth, and additional members of a family unit, annual grants of $300, $180, and $120 were suggested. The allowance would have been reduced by $1 for every $2 of earnings above $3600 annually.

regular public or private employment is that the WA was successful in the latter case but not in the former. While the regular employee gains the benefits of a wage that is likely to be at least three-quarters of the national minimum plus both the wage subsidy and the earnings bonus, the public service employee does not. This inequity is the price required to maintain the incentive for public service employees to seek regular employment.

The third provision resulting in horizontal inequities is the generous provision of child care to mothers employed directly by the WA in public service jobs. For these participants, provision of child care would be given highest priority and would be fully subsidized. Other working mothers not employed by the WA may have equally low incomes but would apparently be assigned a lower priority for provision of day care services. They would be unlikely to receive full subsidization of such services.

A further provision encouraging horizontal inequity is that which leaves the decision of supplementation open to the states. As a result, those welfare beneficiaries or work program participants residing in states that legislate generous state supplementation plans would have higher total incomes than equally poor residents in low-supplementation states. However, because the committee bill enables states to raise benefit levels for welfare benefits to $2400 for a family of four at no additional state cost, this inequity would be reduced from the one existing in the current welfare system.

Efficiency Effects

A second criterion used to evaluate the effectiveness of a government expenditure program is economic efficiency, which focuses on the resource allocation effect of a policy change. When this criterion is applied to an income transfer policy, impact on the work–leisure choice is a primary issue. In this regard, a work-conditioned, income supplementation strategy embodies a quite different set of incentives than do the current welfare system, H.R. 1, or proposed negative income tax or credit income tax plans.

For example, as noted in the first section, H.R. 1, when integrated with payroll taxes and state supplements, would have imposed a marginal tax rate of at least 80 percent or more on recipient earnings. The effect of this, together with the guaranteed income obtainable without work, would have been to erode seriously the incentive for work efforts for both current AFDC recipients and the working poor. The committee bill, on the other hand, incorporates three characteristics that induce work effort.

The first characteristic is the requirement that those who are employable must engage in productive employment (not merely be available to work) in order to be eligible for an income supplement. The second is the inducement for work effort implied in the work subsidy provision. As an example of the difference in work incentives between a negative income tax type plan and a work-conditioned subsidy scheme, Table 4.4 compares the marginal tax rates of a few individuals in different circumstances under H.R. 1 and under the committee bill. In all cases, the marginal tax rate on earnings is substantially lower in the committee bill than in H.R. 1. In one-half of the cases shown for the committee bill, the marginal tax rate is negative, implying that a $1 increase in earnings results in an increase in income of more than $1. The pattern of benefits and marginal tax rates for both schemes are also shown in Figures 4.2 and 4.3. Figure 4.2 shows the relationship of total income and earnings when increased earnings result from increased wage rates. The lower schedule displays the relationship of earned income to total money income; the upper schedule displays the relationship of earned income to total money income *plus* day care subsidies. In the upper schedule, it is assumed that the family is eligible for day care support of $800 per child, for three children. Figure 4.3 shows the relationship when increased hours-worked account for increased earnings. The dashed line in Figure 4.3 shows the relationship when increased earnings are obtained by full-time work at a wage rate that increases from $1.00 to $1.50 to $1.80 to $2.00 per hour.

A third positive work incentive provision in the committee proposal affords family heads who are working part time in regular employment the opportunity for additional work in public service employment up to a total of forty hours per week. By affording additional opportunities to those seeking income beyond that attainable through part-time employment, it is likely to stimulate additional work effort by at least some workers.

Although these positive inducements for work effort are substantial, the committee bill is not uniform in its labor supply effects. As noted in Figures 4.2 and 4.3, the marginal tax rates vary significantly depending on whether incremental earnings are attributable to an increase in hours worked or an increase in wage rates. Because the wage rate subsidy is based on the differential between the actual wage rate and the national minimum wage rate, the volume of subsidy at a given wage rate is a direct and linear function of the number of hours worked. However, efforts to increase earnings through seeking higher-paid employment are not so rewarded. Indeed, increased earnings from higher wage rates erode the per-hour subsidy, permitting the worker to retain only a fraction of the increased earnings from the higher-paying jobs. As seen in Table 4.4 and

Table 4.4 Some Illustrations of Benefits and Marginal Tax Rates for H.R. 1 and the Senate Finance Committee Bill

| | | H.R. 1[a] | | Senate Finance proposal[a] | | |
| | | | | | MTR[b] (percent) | |
	Earnings	Total income	MTR[b] (percent)	Total income	Hours variable[c]	Wage rate variable[c]
Case 1: Family with head employed at $1.40 per hour	$2,800	$3,662	+72.2	$3,080	-4.8	-4.8
Case 2: Family with head employed at $1.60 per hour	3,200	3,773	+72.2	4,120	-23.8	+70.2
Case 3: Family with head employed at $2.25 per hour	4,500	4,119	+86.2	4,775	+30.2	+30.2
		(4,050)	(+119.2)[d]			

[a] For both H.R. 1 and the Senate Finance Committee bill, the cases shown assume that the family head is the only working family member and that he or she is employed in a regular public or private job. The benefits implied in the data exclude any public service employment income, state supplemental benefits, child care subsidies, or any other benefits in addition to the basic program.

[b] The estimate of the marginal tax rate on earnings cumulates the payroll tax rate of 5.2 percent, the federal income tax rate of 14.0 percent on earnings above $4300, and the marginal tax rate implicit in the plan for both H.R. 1 and the Senate Finance Committee bill. Those tax rates shown with a plus sign in the table are tax rates in the conventional sense; those with a minus sign are negative marginal tax rates or marginal subsidy rates. In the latter case, a $1 increase in earnings results in an increase of after-tax income that is greater than $1.

[c] For the Senate Finance Committee proposal, two marginal tax rates are shown. In the first case, it is assumed that the increase in earnings is generated by an increase in *hours* worked, wage rate constant. In the second case, it is assumed that the increase in earnings is generated by an increase in the *wage rate*, hours worked held constant.

[d] This extreme tax rate is due to the provision in H.R. 1 that, beyond the federal break-even, states may impose 100 percent tax rates on earnings. This figure assumes that states exercise this option.

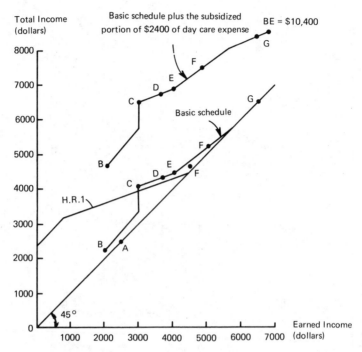

Figure 4.2. Income supplements to a family with head employed full time in regular employment—H.R. 1 and Senate Finance Committee bill. The upper curve includes child care subsidies; the lower curve displays only work subsidies—the wage rate subsidy and the employment bonus. The curves display the positions attained by increasing earnings through increasing wage rates, assuming full-time work. A, family head working full time in public service employment program, requiring day care for three children; B, family head working full time in regular employment, requiring day care for three children, earning $1.00 per hour; C (D), family head working full time in regular employment, requiring day care for three children, earning $1.50 ($1.80) per hour; E, family head working full time in regular employment, requiring day care for three children, earning $2.00 per hour; F, family head working full time in regular employment, requiring day care for three children, earning $2.50 per hour; G, family head working full time in regular employment, requiring day care for three children, earning $3.25 per hour (assuming that day care subsidy decreased by 50 percent of additional earnings beyond $5000).

Figure 4.3, the implicit marginal tax rate on increases in earnings due to increases in wage rate is over 70 percent through some earnings ranges.

Moreover, while the committee wishes to encourage female family heads eligible for cash transfers unrelated to work effort to participate in the employment program on a voluntary basis, it has stipulated a tax rate on earnings for such employment (except for a small disregard) to be 100 percent.

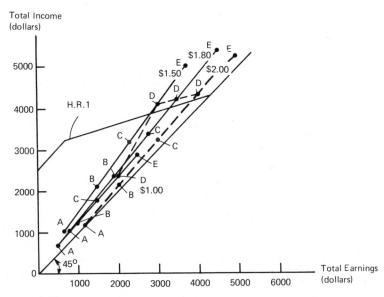

Figure 4.3. Income supplements to a family head employed at various wage rates with varying hours worked—H.R. 1 and Senate Finance Committee proposal. The three solid lines and the heavy dashed line show income levels related to earnings as earnings increase by increases in hours worked, wage rate constant. From highest to lowest, the solid lines represent wage rates of $1.50, $1.80, and $1.00. The heavy dashed line represents a wage rate of $2.00. On each curve, the points A, B, C, D, and E refer to 10, 20, 30, 40, and 50 hours worked per week, respectively. The dotted line connecting the Ds indicates the schedules for increasing earnings by increasing wage rates, hours worked constant.

Finally, the committee bill contains two provisions that would discourage participants in the employment program from engaging in job training programs. As described already, while the proposal permits participants in public service employment to opt for training rather than work, it places those who choose to do so at a financial disadvantage by delaying the time at which some income is received. Further, because the wage rate subsidy imposes high marginal tax rates on increased earnings from higher wage rates, the incentive to upgrade one's skills and wage rate potential is weakened.

This problem of high marginal tax rates on increased earnings from higher wage rates is further exacerbated by the failure of the committee to deal explicitly with the other income-conditioned programs from which work subsidy recipients can draw benefits. While the Medicaid program would be modified by the committee to eliminate the notch, the income-conditioned nature of the benefits would persist. In addition, public housing, higher education subsidies, and the positive income and Social Security taxes would all add their tax rates on earned incomes to the cumulation. When all of these are considered, some work subsidy recipients would be no better off in terms of net spendable income by accepting a higher-paying position. Moreover, the positive incentives for increases in earnings through increases in hours worked would be reduced by these cumulative tax rates.

In addition to the effects of the proposal on the labor–leisure choice, there are other important economic efficiency effects of the proposal. One of the most significant of these is the effect on real output of diverting mothers from the production of "home services" to the employment program. Clearly, a net social gain from this diversion exists if the marginal product of such a worker (as indicated by her market wage) is in excess of the value of her home services (perhaps as indicated by the costs of hiring a housekeeper in her place) plus the consumption value she places on being at home. While it is difficult to ascertain reliable estimates of these values, it is not obvious that a female family head with low skills and marginal employability will produce more in, say, a public employment program than she would have by remaining a homemaker. While the net increase in work effort outside the home (in either private or public service employment) surely represents a gross increment to social output, it must be compared with the value of home services forgone (including the consumption value of home work) in ascertaining the net efficiency effect of required employment outside the home.

A further efficiency effect concerns the impact of the wage rate subsidy on factor input combinations. Viewing that subsidy as an artificial alteration in the market price of workers receiving the subsidy, employers are likely to substitute labor subject to the subsidy for both capital and labor that is not subsidized. To the extent that this artificial alteration in effective wage rates induces inefficient input substitutions—as standard economic theory would suggest—a real welfare loss must be attributed to the policy. Again, the magnitude of this efficiency effect is unknown and, in all likelihood, unknowable.

In summary, the committee bill would, in all likelihood, increase the amount of work effort by low-income family heads. It would do so by requiring employable family heads to work in order to qualify for subsidization, by raising their effective wage rates by direct subsidization, and by guaranteeing employment to those seeking work. However, the bill provides substantially greater incentives for a family head to increase earnings by increasing the number of hours worked rather than increasing his or her rate of pay. By failing to integrate the full program with other income-conditioned subsidies, the bill would confront some recipients with tax rates of nearly 100 percent on increments to earnings from improved skill levels, promotions, or job changes. Further, the bill almost completely discourages work effort by families eligible for direct cash transfers and may generate reductions in real social output through inducing inefficient substitution of employment outside the home for home work, and inefficient substitution of subsidized low-wage inputs for unsubsidized labor and capital.

Effects on the National Wage Structure

According to standard economic analysis, a wage rate subsidy, by itself, would tend to erode the structure of wages in any given labor market. The logic is as follows. As viewed by low-wage workers, the effect of a wage rate subsidy is to increase the effective price at which they can sell their labor. With a labor supply curve of positive elasticity, workers will respond to the higher effective price by making available an increased supply of labor. The labor market, in turn, will respond to this shift in supply by establishing a lower observed price or wage rate. At this lower market wage rate, those workers whose wage rates are subsidized will still be better off than before the subsidy—assuming that the decrease in the market wage rate is not equal to the subsidy.

However, because of this artificially induced reduction in the market wage rate for low-wage workers covered by the subsidy, employers will have incentive to substitute such labor for higher-wage, noncovered (and presumably higher-skilled) workers and for capital. The effect of this substitution would be a reduction in the demand for both higher-skilled labor and capital inputs, which the market would transform into lower wage rates for higher-skilled workers and a lower return on capital.[21]

Those employers able to make such substitutions would experience a reduction in production costs which, if they sold their goods in a competitive market, would result in some reduction in the price of their output. Through this mechanism, some of the wage subsidy paid to low-wage workers would be passed along to consumers in the form of lower prices.

---

[21] If, for some reason, the market price for these inputs (higher-skilled labor) were inflexible downward, the effect of the wage subsidy would be to move some of the higher-skilled labor into the lower-skill labor market, further increasing the labor supply in that market and further decreasing the market wage rate in that market. Under these circumstances, it is possible that the wage rate in this market would fall to such an extent that low-wage workers receiving the subsidy might be worse off than before the subsidy was put into effect.

To some extent, these decreases in observed wage rates in both high- and low-skill markets will be offset by an output effect. Because of the net increase in labor supply induced by the subsidy, real output in the economy will rise. This in turn will increase the demand for labor in both high- and low-skill markets, providing some offset to the first-round wage rate decreases. In the absence of rigidities, however, observed wage rates are likely to show some net reduction.[22]

Under some combinations of labor market circumstances, then, one might perceive the following adverse effects from a wage subsidy:[23]

1. A reduction in the market wage rate for both low-wage workers covered by the subsidy and those who are not.
2. Under certain extreme labor market conditions, a reduction in the market wage rate for low-skill labor sufficient to override the subsidy, leaving the low-wage worker worse off than before.
3. A reduction in the demand for—and wage rates paid to—higher-skill, higher-wage labor.
4. Under certain labor market conditions, more competition between higher- and lower-skilled workers in the lower-skilled labor market and/or increased unemployment for low-skilled workers.

Given the current state of knowledge, it is impossible to discern which, if any, of these impacts might accompany the institution of a wage subsidy for low-wage workers. The net effect depends upon the nature of labor market imperfections, the elasticities of the supply and demand for both higher- and lower-skilled workers, the elasticity of substitution of high- and low-skill workers within firms and industries, and the nature of supply, demand, and cross-elasticities in product markets. Simultaneous determination of the interacting effects of all these relationships is required to answer the question with any certainty. Currently, neither the data nor the general equilibrium models are available for such estimation.[24]

This is not to imply, however, that nothing can be said about the likelihood of any of these effects developing from any specific legislative proposal incorporating a wage subsidy. Consider a wage subsidy aimed at

---

[22] It should be noted that, if the wage rate in the market for low-wage workers were inflexible downward, the increase in labor supply induced by the wage subsidy would force some low-wage workers into unemployment. However, a possible offset to this could occur if some family heads left private sector jobs for public service employment, thus opening up low-wage slots for nonheads of families.

[23] Again, offsetting these adverse effects is the real output effect that would tend to increase the demand for both high- and low-skilled labor.

[24] Neil Weiner, Robert D. Lamson, and Henry M. Peskin, "Report on the Feasibility of Estimating the Effects of a National Wage Bill Subsidy," Paper HQ 69-10725, Institute for Defense Analysis, September 1969.

low-wage workers (say, those with wage rates below the national minimum) consistent with a Finance Committee type work-conditioned, income supplementation strategy. Presume the existence of two separate labor markets: that covered by minimum wage legislation and that not covered by the minimum wage law. Assume also a public service employment guarantee for any family head whose regular employment alternatives are less desirable than the guaranteed public employment. Finally, assume that minimum wage legislation constrains most employers from substituting workers not covered by the minimum wage law for workers who are.

In this context, is seems unlikely that the demand for higher-skill workers and the prevailing wage paid them would be greatly undermined by the wage subsidy provision of the program. This erosion can occur only if employers can easily substitute low- for high-skill workers in response to a change in relative prices.[25] Such substitution is difficult given the influence of labor organizations and the industrial coverage of minimum wage legislation.[26]

Without this erosion in the market for higher-skill labor, it seems unlikely that substantial additional competition between high and low skill would be induced. As a result, it is most unlikely that workers newly covered by the subsidy could receive lower net wages after the institution of the subsidy than before.

However, if by some set of circumstances—perhaps wage inflexibility again—some workers in the low-skill (covered) labor markets are forced into unemployment because of the increase in labor supply induced by the subsidy, real costs could occur. It is with respect to such occurrences that the strategy provides the guarantee of public service employment. With the guarantee, low-wage workers experiencing unemployment or wage rate reduction are presented with an alternative that may be superior to their situation prior to the effects of the wage rate subsidy, let alone after the possible adverse effects of the subsidy have occurred.

On the basis of these considerations, it appears that, especially in the face of existing labor market inflexibilities caused by minimum wage laws and labor organizations, the work-conditioned, income supplementation strategy offers protection against many of the possible adverse effects of a wage rate subsidy on workers in most skill and wage rate categories. Due to industry coverage of the minimum wage, the subsidization of low-

---

[25] It should be noted, however, that some substitution of this sort will occur as a matter of course if the price of goods produced by low-skill-intensive industries falls relative to the price of goods produced by high-skill-intensive industries.

[26] Again, recall the real output offset to the reduced demand for both high- and low-skill labor.

wage workers, and the guarantee of public service employment, few workers are likely to be adversely affected by potential wage rate erosion induced by the wage subsidy.[27]

Finally, the small size of the subsidy relative to the market for low-wage workers should be noted. In 1966, approximately 32 million workers had wage rates below $2 per hour according to the Survey of Economic Opportunity. This group of workers earned in excess of $50 billion. It seems highly unlikely that a $2–$3 billion wage rate subsidy aimed at this group of workers would seriously erode the wage structure of the labor markets in which they operate.

Questions of Administrative Feasibility

It seems to be an axiom that issues of administration pose serious questions of feasibility for all proposed modifications of the Public Assistance system. Issues of administrative discretion regarding categorization, reporting, eligibility and benefit determination, termination, and social service provision have plagued the current welfare system for many years. Neither H.R. 1 nor the Finance Committee proposal avoids these problems. In fact, because the committee proposal (and, to a lesser extent, H.R. 1) would mean the integration of public employment and additional in-kind benefit and service programs with cash transfers, the problem of discretion is likely to be exacerbated. Moreover, the difficulties inherent in implementing programs requiring interagency coordination are expanded severalfold in both these proposals. For example, the Finance Committee proposal would not only establish several new programs, it also imposes administrative responsibilities on three separate agencies. Any person covered by legislation could receive benefits and services from three or four different programs and from as many different offices.

One of the primary new administrative tasks implied by the committee proposal is the separation of the population of current welfare recipients into employables and welfare eligibles. While the basic rules for distinguishing the status of different recipients have been suggested, numerous special situations are inevitable and unspecified in the rules. With such special situations, the basic difficulty of categorization becomes even more severe and the opportunity for horizontal inequities through administrative discretion becomes enormous.[28]

---

[27] Most of those adversely affected will be nonheads, who are not eligible for wage subsidization or public service employment.

[28] It should be noted that H.R. 1 also required a separation of those families with and without an employable head and was thus subject to these same difficulties.

A second major set of administrative responsibilities and difficulties is associated with the operation of the Work Administration. As described in the proposal, the WA will have a number of options in dealing with an employable family head who is guaranteed public service employment but who does not already have a job:

1. The WA can work with private sector employers to secure regular employment for applicants. In this case, the applicant, once placed in a job, would deal directly with the employer in negotiating the terms of employment.
2. It can work with public sector employers in much the same way to gain regular employment for applicants.
3. It can provide special public service employment to applicants who cannot be placed in regular public or private employment. This requires the WA either to create an enterprise employing labor and producing outputs or services for "the betterment of the community," or to hire out employees to private or regular public employers on a temporary basis.[29]

All these activities imply enormous new responsibilities in the areas of job development and job placement.[30] To accomplish them with creativity, efficiency, and equity is a major, new and difficult undertaking. Consider, for example: How does the WA deal with a worker who refuses to accept private sector employment to which he is referred? How does the WA determine if a private sector job is appropriate for regular placement of an applicant or if the job is a temporary one that the employer should contract out to the WA? On what basis does the WA declare that a rural applicant is too remote from a WA office to require public service employment in order to be eligible for benefits? How is the danger of "dead-end" jobs to be avoided as the WA seeks to create jobs for "the betterment of the community"? How does the WA deal with recalcitrant employees in the special public service part of the program? What is the maximum length of time that a person can remain in special public service employment? What can the WA offer to employers to induce them to deal with it rather than fill job openings in the open market? The alternatives open to the WA in all of these areas imply the necessity of exercising enormous administrative discretion.

[29] In the latter case, the payment would be made directly from the employer to the WA and wages would be paid by the WA to the workers.
[30] As noted earlier, the development of a large-scale day care program and the employment of participants in the employment program in it is also envisioned as one of the primary responsibilities of the WA.

As the proposal is now structured, a person could be in several different programs over the course of a year. For example, a person could be in special public service employment and, hence, ineligible for the wage rate subsidy or earnings bonus, in regular employment in the private sector and either eligible or ineligible for both the subsidy and the bonus, or in the residual AFDC program. In each of these situations, the individual would be eligible for packages of benefits of one type or another. The record-keeping effort required to account for these changing situations for, say, 10 million families is mind boggling. Moreover, depending on the accounting periods used for determining payments and the mode of payment, these basic difficulties could be compounded.

A further administrative difficulty stems from the dependence of the wage rate subsidy on the reported wage rate. Because of this dependence, an incentive is created for both the subsidized worker and his employer to collude in reporting a lower-than-actual wage rate and a larger number of hours than actually worked for any given earnings level. In this way, the subsidy payment would be increased over its appropriate level, and both employer and employee could gain. The enforcement of prohibitions against this practice would be a difficult undertaking. Moreover, because the standard employee paycheck shows only total earnings, it fails to yield the information required to determine eligibility for the subsidy and the amount of subsidy to be paid. As a consequence, special record-keeping would be required for determination of the appropriate subsidy to be paid.

In addition to these administrative difficulties, a number of additional problems inhibit the implementation of the special public service employment program. The first of these is the inevitable competition of special public service employees with regular public employees if the WA negotiates such special positions within government agencies. A second problem is that of locating appropriate work for a population that is primarily female when most tasks in the public sector are thought of by many as "male jobs."[31] Finally, it appears that many state governments would be reluctant to participate in such a program if the federal government paid only the salary of special public service employees. State governments have emphasized the need for the federal government to cover other associated costs of the program—supervisory, equipment, space, and supply costs—if they are to be induced to accept special public service employees.

[31] This point was emphasized by several state governors who responded to questions of the Senate Finance Committee regarding the potential of such a program.

IV. An Alternative Work-Conditioned, Income Supplementation Program: The Earnings Subsidy

While the Senate Finance Committee bill has a number of equity, efficiency, and administrative problems, it represents an income maintenance strategy with work incentive and income support characteristics that are attractive to many. In this section, the dimensions of an alternative program of work-conditioned subsidies is described and criticized. The object is to retain some of the desirable characteristics of the committee bill while correcting several of its structural problems. This alternative incorporates all three of the attributes essential to a work-conditioned, income supplementation strategy—direct cash transfers for those not expected to work, work subsidies for low-income family heads with jobs, and guaranteed employment for poor families with employable heads unable to secure a job. Its major provisions are as follows.

1. *An employability criterion.* This proposal, like that of the Finance Committee and H.R. 1, would require the categorization of low-income family heads into two groups: those who are employable and those who, because of disability or severe child care responsibilities, are not expected to work. While the criterion proposed by the Senate Committee recognizes a number of the determinants of "employability," a more comprehensive criterion is required. This criterion should perhaps consider the number of children as well as the age of the youngest child. If the program is to be integrated with day care subsidies, the determination of employability on the basis of number of children can be justified on efficiency grounds. It should also incorporate comprehensive standards for determining the seriousness of partial disabilities.

2. *A cash transfer program.* Both male and female single-parent families without an employable head would be eligible for direct cash benefits unrelated to work effort. A federal minimum of $3000 for a family of four would be guaranteed, with states remaining free to supplement incomes above the federal minimum but with no added federal funding. The guarantee would be reduced by $2 for every $3 of other income—earned and unearned. The federal government would administer the program.

3. *A public service employment program.* All family heads found to be employable would be guaranteed a special public service job paying three-fourths of the national minimum wage. Assuming the national minimum wage to be $2.00 per hour, this implies a public service wage rate

of $1.50. Work for up to forty hours per week would be offered, imply-
ing an income guarantee of $3000 per year.

4. *An earnings subsidy.* All families would be eligible for a subsidy
on their earnings from regular public or private sector jobs. Moreover,
low-income family heads could add special public service employment
income to subsidized earnings up to a total income level of $3000 per
year without facing a positive marginal tax rate.

The earnings subsidy would be equal to 50 percent of regular family
(sum of husband's and wife's) earnings up to $2000. Hence, a family
head working one-half time at the minimum wage rate of $2 per hour
(hence earning $2000) would receive a subsidy of $1000, yielding a total
income of $3000. Beyond earnings of $2000, the worker would fall on a
schedule implying a positive marginal tax rate of 33 percent. The break-
even point would occur at $5000. Table 4.5 illustrates the earnings subsidy
schedule applicable for low-income families who engage only in regular
private or public sector employment.

In addition to either being in the special public service employment
program (without the earnings subsidy but guaranteeing an income level
of $3000) or employed in a regular private or public job, a worker could
combine both. For a worker with some regular earnings, the special public
service program could be used to supplement private matched earnings
up to a total of $3000 without an erosion of marginal earnings through the
implicit tax rate. Beyond $3000, incremental public service program earn-
ings would be subject to the 33 percent tax rate. Similarly, a worker with
some special public service earnings could use regular (subsidized) earnings to supplement public earnings up to the $3000 level without an

Table 4.5 Net Allowances from the Earnings Subsidy for a Family with
Regular Employment Income

Family income before allowance	Net allowance	Income after allowance	Marginal tax rate
0	0	0	—
$500	$250	$750	−50%
1000	500	1500	−50
1500	750	2250	−50
2000	1000	3000	−50
2500	883	3337	+33
3000	666	3666	+33
3500	500	4000	+33
4000	333	4333	+33
4500	167	4667	+33
5000	0	5000	+33

erosion of marginal earnings. Again, total earnings in excess of $3000, but below the break-even point, would be subject to the implicit 33 percent tax rate. Table 4.6 illustrates the total income pattern for low-income workers who engage in either regular public or private sector employment or special public service employment or who combine these alternatives in various proportions.

In Table 4.6, several patterns are of special interest. First, the very large incentive for increased regular employment (provided by the 50 percent subsidy on private earned income up to $2000) is seen in the first column. As regular earned income increases from $500 to $1000 to $1500 to $2000, total income increases from $750 to $1500 to $2250 to $3000. This incentive for increased regular employment is also seen by reading across the rows. For any level of earned income up to $4000, the level of total income is inversely related to the proportion of it that is earned in the special public service employment.

Second, the effect of the 33 percent tax rate on income over $3000 is seen by reading down any of the columns. This tax rate—which assures that the break-even income level will not exceed approximately $5000— has yet another impact that is observable in the table. While individuals who have some income from regular employment would be eligible for a total of $3000 of public service income, any such income earned after

Table 4.6 Total Income by Earned Income Level and by the Regular Employment–Public Service Employment Division of Earned Income for a Family Head

Earned income	100 percent private	75 percent private, 25 percent public	50 percent private, 50 percent public	25 percent private, 75 percent public	100 percent public
$500	$750[a]	$687[a]	$625[a]	$562[a]	$500[a]
1000	1500[a]	1375[a]	1250[a]	1125[a]	1000[a]
1500	2250[a]	2063[a]	1875[a]	1687[a]	1500[a]
2000	3000	2750[a]	2500[a]	2250[a]	2000[a]
2500	3337	3293	3083	2812[a]	2500[a]
3000	3666	3666	3500	3250	3000
3500	4000	4000	3912	3625	[b]
4000	4333	4333	4333	4000	[b]
4500	4667	4667	4667	[b]	[b]
5000	5000	5000	5000	[b]	[b]

[a] Any individual with total income below $3000 is eligible for additional public sector earnings equal to the difference between the total income figure shown and $3000 without an erosion of marginal earnings.

[b] Not applicable, in that public sector earnings cannot exceed $3000 per worker.

a total income level of $3000 has been attained would be subject to the 33 percent tax rate. In effect, such earnings would entail employment at 67 percent of the hourly wage rate paid for special public service employment—or about $1 per hour. Few would be expected to make themselves available for the public program at this hourly rate. Consequently, this provision assures that excessive use of the public program will be minimal.

Finally, it should be emphasized that, in all cases in the table showing total income of less than $3000, family heads could obtain additional tax-free income by taking advantage of the special public service employment guarantee. (These cases are denoted by footnote reference *a*, Table 4.6.) As shown in the table, then, these cases represent individuals who choose not to avail themselves of the $3000 public service guarantee that is open to them. Several of the combinations implicit in Table 4.6 are shown in Figure 4.4.

5. *A children's allowance.* A notable characteristic of the earnings subsidy and public service employment programs is the absence of differential subsidization based on family size. To condition employment-based

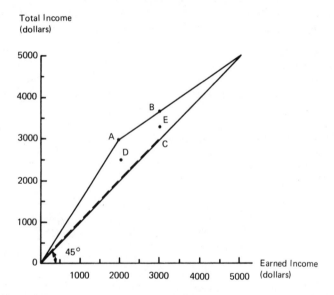

Figure 4.4. Earnings supplements to families with various earnings levels and combinations of regular and special public service employment under the proposed earnings subsidy plan. A, Family head earning $2000 in regular employment (Total income = $3000); B, Family head earning $3000 in regular employment (Total income = $3666); C, Family head earning $3000 in special public service employment (Total income = $3000); D, Family head earning $1000 in regular and $1000 in special public service employment; E, Family head earning $750 in regular and $2250 in special public service employment.

subsidies on family size would entail the payment of a variety of wage rates for the same work effort, hence violating the principle of "equal pay for equal work."

To provide some family-size-conditioned subsidy differential, the structure of low-income subsidies described in points 2 and 4 would be supplemented by the payment of a children's allowance for families in excess of four members. In order to recognize the economies of scale in family size, grants of, say, $300, $180, and $120 would be provided for the fifth, sixth, and additional members of a family unit.

Such family-size-conditioned subsidies are most important for large families with very low incomes. At higher income levels, not only is the ability to support large families greater but, in addition, through the personal exemptions of the federal income tax, large families that pay federal taxes receive substantial implicit family-size-conditioned subsidies. To accommodate the goal of targeting the family-size-conditioned benefit on those with very low incomes, these means are proposed:

a. The total children's allowance benefit would be reduced by $.10 for every dollar earned in special public service employment.[32]

b. The total children's allowance benefit would be reduced by $.15 for every dollar earned that was subject to the earnings subsidy.[33]

The total benefit schedule for a family of six members with earnings only from regular employment is shown in Figure 4.5.

6. *Integration with child care subsidies.* Substituting a work-conditioned, income supplementation strategy for the current welfare system would require additional work effort from numerous female heads with school-age children and from long-term unemployed male family heads. Hence, subsidization of after-school and full-time summer day care would appear to be an essential part of such a policy shift.

There are two standard means of integrating a program of child care support with an income supplementation program. The first is through a system of child care expense deductions from gross earnings. The second is through either direct governmental provision of child care services or direct governmental payment of child care expenses privately purchased.

---

[32] Hence, the head of a five-member family working full time in special public service employment would receive no net children's allowance. If the family had six members, children's allowance benefits would be $180.

[33] The head of a family of five (six) with only regular employment earnings would experience a break-even earnings level on children's allowance benefits of $2000 ($3200). It should be noted that the differential marginal tax rate modestly reduces the relative incentive to seek regular employment as opposed to special public service employment.

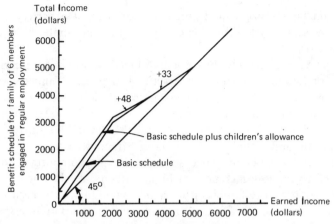

Figure 4.5. Earnings supplements and children's allowance to families under the proposed earnings subsidy plan.

In the first case—deductibility of child care expenses from gross income—the implicit marginal tax rate on earnings determines the portion of child care costs that are borne by the government and the portion borne by the family. Hence, if the marginal tax rate is .5, child care expenses will be shared equally by the program and the family: If the marginal tax rate is .67, the government will bear two-thirds of the cost of child care.

Subsidization of child care through deductibility is impossible under an income supplementation program in which there are negative marginal tax rates on earnings, as in both the earnings and wage rate subsidy plans. A standard deductible arrangement here would entail the family's bearing more than 100 percent of the cost of child care.

The alternative method of integrating child care with an income supplementation plan would be either direct government provision of services or reimbursement for services purchased privately. If this form of subsidization is to be targeted on the poor, the subsidy must be income-conditioned. Two difficulties are encountered with this form of subsidization. First, because such income-conditioned child care subsidies cause the break-even income level to be extended beyond that implied by cash subsidies, the budgetary costs of the program become very large. The target efficiency of the program becomes simultaneously reduced. The second difficulty is the standard one of cumulative tax rates. Given the substantial costs of child care services, the implicit tax rate required to achieve an acceptable break-even level may be very high. When this tax rate is combined with the tax rate on income-conditioned cash subsidies, the cumulative tax rate may be prohibitive.

One possible way of alleviating these problems for families receiving the 50 percent earnings subsidy is to require the family to begin sharing the costs of child care in the income range at which the subsidy is still in effect. This would reduce the need for a high implicit marginal tax rate through the income range where tax rate cumulation is a problem. Such an arrangement is shown in Figure 4.6 for child care expenses of $500 and $1000. In this situation, the full cost of child care would be borne by the government while family earnings were less than or equal to child care costs. From that earnings level to $2000 of earnings—at which level the 50 percent earnings subsidy is replaced by a 33 percent tax rate—an implicit tax rate of 20 percent would be imposed on earnings in order to reduce gross child care subsidy. This would effectively reduce the earnings subsidy from 50 to 30 percent through this range. Beyond $2000 of earnings (implying at least $3000 of total income for workers in regular employment), the child care subsidy would be taxed at a rate of 10 percent. This implies a cumulative tax rate of 43 percent from $2000 to either the new higher break-even point or the earnings level beyond which no child care subsidy is provided.

In Figure 4.7, the integrated benefit schedule is shown for a family of six with earnings from regular employment, children's allowances of $480 at zero earnings, and $1000 of child care expense. The upper solid line shows that the cumulative tax rate varies from −35 percent to +58 percent. The high tax rate of 58 percent is the result of the implicit tax rates

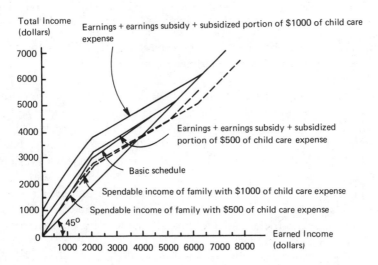

Figure 4.6. Earnings supplements and child care subsidies of $500 and $1000 to families under the proposed earnings subsidy plan.

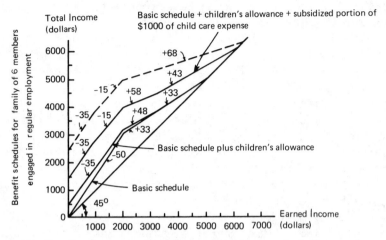

Figure 4.7. Benefits from proposed earnings subsidy plan—including earnings supplements, children's allowance, child care subsidy, and state supplemental benefits.

on the earnings subsidy (33 percent), the children's allowance (15 percent), and the day care subsidy (10 percent). The break-even earnings level for such a family is about $6200.

7. *Integration with state supplementation.* States would be permitted to supplement the incomes of families whose heads are employed in special public service jobs or whose earnings from regular employment are subsidized. However, such supplementation programs would be constrained in the following ways:

a. State supplemental benefits would be based on the assumption that total income (including federal subsidies) is at least $3000, even if it is less than $3000.

b. Where children's allowance subsidies do not extend above earnings levels of $2000 (families of less than six members), the supplementation program would be limited to a marginal tax rate of 25 percent. This tax rate would apply to earned income from $2000 to $5000. For incomes above $5000, the program would be limited to a tax rate equal to the sum of the tax rate on the supplemental program (25 percent) and the tax rate on the federal earnings subsidy (33 percent). This implies a maximum combined tax rate from federal and state income supplementation programs of 58 percent. Including child care subsidies, the maximum marginal tax rate would be 68 percent.

c. Where children's allowance subsidies do extend above earnings levels of $2000 (families of six or more), the supplementation program would be limited to a tax rate of 10 percent over the earnings range through which children's allowance subsidies are paid. For earnings ranges above that amount, the provisions of (b) would apply.

The benefit schedule for a family of six with $1000 of child care expense and with state supplemental benefits of $1000 is shown as the dashed line in Figure 4.7. This schedule incorporates the provision for adjusted tax rates for families with children's allowance subsidies that extend above earnings levels of $2000.

8. *Refund of payroll taxes.* Families with earnings from special public service employment or those receiving the earnings subsidy would receive a refund of Social Security taxes paid on earnings.

9. *A ceiling on the number of programs in which a family may participate.* As the preceding analysis has shown, marginal tax rates rise to a significant level when a family participates in the earnings subsidy program, the children's allowance program, the child care subsidy program, and the program of state benefit supplementation. These programs by no means exhaust the list of federal in-kind and cash transfer programs with benefit levels that are income-conditioned. Consider, for example, existing medical care programs, public housing programs and other housing subsidies, higher education subsidy programs, veterans' benefit programs, Unemployment Compensation benefits, and Social Security survivor benefits. Moreover, recent proposals for subsidized health care have high benefit levels and implicit marginal tax rates of 25 percent or more on earnings. Participation in several of these programs implies marginal tax rates well in excess of 100 percent and a total elimination of work incentives.

A number of techniques exist for reducing cumulative tax rates, including the imposition of a tax ceiling, the sequencing of programs, and the use of the deductibility procedure.[34] While each of these techniques can reduce the cumulative tax rate below the simple sum of component program tax rates and below 100 percent, none keep the cumulative tax rate from closely approaching the 100 percent level. An alternative to these techniques, which could restrain the cumulative tax, would be to establish a ceiling on the number of programs from which a family can receive benefits. Having established the ceiling, families could choose among that set of available program benefits which best fit their needs and tastes.

For example, a standard integrated income supplementation program for the nation's families could be defined to be the earnings subsidy, children's allowance, child care, and state supplementation programs, the

---

[34] These techniques are analyzed by Henry J. Aaron and by Thad W. Mirer in this volume.

integrated benefit schedule of which is shown in Figure 4.7.[35] Any family
that desired to draw benefits from a program not included in this set (say,
public housing or veterans' benefits) would have to agree to cede benefits
from any one of the included programs (say, state supplements) at its
own choosing. Participation in two nonincluded programs would require
the ceding of benefits from any two included programs. This provision
would be combined with a maximum implicit tax rate on any nonincluded
program of, say, 10 to 15 percent. This sort of ceiling could restrain the
cumulated tax rate from ever exceeding approximately 70 percent.

Such a ceiling on participation would require coordination among the
various programs to insure that benefits were not being received from an
excessive number of programs by any given family. While such a ceiling
on program participation restricts the extensiveness of program participation in order to place an effective maximum on the cumulated tax rate, it
does provide substantial choice among beneficiaries concerning program
participation.

V. Evaluation of the Earnings Subsidy Proposal

The alternative program of work-conditioned income supplementation described here was designed to correct some of the structural problems in the Senate Finance Committee proposal, while retaining its
desirable work-incentive characteristics. In addition, it was designed to
highlight the difficulties of integrating the several components of income
support inherent in the strategy (and in all other welfare reform proposals) with the plethora of other income-conditioned subsidy programs.
In considering the problem of program integration, it was concluded that
the devices of program sequencing and deductibility would not keep the
cumulative tax rate from approaching 90 percent or more. The proposed
ceiling on the number of programs from which a family could draw
benefits could constrain the cumulative tax rate to below 70 percent.

The major difference between the alternative proposal and that of
the Senate Committee is the substitution of the earnings subsidy for the
wage rate subsidy and earnings bonus. In addition to increasing the negative marginal tax rate on earnings to give additional work incentive and
subsidization to low-income families, the earnings subsidy simplifies administration of the program by replacing two work-related programs by

---

[35] One might also wish to include the national health care program covering poor
families.

one. Further, it eliminates both the incentive for beneficiary fraud implicit in a subsidy focused on the wage rate and the comparative disincentive for seeking job training, advancement, and new positions with higher wage rates as opposed to working more hours, which is also implicit in the wage rate subsidy. Finally, the important incentives to seek regular employment rather than accept special public service employment are strengthened in the alternative proposal.

However, because it would also lead to an increase in the supply of low-wage workers, the alternative proposal would have much the same sort of effect on market wages and the combination of low-wage workers, high-wage workers, and capital inputs employed in the economy. However, as indicated earlier, while the direction of the effects of these changes is known, their size is not likely to be substantial.

Because this alternative combines the basic components of the committee bill, it too would have a high target efficiency (or antipoverty effectiveness). The larger earnings subsidy that it provides to families earning very low wage rates or working part time—likely characteristics of current welfare recipients who would be declared employable—would tend to increase the target efficiency of the program.

By incorporating a children's allowance, the alternative eliminates the lack of family-size-conditioned subsidies inherent in the Senate bill. Because many of the poorest families are the very large families, this provision would also have a high target efficiency. While these are attractive equity effects of the alternative, it does very little to remove the several horizontal inequities of the Finance Committee bill.

Finally, by eliminating one incentive for fraud, the alternative eliminates a major administrative problem with the Senate bill. However, most of the other administrative difficulties inherent in that bill are also present in the alternative proposal. These include the difficult—and perhaps insoluble—administrative problems in implementing a major public service employment program and the leeway for substantial discretion in applying a criterion for categorizing the poor.

In conclusion, then, the alternative proposal remedies many of the maladies of the Finance Committee bill and moves toward integration of a work-conditioned, income-supplementation strategy with other income-conditioned programs. However, it does not eliminate other difficulties of such an income maintenance strategy. Because of its emphasis on the employment of the heads of single-parent families, the proposal is still subject to the criticisms levied against any "workfare" proposal. It, however, strives to avoid the epithet of "slavefare." While requiring work effort, the proposal not only guarantees employment but provides sizable financial supplements to earnings. At a minimum, the alternative proposal should enable the work-conditioned, income supplementation strategy to be considered without the unnecessary difficulties of the Finance Committee proposal.

Acknowledgments

The research reported here was supported by funds granted to the Institute for Research on Poverty by the Office of Economic Opportunity pursuant to the provisions of the Economic Opportunity Act of 1964. The helpful comments of Irwin Garfinkel, W. Joseph Heffernan, Hirschel Kasper, Russell Lidman, Irene Lurie, and, especially, Robert Lampman are gratefully acknowledged. The conclusions are the sole responsibility of the author.

Addendum

Subsequent to the preparation of this chapter, a major development came about suddenly and is now federal law. A component of the major Tax Reduction Act of 1975 is a $1.7 billion earnings bonus or earnings subsidy, as discussed in this chapter. Sponsored by Senator Russell Long and the Senate Finance Committee, this provision will subsidize earnings up to $4000 at a 10 percent rate (for a maximum subsidy of $400). The earnings subsidy will be phased out at an earnings level of $8000. The new law is now part of the federal tax code and represents a major new component to the nation's income transfer system—a component that extends direct cash support to male-headed working poor families.

5

Alternative Approaches to Integrating Income Transfer Programs

Thad W. Mirer

I. Introduction

The nature of existing income transfer programs and the problems of reforming them are now receiving considerable attention. One of the most significant problems is how to coordinate the many programs so that the resulting system will be equitable and will contain positive work incentive features. This chapter examines alternative schemes that might be used to link programs and provides an example of how the schemes can be used to design an integrated system.

The mélange of current income maintenance and related programs appears chaotic and irrational because most of the programs have been designed to achieve a limited set of goals, with relatively little concern for the overall effects of the entire set of programs. The results are work disincentives due to high tax rates for many people over broad ranges of income, gross inequities among persons and families of similar characteristics, and general dissatisfaction among recipients and taxpayers alike.

Less-than-comprehensive welfare reform may result in the demise of some programs, but it will leave the operation of many basically unchanged. Each of the remaining programs probably will continue to operate with its own set of goals and requirements. Public housing programs, for example, may continue to offer decent housing to only a fraction of the persons eligible and may need to generate revenue through rent collection to cover some part of their total cost. Medical insurance will continue for the aged and the poor and may be extended to the entire population. In coordinating the various remaining programs, it will be essential to identify and analyze the purposes and unique features of each, in order that the basic integrity of each not be destroyed. However, some aspects of various programs' operations are not essential to their integrity and justifiably may be changed in the reform process. What "reform" is eventually achieved depends, in part, on the rules by which the various programs are linked, or integrated.

A rational approach to designing a well-integrated system of transfer programs entails identifying the main goals of the system as a whole and the constraints placed on the system, and then establishing links among the various programs so as best to achieve these goals. In an overall view, the properties of the system as a whole are more important than those of the individual programs.

General agreement probably can be reached on two main goals for a new transfer system: (*1*) fostering equity, both vertical and horizontal, and (*2*) encouraging work effort. The difficulty is that a plan to promote one goal is likely to be detrimental to the other.

The equity goal of the system is to improve the lives of the nation's poor by redistributing resources to them from those who are better off. The system should try to assure some minimal standard of living for all citizens. In addition, it should be designed with the need for horizontal equity in mind, for reasons ranging from social philosophy to constitutional law. Serious breaches of this principle occur when assistance programs, such as public housing, are made available to fewer than all eligible persons, and when aid to different "categories" varies in generosity.

Encouraging work effort must be recognized as a goal of the welfare system for social, economic, and political reasons. Most analysts consider the cumulative marginal tax rate on earnings, which is a combination of the nominal marginal tax rates in each program in the system, to be quite important in this regard. Although the available evidence yields a wide range of estimates, it is generally reasoned that a low tax rate encourages work effort more than a high one. In any case, it seems certain that tax rates on earnings in excess of 100 percent are socially unjust. Cumulative marginal tax rates in the range of 50–70 percent may be reasonable for current welfare program recipients because these rates are lower than those that they now face, at least nominally; but, if a reformed system extends income transfers to large numbers of persons not now covered, these rates may come to be viewed as excessive. The difficulty with establishing low rates, of course, is that this causes program costs to soar.

Achievement of these goals is subject to the political and economic constraint of keeping these total income transfer costs low. The lower the total system's costs, the less will be the achievement of its goals. But the political prospects for welfare reform may be enhanced if costs are kept low. The costs attributable to particular programs under alternative plans for welfare reform may also be important in the choice to be made among them.

In the next section of this chapter, alternative schemes for linking programs in a reformed income transfer system are considered in relation to these goals and constraints. The approach focuses on the relationships between the benefit schedules and tax rates of individual programs and the benefit schedule and tax rates of the entire system.

II. Schemes for Linking Transfer Programs

An important concept in the determination of a recipient's benefit under an income-conditioned transfer program is that of countable income. Typically, a transfer program offers a recipient a lump sum gross benefit, or "guarantee," and then diminishes the net benefit as "countable income" increases; in effect, there is a tax on countable income. Each program may have its own definition of countable income. Usually, countable income includes earnings and property income, minus some deductible items. Some programs consider the benefits of other transfer programs as countable income—and thereby tax these other benefits—while others do not. The various components of countable income may be taxed at the same or different rates by each program. Other important aspects of the definition of countable income are the recipient unit, which is usually the family, and the accounting periods. As will be seen, the definition of countable income used by each program is one of the most important determinants of how the various programs operate together.

Six schemes for linking transfer programs will be analyzed here by examining some simple cases. The building blocks of the analysis are two hypothetical transfer programs named T (for transfer) and NIT (for negative income tax). Heuristically, the first transfer program may be thought of as a commodity program, such as housing, or a cash program, such as Social Security, and the second as a negative income tax program. These names make the analysis more interesting, but the conclusions do not depend on the identity of either program. In addition to these two transfer programs, the family's earnings (E) and its net income (Y) will be considered in each case.

The net benefit from each program or the net amount of income of each type for a family are denoted as

E	earnings
$T = G_1 - t_1 \cdot Y_T$	first transfer program
$NIT = G_2 - t_2 \cdot Y_{NIT}$	second transfer program
$Y = E + T + NIT$	net family income

where G_1 and G_2 are the guarantee payments, t_1 and t_2 are the marginal tax rates, and Y_T and Y_{NIT} are the countable incomes for the first and second transfer programs, respectively. The system's cumulative marginal tax rate on earnings (θ), expressed as a fraction, is equal to 1 minus the change in net family income that results from a $1 increase in earnings; in calculus notation, $\theta = 1 - dY/dE$. Property income is assumed to equal zero in these examples, but this does not affect the qualitative conclusions that are drawn.

Associated with each transfer program is a "natural break-even point" —the level of countable income (Y_T or Y_{NIT}) at which net benefits of the program become zero and above which a family is phased out of the program. The natural break-even points of the two transfer programs examined here are $Y_T = G_1/t_1$ and $Y_{NIT} = G_2/t_2$, respectively, determined by setting the net benefit in each program equal to zero and solving each resulting equation. The "earnings break-even point"—the level of earnings (E) at which net benefits of the program become zero—can be computed for each program only when all the links in the transfer system have been completely specified.

In the simple cases examined later, specific values for the programs' guarantees and tax rates will be assumed. For the T program, G_1 is set equal to $1000 and t_1 is set equal to $\frac{1}{4}$ in most examples; these parameters are representative of existing public housing programs. For the NIT program, G_2 is set equal to $2400 and t_2 is set equal to $\frac{2}{3}$; these are similar to the parameters of the Family Assistance Plan passed by the House of Representatives in 1971.

By considering only two programs at a time, it is possible to focus on how the alternative linking schemes affect the goals and constraints discussed earlier. Later, a more complex analysis in which taxes and other transfer programs are explicitly considered is presented.

Scheme I: Independent Addition

The case of independent addition serves as a base to which other schemes are compared. Under independent addition, countable income is defined as earnings (E) for both transfer programs, and the programs ignore each other.

$$NIT = \$2400 - \tfrac{2}{3} \cdot E$$
$$T = \$1000 - \tfrac{1}{4} \cdot E$$
$$Y = E + NIT + T$$

In Table 5.1, the basic nature of these programs is shown. The system's cumulative tax rate on earnings (θ) is the sum of the tax rates of the programs operating in any earnings range. The cumulative tax rate

Table 5.1 Independent Addition

E	NIT	(Y_1)	T	(Y_2)	Y	θ
$0	$2400	$2400	$1000	$1000	$3400	
1000	1733	2733	750	1750	3483	
2000	1066	3066	500	2500	3566	$\tfrac{11}{12}$
3000	400	3400	250	3250	3650	
3360	160	3520	160	3520	3680	
3467	88	3555	133	3600	3688	
3600	0	3600	100	3700	3700	
4000	0	4000	0	4000	4000	$\tfrac{1}{4}$
5000	0	5000	0	5000	5000	
5100	0	5100	0	5100	5100	0
6000	0	6000	0	6000	6000	

declines in steps (from $\tfrac{11}{12}$ to $\tfrac{1}{4}$ to 0) as earnings rise, because the family is phased out of the programs at different earnings levels. The table also shows the net real income, Y_1, resulting from a system consisting of only the NIT program, and the net real income, Y_2, resulting from a system consisting of only the T program.

If the tax rates under the individual programs were to sum to more than 100 percent, the cumulative tax rate on earnings of the entire system would exceed 100 percent: A family would be worse off by earning more money.

Scheme II: A Tax Ceiling Program

In this scheme, also, countable income for each program is defined as earnings, but the tax rate in the *NIT* program is adjusted so that the cumulative rate θ does not exceed some specified level, for example, $\frac{2}{3}$.

$$T = \$1000 - (\tfrac{1}{4}) \cdot E$$
$$NIT = \$2400 - t \cdot E$$

such that $\theta \leqslant \frac{2}{3}$

$$Y = E + T + NIT.$$

As shown in Table 5.2, the *T* program is unaffected relative to its operation under the independent scheme. The family remains in the system up to earnings of $5100, always with a cumulative rate $\theta = \frac{2}{3}$. As earnings rise, the *NIT* program reduces its payments at an effective tax rate of $\frac{5}{12}$ while the family is accepting the *T* benefit, and at $\frac{2}{3}$ when not (i.e., $t = \theta - \frac{1}{4}$ in the former situation, and $t = \theta$ in the latter). The family is always at least as well off as it would be under the independent addition scheme.

When the *T* program is like that of the example, the tax ceiling effected by the *NIT* program makes the system equivalent to simply add-

Table 5.2 A Tax Ceiling Program

E	T	NIT	Y	θ
$0	$1000	$2400	$3400	
1000	750	1983	3733	
2000	500	1566	4066	
3000	250	1150	4400	
3360				
3467				$\frac{2}{3}$
3600	100	900	4600	
4000	0	733	4733	
5000	0	67	5067	
5100	0	0	5100	
6000	0	0	6000	0

ing the T guarantee ($1000) to the NIT basic guarantee. If the T program had a much higher guarantee (higher than $1440, which would result in the T and NIT programs both phasing out at $E = \$5760$), the result would be modified: NIT would be phased out before T, and the recipient would continue in the T program at a $\frac{1}{4}$ tax rate.

When effecting a ceiling rate, the NIT program covers more families than under the independent addition scheme and pays higher benefits at all earnings levels. The T program operates as under independent addition.

Under the 1971 House-passed version of H.R. 1, state supplementation programs to the basic FAP benefit plan were constrained to operate under a scheme similar to that of a ceiling rate program, at least within some range.

Scheme III: Sequencing Programs

The rule of sequencing is that the countable income taxed by any program includes earnings plus the net benefit of all "previous" programs in which the individual participates, with the order of programs established by law. If some set of programs is sequenced, the cumulative tax rate of the set will be less than 100 percent, even if the sum of the programs' tax rates is greater than 100 percent. At any earnings level, the cumulative tax rate depends on the programs in which the person participates and is less than the sum of the tax rates of these programs:

$$\theta = 1 - (1 - t_1) \cdot (1 - t_2) < 1$$
$$\theta < t_1 + t_2 \text{ (for } 0 < t_1, t_2 < 1).$$

These results are obtained by substituting the program formulas into the identity for net family income, differentiating to calculate θ, and rearranging terms.

While the order of the sequencing does not affect the cumulative tax rate for the programs' participants, the order does affect (1) the net benefits of each program, (2) the earnings ranges in which the person can participate in some programs, and (3) the total system benefits. Two sequences are illustrated:

Taking NIT first:
$$Y_{NIT} = E$$
$$NIT = \$2400 - (\tfrac{2}{3}) \cdot Y_{NIT}$$
$$Y_T = Y_{NIT} + NIT$$
$$T = \$1000 - (\tfrac{1}{4}) \cdot Y_T$$
$$Y = Y_T + T$$

Taking NIT second:
$$Y_T = E$$
$$T = \$1000 - (\tfrac{1}{4}) \cdot Y_T$$
$$Y_{NIT} = Y_T + T$$
$$NIT = \$2400 - (\tfrac{2}{3}) \cdot Y_{NIT}$$
$$Y = Y_{NIT} + NIT$$

1. In the second sequence (Table 5.3), benefits from the T program are determined as in the independent case. The NIT program "taxes" Y_{NIT} (not just E) at the nominal rate of $\frac{2}{3}$, which amounts to taxing E at a cumulative rate of $\frac{1}{2}$; the benefits that it pays are reduced relative to its operation as an independent program. In the first sequence (Table 5.4), it is the T program whose benefit schedule is reduced; in the range of earnings in which a family participates in both programs, the T program's effective rate of tax on earnings is only $\frac{1}{12}$.

2. The cumulative rate of tax on earnings for the system as a whole is $\frac{3}{4}$ when the family participates in both programs, the same for both sequences because $\theta = 1 - (1 - t_1) \cdot (1 - t_2)$. In the first sequence (when NIT is the "first" program), the NIT program acts as in the independent case, with its earnings break-even point equal to its natural break-even point (here, $E = \$3600$). By contrast, in the second sequence (when NIT is the "second" program), NIT phases out with a lower earnings break-even point (here, $E = \$3467$). In this second sequence, the NIT program will have a lower earnings break-even point the higher the guarantee or the lower the nominal tax rate in the T program.

3. The systems are not equally generous: The first yields a higher net real income, Y, for all earnings levels. Either order makes the net

Table 5.3 Sequencing Programs (2)

E	T	Y_{NIT}	NIT	Y	θ
$0	$1000	$1000	$1733	$2733	
1000	750	1750	1233	2983	
2000	500	2500	733	3233	$\frac{3}{4}$
3000	250	3250	233	3483	
3360					
3467	133	3600	0	3600	
3600	100	3700	0	3700	$\frac{1}{4}$
4000	0	4000	0	4000	
5000	0	5000	0	5000	
5100					0
6000	0	6000	0	6000	

Table 5.4   Sequencing Programs (1)

E	NIT	Y_T	T	Y	θ
$0	$2400	$2400	$400	$2800	
1000	1733	2733	317	3050	
2000	1066	3066	234	3300	$\frac{3}{4}$
3000	400	3400	150	3550	
3360					
3467	89	3556	111	3667	
3600	0	3600	100	3700	
4000	0	4000	0	4000	$\frac{1}{4}$
5000	0	5000	0	5000	
5100					0
6000	0	6000	0	6000	

benefits of the sequencing scheme less generous than those of the independent addition scheme.

Currently, Food Stamp benefits are determined by including AFDC benefits in the calculation of countable income; this is an example of sequencing programs.

Scheme IV: Full Benefit Offset

This linking scheme, which is a special case of sequencing, was proposed in H.R. 1 (92d Congress) for determining FAP benefits for persons who also receive Social Security. The net benefits of the T program are taxed at 100 percent by the NIT program, that is, the net T benefit is subtracted from the NIT benefit that would otherwise be given:

$$T = \$1000 - \left(\tfrac{1}{4}\right) \cdot E$$
$$NIT = \$2400 - \left(\tfrac{2}{3}\right) \cdot E - T$$
$$Y = E + T + NIT.$$

As illustrated in Table 5.5, the entire system yields the same benefits as would NIT alone, up to the point where NIT is phased out ($E = \$3360$). Above that level of E, the family continues to participate in the T program with a $\tfrac{1}{4}$ tax rate on E. The T program is unaffected relative to

Table 5.5   Full Benefit Offset (1)

E	T	NIT	Y	θ
$0	$1000	$1400	$2400	
1000	750	983	2733	
2000	500	566	3066	$\frac{2}{3}$
3000	250	150	3400	
3360	160	0	3520	
3467				
3600	100	0	3700	$\frac{1}{4}$
4000	0	0	4000	
5000	0	0	5000	
5100				0
6000	0	0	6000	

the independent case, and the NIT benefits are reduced. The effective tax rate on E of the NIT program is $t_2 - t_1$, or $\frac{5}{12}$.

If the natural break-even point of the T program were lower than that of the NIT program—as would be achieved if the tax rate of the T program were raised to $\frac{1}{2}$ (see Table 5.6)—then the full benefit offset linkage makes the whole system's net benefit schedule identical to that of the NIT program operating independently. If the T program were more generous than NIT, say $T = \$2500 - (\frac{1}{2}) \cdot E$, then the family would not enroll in the NIT program.

AFDC programs currently apply the full benefit offset to some other programs' benefits, such as Unemployment Insurance. However, the true effect of this scheme in AFDC is difficult to ascertain because of the peculiarities of various states' plans, such as allowing deductibles against unearned income and paying only a fraction of recognized need.

Scheme V: Expense Deductibility

One way to encourage the use of a government or privately sold service, such as day care, is to allow the expenditures on the service to be deducted from the countable income to be "taxed" by some other program. In some cases, these deductions also may serve to promote horizontal equity among different groups of recipients.

Table 5.6   Full Benefit Offset (2)

E	T	NIT	Y	θ
$0	$1000	$1400	$2400	
1000	500	1233	2733	
2000	0	1066	3066	$\frac{2}{3}$
3000	0	400	3400	
3360	0	160	3520	
3467				
3600	0	0	3600	
4000	0	0	4000	
5000	0	0	5000	0
5100				
6000	0	0	6000	

For example, the *NIT* program might be structured

$$NIT = \$2400 - \left(\tfrac{2}{3}\right) \cdot (E - bD)$$

where D is the expenses and b is the proportion of them that is deductible. In analyzing the properties of this scheme, a clear statement of whether or not the deductible expenses are required to be less than total earnings can be important. Consider the case where this constraint is not binding, or where $bD > E$ is allowed and the negative tax is paid as a benefit. The program formula can be rewritten

$$NIT = \$2400 - \left(\tfrac{2}{3}\right) \cdot E + \left(\tfrac{2}{3}\right) \cdot bD.$$

The parameter b could be set to allow partial, full, or multiple deductibility. For example, if b is equal to the inverse of the tax rate ($b = \tfrac{3}{2}$), then the deductibility scheme would be equivalent to an increase in the guarantee equal to the full cost of day care: Day care would be "free."

If earnings increase while day care expenses remain constant (such as would happen if the worker received a wage increase), $\theta = \tfrac{2}{3}$ and the day care deduction remains an augmentation of the *NIT* guarantee. If day care costs increase proportionately with earnings (such as would happen if earnings increased because of more weeks worked per year or because the charge for day care varied with earnings) then $D = kE$, and the cumulative tax rate on earnings would be less than $\frac{2}{3}$ so long as deductible day care expenses were less than total earnings ($bk < 1$):

$$NIT = \$2400 - (\tfrac{2}{3}) \cdot (E - b(kE))$$
$$NIT = \$2400 - (\tfrac{2}{3}) \cdot (1 - bk) \cdot E.$$

If the deductible expenses are really "work expenses," then net family income as defined here is not the same as the familiar concept of "disposable income."

Scheme VI: Tax Reimbursement

If the "taxes" paid in the T program are reimbursed by the NIT, this scheme has the effect of decreasing the tax rate of the NIT program.

$$T = - (\tfrac{1}{12}) \cdot E$$
$$NIT = \$2400 - (\tfrac{2}{3}) \cdot E + (\tfrac{1}{12}) \cdot E$$
$$NIT = \$2400 - (\tfrac{7}{12}) \cdot E.$$

The earnings break-even point of NIT is raised and so are the net benefits payable at all levels of earnings.

Such a scheme is now in effect in most states in calculating AFDC benefits for working women who pay income taxes. Their AFDC benefits are adjusted to compensate them fully for income and other payroll taxes paid.

Other Schemes

Other schemes for integrating various programs in an income transfer system serve to separate rather than link them. One possibility is to prohibit persons enrolled in one program from participating in another. Another is to limit the number of different programs in which any family may enroll. These schemes may prove to be politically acceptable or administratively convenient, and they may provide somewhat more horizontal equity than is found in the current system without involving alteration of the operations of any programs.

III. An Example of Designing an Integrated Set of Transfer Programs

A rational way to approach the problem of system design might be to group the programs according to their purpose and operation. Within each group, some scheme or combination of schemes can be used to link the programs into a block. Each of the blocks then can be linked to form an integrated system. The linking schemes need not be the same within each of the blocks, nor the same among blocks as within them.

A hypothetical example, based on one view of the world and the trade-offs between system goals, can be made from the following list of items that affect family income and programs that might exist after an overall reform. This list is already sorted into blocks.

1. Nonlabor private income (pensions, income from wealth, alimony)
2. Earnings
3. Payroll and income taxes
4. Housing assistance, day care assistance, and health care assistance
5. Social insurance benefits, veterans' payments, and basic income maintenance benefits
6. General (local) assistance and private charity

The first two blocks comprise the nontransfer sources of income for a family, and when payroll and income taxes (the third block) are subtracted, a net private income can be calculated. In a more detailed system, business and work expenses might be put in the third block, and then they could be deducted in calculating net private income.

The fourth block contains programs predominantly serving to subsidize and influence family budget decisions for housing, child care, and health care items. Within the block, these programs could be allowed to "add up," as in the independent addition scheme.

The fifth block contains three programs that serve predominantly to provide cash income and that are, therefore, substitutes for one another. One of the three, a new "basic income maintenance" program, such as a negative income tax, might serve as a residual program: Eligibility would be universal, and social insurance benefits and veterans' payments would be taxed at 100 percent (full benefit offset). If one wanted to reward those eligible for either of these other two programs, a simple arrangement would be to add a small flat sum to the basic income maintenance program's guarantee.

The linking of the fourth and fifth blocks presents the most difficulty in designing the whole system. The plan here is to sequence the budget subsidy block before the cash payments block, so that countable income for determining benefits from budget subsidy programs is net private income, while countable income for the cash payments block is net private income plus net benefits from the fourth block. The valuation of benefits from the budget subsidy programs presents some thorny problems of economic analysis, but it must be done. The fifth block's tax rate on the fourth block's net benefits might be the same as that on private income, or it might vary up to 100 percent (which would amount to a full benefit offset). An advantage of this sequence, especially with a high fifth block tax rate on the fourth block's net benefits, is that it achieves greater horizontal equity than would be possible if the sequence of the two blocks were reversed. A disadvantage is that program costs in the fourth block are made higher. If it is desired to attract families into the budget subsidy (fourth block) programs, the tax rate in the fifth block on these programs' net benefits should be less than 100 percent.

The sixth block (general assistance and charity) could be allowed to operate with considerable discretionary authority, even undermining the work incentives built up by the rest of the system, in order to care for special and emergency cases. Benefits from this block would not be taxed by any others.

The methods of integration used in this example depend on a particular set of analyses of program purposes and effects and on a particular view of system goals. These views may not be consensus views. For instance, day care has been implicitly classified as an expense of raising children, not of going to work, and hence is put into the block of budget subsidy programs. In this example, families are free to participate in publicly owned housing and day care facilities if they wish, and the programs are viewed predominantly as efforts to correct private market supply failures. Within the cash payments block, a social insurance program operating like the current Old Age Insurance program is treated as a publicly determined transfer rather than as a privately earned insurance benefit; hence, taxation of these benefits at a high level—perhaps 100 percent—is recommended. A reformed social insurance program in which benefits are more closely related to contributions might well be classified in block 1.

The particular sequence of the fourth and fifth blocks, which results in a high tax rate on budget programs, derives from placing a high value on the goal of horizontal equity and from a concern for total system cost.

Other difficulties in designing an integrated system of transfer programs cannot be overlooked. What is most important to do in the field of welfare reform seems to be what is most difficult to do in the realm of political decision-making: The rules and regulations of each program must be designed with an understanding of how it is to be integrated with other programs and how it will affect the entire system.

Acknowledgments

This paper was stimulated by Henry J. Aaron's paper, "Alternative Ways to Increase Work Effort under Income Maintenance Systems," which is Chapter 6 in this volume. The research reported here was supported by funds granted to the Institute for Research on Poverty at the University of Wisconsin by the Office of Economic Opportunity pursuant to the Economic Opportunity Act of 1964. The author, formerly a research associate at the institute, thanks Robert Lampman and Irene Lurie for fostering this paper, and retains responsibility for all views expressed herein.

6

Alternative Ways to Increase Work Effort under Income Maintenance Systems

Henry J. Aaron

I. Introduction

The problem of high marginal tax rates within the welfare system, particularly in the Aid to Families with Dependent Children (AFDC) program, has increasingly troubled and frustrated reformers interested in improving the welfare system. These tax rates, generated by the reduction in cash assistance and in-kind benefits as income increases, rival or exceed the highest rates imposed under the personal income tax.

Reducing these tax rates is important because they affect the incentives to work that welfare recipients face. The economic effect of income support is still uncertain. Using data collected for other purposes, several economists have tried to determine how sensitive low-income families are to high tax rates.[1] Their studies agree that a large transfer of cash causes

This chapter is based on parts of a staff paper by Henry J. Aaron in a book of papers, *Why Is Welfare So Hard To Reform?* © 1973 by the Brookings Institution, Washington, D.C. Reprinted by permission.
[1] See, for example, Glen G. Cain and Harold W. Watts, *Income Maintenance and Labor Supply: Econometric Studies* (Chicago: Markham, 1973), for a review of currently available evidence. See also Sandra S. Christensen, "Income Maintenance and the Labor Supply" (Ph.D. diss., University of Wisconsin, Madison, 1972); Christopher Green and Alfred Tella, "Effect of Nonemployment Income and Wage

some to either work fewer hours or withdraw from the labor force altogether, and that higher tax rates also tend to reduce work effort. They
also suggest that groups marginally attached to the labor force, such as
teenagers and women, are more sensitive to both these influences than are
prime-age men, particularly men who are parents of school-age children.

The marginal tax rates faced by welfare recipients are high because
(*1*) AFDC benefits decline fairly sharply as income increases beyond certain levels and (*2*) many AFDC recipients also receive in-kind benefits
that are reduced as income rises. Although actual reductions in benefits as
incomes rise are smaller than the legal provisions indicate, Hausman has
found average rates, calculated over wide ranges of income, that run from
61 percent to 91 percent in four major cities.[2]

In recent years, three major proposals have been advanced to reform
AFDC. All claimed to improve work incentives by reducing marginal tax
rates. All failed to do so, in large part because they ignored the implicit
tax rates in other programs that provide in-kind benefits, or they so
altered these programs that, unwittingly, cumulative tax rates were made
even worse.

H.R. 1, the second version of President Nixon's proposals for welfare
reform enacted by the House of Representatives, illustrates the problem.
This plan promised to pay $1600 to a parent and one child with no outside
income, an additional $400 for each of the next three family members,
and $300 for each additional family member. Benefits were to be reduced
by two-thirds of earnings in excess of $720 per year. Figure 6.1 shows the
marginal tax rate faced by a family of four eligible under H.R. 1, alternatively for cash assistance only or for cash assistance, Medicaid, and housing
assistance. Figures 6.1–6.3 are based on the assumption that eligible families
pay Social Security taxes at 5 percent, federal personal income taxes at
1972 statutory rates, state income taxes at 2 percent on earnings between
$5000 and $7000 per year and 4 percent on earnings above $7000, and
incur work-related expenses equal to one-fifth of the first $3000 of earn-
ings; that housing assistance is worth $1800 − .25 [.9 ($E − T$) + CA]
where E = earnings, T = taxes, and CA = cash assistance; that a family of

---

Rates on the Work Incentives of the Poor," *Review of Economics and Statistics* 51
(November 1969): 399–408; Robert E. Hall, "Wages, Income and Hours of Work in
the U.S. Labor Force," Working Paper No. 62 (Massachusetts Institute of Tech-
nology, Cambridge, Mass., August 1970); Michael J. Boskin, "Income Maintenance
Policy, Labor Supply and Income Redistribution," Research Memorandum No. 111
(Stanford University, Research Center in Economic Growth, May 1971); Edward
D. Kalachek and Fredric Q. Raines, "Labor Supply of Lower Income Workers," in
Technical Studies, The President's Commission on Income Maintenance Programs,
(Washington, D.C.: U.S. Government Printing Office, 1970), pp. 159–185.
[2] Leonard J. Hausman, see Chapter 2.

Marginal Tax Rate (percent)

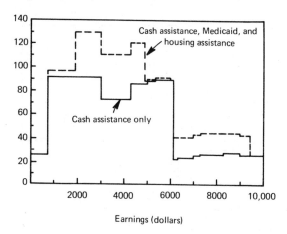

Earnings (dollars)

Figure 6.1. Tax rates for a family of four under H.R. 1 alone and in combination with in-kind benefits, by earnings level.

Note—Derived using the following assumptions: Under H.R. 1, a family of four receives a $2400 federal guarantee and a $1200 state supplement. The state tax rate, like that imposed by the federal government, is 66⅔ percent. Recipients pay Social Security taxes at 5 percent of earnings, federal personal income taxes at 1972 statutory rates, state income taxes at 2 percent of earnings above $5000 and below $7000 and 4 percent on earnings above $7000; they incur work-related expenses equal to one-fifth of the first $3000 in earnings. Medical benefits are worth $1000 and actual medical expenses are $1000. The 33⅓ percent deductible applies to earnings between $1920 and $4920 per year. Housing assistance is equal to $1800 − .25(.9($E − T$) + CA), where E denotes earnings; T, taxes; and CA, cash assistance.

four receives a $1200 state supplement; that the state supplement tax rate, like the federal, is 66⅔ percent; that actual medical expenses and Medicaid benefits are both $1000; and that a deductible equal to 33⅓ percent of income is imposed on Medicaid beneficiaries. As is apparent, tax rates under H.R. 1 would have been super-confiscatory over certain ranges, actually penalizing households for added work.

The Senate Finance Committee, headed by Senator Russell Long, reported out a quite different wage subsidy plan. Under the Long plan, the federal government would have supplemented hourly wages of workers paid at least $1.50 per hour by offering them (*1*) a wage subsidy equal to three-fourths of the difference between $2.00 per hour and their actual hourly wage and (*2*) an earnings subsidy equal to 10 percent of the first $4000 of earnings. The maximum subsidy, $1050 per year, did not vary by family size. These benefits would have been reduced by $1.00 for each $4.00 of earnings over $4000 per year. The Long plan initially appeared to

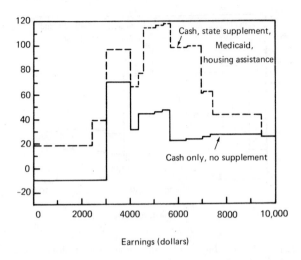

Marginal Tax Rate (percent)

Earnings (dollars)

Figure 6.2. Tax rates for a family of four under the Long plan alone and in combination with in-kind benefits, by earnings level.
Note–Derived using the following assumptions: The worker is employed at $1.50 per hour for the first $3000 of annual earnings and thereafter at a gradually increasing rate that reaches $5.00 per hour at $10,000 annual earnings. In Case A, the worker receives Long plan benefits only. In Case B, he receives Long plan benefits plus a $1200 state supplement phased out at the rate of $1.00 for each $2.00 of earnings over $4500, Medicaid benefits worth $1000 for which he pays a premium equal to one-fifth of earnings between $2400 and $7400, and housing assistance computed as in Figure 6.1.

contain positive incentives for work by beneficiaries. As Figure 6.2 shows, this claim was valid only for households earning $3000 or less per year and who received no supplemental cash assistance or benefits in kind. Households receiving supplemental state benefits, Medicaid, and housing assistance faced tax rates that approached or exceeded 100 percent over wide ranges. This figure is based on the assumption that the worker is employed at $1.50 per hour for the first $3000 of annual earnings, and thereafter at a gradually increasing rate that reaches $5.00 per hour at $10,000 annual earnings; that a state supplement of $1200 is paid that is phased out at the rate of $1.00 for each $2.00 of earnings over $4500; and that the worker pays for Medicaid benefits worth $1000 a premium equal to one-fifth of earnings between $2400 and $7400.

During the 1972 campaign for the Democratic presidential nomination, Senator George McGovern proposed a system of demogrants under which a family of four would receive about $4000 per year if it had no

Marginal Tax Rate (percent)

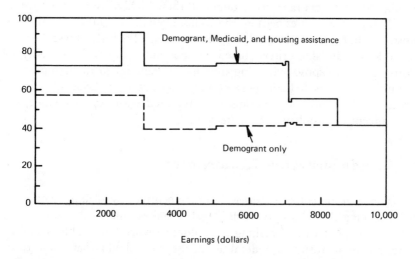

Earnings (dollars)

Figure 6.3. Tax rates for a family of four under a demogrant system alone and in combination with in-kind benefits, by earnings level.
Note—Derived using the following assumptions: Demogrants are $3600 per year for a family of four. The family pays Social Security and state income taxes and incurs unreimbursed work-related expenses at the same level as in Figure 6.1. Federal income taxes are set equal to 33⅓ percent of earnings without deductions or exemptions. Medicaid is treated as under the Long plan. Housing assistance is computed as in Figure 6.1.

income, and face a tax rate of about 33⅓ percent on all earnings. This system would have replaced AFDC, the personal income tax (but not the Social Security payroll tax), and possibly other federal programs as well. As shown in Figure 6.3, families eligible only for the demogrant would have faced relatively modest tax rates, but those eligible for Medicaid and housing assistance would have confronted marginal tax rates of 70 percent and more. This figure treats Medicaid as under the Long plan. Under this form of cash assistance, tax rates that are relatively modest become prohibitive if recipients qualify also for Medicaid and housing assistance, which underlines the importance of coordinating cash assistance with benefits in kind.

The striking tax rates that AFDC, H.R. 1, the Long plan, and demogrants share should not obscure the profound political, economic, and administrative differences among them. They are based on different views of the welfare problem and of the poor; they would provide substantially different benefits and reach different people; they would entail quite different degrees of administrative discretion and would distribute this power differently. Nevertheless, the work disincentive problem caused by high marginal tax rates arises under all these highly disparate programs.

This problem arises because the welfare system includes not only cash assistance but various in-kind benefits as well. To make these benefits available on equitable criteria based on economic need will inevitably be costly and will expose increasing numbers of families to the complexities of multiple benefits, to high tax rates, and to serious work disincentives. Unless the various in-kind programs are integrated with cash assistance, the work incentive problem cannot be solved.

II. Administrative Requirements

The government can increase work incentives by making work pay or by making the failure to work illegal or unbearable.

The simplest way of making the failure to work unbearable would be to terminate all forms of federal assistance. Few doubt that labor force participation of welfare recipients would rise if welfare were ended. But despite periodic efforts to cut welfare rolls, this method of increasing work incentives enjoys little support. The record of public assistance clearly indicates that however anxious Congress and state legislatures may be to strip benefits from welfare cheaters or from those thought capable of working, most legislators are prepared to aid large numbers of the poor, particularly those who have tried sincerely but failed to find work.

Once a welfare system exists, a fundamental decision must be made, whether to handle the problem of work incentives by inducing recipients to work or by requiring them to do so as a condition for aid. This decision implies certain choices in determining eligibility and benefits. On the one hand, eligibility might be based solely on the economic circumstances of applicants. The present system does not follow this course; it excludes childless households and most families headed by men, partly on the ground that adults in such households have no excuse for not working. Late in 1971, Congress stipulated that all adult welfare recipients, except mothers of preschool children, must register for work or training. H.R. 1 contained a similar requirement. Such work requirements are attractive to those who believe that welfare recipients are slackers, and especially to those, like mothers of preschool children now in the labor force, who find work a chore and inconvenience and wonder why others should be spared.

Unfortunately, administrative requirements are unlikely to solve the work incentive problem unless work also pays. The lessons of other income support programs are instructive. From the very beginning, recipients of unemployment insurance have had to accept reasonable job offers or face loss of benefits. To prevent abuses, however, the law contained a "suitability test": Jobs had to be appropriate to the skills and training of the unemployed person and within reasonable commuting distance. In practice, many available jobs are found to be "unsuitable" for the unemployed worker. College graduates have not been required to dig ditches, nor grammar school graduates to program computers. Furthermore, the fact that the unemployed have often outnumbered the available jobs has made it even harder to determine whether or not the applicant turned away by an employer really tried to get the job. In any case, nearly anyone can arrange to be rejected if he is disinclined to accept the job.

It would be even harder to enforce a work requirement on recipients of Public Assistance, Food Stamps, housing assistance, or Medicaid than on recipients of Unemployment Insurance. On the average, people served by these programs are less well-educated and have fewer marketable skills than those served by Unemployment Insurance. In the absence of persuasive incentives, an employer is less likely to inform governmental agencies of job openings for welfare recipients. Consequently, such applicants probably will outnumber available jobs. Moreover, they may intentionally or unintentionally behave so as not to be hired or, once hired, to be fired. Unless it were possible to distinguish those who can work but refuse to do so from all other recipients of assistance, a work requirement would be ineffectual against those who resolved to evade it. How to make this distinction raises difficulties that are probably insuperable.

> For example, should a carwasher who is laid off during a rainy spell be required to take a different job? . . . What should be done about an ice cream vendor in the winter? What kind of work will be defined as "suitable" for a mother with no previous work experience, and what kind of job will she be required to accept to maintain her portion of . . . benefits? These questions are intended to suggest the difficulty of administering a work test, especially for a population of marginal workers whose work patterns are typically unstable.[3]

Removal of the "suitability test" would simplify many of these problems. Administrators would not have to make complex judgments, for example, about the reasonableness of requiring a particular recipient to commute a particular distance to a particular job. The Talmadge amendment, requiring AFDC recipients to register for work and training, does not contain a suitability test. Neither did H.R. 1 or the Long plan.

But some observers fear that work requirements, even those circumscribed by a suitability test, would foster administrative abuse. In small towns and rural areas, particularly those with one employer or highly

[3] D. Lee Bawden, Glen G. Cain, and Leonard J. Hausman, "The Family Assistance Plan: An Analysis and Evaluation," *Public Policy* 19 (Spring 1971): 345.

seasonal demands for labor, the requirement could be administered to foster an abundant labor supply, to hold down wages, or to maintain racial subjugation.[4] Such critics allege that a work requirement would create a pool of workers forced by the threat of starvation to take any job, however repulsive, at any wage, however low; that supporters of work requirements want, among other things, to ensure a plentiful supply of cheap, menial labor,[5] in short, that a work requirement will enslave the poor by requiring that they do the bidding of the authorities to get food for their children. Removal of the suitability test would create greater opportunities for abuse. Many critics oppose a work requirement, also, from a belief that the government of a country as wealthy as the United States is morally obliged to prevent starvation or gross poverty and that cash assistance should be available to the poor as a matter of right.

The criticism that a work requirement would be abused is obviously serious. But the criticisms stressed here allege that, if work does not pay, a work requirement in most places and times would be ineffectual and inoperative, a costly and largely futile effort to compel the poor to behave in ways contrary to their own self-interest. It is unimaginable that a large bureaucracy would be capable of sifting millions of individual cases, each fraught with special problems, needs, and ambiguity, all requiring judgment if not wisdom. To inspire hard work is a laudable goal, but one not likely to be achieved through a work requirement without more authoritarian administration than most Americans are likely to accept.

III. Economic Incentives

The other way to create work incentives is to make work pay. The person who earns more must derive sufficient gain to make the extra work worthwhile. For some adults, including many recipients of welfare, work is an end in itself, a means to personal satisfaction and social status; such people will work for psychic gains even if the financial reward is small.[6]

[4] The AFDC system is alleged to operate in this manner in much of the South and in rural California.

[5] The proposal of Senator Russell B. Long to permit tax deductions for wages paid to domestics who would otherwise be on welfare lends credence to this allegation, as does Governor Lester Maddox's statement that, if the Family Assistance Plan passed, "You're not going to be able to find anyone willing to work as maids or janitors or housekeepers" (*Wall Street Journal*, 15 December 1970).

[6] For evidence that the work motivation of the poor closely resembles that of other groups, see Leonard Goodwin, *Do the Poor Want to Work? A Social–Psychological Study of Work Orientations* (Washington, D.C.: Brookings Institution, 1972).

Other adults refuse work even if the gains are great; for them, the rewards of leisure suffice. For many, however, the decision to report daily to a job that is neither repugnant nor very attractive may be influenced by economic considerations. In some cases, the influence may be direct, in others, indirect, through peer-group pressures that in turn are shaped by economic influences. Whether the importance of economic incentives is real or only apparent, many political leaders believe that such incentives significantly affect work effort. In either case, the success of efforts to reform welfare will be promoted by the creation of genuine work incentives in a restructured system.

Negative Income Taxes

For well over a decade, economists have advocated introducing a negative income tax as an alternative to Public Assistance. Some have proposed that a negative income tax replace in-kind assistance as well.[7]

A negative income tax assures to all eligible households, without other income, basic support related to family size. As earned income rises, the family is subject to an implicit tax through reductions in support payments. The basic support levels and the implicit tax define the income range of eligible families.[8] The negative income tax may be restricted to certain groups, such as families with children, or may be universal. The amount of support may depend on family net worth as well as on income. In fact, the problems of creating a negative income tax parallel those of the (positive) personal income tax.[9]

In a trivial sense, the United States already has a negative income tax: AFDC provides certain kinds of families with children a geographically variable guarantee whose implicit tax rate is $66\frac{2}{3}$ percent of earned income

---

[7] For example, Milton Friedman initially favored the negative income tax as an alternative also for Social Security, unemployment insurance, and farm price supports; see his *Capitalism and Freedom* (Chicago: University of Chicago Press, 1962), especially Chs. 12 and 13.

[8] For example, a plan that provides $3000 for a family of four and that reduces benefits $1 for every $2 of earnings (a 50 percent tax rate) will provide benefits to all four-person families with earnings of less than $6000. The negative income tax is "negative" in the sense that the *average* tax rate is negative; that is, a transfer is paid rather than a tax collected. Most popularly discussed negative income taxes have high *positive marginal* tax rates on increments to earnings. See Christopher Green, *Negative Taxes and the Poverty Problem* (Washington, D C.: Brookings Institution, 1967), pp. 62–67, for a discussion of the relationship among the guarantee level, the implicit tax rate, and the eligibility ceiling.

[9] James Tobin, Joseph A. Pechman, and Peter M. Mieszkowski discuss these problems at length and propose solutions to them in "Is a Negative Income Tax Practical?" *Yale Law Journal* 77 (November 1967): 1–27.

over $360 per year with credit for taxes paid and work-related expenses, and 100 percent of unearned income. H.R. 1 and demogrants combined with tax reform are kinds of negative income taxes. The former was limited to families with children; the basic support level of $2400 for a family of four was not geographically variable although states could have supplemented this payment; the implicit tax was 66⅔ percent of earnings over $720 per year without any credit for taxes paid or work-related expenses; it replaced AFDC and one form of in-kind assistance, Food Stamps, but retained other forms of in-kind assistance. Demogrants are payable to everyone: They guarantee $3600 to a family of four, for example; the implicit tax rate is, say, 33⅓ percent on income; deductions or credits could be incorporated without altering the basic structure.

If AFDC, H.R. 1, or demogrants are viewed in this light, the issue is not whether or not to adopt a negative income tax but what features it should have to reinforce work incentives and to achieve more equitable eligibility standards and benefit levels. These plans also make clear that to advocate replacement of the existing system with a negative income tax is meaningless until one specifies the attributes of the assistance program one espouses. Then the discussion can turn to these attributes and need not center on an empty, but frequently emotional, debate about the desirability of negative income taxes.

The preceding figures that relate to AFDC, H.R. 1, and demogrants make clear that a negative income tax like these plans does not solve the work incentive problem. At least three features contribute to that failure: the high implicit tax rate contained in these forms of the negative income tax, the failure to terminate in-kind benefits or to integrate them with the cash assistance program, and the failure to take income and payroll taxes and work-related expenses into account in computing family income.[10] The remainder of this chapter will review alternative methods of amending these three features of assistance programs to improve work incentives.

Reducing the Tax Rate

The most obvious way to improve work incentives appears to be to lower the implicit tax rate under cash assistance—from 66⅔ percent to, say, 50, 40, or 33⅓ percent. A 66⅔ percent tax permits the worker to keep $1.00 when he earns $3.00; a 50 percent tax lets him keep $1.50; a 33⅓ percent tax, $2.00.

Unfortunately, this approach is exceedingly costly; but what is worse, it does not work. The tax rate under the illustrative demogrant system is

[10] H.R. 1 would have allowed day care costs to be deducted.

only 33⅓ percent. The tax rate embodied in the Long plan is even lower over certain income brackets for low-wage workers. When combined with in-kind assistance, however, the rates swell to 70 percent or more (see Figures 6.2 and 6.3). For this reason, the simple approach of cutting the tax rate under cash assistance is inadequate to make work pay. No matter how far Congress moves to build work incentives into cash assistance, the effort will fail unless in-kind assistance is also reformed.[11]

Lowering the tax rates for lower-income brackets requires that assistance be paid to families in the middle-income brackets; that step vastly increases the cost of assistance. The cost of a $2400 guarantee with a 50 percent tax rate is nearly one-half greater than that of a $2400 guarantee with a 66⅔ percent tax, and one with a 33⅓ percent tax costs more than four times as much. Lowering the tax rate costs so much partly because most families who receive some assistance when the tax rate is high receive more when it is low. More important, reducing the tax rate increases the number of families assisted. A $2400 guarantee (with $720 of earnings disregarded) reaches families with earnings up to $4320 when the tax rate is 66⅔ percent, $5520 when the tax rate is 50 percent, $7920 when the tax rate is 33⅓ percent. Lowering the tax rate opens up eligibility in earnings brackets that are more and more thickly populated.

Lowering the tax rate also spreads the work incentive problem widely because it exposes middle-income families to much higher marginal tax rates than they face under current law. Even if the effect on work effort of each family is small, the total effect may be considerable. Because of the large number and high labor force participation of families in such brackets, the increase in their marginal tax rate may well cost more—in terms of their reduced work effort—than is gained by reducing the tax rate on low-income families.

"Cashing Out" In-Kind Assistance

One approach would be to replace, or "cash out," in-kind assistance with more generous cash assistance. This position receives support both from those who believe that the federal government has no business telling people how to spend their incomes and from those who feel that federal efforts to influence the composition of private outlays often fail or produce

[11] For these reasons, proposals, such as that introduced by Senator Gaylord Nelson (U.S., Congress, *Congressional Record*, daily edition, 92d Cong., 2d sess., 5 April 1972, pp. S5385–86), to limit the reduction in cash assistance under H.R. 1 to 50 percent of earnings in excess of $720, do not materially alleviate the work disincentive problem.

unintended consequences.[12] It is not possible simultaneously to cash out in-kind benefits for all recipients of cash assistance and to keep down implicit tax rates without extending assistance to a large fraction of the American population, thus vastly increasing total benefits and substantially raising taxes on the remainder of the population to finance them.

Furthermore, alongside its grudging willingness to give money to the poor, Congress has repeatedly expressed through legislation a desire to improve housing or provide free medical assistance or subsidized food. The initial passage of assistance in kind requires no explanation more profound than that legislators are more pained to know that children are hungry, that the sick are neglected, or that squalid housing blights their city than they are about less obtrusive or disturbing forms of deprivation. To the extent that those who pay taxes feel more concerned about the health or housing than about the clothing or recreation of the poor, the case for commodity assistance, as opposed to general cash assistance, is strengthened.[13]

Especially if some motives for in-kind assistance are unrelated to the welfare of recipients—for example, reduction of food stocks, in the case of food distribution—cash assistance is hardly an answer. At an equally mundane level, the existence of housing, medical, and food assistance means that congressional committees, subcommittees, and their staffs, and federal agencies have a special concern with these programs. While they may support amendments in them, they are quite likely to resist repeal. Whether based on parochial self-interest or on special knowledge, the views of these powerful groups must be recognized.

Recent actions of Congress suggest that assistance in kind can be curtailed in some circumstances. Both H.R. 1 and the Long plan would have denied food assistance to recipients of the basic federal guarantee. The prospects and the desirability of similarly restricting housing and medical assistance to the poor are far more questionable, however, largely because no income maintenance scheme in sight would cause recipients voluntarily to buy the quantity of housing and medical services that federal legislation indicates the nation views as "basic." Furthermore, most housing assistance is provided on dwellings built with the guarantee of government

---

[12] For an example of the first group, see Friedman, *Capitalism and Freedom*, Ch. 11; representative of the second are Gilbert Y. Steiner, *The State of Welfare* (Washington, D.C.: Brookings Institution, 1971), Ch. 1, and Theodore J. Lowi, *The End of Liberalism: Ideology, Policy, and the Crisis of Public Authority* (New York: W. W. Norton, 1969), especially Ch. 9.

[13] See Henry J. Aaron and George M. von Furstenberg, "The Inefficiency of Transfers in Kind: The Case of Housing Assistance," *Western Economic Journal* 9 (June 1971): 184–191; Harold M. Hochman and James D. Rodgers, "Pareto Optimal Redistribution," *American Economic Review* 59 (September 1969): 542–557.

subsidies for up to fifty years; the subsidies on existing units cannot in fact be terminated.

Cash or In-Kind Benefits—Not Both

Recipients of cash assistance might be given the option of refusing in-kind benefits or of treating the value of in-kind benefits as part of that assistance. For example, a family eligible for $2400 in cash that receives a housing subsidy of, say, $1000 could be given the choice of retaining the housing subsidy and being paid only $1400 in cash, or giving up the subsidy and being paid $2400 in cash. Alternatively, a family opting for the housing subsidy could have its cash grant reduced by some fraction of the value of the housing subsidy. Medicaid or day care subsidies might be treated similarly.

This approach would reduce the aggregate value of benefits for some families now eligible under two or more programs, especially in relatively generous states. It would confront them with the painful choice between refusing health or housing subsidies or surrendering a large share of their cash assistance in order to retain them. If the reduction in the cash payment equaled the full value of the in-kind subsidy, most families would refuse the subsidy and retain their expenditure options. As a result, the very poorest families, with no money income other than cash assistance, would be compelled to give up Medicaid or subsidized housing; those who received little or no cash assistance because of outside income, but who were eligible for in-kind benefits, would opt for them. That the poor would be unable to afford "standard" housing or comprehensive health insurance would mean that many of the very poorest families would have housing or medical care below national standards. It is doubtful whether an explicit policy of excluding those most in need from health or housing assistance would command widespread support.

A Tax Ceiling

If in-kind assistance continues, some method must be found to prevent implicit tax rates under these programs and cash assistance from cumulating into intolerable work disincentives. A possible approach is to use *one* program to guarantee each recipient under *any* program that the cumulative tax rates to which he is exposed will not exceed some maximum, such as 50, 60, or $66\frac{2}{3}$ percent. The most obvious candidate for this role is cash assistance.

This approach could work as follows: A family that was eligible for cash assistance only would face, say, a $.50 reduction in assistance for each additional $1.00 in earnings—a 50 percent tax. Another family, which received in addition housing assistance that was cut by $.25 for each additional $1.00 in earnings, would have its cash assistance cut by only $.25, making a $.50 reduction overall. Alternatively, the implicit tax rate on families receiving benefits under two or more programs might be allowed to exceed slightly the tax on families receiving cash assistance alone. In the example, when earnings rise $1.00 and housing assistance thus falls by $.25, cash assistance might be reduced by, say, $.35, making a 60 percent tax.

This approach appears to permit solution of the work incentives problem without revising assistance in kind. It would, in one motion, assure that poor households would not confront tax rates above some agreed maximum. Unfortunately, it would create serious problems for federal–state fiscal relations. Moreover, the costs of this solution are likely to approach those of cashing out in-kind benefits. A simple example illustrates the problem. Assume that the basic federal guarantee is similar to that contained in H.R. 1—$2400 per year for a family of four; that the first $720 per year of earnings will be disregarded in computing cash or in-kind assistance; and that the total tax rate on earnings above $720 will not exceed 50 percent. Consider three four-member families, *A*, *B*, and *C*. Family *A* earns $4000 and receives no housing assistance in a low-benefit state that does not supplement the basic guarantee but provides modest health benefits worth an average of $200 per year. Family *B* lives in the same state and earns $9000. Family *C* earns $9000 but lives in a high-benefit state that pays a supplement of $1800 per year and medical benefits worth $1000 per year to a family of four with no earnings; family *C* also lives in subsidized housing worth $1800 per year, for which it pays one-fourth of net income. Family *A* receives benefits worth $960 and would receive some until its earnings rose to $5920. Family *B* receives no assistance. Family *C* receives benefits worth $1810 and would receive some until its income reached $12,620.

This system would encourage not only the poor, but also the middle class, to migrate from low-benefit to high-benefit states. AFDC has been criticized for encouraging such migration among the poor, a group known to be far less mobile than the middle class.

Furthermore, in order to enforce a maximum tax rate, the federal government would have to restrict the rates states could apply on earnings in computing state supplementary payments. If earnings led first to a reduction in state supplementary payments and then to a reduction in the federal payment, states could bring about a vast increase in federal transfers to their residents at relatively modest costs in higher state transfers. State legislators would feel an enormous incentive to raise supplements which would impose only moderate costs on the state treasury but would force the federal government to assist the lower-middle- and middle-income families at the expense of the nation at large. If earnings led to a reduction first in the federal payment and then in state supplements (as under H.R. 1), the cost to the states from liberalization of the federal guarantee would be substantial, unless they curtailed supplementary payments. Such a reaction by a state would create hardship for its recipients of cash assistance who did not also receive in-kind assistance. Federal increases in, say, housing assistance might trigger equal declines in state-financed cash assistance; recipients of both would lose some control over how they spent their assistance, but recipients solely of cash assistance would clearly suffer.

In summary, federal efforts to put a ceiling on the implicit tax rate on recipients of assistance will create or perpetuate problems—insupportable costs or inter- or intrastate inequities—that are nearly as serious as those solved by a ceiling, particularly if states pay widely differing amounts of supplementary cash assistance and if other types of assistance cover some, but not all, recipients of cash assistance.

Integration of Methods of Computing Taxes

One flaw produced by the disconnected history of assistance programs is easily repaired. Unfortunately, the gains would be small. The flaw is that the implicit tax rates under each program do not always take account of those under other programs. For example, rents in low-rent public housing or in rental assistance housing, and mortgage payments in homeownership assistance housing, are based on cash income including public assistance and earnings; no allowance is made for federal or state income taxes paid, although certain deductions are permitted. Under H.R. 1, cash assistance and the Medicaid deductible would have been based on gross earnings without regard for payroll taxes or federal and state income taxes (let alone work-related expenses); housing benefits would have taken no account of Medicaid benefits or of the implicit tax on them. The Long plan would have imposed a premium for Medicaid based on gross earnings rather than net income. Because of this lack of coordination, tax rates can easily cumulate to more than 100 percent—more easily under H.R. 1 than under the existing system, the Long plan, or demogrants.

This problem can be mitigated, however, if the rates are applied sequentially to net resources—the sum of all cash assistance and earnings plus the market value of assistance in kind less all taxes, fees, and charges. This procedure prevents the most serious work disincentive—the circumstance in which an increase in earnings reduces a family's net income. To illustrate, as earnings rise, a four-person family must pay Social Security payroll taxes from the first dollar of earnings, federal income taxes on earnings in excess of $4300 (if the family uses the low-income allowance), and state income taxes for its earnings level. Cash assistance should be based on earnings net of these taxes, rather than gross earnings (unless, as in many states, a full credit is given for taxes paid). The sum of net earnings and cash assistance equals disposable cash income. The net value of, say, Medicaid should be added to disposable cash income. The charges imposed for, say, assisted housing (or the size of a housing allowance) should depend on the sum of disposable cash income and the net value of medical coverage. And so on for any other commodity assistance, such as subsidized day care.[14]

This arrangement would assure only that the cumulative tax rate did not exceed 100 percent. Unless the rates were kept to moderate levels, the cumulative rate might be so close to 100 percent as to leave assistance recipients only meager recompense for work.[15]

IV. Program Redesign

Cash Assistance

AFDC, H.R. 1, and demogrants all guarantee a basic payment to eligible families with no earnings or other income, and they all impose a positive marginal tax on earnings. Indeed, the high positive marginal tax rates under cash and commodity assistance are jointly responsible for the work disincentive problem. As far as benefit and tax schedules are concerned, no distinction is made between the employable and unemployable. These plans are unitary. The Long plan would have continued AFDC for those not required to work and would introduce a wage subsidy for

[14] Symbolically, let t_i represent the implicit tax rate for assistance of form i $(i = 1, \ldots, n)$; D_i the amount of income disregarded in computing the benefits; and A_i the amount of assistance when family disposable income including net transfers is D_i. Then family income after the ith transfer program, y_i, s equal to $y_{i-1} + A_i - t_i(y_{i-1} - D_i)$, where $y_0 = E$, earnings. An increase in earnings must raise y_i if $t_i < 1$ for all i, since $dy_i/dE = (dy_i/dy_{i-1}) (dy_{i-1}/dy_{i-2}) \ldots (dy_1/dy_0) = (1 - t_i)(1 - t_{i-1}) \ldots (1 - t_1)$, which is necessarily positive.

[15] To illustrate, a worker who paid payroll taxes of 5 percent and federal income taxes of 14 percent, and who suffered a reduction in cash assistance of $66\frac{2}{3}$ percent, in medical assistance of 20 percent, and in housing assistance of 25 percent, would face a cumulative tax rate of 84 percent, thus: $(1 - .05 - .14)(1 - .66)(1 - .2)$ $(1 - .25) = .165$. For further examples of how to integrate tax rates under various programs, see Thad W. Mirer, Chapter 5, in this volume.

those deemed employable. A relatively high benefit and a high tax rate are contained by AFDC; the Long plan provided no benefit when there were no earnings, but contained genuinely negative tax rates. The Long plan was binary.[16]

In a binary system, families may be able to choose the part of the system into which they fall. Under the Long plan, for example, a woman could have stayed under the AFDC system by allowing no more than six years between births. A man who cannot find private employment and rejects the public employment offered to him, or who earns less than he thinks his family needs, could leave his family, thereby making them eligible for AFDC. There is no evidence that significant numbers of families respond to the similar incentives in the AFDC system. But the lack of evidence has not prevented critics of AFDC from condemning the system for these faults.[17] Those, including Senator Long, who fault the AFDC system for these incentives should not look to measures like H.R. 1 or the Long plan for redress.[18]

The preceding comparison of AFDC and the Long plan illustrates the kinds of problems that may arise within any binary system if families have discretion over their own benefits. This possibility is particularly disturbing when it involves decisions about such basic matters as marriage or cohabitation and the number of children.

Despite these problems of binary systems, experts on income maintenance remain attracted to them, because the problems of the family with no potential earner differ significantly from those of the family with an unemployed or low-skilled worker. Some have proposed wage subsidies; some, earnings subsidies.[19]

---

[16] In principle, it would be possible to have three or more plans for separate groups. The separate programs for the aged, blind, and disabled may be viewed in this light.

[17] On this subject, see Steiner, *State of Welfare*, especially Ch. 3.

[18] H.R. 1 raised the same issue in more acute form. After 1974, mothers without children under the age of three were to be required to accept jobs or training as a condition for benefits. While the justice of this requirement is debatable, the fact remains that any mother who felt deeply she should be with her three-year-old, or who simply did not want to work, could follow her inclination by having another child.

[19] For an example of the wage subsidy proposal, see Richard J. Zeckhauser, "Optimal Mechanisms for Income Transfer," *American Economic Review* 61 (June 1971): 324–334; also, in "An Alternative to the Nixon Income Maintenance Plan," *Public Interest*, No. 19 (Spring 1970): 120–130. Zeckhauser and Peter Schuck propose a wage subsidy equal to half the difference between the worker's hourly wage and $3 per hour. An example of the earnings subsidy proposal appears in Robert Haveman

Proponents of wage and earnings subsidies focus on the sensitive work incentive question. The case for wage supplements instead of earnings subsidies rests on a politically and economically significant distinction between the implicit tax rate on increases in earnings due to an increase in hours worked on the one hand and in hourly wages on the other.[20] Public statements suggest that congressmen are concerned more about the person who does not work at all than about the person who works but refuses an increase in wages. An assistance program that applied a lower tax rate to increased earnings due to a rise in hours worked rather than to those due to increased hourly wages would meet a politically relevant concern.

A plan that applies a lower tax rate to increased earnings due to a rise in hours worked than to those due to increased hourly wages can be described by the following benefit formula:

$$B = B' + W,$$

where

$$B' = \$2640 - .3H(\$1.60) - .6H(E - \$1.60)$$

and

$$W = .3H.$$

In the formula, B represents benefits; B', intermediate benefits; W, work expenses allowances; H, hours worked; E, hourly earnings. B and W are constrained as follows: Maximum benefit $= \$2400$, minimum benefit $= \$0$, and maximum work allowance $= \$450$. This plan is neither a wage nor an earnings subsidy, since benefits do not at any point increase with earnings, and families are guaranteed income regardless of whether or not they work. It is, however, a unitary system. This means that all people within the system are treated alike, thereby reducing incentives to alter family arrangements.

Table 6.1 illustrates the plan. It shows the benefits payable to a family of four for various numbers of hours worked and hourly wages. The benefit for a family with no earnings is $2400, the same amount provided in H.R. 1 and assured to public employees under the Long plan. Workers can earn $2133 net of taxes without loss of benefits if net earnings are $1.60 per hour but only $593 if they earn $4.00 per hour. Each employee receives an allowance for work expenses of $.30 per hour worked up to a

---

and Robert Lampman, *Two Alternatives to FAP's Treatment of the Working Poor*, University of Wisconsin, Institute for Research on Poverty Discussion Paper No. 94–71. These authors suggest a 100 percent earnings subsidy on earnings up to $1300 per year for a four-person family, recaptured by a 50 percent tax on earnings between $1300 and $3900 per year. Haveman and Lampman advocate a binary system.

[20] The Zeckhauser–Schuck wage supplement applies a 50 percent tax on increased earnings due to rises in wage rates, and pays a subsidy at a rate that ranges from 44 percent (at the minimum wage, $1.60 per hour) to zero (at $3.00 per hour) for additional hours worked.

Table 6.1   Work Incentive Benefits under Unitary Formula with Maximum Annual Benefits of $2400 for a Family of Four, by Hourly Earnings and Hours Worked

Hourly earnings net of payroll and income taxes	Hours worked per year					
	100	250	500	1000	1500	2000
1.60	2400	2400	2400	2400	2370	2130
1.80	2400	2400	2400	2340	2190	1890
2.00	2400	2400	2400	2220	2010	1650
2.20	2400	2400	2370	2100	1830	1410
2.40	2400	2400	2310	1980	1650	1170
2.60	2400	2400	2250	1860	1470	930
2.80	2400	2400	2190	1740	1290	690
3.00	2400	2385	2130	1620	1110	450
3.20	2400	2355	2070	1500	930	210
3.40	2400	2325	2010	1380	750	0
3.60	2400	2295	1950	1260	570	0
3.80	2400	2265	1890	1140	390	0
4.00	2400	2235	1830	1020	210	0
4.20	2400	2205	1770	900	30	0
4.40	2400	2175	1710	780	0	0
4.60	2400	2145	1650	660	0	0
4.80	2400	2115	1590	540	0	0

Source–Prepared by author.
Note–All amounts in dollars.

maximum of $450. The implicit tax rate on net earnings due to increases in hours worked for a worker employed at the minimum wage ranges from zero for workers employed less than 1333 hours to 30 percent for those employed more than 1500 hours. For workers earning $3.00 per hour, the tax rate ranges from zero for those who work less than 235 hours to 44 percent for those who work more than 1500 hours. Benefits would be reduced by 60 percent of additional earnings due solely to increases in average hourly earnings.

This formula encourages earners to work additional hours, a decision over which some workers, particularly women and casual laborers, exercise considerable discretion. A major shortcoming is that it provides smaller—though still positive—incentives to accept or seek employment at higher wages. A maximum of, say, 2000 hours (that is, year-round full-time employment) would be used in computing benefits. Such a rule would subject overtime wages and earnings by secondary workers to the 60 percent tax.

This formula offers low-wage workers great incentive to supplement the federal grant with earnings and is likely to attract low-wage and part-time workers into the labor force. It also assures a substantial average wage to higher-wage workers, who must choose between full-time employment and none at all because of job rules.[21] By exposing low earnings to no tax, and modest increases in earnings from working longer hours to a low tax, this type of benefit formula promotes work effort by low-wage, part-time, and marginal workers who are sensitive to the tax rate, at the same time that it offers a large *average* gain to higher-wage, regular workers who have been shown to be less sensitive to marginal tax rates.

This formula is purely illustrative. Alternatives could be designed to reward more generously hours worked by high-wage workers, to encourage overtime work or secondary workers, or to reduce the implicit tax on increased hourly earnings. The essential characteristic is that this formula differentiates between hours worked and hourly earnings in determining benefit levels. The chief consequence is that, even if their total earnings are the same, a worker who is employed more hours at a lower hourly wage than another worker will receive more cash assistance. As a result, fewer workers would withdraw completely from the labor force than would be induced to do so by plans like H.R. 1, which subjects to high tax rates increases in wages due to additional hours worked.

A benefit formula that distinguishes changes in earnings related to hours worked from those due to wage rates requires two sets of implicit taxes and data on both hours worked and wage rates. Such a formula may encourage collusion between employers and employees to understate hourly earnings and overstate hours. To reduce the problem, earnings of less than, say, $1200 per year might be deemed to have been at the minimum wage. A benefit formula based solely on earnings avoids this problem but fails to distinguish between hours worked and wages earned in the determination of benefits.

Housing

Federal housing programs provide very large benefits, averaging approximately $1000 per year per family. Most beneficiaries are families with incomes near or beyond the income limits for cash assistance. There are two distinct reasons why housing might be subsidized. First, the nation has declared repeatedly through legislation its interest in assuring decent

---

[21] A worker who earns $5.00 per hour gross wages will lose only about $62.50 in transfers for his first $1187.50 of net after-tax earnings. After payment of taxes, the net hourly wage of such a worker who heads a family of four is $4.75; 250 hours of employment yields net earnings of $1175.50.

housing for all. Unfortunately, the methods it has adopted to achieve this objective have contained inefficiencies[22] and have contributed to work disincentives. Second, variations in housing costs are the major cause of interregional differences in the cost of living. Housing allowances that supplement cash assistance can remove these regional disparities. The supplement could vary from zero in the lowest-cost areas to an amount equal to the difference between housing costs there and in the highest-cost areas. Housing allowances have the advantage of permitting beneficiaries to buy the mix of housing, location, and neighborhood characteristics that best suit perceived needs and can be used for existing, as well as new, housing. Existing programs, in contrast, provide subsidies for specified units, usually newly constructed, in particular places, and are so scarce that eligible families must take what is offered. Since allowances would be paid to the eligible household, recipients could retain them when they move; existing subsidized units are so scarce that an occupant cannot count on finding another subsidized unit if he vacates the one he occupies.

Existing housing programs pose work disincentives because families are expected to spend 20–25 percent of income on assisted units, with the government making up the difference between this amount and full costs. Since the subsidies are tied to particular units, the cost of housing to assisted families rises with their income, but they do not have the option of moving to better housing. By defraying a portion of the rent or housing costs of low-income households so that aid rises with housing expenditure but declines with income, the nation could better foster its goal of good housing without inflicting work disincentives as serious as those operating today. It would be entirely reasonable for this form of housing assistance to extend beyond the income range eligible for general income support, since the declared interest in housing standards (in contrast with the silence about adequate provision of many other goods) implies society's greater concern with adequate housing.

A housing allowance could be of the following form: For families with resources of $2500 per year or less and housing costs of H, benefits are

$$B_H^* = .5(H - \$100),$$
$$B_H^* \text{ (maximum)} = \$600.$$

For families with higher annual money resources Y, and housing expenditure H, the benefit is

$$B_H = B_H^* - .1(Y - \$2500).$$

[22] See Henry J. Aaron, *Shelter and Subsidies: Who Benefits from Federal Housing Policies?* (Washington, D.C.: Brookings Institution, 1972).

Table 6.2 Annual Housing Allowance under Formula with $600 Maximum and Family Housing Expenditure from Own Resources, by Selected Incomes

Total housing outlays	Disposable resources					
	2500 or less	3500	4500	5500	6500	7500
500	200	100	0	0	0	0
	(300)	(400)	(500)	(500)	(500)	(500)
700	300	200	100	0	0	0
	(400)	(500)	(600)	(700)	(700)	(700)
900	400	300	200	100	0	0
	(500)	(600)	(700)	(800)	(900)	(900)
1100	500	400	300	200	100	0
	(600)	(700)	(800)	(900)	(1000)	(1100)
1300	600	500	400	300	200	100
	(700)	(800)	(900)	(1000)	(1100)	(1200)
1500	600	500	400	300	200	100
	(900)	(1000)	(1100)	(1200)	(1300)	(1400)
1800	600	500	400	300	200	100
	(1200)	(1300)	(1400)	(1500)	(1600)	(1700)

Source—Prepared by author.
Note—All amounts in dollars; family expenditure in parentheses.

Table 6.2 presents such a housing allowance. It is much below the average assistance available to the minority of low-income households eligible under existing housing programs, but it is presumed to be generally available. The housing assistance formula is constructed so that households with $2500 in net income that spend one-fifth of their own resources on housing receive $400 in housing allowances. The government would pay 50 percent of additional housing costs up to a maximum that would decline with income, from $600 per year for a family with $2500 per year total income to $0 for a family with $8500 per year income. No family would face a housing tax of greater than 10 percent of disposable income. The effective tax rate on earnings would be considerably lower, since disposable income would rise less rapidly than earnings.

Medical Care

Medical care raises the same tax issues as does housing assistance. The "notch" in the present Medicaid formula, the 33⅓ percent implicit tax contained in H.R. 1, and the 20 percent premium for Medicaid in the Long plan, create formidable work disincentives. The limitation of these programs to the poor contributes to their peculiar design. The need to curtail benefits sharply as income rises would be reduced if medical assistance for the poor were imbedded in a broader health protection plan.

It is possible to design comprehensive health insurance schemes that establish premiums graduated with respect to income, yet that impose far more modest tax rates than does H.R. 1. For example, the national health insurance program proposed by Feldstein, Friedman, and Luft would cover all families and individuals, and would involve a premium, a deductible (the amount that must be paid before the insurer begins to pay any share of the medical expense), and co-insurance (a portion of medical costs above the deductible that is paid by the insured person), all varying with income.[23] The formula would require that families pay (*1*) a premium equal to $50 plus 1 percent of income in excess of $3000 per year but less than $12,000 per year; (*2*) a deductible of $50 per adult plus $25 per child plus 5 percent of income in excess of $3000 but less than $12,000 per year; and (*3*) a portion of medical costs in excess of the deductible equal to 8 percent plus 4 percent for each $1000 of income up to $12,000. Net benefits for a family with income of $2000 per year or less would average $414.

The implicit tax rate in their formula would vary according to income, family size, and gross costs of medical care. For a family of four with $3000 in income and $500 in medical care costs, the implicit tax rate would be 8 percent. If income were $10,000 and medical costs were $1000, the tax rate would be 10 percent. If total resources (earnings plus benefits) are used as the base, the tax rate works out to considerably less. According to Feldstein and his co-workers, this plan would not be self-financing. General revenues or earmarked taxes of $9.5 billion would be necessary to supplement income from premiums, deductibles, and co-insurance if these charges were based on the ordinary definition of income. The cost would be higher if these charges were based on net family resources.

Program Redesign—Cumulative Effect

If cash, housing, and medical assistance were awarded according to the formulas just described and if the tax rates were imposed sequentially, the basic benefit for a family of four with no outside earnings would be worth $3410 (see Figures 6.4 and 6.5). Some cash benefits would be avail-

[23] See Martin Feldstein, Bernard Friedman, and Harold Luft, "Distributional Aspects of National Health Insurance Benefits and Finance," Discussion Paper No. 248 (Harvard University, Harvard Institute of Economic Research, August 1972).

Marginal Tax Rate (percent)

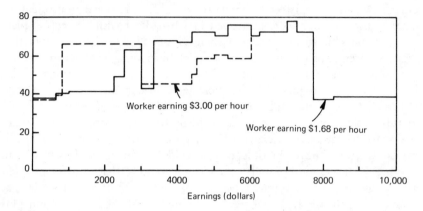

Figure 6.4. Tax rates for a family of four under proposed alternative assistance programs.
Note—Cash assistance is assumed to be distributed in the pattern shown in Table 6.1, housing assistance as in Table 6.2. Medical assistance is distributed according to the formula described on p. 183 for a family with medical expenditure of $1000. Employees are assumed to incur work-related expenses, Social Security, and federal and state income taxes as in Figure 6.1.

Net Income (dollars)

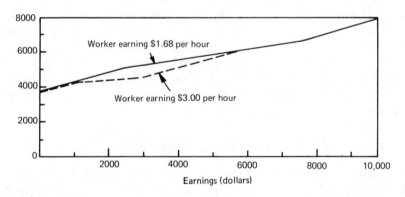

Figure 6.5. Value of benefits under proposed alternative assistance programs, by earnings level.
Note—Cash assistance is assumed to be distributed in the pattern shown in Table 6.1, housing assistance as in Table 6.2. Medical assistance is distributed according to the formula described on p. 183 for a family with medical expenditure of $1000. Employees are assumed to incur work-related expenses, Social Security, and federal and state income taxes as in Figure 6.1.

able until earnings reached $7728.[24] Some housing assistance would be received by families of four until gross earnings exceeded $10,000 per year. The average value of medical care benefits for such a family would range from $414 for families with incomes below $2000 per year to -$951 for families with incomes over $25,000 per year. Positive medical benefits cease altogether at about $7600. Removal of Social Security payroll taxes for low-income workers and further increases in their allowances would improve their work incentives somewhat.

The total benefit for a family with no earnings, $3410, is much less than total benefits available today in the more generous states. This level is purely illustrative, but much larger universal benefits, worth $4500 or $5000 per year, are likely to be so costly as to be politically unacceptable. Some states, doubtless, would choose to supplement benefits at this level. They should be free to do so, provided that the tax rates imposed by them do not thwart incentives. For example, states might be required to follow the basic formula shown in Table 6.1 but with state supplements added on. The costs of permissible supplements might be viewed as excessive by many states. A dilemma for the states would result—to maintain incentives at the cost of curtailing benefits for some families or to maintain benefits at high cost to the state.

Figure 6.4 shows the marginal tax rates facing two families. One earns $1.68 per hour gross; increases in earnings are due to increases in hours worked until the worker is employed 2000 hours per year, and after that to increases in hourly wage rates. The other earns $3.00 per hour. As is apparent, the worker who earns more per hour faces a higher rate.

Both workers have substantial work incentives, however. The low-wage worker faces a tax rate averaging 44 percent if he works less than full time; for the higher-wage worker, the rate is 56 percent, but the increase in his after-tax resources is larger than that of the low-wage worker. These tax rates show the amount by which reductions in benefits under the system of cash assistance shown in Table 6.1, the housing allowance shown in Table 6.2, and the medical care plan described on pages 182–183 offset any increase in earnings. The tax rates under these programs, respectively, are sequenced for purposes of computing benefits under the next program, as suggested on pages 175–176. The low-wage worker gains $1878 from full-time employment after work-related expenses are deducted and assistance is reduced; the high-wage worker gains $2630. Increases in earnings due to increases in hourly wages or to overtime work would be exposed to higher tax rates. In other words, workers would lose more by

[24] This calculation presumes that the worker is employed 2000 hours. Cash benefits would phase out at lower earnings if the worker were employed less than full time at a higher wage.

curtailing (or gain more by increasing) work hours, and relatively less from increasing or decreasing hourly earnings.

Conversion of the existing welfare system to the integrated, three-part system described here would vastly improve equity and would substantially raise work incentives for families now receiving cash assistance. It would extend benefits to the working poor and lower-middle class. Along with these benefits, these groups would face tax rates that would be relatively low only by comparison with those under AFDC or H.R. 1; they would be far higher than those that now apply. Both the transfer and the increased tax rates would tend to cause low-income workers to reduce work effort, although it is impossible at this time to say by how much. Unlike demogrants, this system would not provide transfer or tax relief to middle-income workers.

Reform of the assistance system will create some new problems. The first question concerns the in-kind benefits not treated in this chapter. Continuation of the Food Stamp program would require yet another implicit tax on increased earnings. A food aid formula could be designed so that the additional reduction in work incentives was modest. Nevertheless, it is assumed here that food assistance would be terminated.[25] This assumption is consistent with H.R. 1 and the Long plan, both of which would have terminated Food Stamps for all households receiving federal cash assistance.

In addition to Food Stamps, federal college tuition assistance is income-tested, and day care and other present or prospective benefits might be. An income test means a tax rate. All such programs should be integrated with the major programs described here.

The second problem concerns the proper treatment of adults who do not work. H.R. 1 and the Long plan established a work requirement for fathers and mothers of children over three and over six, respectively. The latter also guaranteed a public service job, newly created if necessary. The former approach, as argued earlier, is likely to be ineffective or repressive or both. The latter is likely to be extraordinarily difficult and costly to administer if the public employment opportunities are to be adequate to absorb all who become unemployed and needy over the business cycle. The size of this group fluctuates widely. If the number of jobs does not keep pace with the demand for them, the guarantee will be an empty gesture for some. The effort to provide public employment or to find jobs for the unemployed may well be a good investment of public funds.

[25] The program could be terminated in effect without doing so in fact. One means would be to pay a fraction of cash assistance in Food Stamps. If the value of the stamps were lower than typical food expenditures, the substitution would have little effect (except for any stigma that attaches to the use of Food Stamps).

The propositions advanced here are that (*1*) such efforts are more likely to succeed the better the work pays and (*2*) under the best of circumstances, they can reduce the scope of, but cannot replace, cash assistance.

V. Summary

By now it should be clear that the problems Congress faces in reforming welfare are inherent in a system that provides highly variable and locally generous benefits under several independent and uncoordinated programs on the basis of geographically variable eligibility. The reason Congress has found it difficult to find a plan that provides universal benefits at a level regarded as reasonable, that preserves work incentives, and that is not vastly more expensive than President Nixon's proposals is that no such plan exists or can be devised: These objectives are mutually inconsistent.

In this predicament, policymakers might be tempted "to leave bad enough alone." This choice is a chimera. The recent growth of federal housing assistance and the likely provision of subsidized day care for the poor assure that the number of low-income families exposed to several implicit taxes in addition to explicit payroll and income taxes will grow rapidly. The current Medicaid notches and spend-downs confront the poor with utterly grotesque choices. If policymakers do not face the work incentive problem, it will rapidly get worse.

A major forward step in thinking about welfare reform would be widespread recognition of the following and of its implication: Creation of effective work incentives requires simultaneous reform of all major income-tested programs. The committee structure within Congress and the departmental bureaucracy of the executive probably exclude the organizational embodiment of such recognition. A useful compromise among the relevant committees and departments would be specific agreement concerning the "sequence" of assistance, that is, the order in which tax rates will be applied. Housing assistance should be broadened to include all those with incomes too meager to buy acceptable housing, whether or not they choose to live in units constructed under federal housing programs. The formula for Medicaid assistance should be revised to remove the unconscionable notches and spend-downs that now operate.

The reforms described here are based on an "incrementalist" view of the American political process. They suggest major evolutionary changes in existing programs, based on three technical principles. First, the tax rate need not be the same on increases in earnings from longer working hours as on increases from higher hourly wages. A second, related, principle, incorporated in the housing and medical assistance formulas described previously, is that the government may subsidize increased expenditures at the same time that higher incomes tend to reduce subsidies.

Third, a number of marginal changes in existing programs are in order. In making them, one criterion should be how well they will facilitate subsequent reform. To reduce the wide disparities in state benefits and administrative practice that pose the most serious obstacle to reform, uniform national standards should be established for defining work-related expenses. At present, gross variations in state rules operate to create large differences in the actual benefits. Uniform computational procedures should be established under which benefits would be reduced as earnings rose. Uniform procedures should be adopted regarding the earmarking of cash payments for specific family expenditures.

The history of efforts to reform welfare during the years 1969–1972 makes clear that none of the several minorities seeking diverse and inconsistent changes in the present system has the power to impose its will on the others. This predicament emerged most clearly in 1972 when eleventh-hour efforts on the floor of the Senate to enact the House-passed welfare reform proposals contained in H.R. 1, to liberalize them, and to substitute the Long plan for them all failed. Welfare reform will succeed only when a coalition has been organized uniting two or more of the groups. If those who seek more generous and uniform benefits are to succeed, they must win over some of those whose concern over work incentives led them to oppose H.R. 1 and more liberal substitutes.

The evolution of the welfare system depends on far broader considerations than the technical matters examined in this chapter: It rests on such issues as how much income should be redistributed and to which income classes, how automatic or discretionary such redistribution should be, who should exercise the discretion. Answers to these questions will define the size of a new public assistance program or whatever replaces the current system.

7

When Do Recipients Value Transfers at Their Costs to Taxpayers?

Maria Schmundt / Eugene Smolensky /
Leanna Stiefel

I. Introduction: A Theorem Used and Abused

A long-standing theorem of economics is that, if governments wish to make poor people as well off as they can be made for any given total expenditure level, aid should take the form of cash rather than goods and services. The argument is simply that, if cash is given, the recipient can buy what he has been receiving in goods, if that is what he wants; but if he would prefer something else, say less food and more housing than he is being given, he will be worse off receiving goods than if he were given cash.

This theorem has been used in two important ways. First, it has been used to impugn the motives of government and to imply that hidden objectives are producing inefficient expenditure patterns. The several such arguments are straightforward. If cash is best from the point of view of the poor, then giving other than cash must mean that the givers do not have the best interests of the recipients at heart. "Bang for the buck" (to borrow a Pentagon metaphor) has been sacrificed to provide income for union men, for farmers, or for social workers who provide the goods and services. Or else it is alleged that the welfare of the poor has been sacrificed to paternalism: The poor will be forced to buy what the government thinks to be best for them. Or, even more Machiavellian—though perhaps economically efficient—the poor are being bribed to do things that make the nonpoor better off. For example, the poor are locked away in public housing so their slums do not lower other people's property values.

The second, more technical, employment of the theorem has been to argue that the statistics that purport to show how the government has helped the poor overstate that help by using the cost to the government as a measure of benefits. If all benefits were cash transfers, then benefits would equal cost; but if benefits are in kind, then in general it follows from the theorem that benefits to the poor are likely to be less than costs. Less aid, but in cash, would keep the poor as well off as they are with their in-kind transfers.

There are many reasons, however, for believing that the theorem is not so generally relevant as is assumed. In many circumstances, recipients may be as well off as they would be if they were given the cost of their in-kind transfers in cash. In this chapter, those circumstances will be rigorously derived from consumer theory. Whether or not the mass of recipients of in-kind transfers are just as well off as they would be with the money cannot be determined except by empirical analyses. Such analyses are under way, but not completed. However, we will demonstrate the significance for policymakers of knowing just how much cash would be required to keep in-kind transfer recipients exactly as well off as they are now. Some general policy implications that follow from the analysis are also drawn.

II. Benefit Weights for In-Kind Transfers

Introduction

The simplest and most frequently used method to measure the benefits of transfer programs is to add the government cost of the income or in-kind transfer to the recipients' pretransfer income.[1] There are three major objections to this procedure.

1. If the programs or program changes examined are substantial, they may cause changes in relative factor and commodity prices and thus pretransfer incomes. Though this problem is important (and has received increasing attention in the tax incidence literature), we will ignore it in

[1] For example, W. Irwin Gillespie, "The Effect of Public Expenditures on the Distribution of Income: An Empirical Investigation" (Ph.D. diss., Johns Hopkins University, Baltimore, 1963), or W. Irwin Gillespie, "Effect of Public Expenditures on the Distribution of Income," in *Essays in Fiscal Federalism*, ed. R. A. Musgrave (Washington, D.C.: Brookings Institution, 1965).

the context of this chapter by assuming that, in the relevant range, changes in the composition of demand and output due to in-kind transfers are not sufficiently large to influence relative prices and that transfer programs do not affect individual factor supplies.[2]

Of course, it is probably not true that factor supplies are independent of transfers. The high implicit tax rate built into the transfer programs as earned income rises probably has a substantial effect on work effort, especially since many programs are cumulative (for example, certain cash transfers lead to automatic eligibility for a whole bundle of in-kind benefits). Although this objection is often important when the aggregate effect of the entire government sector is under consideration, it can be ignored in the context of this chapter, since the consequences of in-kind programs will only be compared to equivalent cash transfers, which would presumably affect factor supplies in similar ways.

2. The benefits from transfer programs may accrue not only to recipients but to other groups as well, if recipient characteristics influenced by such programs create externalities. If the political process is Pareto efficient in the sense that the transfer programs make nobody worse off, the cost of the program is a lower-limit estimate of total benefits to those who bear the burden of financing the programs.[3] That is, the cost may be as appropriate a measure of benefits to nonrecipients as to recipients. This objection will not be treated here, but it does not affect the substance of what follows.

---

[2] If factor supplies are independent of the income distribution, sufficient conditions for the invariance of relative market prices are constant returns to scale production functions, identical factor proportions for all industries, and perfect markets (including government market activities). The production possibility surface will be flat, and commodity as well as factor prices are invariant under output changes.

Note that certain market imperfections—like constant relative price differentials—would not impair the independence of relative prices from demand and output structure changes. The more stringent assumption of perfect markets eliminates some complications when the benefit and cost sides are integrated: Market values equal resource cost. But it is likely that certain in-kind programs are motivated by imperfections. For example, the oversupply of farm products and the negative effect on the nonfarm poor caused by the agricultural price support program may have provided the incentive for many in-kind programs administered by the Department of Agriculture.

[3] If the programs make those who finance them better off, total donor benefits exceed the program cost. This statement does not imply that donor benefits should be accounted for at a higher value than their cost price, unless transfer programs are of an all-or-nothing type. If donors are in a position to decide on the extent of these programs in the same way they determine their "private goods" consumption, inframarginal program units should be evaluated at marginal benefits. That is, if donors equate marginal program benefits to marginal program cost, donor benefits equal donor cost, irrespective of the "donor surplus" involved.

3. The objection that will be dealt with is that recipients may not evaluate transfer benefits as equal to their cost. If recipients "purchased" these transfers in the market place, or if they could resell their options at market prices without incurring transactions costs, or if the quantities transferred were generally less than or equal to what recipients would have consumed had there been costless reselling opportunities, then, of course, recipients would value their in-kind transfers at their market price. Quite apart from the possibility that market values and resource cost may differ, these conditions are not characteristic of existing programs.

Given that relative prices and individual factor supplies remain unaffected, the theorem from welfare theory tells us that recipients are at least as well off, but very likely are better off, under direct cash transfers than under in-kind transfer programs of equal market value.[4] The value a recipient puts on the transfers he receives differs, therefore, according to the form in which they are given. In the next section, a measure of the evaluation by recipients of the various transfer programs is developed that takes the form of the transfer into account.

Range of Benefit Weights

For all practical purposes, income (and/or wealth) rather than utility obtained seems to be the only manageable measure of benefits. Accepting income as a measure of welfare means that the value to recipients of cash subsidies is equal to their money value, but that, for measurement purposes, in-kind transfer expenditures will need to be transformed by appropriate weights into the same units. To express in-kind benefits in income-equivalent units, that cash transfer has to be derived that would leave the recipient's welfare unaffected, if the in-kind programs were to be discontinued and the cash transfer simultaneously substituted.[5] The

[4] The welfare theoretical argument follows the salvageable part of the standard pre-Little argument concerning the superiority of an income over an excise tax. It will be assumed throughout that indifference curve maps are convex.

Irrational behavior, lack of information, and, especially, multi-person households where budget decisions are made by "proxy," may lead to a nonmaximizing use of income. This gives rise to the argument that in-kind transfers may yield higher benefits to recipient units than do cash programs. But, unless it can be shown that recipient budget decisions are systematically inferior to those of nonrecipients (from the individual spending unit's point of view), this objection applies to all households and would necessitate adjustments in the valuation of national income in general.

[5] By analogy to the taxpayer benefit evaluation (see footnote 3), it could be objected that recipient benefits of in-kind programs should be evaluated according to the marginal cash transfer necessary to compensate for a marginal reduction of in-kind

benefit weight to be applied by each recipient to each transfer bundle received will be the ratio of that recipient's evaluation of his transfer benefits (the welfare equivalent cash transfer) to the cost to taxpayers of those transfers. (The benefit weights must be computed simultaneously for the entire bundle of programs in which a recipient participates. The reason benefit weights cannot be computed program by program is explained in the appendix to this chapter.)

THE BENEFIT WEIGHT CAN BE GREATER THAN UNITY

In general, the benefit weight is *at most* equal to unity, with two possible exceptions. If recipients are unable to purchase the commodities being transferred at market prices due to recipient-specific market imperfections (such as racial discrimination) *and* if the in-kind program alleviates this kind of supply discrimination, the benefit weights may exceed unity. This might be the case when the price faced by recipients, even without a subsidy, is lower under the in-kind program than under a cash transfer program. A similar situation occurs when program expenditures are less than the market value of the in-kind transfer. For example, the government may be more efficient than the market, or it may command resources at lower-than-market prices. In these cases, the effective reduction in market prices (the effective subsidy) faced by recipients may be larger than the nominal subsidy provided by taxpayers. The theorem, which is based on the market value of commodities, need no longer hold. Of course, if a government is less efficient than the private sector, or if the government pursues (costly) secondary objectives with those programs, the benefit weight may be less than implied by the theorem.

Until stated otherwise, the market values of subsidies will be assumed to equal program expenditures, regardless of the form in which the transfer is given.

THE BENEFIT WEIGHT CAN BE UNITY

With these qualifications, the benefit weight reaches its upper limit of unity when it is cash that is transferred. Under certain conditions, the benefit weight may equal unity for in-kind program expenditures as well. To informally explore those conditions, assume that a recipient consumes

---

programs, if consistency with the evaluation of other goods is to be maintained. But recipients do not have the option to substitute equivalent cash transfers for in-kind transfers at the margin; that is, for recipients in-kind programs are of the all-or-nothing type, and the "average" evaluation of marginal and inframarginal program units, as outlined previously, is legitimate.

only two goods, one of them being subject to an in-kind program. The benefit weight is unity, if one of the following conditions prevails:

1. The other commodity is a perfect substitute for the subsidized good (that is, the indifference curves between them are linear). This will be true whether or not there are restrictions on the quantity of the subsidized commodity that any individual may consume.[6]
2. At the other extreme, the indifference curves between the program commodity and the other good are rectangular, and the program imposes no restrictions on the quantity of the subsidized commodity consumed that would force the recipient to consume excess quantities for which he has no use.
3. The program restricts consumption of the subsidized good to the exact quantity the recipient would have consumed had he received the market value of the implied subsidy as a cash transfer.
4. The program restricts consumption of the subsidized commodity to less than the quantity just mentioned, but the recipient is free to purchase additional units at market prices and does so. The subsidy then applies only to inframarginal units.

Furthermore, if both commodities are subject to an in-kind program, the benefit weight is unity, if

5. Both goods are subsidized at the same rate, and quantity restrictions are absent.[7]

THE BENEFIT WEIGHT CAN BE NEGATIVE

A sufficient condition for the lower limit of the benefit weight to exceed zero is that the recipient purchase as much as he wishes at the subsidized price and that he purchase some positive amount. Even if there are quantity restrictions in the program, the benefit weights are certain to be nonnegative, if recipients are free to opt out of in-kind programs. In the absence of this option, negative benefit weights are theoretically possible. They occur if the quantity prescribed forces the recipient to a point that lies outside his pre-transfer budget constraint but below his pre-transfer indifference curve surface.[8]

[6] By consumption restriction we mean that the recipient is required to purchase a certain quantity of the commodity, which may exceed or fall short of the amount he desires at the subsidized price.
[7] For policy implications, it should be noted that the recipient's consumption pattern in cases 2–5 is identical to the pattern that would have resulted had the in-kind transfer been given in the form of a direct cash subsidy.
[8] A point above the pre-transfer budget constraint implies positive program cost, that

A procedure for deriving the benefit weights and a formal statement of the independent variables that enter the weights, and the various characteristics of public programs that influence them, are presented in the appendix to this chapter. We turn now to policy implications.

Significance of the Benefit Weight Calculations

Since benefit weights can range from negative values[9] to values in excess of unity, the program cost attributable to recipients may bear no relationship to their cash equivalent. Using expenditure data to measure the welfare benefits of in-kind programs can be not only misleading but biased. Unless benefit weights turn out to be close to unity, the redistributive effect of recipient in-kind benefits should be measured in terms of the welfare equivalent cash transfer.[10]

The welfare equivalent cash transfer measure is important not only to judge the extent of redistribution: It is also necessary to design transfer programs that promote horizontal and vertical equity and that stimulate work effort. For example, the effective tax rates faced by recipients cannot be derived by looking at the change in expenditures on behalf of recipients when their earned income or income from transfers changes. This is true—as should now be clear—when the program bundle leads to a nonunitary benefit weight. It is also true, however, when the income change modifies the program bundle in a way that alters the benefit weight, and a change in any one program may very well influence the evaluation of the others. Suppose an aged public housing tenant receiving Food Stamps gets an increase in his Social Security payments. His benefit weight may change because of his getting more cash, and/or because his rent payments and the cost of his Food Stamps increase.

Similarly, adding program cost to recipient income before a uniform negative income tax schedule is applied may not lead to equity, because

is, the denominator of the benefit weight is positive. A point below the pre-transfer indifference surface implies a negative welfare-equivalent cash transfer; that is, the numerator of the benefit weight is negative.

[9] If "free" education combined with high minimum school attendance laws were the only major program open to some recipients, a negative benefit weight might be more than just a theoretical possibility.

[10] If program costs deviate from recipient benefits, the equivalent cash transfer measure makes a revision of national accounting procedures necessary. The present authors have suggested a procedure to eliminate the valuation imbalances resulting from various in-kind programs. (Cf. L. Stiefel, E. Smolensky, and M. Schmundt, "Modifications for In-Kind Transfer Entries in the National Income Accounts," The Impact of Selected Programs on the Distribution of Income, Working Paper No. 7 (University of Wisconsin, 1972).)

cash and various in-kind program combinations need not be evaluated by the recipients in the same way.

Furthermore, the sequential application of tax rates to various transfers, with ceiling below 100 percent, does not guarantee an overall tax ceiling of less than 100 percent, if in-kind programs are present and tax payments are based on program cost.[11] Finally, it will make a difference whether the "tax" consists of a loss in in-kind benefits or disposable cash income.

Consequently, the two most important questions for which the accurate measurement of benefit weights will provide an answer are these:

1. Is the structure of in-kind programs such as to cause benefit weights to approach unity for a large group of recipients, thereby mitigating the major problem connected with the integration of cash and in-kind transfer programs?[12]
2. If deviations of benefit weights from unity do occur and cannot be ignored, is there a systematic relationship between the size of these deviations and socioeconomic characteristics of the different recipient groups? In particular, does there exist a relationship between the benefit weight and recipient income, defined on either a before- or an after-tax and cash-transfer basis?

The present state of ignorance about specific program characteristics, about how the benefits of each program are allocated, and about the extent to which families participate in several in-kind programs permits only a guess as to the answers to these questions. In the following paragraphs, some general considerations are discussed that may aid intuition and facilitate the actual benefit weight calculations, and that indicate the significance of different answers to the two questions just posed.

Unless a recipient is made worse off by being forced to consume an excessive amount of some commodity at high cost to himself (for example, perhaps compulsory education), there is always some nonnegative differ-

---

[11] See Thad W. Mirer, Chapter 5, for an analysis of the effects of sequencing programs.

[12] Henry J. Aaron and George von Furstenberg ("The Inefficiencies of Transfers in Kind: The Case of Housing Assistance," *Western Economic Journal* 9 (June 1971): 184–191) show that the benefit weight for public housing programs is quite close to unity. They use a two-commodity model (housing services and all other goods) and derive a weight of .96 if a Cobb–Douglas utility function is employed and housing service expenditures amount to 25 percent of recipient incomes. Their high benefit weight is mainly because the restriction on the consumption of housing services by recipients comes quite close to what recipients would have consumed had the housing program cost been distributed as direct income transfers. It should be remembered, though, that single-program benefit weight calculations might be quite inaccurate for multiple program recipients.

ential between market values and the cost to the government for these programs that would result in a unitary benefit weight. Even though a recipient may value his in-kind program bundle at less than its market value, he may regard it as equivalent to an equal-cost cash transfer, if the government provides this program bundle at a cost sufficiently below the market price. For example, low-income families may have limited access to the mortgage or health insurance markets; that is, they may face high prices for these services in the market. Under these circumstances, recipients of subsidies under Section 235 of the National Housing Act or Medicaid may not only derive benefits from the nominal government subsidy, but they may also experience a decline in presubsidy mortgage interest or implicit health insurance premiums, such that the distortion caused by the relative subsidy may be compensated for by improvements in availability. In addition, among the five cases listed under "Range of Benefit Weights" that would lead to a benefit weight of unity under the condition that market values equal program cost, only case 1, where goods are perfect substitutes, can be excluded a priori. The other cases may—singly, or in combination—cause benefit weights to come considerably closer to unity than the high single-program subsidy rates might lead one to expect.

Since all programs applicable to a certain recipient are evaluated simultaneously, distortions caused by a subsidy that tends to lower the benefit weight for a single program may be partly offset, because the recipient can purchase other goods at subsidized prices as well. Suppose a family receives an amount of Food Stamps that commits it to a higher level of food consumption than it would have desired if it had received the Food Stamp subsidy in cash. This implies a benefit weight of less than unity. But if, in addition, the family is eligible for public housing, it may be that the benefit weight for the two-program package will rise due to the increase in the desired food consumption, and both subsidies may have been converted, de facto, into a cash transfer. It follows that one way that may be open to governments if they wish to raise the benefit weights of existing programs is to increase the number of programs and the number of goods subsidized.

Furthermore, for certain recipient groups, the quantity restrictions imposed by in-kind programs may be such that recipients supplement their consumption of program commodities at market prices, which means that only intramarginal units are subsidized. This will lead to a unitary benefit weight as long as government is neither more nor less efficient than the private sector in providing the goods. For example, the value of Food Stamps a family receives may buy a smaller amount of food than the family would have wanted under a cost-equivalent cash transfer or (even simpler) than it would have consumed without the food subsidy. In this case, the family would spend at least the value of the stamps on food anyway, so that the subsidy simply frees the value of the in-kind transfer for whatever the family wishes to buy.

The government can raise the benefit weights by appropriately limiting the quantity of goods subsidized. For every set of subsidies confronting a recipient, there exists a set of quantity restrictions that will leave him indifferent between his in-kind transfer and a cash transfer of equal cost. If this set of restrictions is chosen by the government, the benefit weight will be unity. That is, for every set of subsidies confronting a recipient, there exists a set of quantity restrictions that will leave him indifferent between his in-kind transfers and a cash transfer equal to the cost of the in-kind transfer he receives, unless government cost exceeds market values. For example, while the benefit weight for a family receiving an open-ended food and rent subsidy will almost certainly be less than unity, the government can convert the food subsidy into an outright cash subsidy by making the Food Stamp value low enough; and it can offer a particular public housing apartment at a particular subsidy such that the family would rent the same kind of apartment (and, of course, eat the same amount of food) had both in-kind subsidies been given in the form of cash.

Finally, the mix of commodities that the very poor would buy at different relative prices (real income held constant) may be very similar, so that budget distortions caused by subsidy, as such, are of no practical consequence. Under these conditions, a unitary benefit weight would result, if subsidies are de facto open-ended. In sum, benefit weights in the neighborhood of unity may not be uncommon for a considerable number of recipient groups.

Whether a systematic relationship exists between the benefit weights and recipient income levels is an empirical matter. Theoretically, the influence of income on the benefit weight is composed of conflicting tendencies. On the one hand, poorer recipients are likely to be eligible for a larger number of programs and, hence, substitution effects may be small and the benefit weights large. In addition, the substitution possibilities open to poorer recipients may be very limited, in which case de facto open-ended subsidies come close to equal-value cash transfers; and programs with some maximum subsidized quantity are more likely to be de facto open-ended for recipients with low consumption levels.

On the other hand, subsidy rates of certain programs are inversely correlated with income, which will, ceteris paribus, increase the price distortion and thus decrease the benefit weight. Quantity restrictions that prescribe certain minimum consumption levels will tend to lower the benefit weight as well, if they are fixed at relatively high levels. The reason is twofold. The relatively lower substitutability of commodities for poorer recipients makes high prescribed consumption levels of a few commodities comparatively worthless to them. And it is less likely that poorer recipients will supplement or be on the verge of supplementing those subsidized quantities by purchases at market prices.

If these latter factors outweigh the former, benefit weights rise with income. That is, recipient benefits per unit of program expenditures may decline as income declines, and in-kind programs may not only be less redistributive overall but also less progressive within the lower end of the income scale than appears when program costs are allocated by income class. Viewed from the other side, it is probable that the desired distribution of welfare can be achieved with a higher implicit tax rate than would be the case if benefit weights were constant across income classes.

Since benefit weights close to unity may not be exceptional, some further implications of this case should be pointed out. Benefit weights may be unitary for two reasons. Either recipient and program characteristics are such that the recipient evaluates in-kind programs at their market value and government cost equals market values, or the recipient evaluates in-kind programs at less than their market value but government cost is sufficiently lower to make him indifferent between those programs and a cost-equivalent cash transfer. Although it does not matter, for purposes of measurement, why a certain benefit weight is what it is, the two cases need to be distinguished for the following reason.

In recent years, the benefits of redistribution activities to donors who are either taxpayers or private charitable donors have received increasing attention.[13] In-kind transfers have been justified by postulating that donor utility levels depend not only on the overall welfare (income) of recipients but on certain aspects of the recipient's consumption behavior as well.[14] That is, a recipient's possible evaluation of in-kind transfers at less than their cost is compensated for by the additional benefits accruing to donors due to the direct influence on the recipient's consumption pattern.

A benefit weight of unity means that recipients are indifferent between the bundle of in-kind transfers and a cash subsidy of equal cost. But, in addition, it can be shown that the consumption level and structure of these recipients are exactly what they would have been under a cost-

---

[13] Cf. Harold M. Hochman and James D. Rodgers, "Pareto Optimal Redistribution," *American Economic Review* 59 (Part 1, September 1969): 542–557 and subsequent discussion.

[14] See, for example, David B. Johnson, "Some Fundamental Economics of the Charity Market," in *Economics of Charity* (Blacksburg, Va.: Center for the Study of Public Choice, 1970), p. 94; Edgar O. Olsen, "A Normative Theory of Transfers," *Public Choice* 6 (Spring 1969): 42; Edgar O. Olsen, "Some Theorems in the Theory of Efficient Transfers," *Journal of Political Economy* 79 (January/February 1971): 166–176; Mark Pauly, "Efficiency in the Provision of Consumption Subsidies," *Kyklos* 23 (1970): 33–57; Joseph D. De Salvo, "A Methodology for Evaluating Housing Programs," *Journal of Regional Science* 2 (1971): 178–179.

equivalent cash transfer as long as government cost and market prices, that is, effective and nominal subsidies, are the same.[15] The reason is simply that, if the government is neither more nor less efficient than the private sector, a unitary benefit weight is possible only if in-kind programs actually do have the same effect as a value-equivalent cash transfer. An important corollary to this proposition is that the benefit weight must be less than unity, if—from the donor's point of view—a desirable recipient consumption response is to be achieved efficiently when the externalities are caused by certain items of a recipient's consumption bundle and not by the income differential as such.[16] Consequently, if benefit weights turn out to be close to unity, in-kind programs cannot be justified by the Pareto optimal distribution literature, since donors would have no interest in maintaining the in-kind program bundle, which is presumably more expensive to administer than a consolidated cash transfer program. Hence, either in-kind transfers should be terminated or the professional discussion about in-kind transfers should return to where it was in 1968, when a variety of reasons other than the consumption response of recipients were suggested to explain the persistence of in-kind transfers.

Acknowledgments

We are grateful to the Ford Foundation for the bulk of the financial assistance required to carry out this research and for further financial assistance from the Institute for Research on Poverty at the University of Wisconsin, Madison, pursuant to the provisions of the Economic Opportunity Act of 1964. The opinions expressed herein are solely those of the authors.

Appendix

Deriving the Benefit Weights

Some Basic Conceptual Problems

Deriving a system of benefit weights for each transfer for each recipient poses several conceptual problems.

1. Since the welfare-equivalent cash transfer has to be determined, the use of indifference maps and, thus, utility functions cannot be avoided. Since only the

[15] If, on the other hand, a unitary benefit weight is due to the fact that government costs fall short of market prices, the recipient's consumption structure will not be the same under in-kind and cost-equivalent cash programs.
[16] This corollary is implicitly contained in Pauly, "Consumption Subsidies," an article on optimal consumption subsidies.

shape, not the utility index, of the indifference surfaces matters, we need only to choose among classes of utility functions, where a class is defined as a set of utility functions that can be derived from one another by monotonic transformations. But, unless the choice among classes of utility functions is shown to have little influence on the derived benefit weights, or a certain class of utility functions turns out to be particularly suitable, an arbitrary element is thereby introduced.[17]

For practical purposes, the utility function and its parameters have to be asssumed identical for all recipients. A feasible exception to this rule may be to calculate different parameter estimates for recipient units that differ in location (for example, central city, urban, rural), size, age composition, and race.

2. Even if utility functions are assumed to be the same for all recipients, the welfare weight appropriate to any in-kind transfer depends on the recipient's income level, ceteris paribus. If all in-kind programs consisted of outright price subsidization without any restrictions on the amounts consumed by recipients, only utility functions that imply homothetic indifference curve systems would make the welfare weight invariant with respect to income. If, however, all recipients are required to consume the same amount of the subsidized good, the welfare weight would be the same for recipients with different income levels only if marginal utilities were constant for all goods except the commodity subject to the consumption restriction. Clearly, there is no utility function that could guarantee this invariance for a bundle of programs with different characteristics. This means that recipients have to be disaggregated into income classes to compute the appropriate benefit weights, even if they are subject to identical programs.

3. Since different groups of recipients are subject to different bundles of in-kind programs, the simplest procedure would be to derive the benefits for each group as the weighted sum of the program expenditures applicable to this group. In addition, this method would simplify the task of determining the effect of program changes and program additions. Unfortunately, such a procedure is inadmissible, since the benefit weight of any one program for any group depends on what other transfers are received by the group.

Computing the benefit weights of every program for each recipient income class on the basis of the assumption that either no other programs are in effect, or the other programs do exist, may either under- or overstate the aggregate recipient benefits from the actual bundle of transfer programs.[18] Hence, for every recipient

[17] Computational feasibility and data requirements drastically restrict the feasible classes of utility functions. Since we have no direct information about utility function parameters, we have to infer those parameters from demand or expenditure data. This means that the utility function chosen must not only be characterized by parameter economy, it must also lead to a very simple system of demand or expenditure relations such that reasonable parameter estimates or guesses are possible, in spite of the poor quality of budget data for low-income families.

[18] Aggregate recipient benefits are likely to be understated if the bundle of subsidies affects commodities that are mainly substitutes for each other. Loosely speaking and ceteris paribus, the benefit weight is larger, the smaller the substitution effect, and the substitution effect is reduced as more substitutes are subsidized at similar rates. Consequently, the weighted average of program-by-program benefit weights may be smaller than the benefit weight attached to the program bundle as a whole (cf. footnote 3).

Alternatively, aggregate benefits may be overstated if the bundle of subsidies

202 / Maria Schmundt / Eugene Smolensky / Leanna Stiefel

group within each recipient income class that is subjected to different bundles of programs, a separate benefit weight has to be derived. Moreover, for each program change, the same procedure has to be followed for the new program bundles, since the change will affect the benefit weight attached to the old bundle components.[19] Thus, recipient benefits accruing to each recipient group must be calculated simultaneously for all transfer programs.[20]

The Formal Statement

Formally, the computation of the benefit weights would proceed as follows:

All recipient families e, $e = 1, \ldots, M$, are assumed to have the same utility function,[21] with the vector $X_e = (X_{1e}, \ldots, X_{Ne})$ as argument, where X_{ie}, $i = 1, \ldots, N$, $e = 1, \ldots, M$, is the amount of commodity i consumed by recipient e, that is,

(1) $$U_e = U(X_{ie}, \ldots, X_{Ne}) = U(X_e) \qquad e = 1, \ldots, M.$$

Each recipient e has a certain actual net income, excluding direct taxes paid and including cash transfers received, y_e, $e = 1, \ldots, M$, to be spent on the N commodities. And each recipient is confronted by a vector of market prices and some

---

affects largely complementary goods. If we regard this bundle of complementary goods as one composite commodity, the effective subsidy on this commodity is low and, thus, the benefit weights, high, if they are computed on a program-by-program basis. But the cumulative effect of the bundle of subsidies raises the effective subsidization of the composite commodity. And, in general, the benefit weight declines as the effective subsidy increases. Consequently, the benefit weight attached to the program bundle may be lower than the weighted average of the program-by-program benefit weights.

[19] To give an example: Suppose that all but one item in a recipient's budget is subsidized at the same rate and that there are no restrictions on the quantity he can demand. Suppose further that the benefit weight for this program bundle is less than unity. If the last item is now subsidized as well (at the same rate), the benefit weight of this change is at most unity, whether it is computed on the basis of the existence or nonexistence of the other programs. This implies that, after the addition of the new in-kind transfer, recipient benefits are still less than the market value of the new program bundle, though we know that the new program bundle is completely equivalent to a cash transfer.

[20] This means that the increasing number of studies that try to measure recipient benefits of various in-kind programs, concentrating on one program at a time, cannot be used to determine the redistributive effect of the existing set of in-kind transfers unless it can be shown that, as a matter of fact, the aggregation of program-by-program results comes close to the benefit measures based on program bundles.

[21] If the number and age of family members or some other characteristics influence the budget pattern of recipients in the same income class considerably, the utility function parameters should be estimated separately for different family unit characteristics, if the data available permit such a procedure.

bundle of in-kind programs. These programs may influence the recipient's consumption decisions in several ways:[22]

1. They will reduce the prices of certain commodities to the recipient. If $p = (p_1, \ldots, p_N)$ is the (constant) vector of market prices in the absence of in-kind programs—assumed to be the same for all recipients[23]—a recipient e faces a price vector $p (1 - S_e) = [p_1(1 - S_{1e}), \ldots, P_N(1 - S_{Ne})]$, where $S_{ie} \times 100$ is the effective percentage price reduction for commodity i, $i = 1, \ldots, N$, to recipient e, $e = 1, \ldots, M$, and $1 \geqslant S_{ie} \geqslant 0$.[24] Which elements of the subsidy vector S_e are nonzero depends on the programs in which recipient e participates.

2. Recipient e may be required to consume certain minimum quantities of program commodities and cannot or does not wish to supplement these fixed subsidized quantities by additional purchases at market prices (for example, public housing or, possibly, Food Stamps). That is, there may exist some subset K_e of the N goods for which $X_{ke} = \overline{X}_{ke}$, $k \epsilon K_e$, where $\overline{X}_{ke}$ is the quantity of commodity k to which recipient e is effectively committed. Which goods will belong to this category, and the size of $\overline{X}_{ke}$, will depend on specified characteristics of the program and recipient unit e.

3. Related to the group of commodities K_e—but with very different consequences for the benefit weights—are goods for which the quantities subsidized are administratively fixed on the basis of recipient unit e's characteristics, but recipient e has the option *and* the desire to supplement these quantities by additional purchases at market prices. This possibility may occur either if the subsidized consumption levels are prescribed to the recipient (for example, the commodity distribution program) or if there is a certain maximum subsidized consumption level (for example, subsidized mortgage rates). That is, for some subset L_e of the N commodities ($L_e \neq K_e$), we have $X_{le} > \overline{X}_{le}$, $l \epsilon L_e$, where X_{le} is the actual consumption of good l by recipient e and $\overline{X}_{le}$ is the (smaller) subsidized amount. Since the recipient pays $p_l(1 - S_{le})$ for the inframarginal units X_{le} and p_l for the marginal units, that is, for any amount exceeding $\overline{X}_{le}$, the effect of these programs is equivalent to giving recipient e an outright cash transfer of $\sum\limits_{l \epsilon L_e} p_l S_{le} \overline{X}_{le}$, while commodities $l \epsilon L_e$ should be

[22] Throughout, we assume implicitly that the effect of in-kind programs is to change the budget constraints but not the commodity space or the preferences of recipients. Clearly, some government-provided goods are substantially different from their market counterparts, which would require an expansion of the commodity space. And in-kind programs very likely do influence preference patterns. But to take these aspects into account would severely impair implementation.

[23] Data permitting, this assumption can be relaxed. Some locational differentiation seems important and feasible. In addition to the problem of finding the market prices of certain goods, these prices may not be the same to recipients and nonrecipients as well as among recipient groups with different socioeconomic characteristics. But it is likely that many of these latter differences are sufficiently captured by the locational variable.

[24] Note that S_{ie} is the effective subsidy rate, computed on the basis of the price faced by the recipient in the absence of in-kind programs (p_i), not the nominal subsidy rate (S'_{ie}) based on the postprogram, presubsidy price of the commodity (p'_i), which may differ due to direct or indirect government provision. The relation between the two price subsidies is given by $p_i S_{ie} = p'_i S'_{ie} + (p_i - p'_i)$.

regarded as nonsubsidized. Again, whether or not some program commodity is a member of set L_e, and the size of $\overline{X}_{le}$, will depend on recipient and program characteristics.

4. Finally, there are those commodities for which the subsidy is actually or de facto open-ended. De facto open-ended subsidies occur if recipient e has the option *and* wishes to consume less than some maximum subsidized quantities at the subsidized prices (for example, subsidized mortgage rates for low-income families). Together with commodities for which recipient e cannot or does not claim subsidization, these goods constitute the remaining set of commodities $(N - K_e - L_e)$.[25]

It follows from the preceding discussion that recipient e maximizes his utility function (equation (1)) subject to the following constraints:

$$(2) \qquad y_e + \sum_{l \epsilon L_e} p_l S_{le} \overline{X}_{le} = \sum_{i \epsilon (N - K_e - L_e)} p_i (1 - S_{ie}) X_{ie} + \sum_{k \epsilon K_e} p_k (1 - S_{ke}) X_{ke} + \sum_{l \epsilon L_e} p_l X_{le}$$

$$(3) \qquad X_{ke} = \overline{X}_{ke} \quad \text{for all} \quad k \epsilon K_e, e = 1, \ldots, M,$$

where

$$S_{ie} \geqslant 0, \quad i \epsilon (N - K_e - L_e); \quad S_{le} > 0, \quad l \epsilon L_e; \quad S_{ke} > 0, \quad k \epsilon K_e.$$

The (indirect) utility function resulting from this maximization can then be expressed in terms of known parameters:

$$(4) \qquad U_e = V(y_e, p, S_e, \overline{X}_L, \overline{X}_K), \quad e = 1, \ldots, M.$$

To determine the income necessary to make recipient e as well off as under the in-kind programs, Y_e, we compute the indirect utility function, which results from the maximization of equation (1) subject to a budget constraint involving pre-program market prices faced by the recipient:

$$(2') \qquad Y_e = \sum_{j \epsilon N} p_j X_{je}, \quad e = 1, \ldots, M,$$

that is,

$$(5) \qquad U_e = V(Y_e, p).$$

Equate (4) and (5) and solve for the only unknown, Y_e. Consequently, recipient e's evaluation of the in-kind programs is measured as $Y_e - y_e$. That is, $(Y_e - y_e)$ represents the cash transfer that could be substituted for the bundle of in-kind transfers without changing the welfare of recipient e, and constitutes the numerator of the benefit weight.

[25] Although of vital importance for the magnitude of benefit weights, the distinction between group K_e, L_e, and $(N - K_e - L_e)$ commodities creates considerable difficulties. The reason is that, in many cases, the classification will depend on recipient e's utility maximization itself. That is, for many program commodities, we do not know a priori which group they belong to. For a diagrammatic exposition of various cases of program restrictions, cf. Olsen, "Some Theorems."

The denominator of the benefit weight is given by the cost of the in-kind programs incurred on behalf of recipient e:

$$(6) \quad T_e = \overset{i\epsilon}{\underset{(N-K_e-L_e)}{\sum}} p'_i S'_{ie} X_{ie} + \underset{k\epsilon K_e}{\overset{\Sigma}{R}} p' S'_{ke} \overline{X}_{ke} + \underset{l\epsilon L_e}{\overset{\Sigma}{}} p'_l S'_{le} \overline{X}_{le}$$

$$= \overset{i\epsilon}{\underset{(N-K_e-L_e)}{\sum}} [p_i S_{ie} + (p'_i - p_i)] X_{ie} +$$

$$\underset{k\epsilon K_e}{\overset{\Sigma}{}} [p_k S_{ke} + (p'_k - p_k)] \overline{X}_{ke} + \underset{l\epsilon L_e}{\overset{\Sigma}{}} [p_l S_{le} + (p'_l - p_l)] \overline{X}_{le},$$

where p_j is the market price in the absence of the program, p'_j the pre-subsidy price in the presence of in-kind programs, S_{je} is the effective subsidy, S'_{je} the nominal subsidy rate, $j = 1, \ldots , N$. Aggregation of equation (6) over all recipients results in the total expenditures on in-kind programs, that is, the total cost of in-kind programs to taxpayers.

As long as in-kind programs consist of outright market price subsidization without direct or indirect government provision, $p'_j = p_j$ and thus $S'_{je} = S_{je}$, $j = 1, \ldots , N$, and T_e represents the difference between the income a recipient would need in order to purchase the same bundle of goods as under the in-kind programs paying market prices and the recipient's actual cash income, sufficient to purchase this bundle at subsidized prices.

If, alternatively, in-kind programs combine subsidization with direct or indirect government provision, p'_j may not be equal to p_j, and the preceding definition of T_e may no longer hold. The program cost attributable to recipient e can exceed or fall short of the income change necessary to enable recipient e to purchase the same bundle of goods in the absence of in-kind programs.[26]

Given the in-kind program cost attributable to recipient e, the benefit weight that will transform the cost into this cash equivalent is

$$(7) \quad E_e = \frac{(Y_e - y_e)}{T_e} = E(y_e, p, p', S_e, \overline{X}_{Ke}, \overline{X}_{Le}), \quad e = 1, \ldots , M.$$

If recipients can opt out of in-kind programs, E_e is nonnegative.[27] A sufficient, though not necessary, condition for E_e not to exceed unity is that $p' \geqslant p$.

[26] In the case of public housing, for example, p'_j exceeds p_j, possibly because of side effects or subsidiary goals unrelated to redistribution. On the other hand, any program-related improvement in the availability of commodities to recipients will, ceteris paribus, be reflected in a negative $(p'_i - p_j)$ differential. Some insurance-type programs might lead to a price decline due to the risk-reducing effect of large-scale coverage and the absence of a profit margin. It should be noted that the nominal presubsidy program price p'_j might have to be adjusted, if indirect rationing occurs caused by supply limitations of the program commodity.

[27] We labeled the benefit weight E because E is often described as the "efficiency ratio" of in-kind transfer programs, since it is the ratio of the recipient's valuation of his in-kind transfers (which is equal to the taxpayer cost of the welfare-equivalent cash transfer) and the government resource cost of the program expenditures (which is equal to the taxpayer cost of the in-kind program); the percentage "inefficiency" of in-kind transfers usually is measured as $I = 1 - E$, where I is the ratio of the valuation difference and total program expenditures. If there are nonrecipient benefits associated with in-kind transfers, both these labels are misleading.

Relation (7) implies that E_e will differ among groups of recipients even if they live in the same location (identical p and p' vectors) and even though the U-functions and, thus, the E-functions are assumed to be the same. First, initial net income, y_e, may differ. Second, vectors S_e, $\overline{X}_{K_e}$, and $\overline{X}_{L_e}$ may vary from one recipient to another, not only because of y_e differences—which may influence the commodity classification—but because recipients participate in different programs. In addition, regional and urban–rural differences will influence p and p', which may lead to further variations in the benefit weight.

If it turns out that there is little correlation between the level of y_e and the magnitude of the benefit weight, E_e, even after a geographical (for example, by state) and urban–rural disaggregation is carried out, general statements about the redistributive effect of in-kind programs by income class become virtually impossible.

To answer the extremely important political questions, recipients have to be aggregated into groups that are relatively homogeneous with respect to the independent variables and parameters that enter the benefit weight computation, that is, with respect to the following characteristics: (1) size, age composition, race, and possibly urban–rural location, if utility functions are assumed to vary according to these characteristics; (2) net income, excluding in-kind transfers, that is, income after direct taxes, but including cash transfers; and (3) bundles of in-kind programs received and their specific characteristics, like pre- and posttransfer prices, effective or nominal subsidies, consumption restrictions and their effectiveness.

If a cross-classification of family units by these three criteria results in small cell populations, especially if there is little correlation between (2) and (3), after a disaggregation according to (1) has been carried out, the computation and usefulness of benefit weights are severely hampered. The practical problem of calculating a large number of benefit weights would be less serious than the policy implications of small cells. Only if it could be shown that benefit weights are close to unity for a large majority of cell populations could an acceptable policy conclusion be drawn, namely that in-kind and cash transfers should be treated alike for all practical purposes as far as recipients are concerned. But legislators would be unwilling to take significant benefit weight differences into account, unless they were strongly correlated with socioeconomic characteristics like (1) and (2). This means that important horizontal and vertical equity considerations may be disregarded.

At this stage, any discussion about cell sizes and patterns is hypothetical because little relevant information is available. Information about in-kind program overlaps generally, let alone by recipient characteristics, is practically nonexistent. The link between (3) and (1) plus (2) is established via the eligibility rules. These rules may vary widely from state to state, so that disaggregation by state becomes mandatory. Apart from the use of subsidiary criteria for eligibility, the income definitions employed do not correspond to (2) and may differ from one program to another. Furthermore, eligibility need not imply that the good is available to the recipient.

This brings us to the more particular data problems, such as: What are the effective prices a recipient group in a certain location faces in the absence and presence of in-kind programs, if these programs cause quality or availability changes? Should the effective subsidy implied by health programs be measured on the basis of "units of health insurance" or "units of medical services"? How do effective or nominal subsidies and consumption restrictions vary with recipient characteristics?

How do we find out whether program consumption restrictions are effective or ineffective?

Savings by recipients have been ignored thus far. To derive the redistributive effect of in-kind programs, y_e and Y_e may be defined as income net of savings, since the only arguments in the utility function (equation (1)) are commodity quantities consumed during a certain time period. Consequently, the limiting variable in the budget constraints (equations (2) and (2')) is not income, but income minus current saving plus current dissaving. That is, in our model, y_e and Y_e are implicitly defined as total expenditures on goods and services during a certain period. A consistent integration of savings decisions into the utility function and budget constraint seems to be out of the question. The two simplest ways to deal with (avoid) this difficulty are either to assume that, on the average, total expenditure equals income for low-income families, or to assume that saving or dissaving is strictly proportional to total expenditure and then adjust $(Y_e - y_e)$ correspondingly.[28]

[28] Only the first alternative is consistent with the assumption of fixed individual factor supplies.

8

The Social Security Retirement Program and Welfare Reform

Michael K. Taussig

I. Introduction

This chapter surveys the major issues involved in integrating a Social Security retirement program into an expanded income maintenance system in the United States. It is limited mainly to income maintenance issues related to retirement and the aged population. Other income maintenance programs, including the Social Security programs directed at non-aged survivors, the disabled, and the medically needy will not be discussed at all or will be treated only briefly. Thus, the chapter focuses on the Old Age Insurance (OAI) component of the total Old Age, Survivors, Disability, and Health Insurance (OASDHI) Social Security package. The separation of OAI from general Social Security requires a high degree of abstraction, but it has great practical advantages for the kind of analysis attempted in this chapter. Following the usual convention, reference to the "aged" will denote all individuals aged sixty-five and over, although, as later discussion in the chapter will note, the exact boundary between the aged and the non-aged is somewhat blurred and is an important variable in the economics of Social Security. The basic question, then, is how OAI can best be integrated into one of a number of possible general income maintenance systems.

Social Security in the United States is difficult to disentangle from welfare because, in its present form, it serves two related but distinct functions, one of which overlaps with the basic function of welfare. For example, OAI partially replaces the earnings of individuals when they retire, whatever their income level, but, at the same time, it heavily weights its benefit formula to redistribute income among the aged to those retirees presumed to be most needy. The first of these functions may be called *earnings replacement* and the second *income support*.[1] The income support function of OAI inevitably overlaps with existing welfare programs that provide cash or in-kind income support for the aged poor. Once the distinction between the two functions of OAI is established, we need to decide which of the two functions is more important for social policy. I believe that both are valid and should be strengthened in any income maintenance reform. The allocation of resources between the two functions and alternative programs should be a matter for explicit, informed political choice, and any scheme for integrating OAI into a reformed income maintenance system should maximize the possibilities for intelligent social decisions about these programs. Readers who differ with me on the appropriate functions of income maintenance for the aged can readily reinterpret, according to their own views, the discussion that follows.

In the discussion, only two major alternative reforms of the present income maintenance system are considered to be relevant to OAI and the aged: (*1*) a negative income tax program, such as the plan proposed by the President's Commission on Income Maintenance Programs;[2] and (*2*) a universal demogrant, as described in Rolph's credit income tax proposal.[3] A more or less mandatory public employment program as an alternative to either a negative income tax or a demogrant, as was voted in 1972 by the Senate Finance Committee,[4] I judge to be almost completely irrelevant to this chapter. The Senate Finance Committee did not contemplate making public employment a prerequisite for the payment of cash benefits to the aged, and it seems safe to assume that making public employment mandatory for the aged will never gain significant political support. If

[1] In more traditional social insurance terminology, earnings replacement is identified with *individual equity*, while income support is identified with *social adequacy*.

[2] *Poverty amid Plenty: The American Paradox*, Report of the President's Commission on Income Maintenance Programs (Washington, D.C.: U.S. Government Printing Office, 1969).

[3] Earl R. Rolph, "The Case for a Negative Income Tax Device," *Industrial Relations* 6 (February 1967).

[4] U.S., Congress, Senate, Committee on Finance, *Social Security and Welfare Reform. Summary of the Principal Provisions of H.R. 1 as Determined by the Committee on Finance* (Washington, D.C.: U.S. Government Printing Office, 1972).

mandatory public employment programs ever do go into effect for the needy, non-aged population, they will relate to OAI only incidentally in that they will undoubtedly require some payment related to either OAI or federal civil service retirement and, thus, will marginally broaden the coverage of public retirement programs in the future. But aside from this minor connection, we can ignore the Senate Finance Committee's public employment program proposals and concentrate on the negative income tax and demogrant alternatives for income maintenance reform. The general principles involved in integrating OAI into these two types of programs could be extended easily to apply to any other general, income-conditioned alternative approaches to income maintenance reform.

Within the scope of the chapter, as just delimited, the discussion that follows covers the following topics. Part II considers the historical relationship between OAI and welfare and describes the present situation. It also surveys the general issues of costs, benefit adequacy, and economic incentives relevant to the integration of OAI into any income maintenance system. Part III then considers the major program integration problems of the present income maintenance system for the aged. The present system is based on the relationship between OAI and the Supplementary Security Income program (SSI) enacted in 1972 and effective as of January 1, 1974. (At that date, SSI replaced the state-administered Old Age Assistance program (OAA) as the basic public welfare program for the aged.) Integration problems in the present system arise because of the sharing of the income support function for the aged between the OAI and SSI programs. Preservation of the system in anything like its present state is shown to require unacceptably low benefits under SSI, relative to minimum OAI benefits. If benefits under SSI are increased to the levels required on humanitarian grounds, horizontal inequities[5] that already exist in the system would become intolerable. This unpleasant fact leads to consideration of two quite different approaches to reform of the system.

The first, sketched in Part IV, would strip OAI of its income support function and transform it into a pure earnings replacement program while either a negative income tax or a demogrant program would take over all income support responsibilities for the aged and the non-aged alike. The second alternative, discussed in Part V, would rationalize the income maintenance system for the aged within a single program by including all

---

[5] Horizontal inequity means unequal treatment of persons who are equals with respect to income and a few other characteristics related to consumption needs, such as size of the family unit. With respect to the aged, cases of horizontal inequity arise when elderly persons in identical circumstances are subject to different tax burdens or are not eligible for the same total benefits from various income maintenance programs.

the aged within an expanded OAI program while eliminating SSI for the aged and, ideally, all other public retirement programs as well (except as private-pension type supplements to the basic public retirement program). This kind of *unitary* income system for the aged would thus separate the aged from the non-aged for income support purposes in contrast to the first alternative, the *dual* system, which would combine the aged with the non-aged under either a universal negative income tax or demogrant for basic income support while dealing with earnings replacement for aged retirees through a restructured OAI program of more limited scope.

II. The Present Income Maintenance System for the Aged: An Overview

The Historical Development of OAI and OAA

The present income maintenance system for the aged in the United States dates back to the Social Security Act of 1935, which created both OAI and OAA. The intent of Congress in the initial Social Security and welfare arrangement seems to have been the creation of two separate, complementary income maintenance programs for the aged: OAI was intended to be an earnings replacement program with benefits tied closely to accumulated lifetime payments into an OAI trust fund, while OAA was supposed to be an income support program for those aged families or individuals whose own resources, including OAI benefits, were not sufficient to maintain some socially determined minimum standard of living. Thus, the world envisioned by the drafters of the 1935 legislation appears to have been comparable in broad outline to the dual income maintenance model to be discussed in Part IV. Congress apparently hoped in 1935 that OAA would gradually dwindle to a very small residual program once the OAI system matured and most aged, retired individuals became eligible for substantial OAI benefits in addition to their other sources of income.

These original arrangements were changed, however, by the first amendments to the Social Security Act in 1939.[6] The 1939 amendments considerably altered the original income maintenance system for the aged and created a new framework that has persisted, with only modest changes, down to the present time. In brief, the 1939 amendments introduced important elements of income support (social adequacy) into OAI, abandoning its original relatively strict earnings replacement (individual equity) orientation. The basic principle of tying benefits to accumulated

[6] For further details on the development of Social Security in the United States, and for references, see Joseph A. Pechman, Henry J. Aaron, and Michael K. Taussig, *Social Security: Perspectives for Reform* (Washington, D.C.: Brookings Institution, 1968).

lifetime Social Security taxes for each individual was abandoned in favor of basing benefit amounts on the average covered earnings over a minimum time period. Relatively large benefit payments, thus, could be paid sooner than under the 1935 legislation. At the same time, the system was put on a virtual cash or pay-as-you-go basis, and the plan to accumulate a large OAI trust fund was scrapped. Other aspects of the 1939 amendments and subsequent Social Security amendments since 1939 have, for the most part, reinforced the basic decision to give additional weight to the income support function of OAI at the expense of its earnings replacement function. To a large degree, the 1939 amendments were based on the stark reality that millions of aged people were manifestly needy and that the OAA program could not meet their needs because of the unwillingness and inability of the states to give OAA more than minimum financial support. The decision to make available the large OAI revenues for benefits as soon as possible was, thus, the common-sense humanitarian response, and it was further rationalized by academicians with arguments about the appropriateness of "social adequacy" in social insurance programs.

In addition, Keynesian economists could observe that the accumulation of OAI taxes in the OAI trust fund in the late 1930s served no useful function in a period when national savings already exceeded investment at a full employment level of output. Since the trust fund accumulations could not be converted into real investment, and by no stretch of the imagination could they be linked with a faster rate of economic growth, there was no sound macroeconomic reason why the OAI revenues should not have been used to support the aged, even granted an adherence to the principle of strict earnings replacement in the long run.

Thus, for understandable historical reasons, this country developed an OAI social "insurance" program that bears the major cash income support burden for the aged, while OAA and, now, SSI pick up a residual category of the aged for minimum income support. Railroad retirement (closely tied to OAI), veterans' pensions, civil service and military retirement programs, private pensions, and a very small amount of individual and group charity sources of income all play some role in the total system. Public in-kind programs, such as Medicare and Medicaid, supplement these cash income programs. An income maintenance system for the aged that was largely a response to an urgent but short-run need more than three decades ago has persisted, with very little change, until this day with the powerful support of vested interests and social inertia; OAI is now a mature system in most respects. Coverage of workers, with the important exception of government employees, is approaching the maximum limit, and most individuals approaching age sixty-five are now eligible for OAI benefits. Therefore, it is timely to reexamine the question of the optimum income maintenance system for the aged under conditions that approximate the theorist's long-run equilibrium.

The Current Dimensions of OAI and OAA

Some recent data may be helpful in establishing the dimensions of the current income maintenance system for the aged. The number of aged retired worker beneficiaries in OAI current-payment status in September 1972 was 13.0 million and the number of aged dependents and survivors was 5.1 million.[7] With the addition of 426,000 individuals receiving special transitional age seventy-two and over OAI benefits, the total number of aged individuals receiving OAI (or OASI) benefits came to 18.5 million. If we could simply add to that number the approximately 2 million individuals receiving OAA benefits and the well-over-a-million aged beneficiaries of railroad retirement programs, federal civil service retirement programs, and veterans' retirement and disability programs, the total number of aged beneficiaries of public retirement programs would exceed the approximate total of 20.9 million aged individuals in the United States in 1972. Many persons benefit from more than one such program, however, and many aged individuals received no public benefits, either because they earned enough to be made ineligible for OAI benefits by its earnings test or were not covered by OAI and had sufficient income from other sources to be ineligible for OAA benefits, or because they did not qualify for OAA benefits under the conditions established by state and local governments. The enactment of SSI presumably has eliminated the last of these circumstances and broadened the coverage of public income maintenance programs to all the needy aged. In addition to these data, which refer only to individuals aged sixty-five and over, some 2.6 million retired or disabled workers, or dependents or survivors of workers aged sixty-two to sixty-four, were receiving OASDI benefits in September 1972.

As shown by the numbers just cited, the OAI program now dominates the OAA program, but this has not always been true. In 1940, only 1.6 percent of the age sixty-five and over population was receiving OASDHI benefits as compared to 22.5 percent of this same population receiving OAA benefits. By 1950, the number receiving OASDHI benefits had grown to 20.5 percent, while the number receiving OAA benefits remained quite stable at 22.1 percent. By 1960, OASDHI benefits were going to 63.8 percent of the aged population as compared to only 13.7 percent receiving OAA benefits. As of 1971, the same percentages were

[7] *Social Security Bulletin* 36 (January 1973): 49, Table M–14. Aged survivors cannot be exactly allocated between OAI and the survivors' program of the total Social Security program.

85.3 percent for OASDHI and only 9.6 percent for OAA. In 1971, 6.2 percent of the aged population were receiving both OASDHI and OAA benefits.[8] Thus, the maturing of the OAI program has been matched by a corresponding withering away of the OAA program. The SSI program may raise the percentage of the aged on welfare, at least for a short time, both because it provides a national minimum cash income higher than the current maximum OAA benefits amounts available in some states, and because it is intended to be comprehensive in its coverage of all the needy aged.

Total OASI benefits paid in 1971 amounted to $33.4 billion, a figure that gives the approximate dimensions of the OAI program, although it includes payments to non-aged survivors.[9] On the other hand, it does not include hospital insurance (HI) benefits available to the aged. Total OASI benefits have risen very sharply in the past and are expected to continue going up at almost the same rate in the near future. Total OASI benefit payments were only $16.7 billion as recently as 1965 and are projected to rise to $61.3 billion by 1977.[10] In contrast, total OAA benefits have amounted to only about $2 billion a year recently, and the cost of SSI for the aged is projected at only $3.5 billion in 1974.[11]

But while the total cost of public income maintenance programs for the aged is very large and is going up rapidly, benefit levels under these programs do not provide incomes that allow the aged to live at the consumption standards of the non-aged in the absence of other income sources. The minimum OAI benefit amounts, even after the 1972 Social Security amendments, are only $84.50 per month for a retired worker and $126.80 for a retired worker and his wife; SSI cash benefits for the aged are only $130.00 for an individual or $195.00 for a couple. Thus, despite the huge outlays for public income maintenance programs for the aged that must be financed by taxes on the non-aged, income support for the aged does not yet guarantee them decent standards of living.

Economic Aspects of Income Maintenance for the Aged

The preceding section attempted to place the current income maintenance system for the aged in historical and statistical perspective. Now

---

[8] *Social Security Bulletin* 35 (December 1972): 73, Table Q–4.

[9] U.S., Congress, Senate, Committee on Finance, and House, Committee on Ways and Means, *Summary of Social Security Amendments of 1972. Public Law 92–603 (H.R. 1)* (Washington, D.C.: U.S. Government Printing Office, 1972), pp. 34–35, Table 4.

[10] Ibid., pp. 34–35, Table 4.

[11] Ibid., p. 43, Table 11.

let us turn to a brief, very general discussion of some economic relation-ships relevant to any reform or expansion of the system.

The ultimate goal of an income maintenance system for the aged is, of course, to maximize their well-being, subject to the constraints of attaining other urgent social objectives. The present system is far from reaching this goal. The economic status of the aged has been described quite fully in several recent studies.[12] Their major conclusion is that the aged lag far behind the non-aged in average levels of economic welfare. Adjustments of raw income data to take account of differences between the aged and the non-aged in such factors as asset holdings and size of the family unit qualify this conclusion somewhat but do not alter its basic message. Our society has not yet proved willing or able to provide a sufficient income substitute for earnings for the majority of the aged who are retired. The aged who are able and willing to continue to work are relatively young and well off, while the very aged who cannot work are in the worst financial straits. Although only about one-fourth of all aged males and less than one-tenth of all aged females were still in the labor force, data from the 1968 Survey of the Aged indicate that earnings none-theless accounted for 30 percent of the total income of all the aged in 1967.[13] Income from assets accounted for another 25 percent of the total. In contrast, Social Security benefits, the major income source for most of the aged, amounted to only 26 percent of the total in the same year.

These figures give strong support to arguments that economic incen-tives to work and to save for retirement must be preserved in any future development of the income maintenance system for the aged, even in our affluent society. If all the aged retire from work and if non-aged families do not save for retirement, public retirement programs can support the aged even at very low standards of living only at enormous cost. To pro-vide as little as $3000 per capita support for all the 20-plus million aged today would mean an income maintenance bill, for the aged alone, of over $60 billion. The tax rates on the incomes of the non-aged required to foot this bill are probably not politically feasible but, if enacted, could have a serious impact on the funding of social welfare programs for the non-aged.

[12] See, for example, Lenore E. Bixby, "Income of People Aged 65 and Older: Over-view from 1968 Survey of the Aged," *Social Security Bulletin* 33 (April 1970); Robin-son Hollister, "Income Maintenance Reform Issues with Respect to the Aged," in *Income Maintenance: Interdisciplinary Approaches to Research*, ed. Larry L. Orr, Robinson G. Hollister, and Myron J. Lefcowitz (Chicago: Markham, 1971); and Pechman, Aaron, and Taussig, *Social Security*, Ch. 2.
[13] Bixby, "Income of People Aged 65 and Older," p. 14.

A formal statement of the relationship between average OAI benefit levels, B, and the average OAI tax rate on earnings, t, may help to illustrate some facts of life concerning the costs of income maintenance for the aged. If we define W as the mean earnings of workers covered by OAI, N_W as the number of such workers, and N_B as the number of OAI retired worker beneficiaries, then we can write the following as a condition of equality between OAI taxes and benefits in a pay-as-you-go retirement system:

$$tN_WW = N_BB.$$

Solving for t, we obtain[14]

$$t = (N_B/N_W) \cdot (B/W).$$

The second equation tells us that the tax rate on earnings in a pay-as-you-go system varies directly with the ratio of retired beneficiaries to active workers and with the ratio of average benefits to average earnings. The latter ratio reflects a clear choice in redistributing incomes between the non-aged and the aged. The former ratio reflects both demographic and economic factors. The basic demographic factor is, of course, the relative size of the aged population, which depends primarily on fertility and mortality experience. The relative size of the aged population in this country is relatively insensitive to large variations in future demographic developments through the end of this century, and OAI costs are not expected to change much, for this reason, for the next three or four decades. In 1970, the aged population of 20,156,000 was 9.8 percent of the total population. Estimates of the relative size of the aged population in the year 2000 vary only between 9.6 percent (Series C projection) and 11.5 percent (Series F projection), with the former estimate based on quite high, and the latter estimates on quite low, assumptions about future fertility experience.[15] Therefore, income maintenance costs for the aged are unlikely to be greatly affected for some time by this particular variable. After the turn of the century, however, demographic factors are anticipated to raise the costs of OAI sharply.[16]

[14] Note that t in the second equation is the effective average tax rate on all covered earnings. The maximum covered earnings level for OAI taxes determines the statutory tax rate and the distribution of the tax burden among workers at different earnings levels.

[15] U.S., Bureau of the Census, "Projections of the Population of the United States, by Age and Sex: 1972 to 2020," *Current Population Reports*, Ser. P–25, No. 493 (Washington, D.C.: U.S. Government Printing Office, 1972).

[16] See the appendix on actuarial methodology in *1972 Annual Report of the Board of Trustees of the Federal Old-Age and Survivors Insurance and Disability Insurance Trust Funds* (Washington, D.C.: U.S. Government Printing Office, 1972), pp. 35–46.

Given demographic factors, the ratio of retired beneficiaries to workers in OAI, and thus the tax cost per worker to support the program, depends on economic influences. In particular, it depends on the choices aging workers make regarding the timing and extent of retirement. If all individuals aged sixty-five and over retire in the future, OAI costs will rise by between 5 and 10 percent.[17] And if all individuals aged sixty-two and over should also retire, OAI costs would go up by an additional 5 to 10 percent. Either of these very costly developments would seem to be a real possibility if we simply extrapolate into the future the past trends in the labor force participation of the aged. The latter development is probably critically related to the definition of the retirement age in OAI. Pressures have been, and continue to be, strong to redefine the age of eligibility for full OAI benefits as sixty-two, or even sixty, from the present sixty-five. On the other hand, it may be poor economics to forecast higher retirement rates for the aged in the future on the basis of past experience. In the future, the aging worker is more likely to hold a job that requires mental rather than physical skills and that is relatively pleasurable compared to complete retirement. Public policies that preserve work incentives for the aged thus could help in reversing the trend to earlier retirement and could be a significant factor in improving the relative economic status of all the aged—retirees and workers alike.

III. The Present Income Maintenance System for the Aged: The Need for Reform

The income maintenance system for the aged as of January 1, 1974, consists primarily of OAI and SSI. The first candidate for the system of tomorrow is surely the system of today, made up of these same two programs with their basic features intact, and with legislative tinkering only at the margins. Continuation of the present system would seem, on first consideration, to meet the test of political feasibility and certainly would minimize transitional difficulties. The present system has long had its critics, but much of the criticism has come from opposite ends of the political spectrum and has been mostly offsetting. Marginal changes in the system—for example, the provision of special OAI benefits for uncovered individuals aged seventy-two and over, or the progressive relaxation of the OAI earnings test—have patched up its most obvious deficiencies in the past. Furthermore, the enactment of SSI in 1972 apparently has removed

[17] The estimates in the text are based on information generously provided to the author by the Office of the Actuary of the Social Security Administration. They are subject to errors of interpretation by the author.

most of the serious objections to the old state-administered categorical welfare programs, including OAA. Paradoxically, however, the reforms of the OAA program incorporated in SSI raise questions about the rationality of the whole income maintenance system for the aged, with even more insistence than before 1972. Two closely related problems inevitably plague the present system: (*1*) It is full of severe horizontal inequities in its treatment of the low-income aged; and (*2*) its basic structure is inconsistent with the underlying ideological rationale for the OAI social insurance program.

Before elaborating on these points, it may be useful to consider in detail how the SSI and OAI programs interact. As noted previously, the new SSI program provides uniform national minimum income guarantees to all the aged. In so doing, it will tend to remove the most severe horizontal inequities across states which existed in the old OAA program and will relieve the aged poor of the vagaries of the various state welfare regulations defining eligibility. The income guarantees scheduled under SSI are relatively generous by the standards of the past—at least in the low welfare benefit states—$130.00 per month for an aged individual and $195.00 per month for an aged couple. These amounts compare favorably with the minimum OAI benefit of $84.50 per month for a single retired worker and $126.80 for a retired worker and his or her dependent spouse. Further, they are virtually equal to the special minimum OAI benefits of $127.50 for a retired worker and $191.30 for a retired worker and his or her dependent spouse with twenty-five years of covered employment. Thus, the money income guarantees provided by SSI overlap the lower tail of the OAI benefit distribution and do not lie very much below OAI median benefit levels, even in states that do not provide any cash supplements to the basic federal SSI guarantee. Overlap of welfare cash benefits and the lower tail of the OAI benefit distribution existed under the old OAA program in many states prior to the enactment of SSI in 1972. The new SSI program will continue this same program relationship and extend it for all the needy aged, uniformly, across all the states.

A hypothetical, drastically simplified example may be useful in illustrating the work incentive problems involved in the relationship between the OAI and SSI programs.[18] Suppose that, with SSI in effect, an aged couple is eligible for a combined OAI benefit of $1600 per year. Also suppose that the couple has no other sources of income, with the exception

---

[18] For a fuller discussion of the OAI and SSI relationship, see Robert I. Lerman, "Incentive Effects in Public Income Transfer Programs," in *Studies in Public Welfare*, Paper No. 4, *Income Transfer Programs: How They Tax the Poor*, U.S., Congress, Joint Economic Committee, Subcommittee on Fiscal Policy (Washington, D.C.: U.S. Government Printing Office, 1972), pp. 70–78.

of possible cash benefits under SSI and the husband's earnings. The symbols are defined as follows:

Y = net disposable income of the family.

G = maximum SSI cash benefit (= $2340 per annum).

S = maximum OAI benefit (= $1600 per annum).

E = earnings of the husband.

t_1 = implicit SSI tax rate on earnings
      (= 0 for $E \leqslant$ $780 per annum;
      = .50 for $780 < E \leqslant$ break-even level of E for SSI).[19]

t_2 = OAI earnings test tax rate on earnings
      (= 0 for $E \leqslant$ $2100 per annum;
      = .50 for $2100 < E \leqslant$ break-even level of E for OAI).

t_3 = OASDHI tax rate on earnings
      (= .0585 for $E \leqslant$ $12,000).

t_4 = federal personal income tax rate
      (= .14 plus for $E >$ $4000).

The break-even levels for earnings, or the point at which benefit payments are reduced to zero, are $5300 per annum for OAI and $5700 per annum for SSI in this example. The assumptions about federal income tax treatment of the couple are that the present tax structure continues unchanged into 1974 and that both husband and wife are age sixty-five or over and, thus, receive two personal exemptions each, and that they elect to take the low-income allowance rather than to itemize their deductions. The example is complex enough as it stands, but the reader is warned that many other details that could be relevant in many cases are ignored to preserve relative simplicity. In particular, we ignore differences in accounting periods for OAI and SSI, a factor that, in reality, makes things much more complex.

Table 8.1 defines the income possibilities facing the couple under the further assumption that the husband has discretion about whether or not, and how much, to work. Up to an earnings level of $780 per annum, the couple's net income, Y, is given by

$$Y = S + (G - S + \$240) + (1 - t_3)E.$$

That is, the OAI benefit adds to the net income of the couple only because of the $240 disregard for all unearned income provided by the SSI program. Over this range of earnings, the marginal tax rate on earnings is only the 5.85 percent OASDHI employee payroll tax rate, and the in-

[19] In addition, the SSI program permits recipients to deduct $240 of earned or unearned income. A recipient with no unearned income thus faces a zero tax rate on earnings up to $1020 per annum.

Table 8.1   **Hypothetical Income Possibilities for an Aged Couple under H.R. 1 If Labor Force Participation (Earnings) Is a Decision Variable**

Marginal tax rate		Earnings	Social Security (OAI)	Welfare benefit (SSI)	OASDHI employee tax	Federal personal income tax	Net income (equals earnings + OAI + SSI − taxes)
		0	1600	980	0	0	2580
.0585	<						
		780	1600	980	46	0	3314
.5585	<						
		2100	1600	320	123	0	3897
.5585	<						
		4000	650	320	234	0	4736
.6985	<						
		4820	240	320	282	115	4983
.9485	<						
		5000	150	275	293	140	4992
.9585	<						
		5300	0	200	310	185	5005
.7085	<						
		5700	0	0	333	245	5112
.2085	<						
		6000	0	0	351	290	5359

Note—All amounts in dollars.

centive for the aged individual to work is virtually equal to his gross market earning power (minus any work expenses he might incur).

Over the earnings range of $780–$2100 per annum, the family's net income relationship becomes

$$Y = S + (G - S + \$240) + E - t_1(E - \$780) - t_3 E$$
$$= \$2970 + (1 - t_1 - t_3)E.$$

The marginal tax rate on earnings facing the potential aged worker is now the sum of the implicit SSI 50 percent tax rate and the OASDHI payroll tax rate. For earnings between $2100 and $4000 per annum, the net income relationship becomes much more complex algebraically as the OAI and SSI benefit formulas interact. The value of the couple's OAI benefit is given by

$$\text{OAI} = S - t_2(E - \$2100), \quad \text{for } \$2100 < E \leqslant \$5300.$$

Similarly, the value of the SSI benefit may be written as

$$\text{SSI} = G - t_1(E - \$780) - (\text{OAI} - \$240), \quad \text{for } \$780 < E \leqslant \$4820.$$

The family's net income over this range of earnings is then the sum of its earnings net of payroll tax and its net OAI and SSI benefits. After substitution of the assumed values for S and G in this example and after algebraic simplification, the net income relationship can be written again as

$$Y = \$2970 + (1 - t_1 - t_3)E.$$

The combined marginal tax rate over this range of earnings remains the same $(t_1 + t_3)$ because the reduction in OAI benefits due to the OAI 50 percent earnings test is exactly offset by an equivalent increase in SSI entitlement. The earnings test is not operative over this range of earnings, but it does have the effect of greatly increasing the break-even level of earnings for SSI. Above an earnings level of $4000 per annum, the federal personal income tax rate takes effect, and the total marginal tax rate includes the relevant personal income tax bracket rate (equals 14 percent on the first $1000 of taxable income and 15 percent on the second $1000 of taxable income in this example). Thus, over the earnings range of $4000–$4820 per annum, the marginal tax rate increases by another 14 percent, the first bracket rate in the personal income tax.

For the earnings range of $4820–$5300 per annum, the net OAI payment is reduced by the earnings test to less than $240, the amount of unearned income that can be disregarded under SSI. As earnings increase above $4820 and the OAI payment is reduced, the balance of the amount that may be disregarded (= $240 − OAI benefit) is deducted from *earnings* before the SSI marginal rate is applied. That is, when unearned income falls below $240, any "excess" disregard can be deducted from earnings. Thus, the SSI payment is given by

$$\text{SSI} = G - t_1[E - \$780 - (\$240 - \text{OAI})], \qquad \text{for } \$4820 < E \leqslant \$5300.$$

The effect of this is that the SSI entitlement is increased by $.50 for each dollar that the OAI benefit is reduced below $240 per annum. The marginal tax rate over this range of earnings is equal to $t_1 + t_2 + t_3 + t_4 - t_1t_2$. The OAI and SSI marginal tax rates on earnings interact over this earnings range and amount to 75 percent $(= t_1 + t_2 - t_1t_2)$ before the federal personal income tax and OASDHI payroll tax rates are added on top. Above the OAI break-even level of $5300 per annum, the earnings test rate is no longer effective, and up to an earnings level of $5700 per annum, the total marginal tax rate on earnings includes only the SSI, federal personal income tax, and OASDHI payroll tax rates. The SSI benefit formula over this range of earnings reduces to

$$\text{SSI} = G - t_1(E - \$1020), \qquad \text{for } \$5300 < E \leqslant \$5700.$$

Finally, above an earnings level of $5700 per annum, where SSI benefits are reduced to zero by the earnings test, the aged worker faces the same marginal tax rates as non-aged workers.

The example in Table 8.1 presents just one hypothetical case among many, but it has important general implications. Aged households whose economic status resembles that of the hypothetical household in the example—that is, those who are eligible for only low OAI benefits, owning few or no assets and having low earnings capability—must find their net income choices most bewildering. Such aged individuals will probably conclude that the net gain from continuing to work is quite low, especially if they compare their status to that of non-aged individuals who face much lower marginal tax rates on earnings. It should be noted that Congress, in enacting H.R. 1, consciously improved the work incentive features of both SSI (relative to OAA) and of OAI separately, but it is clear from the foregoing example that the work incentive features of the two programs combined are still far from satisfactory. Also, state cash supplements to the basic SSI guarantee, and in-kind welfare programs tied into welfare eligibility, will generally compound the work disincentives given in this example and extend the disincentives to much higher levels of earnings.

In addition to the problem of work incentives, the present system of income maintenance for the aged makes saving for retirement extremely unattractive for many low-income individuals. If aging individuals or couples can foresee that their total income past age sixty-five will be less than the SSI guarantee, they will have a strong incentive to dispose of or consume any assets they own or, at least, to not make the effort to save and acquire additional assets to finance retirement. SSI continues the practice of OAA of taxing all income from assets at a 100 percent rate (above the $240 per annum disregard applying to *all* unearned income) and, thus, strongly discourages saving by rational low-income households. The assets test for eligibility for SSI benefits obviously adds more disincentives for saving for low-income individuals, at least saving in the form of the financial assets included in the test. Such perverse savings disincentives always existed in the old OAA program, but they apply uniformly to all the low-income aged under SSI and affect aged individuals and families over higher ranges of income in the previously low-benefit states.

But the present system of income maintenance for the aged involves much more profound problems for social policy than the built-in work and savings disincentives just discussed. The fundamental problem is that the system creates intolerable horizontal inequities among the aged. Aged individuals receiving SSI benefits can actually become economically better off than previously better-off individuals whose total income, including OAI benefits, is too high to make them eligible for SSI benefits. The switch in relative economic status can occur because the sum of SSI cash benefits plus any state cash supplements plus the imputed dollar value of in-kind benefits, such as Medicaid, that are tied into welfare eligibility can exceed the value of OAI benefits plus income from other sources for low-income retirees. This problem predated the existence of SSI in the states that paid relatively generous OAA benefits; the provisions of H.R. 1 make this anomalous relationship between OAI and welfare for the aged more uniform nationally.[20] Even if new legislation were to cut existing ties between welfare cash and in-kind programs, the provision of relatively high cash benefits alone under SSI and state cash supplementation has to create some degree of horizontal inequity in that it causes a sharp leveling of individuals who previously enjoyed quite different standards of living.

To take an extreme case, an aged couple whose previous covered earnings entitled them to an OAI benefit of $195 per month and who had no other sources of income will, upon retirement, be better off than a previously destitute couple with SSI cash benefits of $195 per month only to the extent of the SSI $20-per-month disregard on all unearned income. Further, some couples eligible for less than $195 per month in OAI benefits are not eligible to receive SSI supplementation up to the $195 federal welfare standard, because they have financial assets in excess of the asset test maximum for a couple of $2250. Under the provisions of H.R. 1, such persons will be forced to choose between disposing of their "excess" assets in return for somewhat higher total benefits immediately or forgoing the welfare supplementation in order to keep all their assets for future contingencies.

A closely related problem with the present system is that it is incompatible with the rationale for the OAI program. The aged couple receiving OAI benefits in the example of the previous paragraph will surely question whether or not $20 per month plus the nonpecuniary advantages of OAI over the SSI welfare program are sufficient compensation for the thousands of tax dollars they paid into the OAI trust funds over the working life of the earner.[21] Further, it should be noted that the federalization of old-age welfare may well remove much of the welfare stigma associated with the old OAA program and, thus, tend to blur former distinctions between social insurance and welfare. Academicians

---

[20] The 20 percent increase in Social Security benefits in 1972 made the perversity of the present system dramatically clear. Journalists reported numerous sad cases of individuals whose increased Social Security benefits made them worse off because their "higher" incomes made them ineligible for welfare cash supplementation and the associated in-kind benefits.

[21] This point holds with even more force if both husband and wife had substantial covered earnings prior to retirement. See Pechman, Aaron, and Taussig, *Social Security*, Ch. 5, for a discussion of this point. And, of course, the text comparison is for cash benefits only.

will surely point out that, once the SSI guarantee plus state supplementation and welfare-associated in-kind benefits approach low to average OAI benefit levels, OAI becomes essentially a welfare system for the low-income aged whose total incomes, including their OAI benefits, are below or not significantly above the old-age welfare standard.

The argument is basically straightforward. Suppose that the OAI program suddenly came to an end under the extreme case of complete equality in the level of OAI benefits and old-age guarantees. The income of every elderly person without significant other sources of income would remain virtually unchanged because welfare benefits would replace the lost OAI benefits. Income taxes would have to rise to finance the higher welfare benefits, thereby substituting for OASDHI payroll taxes after the cessation of payment of OAI benefits. Thus, the only consequence of ending the OAI program under these extreme circumstances would be to shift financing of benefits for the aged from the payroll tax to the income tax. Indeed, once people grasp the notion that much of OAI is essentially a welfare program for the aged, financed by a regressive tax on wages, they will surely doubt that the program makes sense.

This argument is certainly oversimplified and is subject to the objection that the degree of horizontal inequity in the present income maintenance system is tolerable because it affects only a minority of OAI recipients in the lower tail of the OAI benefit distribution and without significant income from other sources. It may further be objected that the advantages of receiving Social Security income rather than welfare cannot be easily compared in simple dollar terms. These objections have some merit, but, in my judgment, they ignore the symbolic importance of even a very few cases of extreme horizontal inequity and, in any event, do not add up to a strong case. The reader can probably envision many different possible responses to the problems inherent in the present income maintenance system for the aged, perhaps including those to be discussed in the next two sections of this chapter. But it should be clear that, if OAI is to remain in anything close to its present form and in anything close to its present relationship to SSI, OAI benefits must always be liberalized in the future as the federal government and the states raise their minimum welfare standards and their income guarantees under SSI and state supplementation. Otherwise, the present horizontal inequities in the income maintenance system for the aged would affect an intolerably large proportion of the aged population. Large increases in OAI benefit levels may be desirable in the future on many grounds, but it is patently absurd to justify such increases just to preserve the present system of income maintenance for the aged.

A negative income tax or a demogrant program is a possible alternative to SSI as a basic income support program for the aged within a reformed income maintenance system. This possibility is the subject of the next section. But within the present system, substitution of either alternative for SSI would not solve the basic integration problems discussed previously, because they would inevitably conflict with the income support function of the present OAI program. For example, suppose that a universal demogrant providing relatively generous benefits to all the aged were substituted for SSI with no substantial concomitant change in the existing OAI program. If OAI benefits were taxed under the demogrant program at a zero or very low rate (perhaps at the rates applicable to ordinary income under the personal income tax), then the demogrant would duplicate the income support function of OAI benefits for the aged, at very great expense to the Treasury. The alternative dual income maintenance system discussed later in Part IV would then seem to be superior on every count to the present system. Alternatively, if OAI benefits were taxed under the demogrant program at a special high rate (in the limit, at 100 percent), then the situation would be exactly the same in essentials as the present situation. In either case, a demogrant program would be clearly inconsistent with the present structure of OAI.

One last observation can conclude the present discussion. Given the arguments in this section and given the humanitarian case for income support of the aged at relatively generous standards of living, the present income maintenance system for the aged does not seem very attractive for the future. The alternative systems to be discussed in Parts IV and V become correspondingly more attractive despite the likelihood that they pose some transitional problems.

IV. Alternative One: A Dual System Incorporating Separate Earnings Replacement and Income Support Programs

If the present income maintenance system for the aged has two different valid objectives and if these two objectives are becoming incompatible within the single main program (OAI) of that system, then one possible line of reform is to split OAI into two separate programs. One new program could incorporate the income support functions of both the present SSI and OAI programs while the other could be devoted to earnings replacement. Such a split of the present system is by no means a new or radical notion. The reports of the 1971 Advisory Council on Social Security contain language that strongly implies support for such a proposal although they do not explicitly call for two separate new programs.

> The Council believes that improvements in public assistance programs will reduce pressures to distort the contributory social insurance program. An adequate public assistance program would make it unnecessary for Social Security to perform functions that are not appropriate to a wage-related program. . . . Social Security benefits could then be kept more closely related to a worker's earnings and the length of time he worked under the program, and thus to the Social Security contributions he had paid than otherwise could be done.[22]

Gordon has discussed the dual approach and has provided some interesting comments on foreign experience with dual systems of income maintenance.[23] Bishop has also given serious consideration to what he calls a two-tier system.[24] Most important of all, Buchanan has worked out a detailed scheme of "radical reform" for OAI with careful consideration of the transitional problems involved in moving toward his proposed system away from the present system.[25]

Let me outline the details of how such a dual system might work, postponing for the moment transitional problems. Income support for the aged would be given over completely to a universal demogrant or negative income tax type of program, the latter perhaps designed along the lines of the proposal of the President's Commission on Income Maintenance Programs. Either would provide a minimum income guarantee for all types of economic units, including the aged; OAI would then be assigned a pure earnings replacement objective. The income support program would have to tax OAI benefits at the rates applicable to all other sources of income if this dual system were to be a significant departure from the present SSI–OAI relationship. Since income redistribution would be the province of the income support program in a dual system, OAI as

[22] *Reports of the 1971 Advisory Council on Social Security,* 92d Cong., 1st sess., H. Doc. 92–80 (Washington, D.C.: U.S. Government Printing Office, 1971), p. 3. Also see the discussion of social insurance programs in President's Commission on Income Maintenance Programs, *Poverty amid Plenty.*

[23] Margaret S. Gordon, "The Case for Earnings-Related Social Security Benefits Restated," *Old Age Income Assurance. Part II: The Aged Population and Retirement Income Programs,* U.S., Congress, Joint Economic Committtee compendium, 90th Cong., 1st sess. (Washington, D.C.: U.S. Government Printing Office, 1967).

[24] George A. Bishop, "Issues in Future Financing of Social Security," *Old Age Income Assurance. Part III: Public Programs,* U.S., Congress, Joint Economic Committee compendium, 90th Cong., 1st sess. (Washington, D.C.: U.S. Government Printing Office, 1967).

[25] James M. Buchanan, "Social Insurance in a Growing Economy: A Proposal for Radical Reform," *National Tax Journal* 21 (December 1968).

a social insurance program could base its benefit payments solely on considerations of individual or household equity. Once OAI no longer had to provide for the income support of the aged, it could be financed at lower payroll tax rates. The payroll tax savings could then be channeled into higher income tax rates to help finance the basic income support program of the dual system.

Simplicity and elementary notions of justice point to the same OAI benefit formula: Benefits payable to an individual or a family unit would be equal to the life annuity value of the present value of its lifetime tax payments to the OAI trust fund. The interest rate used to compute the present value of OAI tax payments would—following Buchanan and based on fundamental contributions to the economics of Social Security by Samuelson and Aaron—most appropriately be the annual rate of growth of money GNP or some other index of aggregate money economic activity.[26] Provided average benefit levels relative to average earnings levels were held roughly constant, and provided that the relative sizes of the aged and the working populations did not vary greatly, such a scheme would automatically produce tax revenues sufficient to finance OAI benefits without changes in tax *rates*.[27] The OAI trust fund, as under the present system, would be sufficient if it just covered perhaps one year's worth of benefit payments. If, in any year, OAI benefits and taxes did not balance closely, the system would be kept on a current cash basis by payments to, or payments from, general Treasury revenues. A large accumulation of funds in the OAI trust fund in this new pure earnings replacement program would make no more sense under a dual system than it does under the present system.[28]

---

[26] Paul A. Samuelson, "An Exact Consumption-Loan Model of Interest with or without the Social Contrivance of Money," *Journal of Political Economy* 66 (December 1958), and Henry J. Aaron, "The Socal Insurance Paradox," *Canadian Journal of Economics and Political Science* 32 (August 1966).

[27] The statement in the text refers to the effective average tax rate on all earnings. Nominal OAI tax rates would vary with changes in the proportion of total earnings covered and taxed by OAI.

[28] This version of an earnings replacement program differs in mechanics from that suggested by Buchanan, "Social Insurance in a Growing Economy," although the basic underlying reasoning is very similar. Buchanan suggests that all individuals be compelled to buy a certain amount of social insurance bonds, which pay a rate of interest equal to the rate of growth of money GNP. His idea is ingenious, but it seems to be a needlessly radical departure from present practices. He also suggests, however, that private firms be allowed to sell securities that would be legal substitutes for the government's GNP bonds, only provided that firms could provide suitable insurance against bankruptcy. Such an idea is not strictly necessary to his basic plan, and it impresses me as a pernicious threat to social insurance. Why should private firms be allowed to select the best risks from the total population for private profit while the government is left with all the worst risks?

The dual system just outlined would solve very neatly many of the knotty problems of program integration in the present system. If the income support program in the dual system were of a negative income tax (NIT) type, OAI benefits would naturally be included in the definition of income for the NIT but, as noted before, would be taxable at a rate well under 100 percent. Thus, even for families at the lowest income levels, OAI benefits would always add significantly to total family income, in contrast to the present system. Similarly, income from assets would be taxed under the NIT at less than a 100 percent rate, thus increasing incentives to save for retirement for poor families relative to the present system. The level of NIT benefits would be of no concern for the viability of the new OAI program in contrast to the present system, since, under the dual system, differentials in OAI benefits would always result in corresponding proportional differentials in family or individual net income. The same points hold for a dual system in which the income support function is achieved by a program of universal demogrants. Presumably, OAI benefits would be included in taxable income in the expanded and reformed federal personal income tax under such a system, while OAI taxes would be made deductible. (Such a change in basic personal income tax law might be advisable as well if a NIT performed the income support function, but it would be less essential to integration of the two programs.) Otherwise, OAI and a demogrant program would mesh just as neatly as OAI and NIT in a dual system.

A dual system would permit scrapping the earnings test for OAI, with a resulting desirable impact on the work incentives for the aged. The earnings test makes sense in the present system only because OAI performs such an important income support role for the aged. The argument for retaining the earnings test under the present system is that it redistributes a usually fixed amount of funds away from potential beneficiaries who are able and willing to work and, thus, are rather well off, to beneficiaries who are out of the labor force and, thus, are rather badly off. But once the income support function of OAI is given over to a new income support program—either a NIT or a demogrant—this redistributional argument loses all force. No redistribution of income will take place within the OAI program in the dual system, since every family's or individual's OAI benefit will be based strictly on the present value of its past OAI tax payments. Under a dual system, work incentive arguments then clearly prevail and call for an end to the earnings test. Aged individuals who continue to work then can reap the benefits of both the additional earnings during their working years and the larger OAI life annuities made possible by paying more OAI taxes while they work beyond the OAI retirement age.

This last point also suggests that a dual system could deal very nicely with the vexing problem of early retirement under the present system of income maintenance for the aged. Today, individuals who retire between ages sixty-two and sixty-five receive permanently reduced OAI benefits calculated to keep constant the actuarial cost of their life annuity benefits to the system. Unfortunately, early retirees under OAI today are predominantly low-income individuals who cannot afford to receive the lower benefits. This fact leads many people to the observation that OAI fails to support adequately the incomes of early retirees and to the policy prescription that the official retirement age at which OAI beneficiaries can claim unreduced benefits be lowered. But lowering the OAI retirement age increases the size of the legally defined aged population, with possible serious effects in the long run on the labor force participation of the currently "almost aged" population, and the consequent undesirable effects outlined in Part III on OAI costs and the adequacy of OAI benefits.

Under the proposed dual system, a NIT or demogrant program would have responsibility for income support of low-income individuals who cannot or will not remain in the labor force up to age sixty-five. Therefore, OAI would be under much less pressure to reduce its official retirement age. Individuals who left the labor force prior to age sixty-five would be eligible for income support payments. Once they reached sixty-five, their income support payments would be partially supplemented or even replaced by their OAI annuity benefits. Individuals who worked past age sixty-five would receive larger OAI benefits, for the two reasons noted previously.

Alternatively, OAI benefits could be made available prior to age sixty-five at some specified age (such as sixty or sixty-two) with permanent reduction of OAI benefits, as under the present system. The latter alternative has the advantage of making retirement a much more flexible process for the aged individual but has the disadvantage for the economy of providing a certain degree of work disincentives for productive workers under age sixty-five. Either alternative, however, is clearly preferable, in my view, to the present system on both income support and work incentive grounds.

One very significant potential advantage of the dual system outlined in this section over the present system is that it would almost automatically solve the very difficult benefit overlap problems that plague the system today.[29] Very briefly, benefits from all public retirement programs, in-

---

[29] These problems are discussed in detail in James R. Storey, "Public Income Transfer Programs: The Incidence of Multiple Benefits and the Issues Raised by Their Receipt," in *Studies in Public Welfare*, Paper No. 1, U.S., Congress, Joint Economic Committee, Subcommittee on Fiscal Policy (Washington, D.C.: U.S. Government Printing Office, 1972).

cluding OAI, railroad retirement, and veterans' pensions, would be taxable income under the income support program in the dual system; OAI benefits and other public and private retirement benefits would be, quite properly, additive. Since OAI benefits would be based on accumulated lifetime OAI taxes rather than on average earnings over some minimum period of OAI coverage, the anomalies that exist today because of individuals who qualify for federal civil service (or other public programs) retirement benefits while paying no OAI taxes, and for OAI benefits on the basis of minimal OAI-covered employment, would automatically be resolved. Under the present system, coverage requirements for OAI benefits are extremely liberal, and the minimum benefit is high relative to average OAI benefits, because of the OAI income support function. The liberality of OAI coverage requirements and the shape of its benefits–average earnings curve in the present system are intended to help the poor, but they also create inequities when well-off individuals use these provisions to qualify for dual public retirement benefits. Under a dual system, however, a NIT or a demogrant would absorb the current income support function of OAI, and the OAI minimum benefit could quite properly be reduced literally to zero. Dual entitlement to retirement benefits thereby would no longer be a problem.

A dual system would also solve another inequity in the present system: the unfair treatment of married women with substantial labor force experience under OAI. The unfairness arises because OAI taxes are paid on the basis of *individual* earnings while OAI benefits are paid on the basis of earnings of the married couple. If only the husband works, the couple is paid 150 percent of the benefit based on his earnings. If both the husband and wife work, they are both entitled to benefits on their own. However, their combined benefits are greater than those given to the former couple only if the benefit based on the wife's earnings is more than 50 percent of the benefit based on the husband's. This inequity again arises because the income support function of OAI calls for a benefit amount based on presumed family need, and presumed family need is greater for a married couple than for a single individual. The inequity is obvious, and it could be alleviated by various ad hoc methods under the present system.[30] But note that, under a dual system, the problem would vanish automatically because of the strict adherence to the principle of individual equity in the restructured OAI program. Total family OAI benefits under a dual system would depend only on the present value of total family lifetime earnings and would simply be the sum of husband's and wife's benefits based on the earnings history of each. The present inequity against married working

[30] See, for example, Pechman, Aaron, and Taussig, *Social Security*, Ch. 5.

women would no longer exist. Similarly, the present differentiation between employees and the self-employed in OAI would no longer hold in
the dual system; OAI benefits would depend only on the total tax payments attributable to any individual worker. If the self-employed continued to pay only three-fourths or less of the total employer–employee
OASDI tax under the dual system, their benefits would also be correspondingly smaller.

Finally, note that almost everything said about OAI in the foregoing
discussion is also applicable to the Survivor's Insurance program (SI). In
the dual system, OAI and SI would remain linked as OASI just as in the
present system, but SI benefits would be computed without regard to
redistributional considerations. In the dual system, SI benefits would appropriately be based on *average* earnings records, however, just as in the
present SI program, rather than on accumulated tax payments as in OAI.
The rationale for this difference in benefit computation is the difference
in the functions of the two programs: SI is basically a group life insurance
program, and its benefits should bear a relationship to average premium
payments rather than to accumulated premiums; but SI benefits under
the dual system would not necessarily vary with family size or presumed
need as under the present system.[31] The income support program of the
dual system would provide for direct redistribution of income to needy
survivors on the same basis as such redistribution would be provided to
other kinds of needy families.

One last matter remains to be discussed here: the problem of transition from the present system to the proposed dual system of income
maintenance for the aged. Once a universal income support program was
put into effect, how could OASI adapt over time to its new pure earnings
replacement role? No one answer could possibly cover all reasonable
responses to this enormously complicated question. If our society makes
the judgment that it is irrevocably committed to the current rules and
benefit schedules in existing Social Security legislation for all individuals
already in the labor force who have paid any Social Security taxes, then
the transition period from the present system to a dual system would be
a very long one. Any new legislation establishing a restructured OASI
program would apply necessarily only to new entrants into the labor
force, and the dual system would evolve out of the present system gradually over three or four decades. A simple option rule could probably
greatly speed the transition process, however. Every individual already
retired or in the labor force could be given the option of receiving bene-

[31] The choice between the present system and a strict private insurance model on
this issue is not clear-cut. Congress could reasonably opt for either choice and remain
within the framework of the dual system.

fits based either on the computation formula of the present law or on the formula of the new law. A necessary exception to this option rule is that individuals who elected to receive benefits under the new income support program of the dual system could not also elect to receive OAI benefits computed under the existing law. (If the minimum income guarantee under the new income support program were as high as the present SSI guarantee, plus the SSI disregard on unearned income, then the option rule would protect individuals from a decrease in net income.) Without such a provision, needless duplication of income support payments would result, as well as the creation of new horizontal inequities among the aged. Such an option rule inevitably would increase somewhat the costs to the government of the income maintenance system for the aged.

If Congress were unwilling to allow the transition period to go on as long as thirty years or so, it could speed the process greatly in a number of ways. For example, it could make the rules of the new OASI program apply automatically to all individuals currently far from retirement, say to everybody under age fifty. Another possibility would be to combine the option rule outlined before with a freeze on OASI benefit levels scheduled under existing law at their present dollar levels for all new benefit awards. Increases in benefit levels, to offset inflation or for other reasons, would thus be limited to existing beneficiaries. A less drastic version of this last measure would be to confine such a freeze *cum* option to all new benefit awards after a transitional period of perhaps ten or twenty years. These frozen-dollar benefit levels in the existing OASI benefit schedule would then rapidly become very unattractive relative to benefit levels under the new OASI program as earnings levels increased over time because of productivity growth and inflation. Other techniques undoubtedly could be devised to speed the transition to a dual system. Congress would face difficult trade-offs between speeding the transition period and either incurring large transitional costs or violating implied benefit commitments to the aged under Social Security.

In principle, then, the transition from the present system of income maintenance for the aged to a dual system seems to be a manageable problem. This is not to deny that the technical problems of transition could be enormously complex, especially if the transition period were a short one. But this is rightfully the subject of another, much longer paper. The political feasibility of effecting such a transition within our political system is another moot issue beyond the scope of this chapter. But if a dual system is judged to be an improvement over the present system, these difficulties should not be used as an excuse to avoid thinking about and acting on change. Both the technical and political problems of a transition to a dual system would certainly be no more difficult than the similar

234 / *Michael K. Taussig*

problems confronted in initiating the programs enacted in the Social Security Act of 1935.

V. Alternative Two: A Unitary System of Income Maintenance for the Aged

The second alternative income maintenance system for the aged would require separating the aged from the non-aged populations for income maintenance purposes. This alternative merits serious consideration because of its relatively high political feasibility. Congress has demonstrated time and again its determination to treat the aged more generously than the general population in many areas, but especially in income maintenance programs. (The provisions enacted in 1972 in H.R. 1 provide just one more example of this point.) A world that could easily develop in the future with only minor transitional problems would have roughly the following characteristics: Income maintenance for the general population would continue along present lines, or would be redesigned to be something like President Nixon's proposed Family Assistance program, or would be handled by a universal (except for the aged) demogrant program. In any event, it would not apply to the aged except that benefit levels provided for the non-aged would obviously set some sort of minimum standard for the aged as well. Income maintenance for the aged would then bring all the aged under OAI or a similar program with a new label, and SSI for the aged would be abolished.[32] In short, the problems of the present system outlined in Part III, which arise from the uneasy relationship between SSI and OAI, would be resolved by coordination of all income support and earnings replacement functions for the aged within a single income maintenance program.

Benefits for the aged within a single program would include both income support and earnings replacement, just as in the present OAI program. Benefits could, in principle, be made identical to any given combined benefits of a dual system. That is, the minimum benefit in the unitary system could be set equal to the guarantee level of the income maintenance program in the dual system. Increments above the minimum benefit in the unitary system could then equal the level of benefits provided under the earnings replacement program of the dual system, less the losses of benefits under the income support program. These losses would occur because dollars of income above the minimum income support benefits would be "taxed" (would reduce benefits). Past the break-even

[32] For one proposal in this spirit, see Bruno Stein, *On Relief* (New York: Basic Books, 1971), pp. 109–111.

point of the income support program, the increments would be set equal to the amounts provided by the earnings replacement program of the dual system without any reduction.

An example will help to illustrate the possible identity of benefits under hypothetical dual and unitary income maintenance systems. Suppose that the guarantee level in the income support program of a dual system were $200 per month for a given type of family unit and that the off-setting tax rate in the program were 33⅓ percent. Then, if an aged family of this type were entitled to $100 per month from the OAI program of the dual system and had no other income sources, its net income would be $267 per month (= $200 income support guarantee + $100 OAI benefit − .333 × $100 income support program tax). Similarly, if its OAI benefits were $200 per month, its net income would be $333 per month under the same assumptions. That is, up to the break-even level of the income support program—$600 in this example—its net income would rise by 66⅔ cents for each additional dollar of OAI benefits to which this family was entitled. Above the break-even level of income, each additional dollar of OAI benefits would add a full dollar to net income. A unitary income maintenance system could, in principle, duplicate this benefit within a single program, at least under the circumstances assumed in this example. The minimum benefit payable to an individual with no covered earnings would be $200 per month. Increments above the minimum benefit would then be $67 per month for each $100 per month life annuity to which the family unit was entitled on the basis of its earnings record up to the point where OAI benefits reach the $600 level. Above that level, OAI benefit increments would rise by a full $100 per month for each additional $100 life annuity "due to" the family.

This example demonstrates only the logical possibility of identity of benefits in hypothetical unitary and dual systems. In practice, substitution of a dual system for a unitary system (or vice versa) would almost certainly not leave the benefits unchanged. Instead, under the unitary system, increments above the minimum benefit level would probably be determined according to the ad hoc methods now used in OAI, with the probable (but not necessary) result that the earnings replacement function of the unitary system would be deemphasized to some degree in favor of the income support function.

A related issue concerns the nature of an earnings (or income) test, if any, in a unitary system of income maintenance for the aged. As in the present system, the temptation for humanitarian administrators and legislators would be to institute relatively tough earnings (or income) tests in the unitary system to redistribute income from the relatively well-off to the relatively poor aged. Bringing the aged into a unitary system would certainly give it a much stronger income support image than exists today for OAI and would reinforce this temptation. Since such a unitary system would undoubtedly be accompanied by a large infusion of funds from general revenue sources to the OAI trust fund to supplement the present tax on wages, Congress would probably put great pressure on the old-age income maintenance administrators to reduce costs as much as possible. An earnings or income test for retirement benefits is an obvious response to such pressure. For these reasons, it is probable that an earnings test or an income test would be much tougher in a unitary system than in the dual system discussed in Part IV above. Also, of course, the earnings or income test under the unitary system would have much more universal scope than an income test under the income support program of a dual system since the latter would apply directly only to those aged individuals with very low incomes. Therefore, a unitary system of income maintenance for the aged is likely to create greater work disincentives than a dual system. If an income test in a unitary system replaces the earnings test under OAI in the present system, it will create greater disincentives for saving as well. The validity of these conjectures depends, of course, on the precise details of any real-world unitary or dual system of income maintenance for the aged. Generalizations about the exact nature of hypothetical alternative programs are risky.

A unitary income maintenance system for the aged is simple and contains only a few problems requiring explicit discussion. The first is the appropriate means of financing the system. As noted previously, a unitary system designed along the lines suggested here would be so openly an income support program that it would call for at least partial general revenue financing. The payroll tax would still be very useful for benefit computation purposes, however, and should probably be retained in form but definitely not in substance. A very simple method of restructuring the payroll tax along desirable lines in a unitary system is to make all or part of the employee's share of the tax just a withholding device for the personal income tax. This objective could be accomplished by allowing the employee share of the tax to be claimed as a credit against the personal income tax, and to refund the full amount of any excess of the sum of the credits for all workers in a family over the personal income tax liability of the family.[33] To restructure the payroll tax even more drastically, all or part of the employer share of the tax could be allowed as a credit against either the corporation income tax or the personal income tax of the proprietors of an unincorporated business. The credit device would leave

[33] See Pechman, Aaron, and Taussig, *Social Security*, Chapter 8, for further details about this technique.

the records and finances of the OASI trust fund intact but would remove all regressive elements from the tax side of Social Security. Of course, personal income tax rates would have to rise correspondingly to meet the cost of the payroll tax credit.[34] In contrast, the dual system would leave the payroll tax intact in its present form, except that rates could be reduced to match the savings of removing all income support from the OAI program. In both systems, however, the net result should be a reallocation of the tax burden away from Social Security payroll taxes to income taxes in order to finance income support of the aged out of a more progressive source of revenue.

A very difficult problem for a unitary system would be the overlap of public retirement benefits that plagues the present system. This problem is difficult to solve in the present system because of institutional inertia and reinforcing political pressures exerted by public sector employees. A new universal income maintenance system for the aged could solve this problem at one stroke by simply making its coverage of earnings universal and including all public employees in basic retirement benefit coverage. Then all public employment benefit programs could be converted into a public sector analog of present private pension programs, with benefits under these programs designed to supplement the basic OAI retirement benefit program. To venture a guess about political realities, such a reform would be as difficult to effect within the framework of a unitary system as it is in the present system. Veterans' pensions would present perhaps an even more embarrassing political issue for a unitary income maintenance system for the aged. These pensions are, in fact, welfare payments for veterans and their dependents and survivors since there is no requirement that the veteran should have incurred a service-connected disability. Thus, in principle, such benefits should simply be abolished under a unitary system, especially if the minimum benefit provided by the new OAI program for the aged were set at a high-enough level. To allow veterans' pensions to be added to the benefits provided by the old-age income maintenance program would be to permit all sorts of horrible horizontal inequities. But political realism suggests that Congress would adopt the latter course.

[34] A tax credit to employers for their share of the payroll tax may seem, on first encounter, a strange and regressive tax proposal. But note that the text discussion couples this proposal with a general increase in income tax rates to maintain a constant total tax yield to the Treasury. The purpose of such a tax credit would not be to provide tax relief to employers but, rather, to increase the demand for labor, which is a function of the gross wage including payroll taxes. If modern tax incidence theory is correct, the long-run result of the tax credit would be a progressive shift in the overall tax burden away from wage incomes covered by OASDHI to all incomes.

A critical problem for a unitary system would be the exact definition of the aged population and the coordination of income maintenance programs for the aged with other Social Security programs directed at the non-aged population. Age sixty-five or any other single age is an arbitrary and artificial boundary between the non-aged and the aged. But, in the unitary system envisioned here, the choice of the critical retirement age is all important if there really is to be a separate income maintenance system based on age. Early retirement is one immediate problem with no obvious resolution. Just as in the present system, a unitary income maintenance system for the aged would have to either allow early retirement with reduced benefits or deny benefits to early retirees (who might or might not qualify for income maintenance benefits for the non-aged). In either case, the income support functions of the system are clearly going to be unsatisfactory to some critics. A related problem suggested by Hollister is that, if benefit levels in the income maintenance program for the aged substantially exceed the benefit levels available for the non-aged, then there will be some incentive to shift dependents from non-aged to aged households.[35] This is just one more example of general, perverse incentive problems with all categorical income maintenance programs.

A further, related issue concerns current Social Security programs directed at the non-aged groups in the population: dependent survivors of workers covered by OASDHI and (some) disabled workers. Should such groups be treated as "honorary aged" as a matter of social policy and be given benefits greater than the benefits provided for other non-aged needy groups not covered by current Social Security programs (the blind and mothers with dependent children, for example)? The differences in treatment between non-aged needy groups covered and not covered by OASDHI are embarrassing enough in the present income maintenance system in the United States with its artificial dichotomy between social "insurance" and welfare. They would become much more embarrassing in a world in which old-age assistance is abolished and all the aged are included in a single categorical income maintenance program. No obvious best solution to these quandaries suggests itself to me.

Alternative Income Maintenance Systems for the Aged

The dual and unitary systems have been intentionally posed in this chapter as clearly defined alternatives. Presenting them in this light is a useful expository device, but it does not give a full description of the choices actually open to reformers of the present system. Elements of

---

[35] Hollister, "Income Maintenance Reform Issues."

both systems can be incorporated more or less logically into some alternative system. For example, one possible alternative might include a system of universal demogrants graduated by age to favor the very old plus an old-age retirement program with a strict earnings replacement function. This alternative is, of course, very close to the dual system outlined in Part IV in essentials. Another alternative, much closer to the unitary system outlined here, would combine a demogrant for the aged plus an old-age retirement program with much less of an income support function plus a separate income maintenance program for the non-aged, perhaps in the form of a negative income tax. Such alternatives blur the distinctions drawn in this chapter between the dual and unitary systems, but the basic integration issues are much the same.

As should already be evident, my own view is that a dual-system approach to income maintenance for the aged is preferable to a unitary approach. I prefer the dual system partly because it seems to offer clear technical advantages over the unitary in solving the vexing integration issues of the present system. But the dual system also seems to me to have broader social and political advantages in that it treats needy people of all ages on a par and clearly separates the two legitimate functions of income maintenance—income support and earnings replacement—into two mutually consistent programs. Such a separation seems desirable because it forces Congress to make explicit decisions about both kinds of programs and, therefore, makes it more likely that both functions of income maintenance will be done justice.

Acknowledgments

The author is grateful to John J. Carroll, Irene Cox, John Snee, Thomas G. Staples, and Alair Townsend for their helpful criticisms of earlier drafts of this chapter. None of these individuals necessarily concurs with the views expressed here, however, and the author is solely responsible for all factual errors that remain.

9

Programming Income Maintenance: The Place of Unemployment Insurance

Raymond Munts

Unemployment Insurance (UI) is part of our Social Security system, a system built on a categorical and contingency approach. Recent proposals for a broad strategy to eliminate poverty, such as negative taxes and demogrants, raise questions for the existing programs in the system. Should UI, as one weapon in the arsenal, be replaced by a more comprehensive new plan of income maintenance, or integrated with it? Is integration feasible? To help the reader pass an informed judgment on these questions, the pages following are directed to three purposes: (*1*) assessment of the income support functions of UI; (*2*) consideration of substituting new programs for existing ones, and, alternatively, integration of new and old plans; and (*3*) description of the design problems that arise under integration.

I. Income Support through UI

UI is designed to perform many functions, and it is somewhat arbitrary to look at some functions while ignoring others. But when analyzing the place of UI under alternative strategies to eliminate poverty, it is appropriate to focus on its income support function.

We shall focus on income support in different ways—first, in terms of aggregate wage-loss replacement, followed by the role of UI in family finances. We then examine work disincentives and benefit inequities, and end with an estimate of UI's antipoverty effectiveness.

Aggregate Wage-Loss Replacement

The aggregate wage-loss replacement rate is a rough measure of how much of the burden of unemployment is in fact lifted from the shoulders of the unemployed. It simply estimates what wages and salaries are lost each year by persons looking for employment, and divides this figure into total UI benefits paid during the same period. Of course, some of the unemployed will not be entitled to benefits, but their earnings loss is also included in the denominator; coverage, eligibility, and duration limitations as well as the wage insurance rates are assessed by this measure.

It has been estimated that about 18 percent of wage loss during the 1950s was replaced by UI, and a similar rate appears to hold for the 1960s.[1] This replacement rate varies with the business cycle.[2]

There are several reasons for this low replacement rate:

1. *Weekly benefit amount.* The norm of weekly benefit payments is usually half of the worker's weekly pay (eleven states add for dependents), but because of low statewide maximums, many workers receive a smaller fraction. Depending on the state, beneficiaries on the average receive about 30 to 45 percent of their weekly pay loss.

---

[1] A study of the period 1948–1960 compares benefits paid in those years with estimates of total wage loss incurred. The results varied somewhat, depending on whether total unemployment was measured or both total and partial unemployment (where the worker has a short work week and is receiving a partial UI benefit). For the thirteen years, all unemployment insurance programs—state, federal employees, veterans, railroad, and temporary extensions—compensated 23 percent for total unemployment and 18 percent for total and partial combined. Richard Lester, *The Economics of Unemployment Compensation* (Princeton, N.J.: Princeton University Press, 1962).

[2] The wage-loss replacement rate is not a constant, but varies with general business conditions. The reasons are complex. In the early stages of a recession, there are likely to be higher wage earners among the insured unemployed and, because of the maximums on payments, these unemployed will receive a smaller proportion replacement of their wage loss. But, at the same time, the portion of the total unemployed who will qualify for benefits is greater than before the downturn. The evidence is that the first effect is overshadowed by the second and that, in the early stages of a recession, the overall replacement rate is higher than it was before the downturn. In the later stages of a recession, the total replacement rate drops considerably, more than unemployment figures would suggest, because an increasing number of persons exhaust their benefits.

2. *Duration and exhaustion.* From 20 to 30 percent of beneficiaries use up their benefit weeks before finding employment. These "exhaustees" had been entitled to an average fifteen weeks of benefits, at worst, to an average twenty-eight weeks, at best, depending on the state.
3. *Disqualifications.* For voluntary job terminations, or failure to be available or to accept suitable work, persons are denied benefits from a few weeks to the full period of their unemployment.
4. *Eligibility.* Some applicants are not eligible because they do not have sufficient evidence of attachment to the work force as measured by base-year earnings, weeks worked, or distribution of work during the year. These requirements exclude workers in marginal and irregular employment as well as new entrants and reentrants to the labor market, the latter accounting for a large share of unemployment in recent times.
5. *Delayed filing and nonfiling.* These account for some of the uncompensated wage loss.
6. *Coverage.* Finally, some persons work in employment that is not covered by the law; no taxes are paid on their behalf and they are not entitled to benefits. In an average month, they constitute about 15 percent of wage and salaried workers.

The low replacement rate is the sum of a partial replacement for some and no replacement for others. For example, in 1967, there were at any given time an average of 3 million unemployed, but only 1 million were being compensated. The distribution in terms of compensability was as shown in Table 9.1.

One might ask whether, with such a low replacement rate, UI is really worth keeping. Could an income maintenance program easily substitute for UI?

This would be a hasty inference. The total amounts paid annually indicate an actuarial value but do not reflect the feeling of security people derive from an insurance program. For instance, the value of life insurance to a family does not await the death of the insured. The UI constituency is not the 5–10 million per year who draw benefits; it is the estimated 70–75 million workers who work in one or more covered jobs during the year and feel a diminished risk. An income maintenance plan that paid $7.5 billion per year (UI payments in the recession year of 1971) would not be regarded as a fair trade.

There is also the fact that UI is regarded as still unfinished business. Coverage has been significantly improved in recent years. Maximums expressed as a percentage of average weekly wages are becoming more prevalent and will help resist the erosion experienced in inflationary times.

Table 9.1 UI Coverage of the Unemployed, 1967

	Number (millions)	Percentage
All unemployed	3.0	100
Compensated UI beneficiaries	1.0	33
Covered by UI but not compensated	.6	22
Eligible unemployed filing for noncompensable waiting weeks	.2	—
Disqualified; not filing for benefits	.3	—
Exhausted UI benefits	.2	—
Not covered by UI	.4	13
New entrants, reentrants (not eligible)	1.0	33

Source—Derived from estimates supplied by the Manpower Administration, U.S. Department of Labor.

Supporting the Standard of Living of the Involuntarily Unemployed

Inherent in the benefit principles of UI is the theory of the declining marginal utility of income. Total utility for the wage earner can be raised by smoothing out his income over all the weeks of the year rather than his receiving more in some weeks and none in others. Since this would argue for weekly benefits equal to weekly wage loss, it is constrained by another principle, that of preserving work incentives. Replacement for a limited period of time is partial in order to encourage the search and acceptance of work.

When UI plans were enacted, it was not clear at what level replacement began to impair incentives (we still do not know). It was assumed to be some proportion of one's weekly wage, and an arbitrary judgment was made that benefits should replace about one-half of the individual's weekly wage loss. (This was less than the two-thirds replacement principle in workmen's compensation, where more objective standards were available to detect malingering.)

This decision was different in conception from that used in England. Sir William Beveridge has said, "Social insurance should aim at guaranteeing the minimum income needed for subsistence."[3] Though we adopted some features of British social insurance, we rejected the subsistence concept. It was felt that the existence of unemployment as a normal feature of free enterprise required recognition that the workers' loss was the important thing, and that the loss was their wage. Since most lived exclu-

[3] Sir William Beveridge, *Social Insurance and Allied Services* (New York: Macmillan, 1942), p. 14.

sively on their own wages, their previous wages are the foundation of their standards of living. Payment of benefits in an adequate proportion to wage loss helps maintain these standards until workers regain their normal employment status. Since there is a wide difference in wage levels and living standards among regions of the country, a wage-determined benefit also provided an automatic adjustment for regional variation.

What is the evidence as to how well UI has succeeded in maintaining its beneficiaries' standards of living? A series of studies made between 1954 and 1958, and one made more recently, have responded to this question by comparing benefits with the claimant's previous wages, family income, and family expenditures.[4]

For most beneficiaries, weekly benefits were less than one-half of their former gross weekly earnings and, in many cases, less than one-half of their take-home pay. The ratio of benefits to earnings (wage-loss replacement) was lower for heads of families than for single persons. This was because of the higher earnings of family heads who were more likely to be affected by state maximums. In wage-loss replacement, single persons fared better than those men in families who were sole or principal earners. And because of their low wage levels, women in families fared best of all.

Unless there was more than one earner, beneficiary families received little income from sources other than UI. In the families of beneficiaries who were sole or major earners, and in single-person households, cash income during unemployment was less than half of the level of cash income during the beneficiaries' employment. Multi-earner families in which the beneficiaries were not principal earners did not, of course, experience as much of a drop in family income during unemployment.

What about benefits relative to expenditures? First, we should note that families with unemployed wage earners did not reduce their expenditures commensurately with their drop in income. A large proportion of families maintained expenditures considerably above income by using up savings, by borrowing, and by receiving help from family or friends. The reductions in expenditures were somewhat higher in recession periods.[5] Benefits appeared to range from 38 to 48 percent of cash expenditures, depending on the state.

[4] Beneficiary surveys conducted by state agencies in cooperation with the U.S. Bureau of Employment Security, reported in *Unemployment Insurance and the Family Finances of the Unemployed*, BES No. U–203, U.S., Bureau of Employment Security (Washington, D.C.: U.S. Government Printing Office, 1961).

[5] This may reflect pessimism about reemployment opportunities, as well as that some were unemployed for longer periods and made more adjustments. Also, more sole or principal wage earners are unemployed in recession times, resulting in heavier income loss.

By postulating a list of nondeferrable expenditures (food, shelter, utilities, medical care), a test of adequacy of UI payments is whether or not. they are sufficient for these necessary expenditures. UI benefits in surveyed families covered only one-half to three-quarters of such expenditures by families whose heads were unemployed. For single beneficiaries, the ratio of benefits to nondeferrable expenditures was more nearly one to one.

In summary, the evidence of these surveys cuts several ways, depending on who is unemployed. First, it shows that UI weekly benefits are not sufficient for families in which the beneficiaries are sole or principal earners. Therefore, they are required to use other means to bridge the gap between income and nondeferrable expenditures. The problem could be remedied by raising maximums so that middle-income workers would also benefit from the half-of-wages replacement principle. More extensive use of dependents' allowances would also help here. For single workers, the program seems to work about as intended, as an economic security system. For additional earners in the family other than the principal earner, it is difficult to evaluate the role of UI without more data about how their earnings figure in family finances.

The duration of unemployment affects the adequacy of benefits, in part because the deferrability of some expenditures diminishes in time and because benefits are eventually terminated. A study in the recession of 1958[6] showed that families of the unemployed decreased savings, postponed buying, borrowed money, piled up bills, and got help from relatives in varying degrees, depending on how long they had been unemployed. The most striking finding, however, was that, as duration of unemployment went beyond thirteen weeks and then beyond twenty-seven weeks, there were drastic adjustments made, such as moving to cheaper quarters, other family members getting jobs, and going on relief. It can be inferred that termination of weekly benefits signals the need for drastic adjustments.

Work Disincentives

There is, then, considerable evidence to suggest that UI does not fully meet its economic security goals of supporting standards of living of the involuntarily unemployed. Is there evidence that benefits interfere with market incentives?

A valuable but frequently overlooked study by Lininger, published

[6] W. J. Cohen, William Haber, and Eva Mueller, *The Impact of Unemployment in the 1958 Recession* (Ann Arbor: Institute of Labor and Industrial Relations, University of Michigan and Wayne State University, 1960), p. 40.

in 1962,[7] investigates whether or not the size of the weekly benefit amount affects the length of time individuals draw benefits. The method of study was to control for different labor-demand factors associated with occupation and industry, length of employment, education, age, sex, race, and place of residence. With variation in duration from these factors accounted for, the remaining variation was assumed to be attributable to differences in the ratio of weekly benefits to the worker's previous wage. The absence of any correlation with the duration of the claims showed workers did not postpone employment because of the benefit–wage ratio. The author concluded that "an increase in the size of weekly unemployment benefits would not lead to longer duration of such benefits."

Another study[8] of state data for the years 1962 and 1967 shows a small effect of benefits on the duration of claims. This study, by Chapin, estimates that a 10 percent increase in the level of benefits would have increased the average duration of benefits in 1967 by one day.[9]

A recent study of "partial benefit" schedules—situations in which UI claimants may work and receive reduced UI benefits—shows that certain kinds of schedules (where work increases result in a net loss of income from work and benefits combined) do restrain work effort to earnings below the critical points of the schedule, thus adversely affecting work behavior.[10]

Studies of exhaustees in several states are inconclusive as to whether or not there is prolongation of unemployment as a result of UI benefits.[11] As might be expected, some persons who terminate their benefits continue to be unemployed, some get work, some withdraw from any further search. The question is whether or not the rates of withdrawal or reemployment jump suddenly with the termination of benefits; if they did, a logical inference would be that benefits had delayed the return to work.[12] But it is

[7] Charles A. Lininger, Jr., *Unemployment Benefits and Duration* (Ann Arbor: Institute for Social Research, University of Michigan, 1962).

[8] See Gene Chapin, "Unemployment Insurance, Job Search, and the Demand for Leisure," *Western Economic Journal* 9 (1971): 102–107.

[9] Chapin's model also shows that the legal maximum duration of UI benefits affects the average duration of unemployment. But, since about one-fifth of claimants exhaust their benefits and since average duration of unemployment is compensated unemployment, the finding is a truism with no implication for the effect of UI on work behavior. Chapin appears to recognize this but does not say so explicitly.

[10] See Raymond Munts, "Partial Benefit Schedules in Unemployment Insurance: Their Effect on Work Incentive," *Journal of Human Resources* 5 (1970).

[11] See U.S., Department of Labor, Bureau of Employment Security, *Major Findings of the 16 State Studies of Claimants Exhausting Unemployment Benefit Rights, 1956–59* (Washington, D.C.: U.S. Government Printing Office, 1961).

[12] The analytical tool here is "survival rate," which is the proportion of claimants in a given week who are still unemployed and available for work the next week.

not clear that an immediate jump of any amount is excessive, given the purpose of UI to provide support until there is "suitable" emloyment.

Other studies have been made on disqualifications and availability criteria, but are somewhat dated. There is room for more empirical work on the wage and mobility effects of UI. From the evidence available, however, there is little reason for fear that UI is severely distorting the operation of the labor market. The exception to this is in certain seasonal employment where labor is attracted by the combination of wage and UI benefits. As for women workers, it is often concluded that they are a special problem for UI because working wives, as so-called secondary wage earners, have less work attachment. However, the labor force participation pattern of women is changing rapidly. Too frequently, conclusions about "women workers" in UI do not distinguish the effects of low earnings and occupational differences that also are associated with female employment.

It would indeed be surprising if UI did not in fact prolong unemployment to some extent. Not only would this be contrary to economic theory, but it would negate what some regard as one of the purposes of UI: namely, to allow unemployed workers to take time to find suitable jobs that make use of their skills and experience. In any final assessment of UI's effect on economic efficiency, some allowance must be made for this contribution to employment stability and productivity.

Benefit Inequities through Interstate Variation

Originally, state UI plans were very similar to each other, largely because the states lacked the expertise to design programs and accepted the recommendations of the Social Security Board. With experience came innovation, and now there is considerable variation. The differences have also been accelerated by the variation in the cost of UI resulting from differences in states' unemployment rates, competitive pressures among the states for industrial development, and the relative strengths of labor and management in policymaking.

The maximum weekly benefit excluding dependent allowances ranges from $45 in Indiana to $105 in the District of Columbia. Potential duration of benefits (number of weeks allowed) ranges from an average potential of 30.6 weeks in the District of Columbia to 19.8 in Florida. Minimum benefits, total annual benefits, eligibility conditions, and disquali-

---

(The survival rate is 1 minus the reemployment and withdrawal rate.) The survival rates suggested by the postexhaustion studies appear to fall within the range of the survival rates for beneficiaries. Further study is needed, however, because survival rates vary by state and the stage of the business cycle.

fication rules all vary considerably. The result is that similar kinds of workers will be treated differently, depending on where they live. An unemployed worker (with no dependents) earning the national average weekly wage ($141 in 1970) would receive weekly benefits of as little as $40 or as much as $77, depending on the state in which he had worked. His benefit would have been equal to 30 percent of his average weekly wage in one state, 30 to 39 percent of his average weekly wage in twelve states, 40 to 49 percent in twenty-five states, and 50 percent or more in fourteen states.

To some extent, weekly benefit levels and the duration of benefits are trade-offs: One state can have higher weekly benefits and shorter duration than another and yet both give beneficiaries about equal total benefit entitlement. Another trade-off is between liberal benefits and tight eligibility and disqualification rules as against low benefits and easy rules.

The cost rate of a state program is one indicator that sums up the liberality of all benefit dimensions considered together. When we further refine the cost rate by estimating it for equal levels of state unemployment (through actuarial procedures), we have a pure measure of how generous a state is toward its unemployment workers.[13] (This can be expressed as statewide benefit expenditures per $100 of total covered payrolls if covered unemployment in the state had averaged 3.5 percent during the year.) The figures for the range in 1960 and 1967 are given in Table 9.2. The conclusion is that some states are twice as generous as others and that, during the first seven years of the 1960s, there was little change in the amount of interstate inequity.

Antipoverty Effectiveness

It is a mistake to think of UI as purely wage-related. Four kinds of compromises have been made with the concept of a social minimal income on the grounds that there is a greater "presumed need" in certain cases.

1. The maximums are statewide ceilings that prevent the half-of-wage-loss principle from operating for the higher earners. They must expect weekly benefits at less than half of their own wage loss, and the exact amount depends on where the statewide maximum has been set. Presumably, this is a concession to the idea that such workers have more savings and other resources to fall back on, and therefore need less than half of their wage loss replaced. (Were this principle rigorously observed,

---

[13] For the methodology, see Raymond Munts, "A Useful Quantitative Measure of State Unemployment Insurance Benefits," Discussion Paper No. 36, Institute for Research on Poverty, University of Wisconsin, Madison, Wisc., 1969.

Table 9.2   Range of UI Cost Rates for 3.5 Percent Unemployment Rates

	Low state (dollars)	High state (dollars)	Low/High (percent)
1960			
All states	.70	1.40	50
Continental states only	.74	1.40	53
1967			
All states	.71	1.60	44
Continental states only	.75	1.44	52

Note—Cost rates are usually expressed per $1 of covered payrolls; here they are stated per $100 for easier interpretation.

we would find a great deal more consistency in maximum benefit amounts relative to statewide average wages than in fact exists.)

2. Nine states compromise the half-of-wages principle so that lower-paid workers get a larger share than this. The state that has carried this the furthest gives the lowest-paid workers a benefit of 68 percent of their weekly wage loss.

3. Eleven states adjust the benefit amount according to family size, or at least add small payments for a specified number of dependents.

4. Eight states and Puerto Rico have a uniform duration of benefits, which allows lower-income persons to receive the same number of potential weeks of benefits as higher-income persons. The other states with benefits of variable duration scale down the number of potential weeks for those of lower earnings or intermittent work records. The effect is that, in the uniform duration states, persons with low earnings in their base year can draw higher total annual benefits than comparable persons in the variable duration states.

With this evidence from the benefit structure, one can presume there is some amount of income redistribution going on within the UI program. But how much? The best source of information comes from the Survey of Economic Opportunity (SEO) of 1967.[14] Although there was substantial

[14] The Survey of Economic Opportunity was conducted for the Office of Economic Opportunity in the spring of 1967 and applied to 1966 income of the respondents. The sample of 30,000 households, or addresses, consists of two parts. The first part is a national self-weighting sample of approximately 18,000 households, drawn in the same way as the Current Population Survey sample. In order to obtain better information concerning the poor, particularly the nonwhite poor, 12,000 additional households were also included in the survey by drawing a sample from areas with large nonwhite populations. Questions were asked about various kinds of income, including unemployment insurance. The survey respondents reported a total that was

underreporting of UI, the SEO suggests the extent of redistribution occurring through UI. The following paragraphs summarize some of the results.

Of the total of all payments reported, 20.4 percent were paid to poor recipient households. Of all the households receiving UI payments, 15.9 percent were poor. These are the best available estimates of the antipoverty effectiveness of the UI program.

The average payment to all families receiving UI in 1967 was $400, and the average to poor families among these was $513, suggesting somewhat more poverty sensitivity than the wage-qualifying requirements and wage-related benefit structure of UI would lead one to suppose. The explanation lies in the compromises with the needs concepts described previously and also the probability that the poorer families were out of work for longer periods.

The $513 average payment was 43 percent of the average poverty gap of the recipient poor families, suggesting wide room for income support in addition to UI. Of the 459,000 poor families receiving UI, about 132,000 (29 percent) were taken out of poverty by their UI benefits. (The other 71 percent would all be eligible for benefits from a guaranteed minimum income plan designed to close the poverty gap.)

UI's insensitivity to family size (only eleven states vary benefits by family size) appears in the finding that benefits did not increase with family size. Single and small families even did substantially better than seven- and eight-person families. The percentage of the poverty gap filled by UI varied from 83 percent for single-person households to 13 percent for eight-person households.

Benefits were highest (over $800) where the head did not work at all during the year, and declined steadily as claimants worked more and more weeks during the year. This was true for all recipient families as well as for poor recipient families.

The SEO reported income for 1966, a year of relatively low unemployment. It would be informative to know the redistribution impact of UI in a year with a higher rate of unemployment. On the one hand, persons of higher income would be out of work and receiving UI in such a year; on the other hand, wage earners would have smaller total earnings for the year. The former effect would reduce UI's poverty effectiveness; the latter effect would increase it. Without information comparable to

---

62.8 percent of all UI program expenditures in 1966. This underreporting is felt by some UI experts to be too serious to warrant use of the SEO data. The findings reported here are from an analysis prepared by Ben Gillingham, "Cash Transfers: How Much Do They Help the Poor?", Institute for Research on Poverty, University of Wisconsin, Madison, Wisc., January 1971.

that provided by the SEO, we cannot know which would be the dominating influence.

II. Roads to Income Maintenance

To explore the mission of UI is to come to the conclusion that income maintenance plans are needed, not as substitutes for UI but in addition to it. UI is for those with interrupted work histories, those who want work and are unable to find it, and those with skills to keep until they are again demanded. It is not for those who are unemployable, nor for those who have obligations that prevent them from being in the labor market, nor is it sufficient for those with incomes far below their minimal needs. UI contributes significantly to the prevention of poverty by cushioning income slides that otherwise can lead to deterioration in morale and family structure. But a strategy for abolishing extant poverty must work through broadly based programs directed to the lowest income families.

These broadly based income maintenance plans are of two types. The income-tested plans (Public Assistance, the Family Assistance Plan, and negative income tax plans) would count UI benefits as income. This reduces the payment of the plan by all or part of the amount of UI benefits. Then there are the demogrants (flat benefit or tax credit plans), under which payments are of uniform amounts irrespective of other income.

When analyzing incentives, the difference between the two types may be more one of degree than one of kind. In the income-tested type, the payments are reduced for receipt of UI benefits and the disincentive effect is experienced on the transfer side. With the demogrant, the UI benefit would probably be taxed by the income tax at the same rate as earnings, and the disincentive effect is felt on the tax side. The benefit reduction rate (sometimes called tax rate) would probably be higher in the income-tested plans than would the tax rate in demogrant plans.

In any case, it is useful to distinguish the two types of plans for purposes of seeing how they might integrate with UI. We look first at problems with the income-tested type.

Integration with Income-Tested Plans

THE ECLIPSE EFFECT

Where an unemployed worker would be entitled to UI benefits and also to payments from an income-tested plan, there might be cases in which there would be no advantage from obtaining UI benefits. This would be the case if UI benefits were totally subtracted from the potential payment level in setting the actual payment, and if UI benefits in a particular case were less than the potential payment. If this were to occur to a majority of the UI constituency, they would lose interest in UI because they would get as much or more from the income-tested plan. In effect, UI would have been eclipsed. This could happen even under rather modest guarantee levels and does occur now in some instances. Some AFDC recipients, for example, receive AFDC supplementation of UI benefits.

To illustrate, it will help to compare the benefits under two specific plans, the Family Assistance Plan (FAP) of the Ninety-second Congress and the UI program of Mississippi. In order to simplify the comparison, it will be assumed that a family has no earnings in the current quarter and that benefits under both programs depend only on earnings in the previous quarter. FAP uses a quarterly carryover accounting period, under which payments are calculated on the basis of estimated income in the current quarter and actual income in the three previous quarters. We simplify by assuming there are no carryovers from the second and third preceding quarters, that there is no income in the previous quarter except earnings, and no income in the current quarter. Earnings net of all deductions in the previous quarter thus becomes the relevant variable. When net earnings are less than the quarterly FAP guarantee, the full FAP guarantee is paid in the current quarter. When net earnings are greater than the FAP guarantee, the excess is carried over to the current quarter and reduces the FAP benefit on a dollar-for-dollar basis.

The relationship between FAP benefits and gross earnings in the previous quarter are illustrated in Figure 9.1(a). For example, a family of four with no income in the current quarter receives $600 if its net earnings in the previous quarter are less than $600. Net earnings in a quarter are equal to gross earnings less $180 and one-third of the remainder, which means that net earnings are $600 when gross earnings are $1080. Each dollar of net earnings above $600 reduces FAP benefits by $1.00, which means that each dollar of gross earnings above $1080 reduces FAP benefits by $.67.

On the UI side, we assume that the base year ended with the date of applications for benefits,[15] and that the high quarter for benefit determination was also the previous quarter. Figure 9.1(b) illustrates how UI benefits in Mississippi vary with earnings in the previous quarter.

---

[15] Actually, Mississippi uses a base year that is the first four of the five quarters preceding the benefit year. Only four states use the preceding quarters. The base period refers to the preceding period of time which is examined to determine whether UI applicants meet the conditions of eligibility (for example, sufficient length of employment above specified minimum levels of pay).

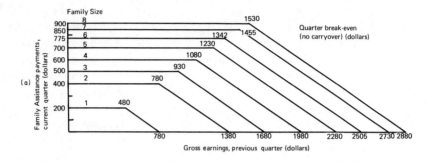

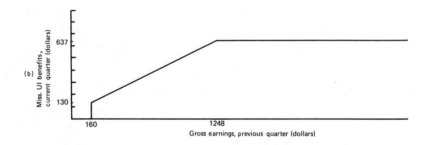

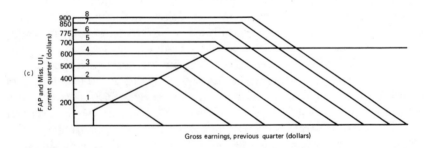

Figure 9.1. Comparison of Family Assistance payments and UI benefits in Mississippi as functions of previous quarterly earnings.

Figures 9.1(a) and 9.1(b) are superimposed in Figure 9.1(c). Wherever the Family Assistance payment is higher than UI, although UI would have to be paid, the total received would be determined by the Family Assistance payment level. This is clearly the case for low-earnings families, and more so for larger than for smaller families. For example, four-person families whose heads earned less than $1086 per quarter, and eight-person families whose heads earned under $1924 per quarter, would in effect have had their UI eclipsed by FAP in Mississippi. According to earnings data from Mississippi,[16] more than half and maybe as many as 70 percent of families have earnings that fall under these levels.

The extent of eclipse will vary positively with the liberality of an income-tested plan, and negatively with the state's earnings level and with the liberality of the UI benefit structure. But after examining other states, it can be concluded that the last is relatively unimportant; that is, the variation in UI plans as now constituted is not a significant factor.

However, the other two factors are quite important, and lead to this conclusion: The variation in income levels around the United States is so significant that, to achieve a satisfactory integration of UI and income-tested plans, such plans must provide for regional variation in their guarantee levels. The alternative is to reduce the payments of an income-tested plan by less than the full amount of UI benefits. This approach is constrained by work disincentive effects, as we shall now see.

TREATMENT OF UI BENEFITS

It is a tenet of social insurance theory that benefits are earned, since the premium or contribution has been paid by the worker or his employer. According to this view, benefits are a form of deferred wages. In the original FAP proposal, UI benefits were treated as deferred wages. The same implicit tax rate was applied to UI benefits as applied to earnings. The Ways and Means Committee changed this to reduce program costs by counting UI as unearned income, reducing the guarantee or potential assistance payments by the full value of any UI benefits. We have already noted one of the consequences of treating UI benefits as unearned income, the possibility of causing an eclipse of UI. There are other consequences as well.[17] But the question here is whether or not there are conflicting objectives in trying both to reduce the eclipse effect and to minimize disincentives.

---

[16] U.S., Department of Health, Education, and Welfare, Social Security Administration, Office of Research and Statistics, *Earnings Distributions in the United States, 1967*, Publication No. 72–11900 (Washington, D.C.: U.S. Government Printing Office, 1971).

[17] Another consequence is that applicants for the income-tested plan may have no interest in obtaining their UI (where it is lower than the plan's guarantee). The Ways and Means Committee "solved" this simply by requiring, as a condition of eligibility for FAP, the application for UI of persons entitled to UI benefits. Requiring entitled persons to claim their UI as a condition for eligibility to an income-tested plan is using the worker as the agent for an intersystem transfer. From one point of view, there is a penalty for failing to perform what is a useless act. The obligation and responsibility for collecting the UI benefit should, more properly, rest with FAP. This is particularly true because of the adversary character of UI administration in which employers review and contest claims.

In this analysis, no light can come from a metaphysical discussion about whether or not UI benefits really are deferred wages. Instead, let us suppose that some of UI had been disregarded—10, 20, 33⅓, or 50 percent. The last two disregards compare with the treatment considered for earnings under FAP. The first two can be regarded as compromises between the "deferred wages" and the "unearned income" treatment. Within these various possibilities, is there any evidence that the total income of beneficiaries would rise to a point that work incentives would be threatened?

The analysis can be made only in terms of a specific structure, and we shall use FAP. Assume families of various sizes, each with a single earner making $100 a week. The single earner has worked steadily for more than three quarters and then is laid off. How will his combined income from UI and FAP in the current quarter compare with his net (after taxes) income in the previous quarter, assuming various disregards of his UI benefits?[18]

The incentive problem here is defined in terms of disposable income when unemployed, divided by disposable income when employed. For a person drawing UI and Family Assistance payments, will the combination fall enough short of his previous net income that he will take back the old job—or one like it—if he has the opportunity? The independent variable of interest is the amount of disregard of UI benefits possible under the Family Assistance or other income-tested plan.

The results are shown (Table 9.3) for two states, Alabama and Connecticut, which have different styles in benefit formula (Connecticut varying with family size) and maximums at extremes that encompass all but five states.

The findings confirm that to have counted UI as earnings (a 67 percent tax rate or 33 percent disregard) would have raised incentive problems, going into the range where current income was 80 percent or better

[18] The method of calculating income in the current (fourth) quarter and relating it to income in the previous quarters is as follows:

$$\frac{Y_4}{Y_3} = \frac{FAB_4 + UI_4}{FAB_3 + E_3} = \frac{FAR - [UI(1-R) + C_{1+2+3}] + UI_4}{FAB_3 + E_3},$$
$$\text{and } FAR - UI(1-R) - C_{1+2+3} \geqslant 0$$

where Y = income, FAB = Family Assistance benefit, E = earnings, FAR = family assistance guarantee for each family size, R = percentage of UI disregarded, C = carryover, UI = jobless benefit, and the subscripts designate the quarter. By subtracting personal income tax withheld and Social Security tax in the third quarter, Y_3 becomes the *net* earnings. See U.S., Congress, House, Committee on Ways and Means, *Report of the Committee on Ways and Means on H.R. 1*, 92d Cong., 1st sess., 20 May 1971, for a description of the benefit provisions in FAP.

Table 9.3   Unemployed Quarter Income As Percentage of Previous Employed Quarter Disposable Income, According to Alternative Treatments of UI Benefits under FAP, Selected States

Percentage of UI benefits disregarded by FAP	Family size						
	1	2	3	4	5	6	7
10							
Alabama	59	57	56	54	67	69	70
Connecticut	65	68	72	76	78	73	72
20							
Alabama	59	57	56	58	72	73	74
Connecticut	65	68	72	77	78	78	79
33							
Alabama	59	57	56	65	79	80	81
Connecticut	65	68	72	76	88	88	88
50							
Alabama	59	57	56	74	88	88	88
Connecticut	65	68	72	65	101	101	100

Note—Assumes single-earner families, earnings $100 weekly in employed quarters, and that only income is earnings, Family Assistance payments, and UI.

of past net income, even in Alabama (for larger families). However, this does not mean it is necessary to go to the other extreme and have no disregard at all. In fact, at a 20 percent disregard, not even large families in Connecticut would reach 80 percent of previous after-tax income. With a 20 percent disregard, there would be some work incentive, and certainly incentive to collect UI.

Cases can arise in which an individual is receiving more than one social insurance benefit. A limiting principle could be applied as follows: In computing the payment, 20 percent of benefits from unemployment insurance plans shall be disregarded; but the total received from social insurance and the payment under this plan shall not exceed 80 percent of the beneficiary's earnings in the previous period (quarter) or one-half of the state's average weekly wage, whichever is greater.[19]

[19] We take our cue here from the "accommodation" made when the Workmen's Compensation constituency began complaining about OASDI supplementation of WC permanent and total benefits. An amendment was added to OASDI that, if a disability claimant is also entitled to WC, his OASDI benefit is reduced in those months in which the total combined OASDI and WC otherwise payable to him and his dependents would exceed 80 percent of his earnings prior to his disability (subject to adjustment for changes in national earnings levels). If the combined benefits exceed this percentage, the OASDI benefits are reduced by the excess. Applying the idea to an income-tested plan may require some additional adjustments. For example, most workers can have their potential wage level defined in terms of

If an income-tested plan does not fully offset the amount of the UI benefit, as here recommended, then there will be an increase in the implicit marginal tax rate on earnings in the integrated system. This occurs because earnings force adjustments in the payments both directly and indirectly through the UI benefits.

An example will show how this works. Assume FAP with a 66⅔ per-cent implicit marginal rate on earnings and a UI plan with a 100 percent implicit rate. If FAP allows 20 percent of UI benefits to be retained, the chain of adjustments for $1.00 of additional earnings is as follows:

$1.00 increase in earnings	+$1.00
Reduction in UI of $1.00	− 1.00
Rise in FAP of $.80	+ .80
Reduction in FAP of $.66⅔	− .66⅔
Increase in income, or 86⅔ percent tax	$ .13⅓

In effect, the 20 percent disregard of UI has altered the overall implicit tax on earnings from 66⅔ to 86⅔ percent.

Some effect is inherent and cannot be escaped, but it can be diminished by lowering the rate reductions used in the UI partial benefit schedule. Connecticut, for example, uses 66⅔ percent rather than 100 percent as in many states. An income-tested plan that treated UI benefits with a 20 percent disregard would have its implicit marginal tax rate raised by thirteen percentage points in Connecticut (that is, from 50 to 63 percent, or 67 to 80 percent) as opposed to twenty percentage points in other states.

INTERACTING MARGINAL TAX RATES

Whatever decision is made as to how an income-tested plan will treat UI benefits, there remains an interesting problem of interacting marginal tax rates between a given state UI program and the income-tested plan. This arises because various states use different partial benefit schedules and because any income-tested plan enacted will probably treat earnings differently than do any of the state UI plans.

If the guarantee level of an individual's UI benefits (for total unemployment) is either well below or well above the guarantee level of the income-tested plan, there is little possibility of their implicit marginal tax rates on earnings interacting. Where the UI benefit is clearly superior,

---

past earnings, but, for those with little previous work experience, an arbitrary definition may be needed, such as some fraction of the average weekly wage of the state.

no payments will be forthcoming from the income-tested plan; for any earnings, the controlling schedule will be the UI partial benefit schedule. Where the guarantee from the income-tested plan is clearly superior to any payable UI benefits, the controlling implicit marginal tax rate on earnings will be that of the income-tested plan, even when UI benefits are also paid. However, when the two guarantees are close together, increments in earnings can cause the superior plan to become inferior.

This may occur frequently, because most of the state UI partial benefit schedules are still heavily dependent on 100 percent implicit tax rates. Among the states with very high tax rates are Alabama, Colorado, Florida, Louisiana, Mississippi, Nevada, and Texas: All have a small earnings disregard followed by benefit reduction dollar-for-dollar of earnings.[20] A claimant could start out on UI with benefits higher than his alternative Family Assistance payment (at a quarterly rate of $800 compared with $600, for example), only to find that, as his earnings go up, he will be entitled to Family Assistance payments[21] (see Figure 9.2).

[20] These schedules are found in U.S., Department of Labor, Manpower Administration, Unemployment Insurance Service, *Comparison of State Unemployment Insurance Laws* (Washington, D.C.: U.S. Government Printing Office, August 1972).
[21] An example will illustrate this. The head of a hard-luck family is laid off and entitled to $62 per week in UI, or $800 per quarter. If he had no UI coming, he would be eligible for $600 quarterly from FAP for his family of four (with no other income, no "carryover"). The UI is clearly better, and he draws. But he finds he has part-time earnings opportunities. In his state, the first $5 of weekly earnings is ignored, but after that, his benefit is reduced by the amount of earnings; FAP ignores the first $180 of earnings in a quarter and then reduces payments by $.67 for each dollar of earnings. When our hard-pressed man starts earning more than $34 per week, he begins to be better off under FAP, and entitled to FAP payments. The following schedule helps show how this works. It is depicted schematically in the first drawing of Figure 9.2.

Earnings		UI benefit (quarter)	UI plus earnings (quarter)	FAP payment (quarter)	FAP plus earnings (quarter)
Weekly	*Quarter*				
$0	$0	$800	$800	$600	$600
5	65	800	865	600	665
10	130	735	865	600	730
20	260	605	865	547	807
30	390	475	865	460	850
40	520	345	865	373	893
50	650	215	865	287	937
60	780	85	865	200	980

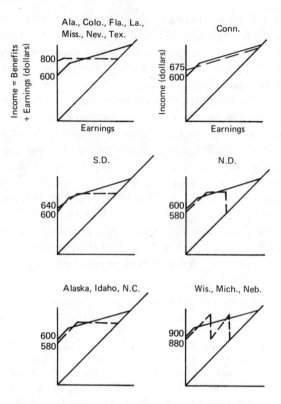

Figure 9.2. Illustrations of interactions between UI partial benefit schedules and the marginal tax rate in the Family Assistance Plan. Broken line (- - -) indicates UI schedules; solid line (—) indicates Family Assistance payments.

A different situation exists in a number of states (North Dakota, Alaska, Idaho, North Carolina, and others) where, at zero earnings in the current quarter, the individual may start off somewhat better on Family Assistance than on UI. But as his earnings in the current quarter rise, the situation will change and the UI benefits will exceed Family Assistance. In some states, as his earnings continue to rise, the relative advantage of UI disappears and he would again be better off on Family Assistance. In the extreme situation (Wisconsin, Michigan, and Nebraska), occasions can arise where, in order to maximize his position, the individual would be changing back and forth between programs five times (Figure 9.2).

Administration of an income-tested plan would have to be extraordinarily competent and sophisticated to follow the marginal rate interactions and respond in the interest of the recipient. It would undoubtedly help if the states all adopted one form of partial benefit schedule, perhaps the one that is used in Connecticut, or a schedule similar in its characteristics to that used by the income-tested plan.[22]

Integration with Demogrants

SUBSTITUTION OF EQUIVALENTS

As we have seen, it is deceptively easy via the eclipse effect to substitute an income-tested plan for UI, even without overtly intending to do so. With a demogrant, an intent to substitute requires positive action repealing UI. Otherwise, UI will be paid in addition to the demogrant. Is it possible to devise a demogrant that will be an acceptable substitute? If the demogrant is large enough, will it be regarded as the equivalent of UI benefits now received?

First, let us take "equivalency" in a political sense of "the greatest good for the greatest number," which overrules individual interests for those of the group. Any particular demogrant can be made progressively more generous until the majority will accept it as a substitute. We assume that each person weighs the loss of UI protection against the gain of a demogrant (though we do not forget that some lose through the demogrant). Assuming the technical problems of knowing individual preferences can be solved,[23] there are two remaining conceptual problems. Is everyone in the society voting, or just those covered by UI? A majority with a direct interest in the UI program may be a majority of the voting

[22] Because UI benefits are scaled at one-half weekly earnings, the break-even point (where benefits decline to zero) has to be less than twice the guarantee and preferably, because of withheld taxes, closer to one-and-one-half times the guarantee.

[23] In the case of each individual now covered by UI, we can presume that it has some value to him, depending on how much he is exposed to the risk of unemployment and how strong his preference is for security over uncertainty. Many people would be willing to buy unemployment insurance if it were optional and offered in the open market, and the price each would pay would depend on the strength of his preference. It is to the point here that, if we had such a hypothetical demand schedule for UI, it would also serve as a kind of demand schedule for a demogrant substitute for UI. The price each individual would pay for UI is also the amount of certain payment he would accept in exchange for giving up UI protection. His preference for a demogrant substitute to UI is mirrored by the cost of giving up UI protection; this is the meaning of equivalency. In the aggregate schedule, there will be some point at which more than half the population will prefer a particular demogrant to UI. All those with a higher equivalency price will simply be outvoted. Unfortunately, this does not get us very far, because we do not know the demand schedule for UI. We could estimate the distribution of beneficiaries by their risk exposure, but in the absence of a market for UI benefits, we know nothing of people's risk tolerance or preference for security although it might be possible to develop proxies using purchase of life or accident insurance.

population. If society enacted UI as a kind of social contract with wage and salary workers to compensate them for their role in an economy dominated by private capital, can this society turn around and outvote a majority of these workers? But the more important difficulty is that, in most states, the size of family does not affect the UI payment, whereas family size could be an important variable for demogrants. Equivalency is a function of both UI preference and family size, and, in the majority voting for the demogrant, there will be larger families than in the minority still preferring UI. Since it makes a difference, does majority mean majority of persons or majority of families?

At the other extreme, there is a different concept of equivalency: namely, that no one should be worse off under the demogrant than he was under UI. Here, the concern is with the largest group of recipients of Unemployment Insurance who have the most at stake. A final determination of equivalency, if one could be made, would be toward some compromise between "no one worse off" and the "greatest good for the greatest number."

What amounts of benefits are paid under the most liberal state programs? The amounts depend on whether or not benefits are defined to include (1) dependents' allowances, which are paid by eleven states, and (2) benefits under the federal–state–triggered extensions, which raise state benefits to a potential thirty-nine weeks. In Table 9.4, the states are shown both with and without the triggered extensions, and with and without dependents' benefits. The largest benefit payable to a single person in the course of a year is more than $5000, but few states pay more than $4000 or even more than $3600.

Now to compare this with payments under a demogrant: There are many possible demogrant payment schedules, depending on whether the amounts are varied by adult–child status, position in the family, or age. Here, we shall assume a schedule that has been shown to have high antipoverty effectiveness as well as administrative simplicity. This schedule provides $1500 for each adult and $300 for each person under eighteen in the family. Okner has calculated the gains and losses from such a demogrant for families of different sizes and income levels.[24] These are shown in Table 9.5.

[24] See Benjamin A. Okner, "The Role of Demogrants As an Income Maintenance Alternative," this volume, particularly Tables 3.8 and 3.9. The loser families (Table 3.8) and the gainer families (Table 3.9) are here combined to give the net demogrant effect for each category of family size and income. For example, on the average, a middle-size family (three to five persons) of $5000 to $10,000 income will be net gainers of about $1143 as a result of the demogrant described here. This is the mean for a family of this size and income category, but a few families in this category are net losers.

Table 9.4 Distribution of States by Maximum Annual Potential Unemployment Insurance Benefits, August 1972

Maximum possible annual UI benefits (in dollars)	*With federal–state extensions[a]*		*Without federal–state extensions*	
	Including dependents' allowance	*Excluding dependents' allowance*	*Including dependents' allowance*	*Excluding dependents' allowance*
5400 to 5000	2	1	—	—
5000 to 4600	—	—	—	—
4600 to 4200	1	—	—	—
4200 to 3800	1	—	—	—
3800 to 3400	5	2	1	1
3400 to 3000	8	9	2	—
3000 to 2600	11	12	3	2
2600 to 2200	18	19	8	6
2200 to 1800	4	6	11	12
1800 to 1400	1	2	24	26
1400 to 1000	—	—	2	4
Total number states[b]	51	51	51	51

[a] Under Employment Security Amendment of 1970.
[b] Includes District of Columbia.

Table 9.5 Average Change in Disposable Income As Result of Demogrant, by Family Size and Income Class

Family size	Benefit schedule	*Change in disposable income by family income class*		
		Under 5000	*5000–10,000*	*10,000–15,000*
1	1500	+840	+71	−720
2	3000			
3	3300			
4	3600	+2095	+1143	+23
5	3900			
6	4200			
7	4500	+3342	+1908	+749
8	4800			

Note–Amounts in dollars.
Source–Computed from Okner, "The Role of Demogrants As an Income Maintenance Alternative," this volume.

The UI levels from Table 9.4 and the demogrant changes from Table 9.5 are compared graphically in Figure 9.3. The comparison suggests that high-risk families who are likely to draw heavily on UI will prefer UI under most conditions, and particularly where the family is small, or where the family is middle-sized with middle or high income, or where the family is middle-sized with low income and is living in one of the states with more liberal UI than the average. Demogrants will be favored even by heavy UI users where the family is both large and low-income, and where the family is large with a middle income but living in a state with low UI benefits.

This conclusion applies to the criterion of "no worse off" in measuring the effect of substituting a particular demogrant for UI. The conclusion does recognize variation among the states in the liberality of their UI benefits. It does not apply the test of "greatest good for the greatest number." Analysis by this criterion requires more knowledge about the strength of people's preference for insurance rather than income.

EFFECT OF HIGHER WITHHOLDING TAX RATES

At the outset, it would appear that integration of UI with a demogrant would be a much simpler and more straightforward process than integration with an income-tested plan. There are no problems of interacting implicit program tax rates although, as will be shown later, there are potential problems with federal income tax rates. There are relationships that are troublesome, not just because they are obscure but because they bear directly on disincentives and the purpose of UI.

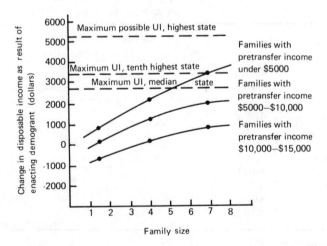

Figure 9.3. Maximum potential UI benefits compared with average change in disposable income under demogrant.

Under a demogrant, taxes and withholding rates are necessarily higher, which has important implications for the ratio of UI benefits to take-home pay. The ratio of all taxes now raised by the federal income tax to a comprehensive tax base is about 20 percent; Okner estimates that, under various demogrant proposals, it could rise to 30 or 40 percent.[25] It is clear that, at almost all levels of income, tax rates would have to be higher under a demogrant. The taxes could be proportional or progressive; when combined with a demogrant, proportional rates give progressive results. However, even if a progressive structure were retained in the rates themselves, higher rates at nearly all levels would still be needed to stay within the limits of a reasonable structure.[26]

If tax rates on earnings are higher under a demogrant, then the worker confronts a different situation. His take-home pay is smaller than before the demogrant, and, when laid off, his wage loss is less. A smaller UI benefit will provide him the same wage-loss replacement rate as formerly, in terms of disposable income. If the withholding rate is substantial, as much as 30 or 40 percent, it becomes impossible to defend the present ratio of weekly benefits to gross wages.

One of the following adjustments would be needed: (*1*) Weekly benefit amounts would have to be calculated as smaller fractions of high quarter earnings; (*2*) weekly benefits would have to be computed in terms of take-home pay rather than gross pay; or (*3*) benefits would have to be made taxable and subject to withholding as are wages and salaries. This last is undoubtedly the simplest adjustment.[27]

SIGNIFICANCE OF THE PAYMENT PERIOD

One possible structure for a demogrant is simply to continue to handle accounts and payments as is done now: In April, the taxpayer calculates his tax and withholding and either makes a payment or receives one, depending on the balance. Under a demogrant, the withholding rate could be estimated with both the tax credit and the expected earnings in mind, and the April accounting would be an adjustment of unanticipated differences. This approach would leave the working parts of UI largely untouched.

[25] Okner, see Chapter 3.
[26] This does not alter in any way the fact that lower- and middle-income persons would usually be much better off under the demogrant.
[27] To compute in terms of take-home pay would introduce inequities because of differences between taxes withheld and actual taxes after end-of-year adjustment. Moreover, states that use quarterly or annual earnings would have no way of applying the take-home pay concept.

A different model, which shall be called the "support model," would provide for regular payment of benefits to the family on a weekly, bi-weekly, or monthly basis. The advantage of this model is that low-income persons would have some form of regular support during the year instead of receiving one big lump sum payment in the spring.

The support model would help UI in two very difficult policy areas, benefit duration and wage-qualifying requirements.

How long should UI be expected to provide benefits? There is general acceptance of state program responsibility up to twenty-six weeks, but beyond that is a no-man's land in which some states have ventured while others fear to go, with the result that Congress sometimes has acted hastily with regard to triggered extended benefit programs. A demogrant of the support model could serve the useful role of relieving UI of concern with persons unemployed beyond six months. For persons of long-term unemployment, there is a strong case for a demogrant rather than UI as a base of support. As time since the last job increases, previous earnings become less relevant, and there develops more justification for applying minimal social needs criteria. Furthermore, long-term benefits are more appropriately financed from general revenues than from a payroll tax.

The problem with wage-qualifying requirements is that, if the minimum benefit is raised, the wage-qualifying requirement gets more restrictive and there is, therefore, no logical way by which UI can improve the situation for low-income, irregularly employed persons. A demogrant would provide support for such persons and also give more flexibility to UI in defining eligibility. States now generally insist on fourteen to twenty weeks of work as minimum evidence of past attachment to the labor market.[28] If state laws were to require twenty weeks of work—and there is some informed opinion that this is desirable—many persons now entitled to UI would not be eligible. However, if a demogrant were in effect, those persons could be declared ineligible for UI and yet not be without income.

The support model of the demogrant could be built in two different ways: Either it could pay every family a weekly (or monthly) amount that would add up over a year to the scheduled tax credit to which they would be entitled; or it could make such periodic payments only to those who are likely to be net recipients after their end-of-year balancing. In the latter case, the regular payments would be based on estimates of the

[28] Minimum required earnings for the high quarter range from $75 to $416 and for the base year from $200 to $1200, depending on the state. These are stated in different ways, sometimes as minimum weeks of work, or base year earnings as multiples of high quarter earnings, or as multiples of the weekly benefit amount.

annual amount divided by twelve for monthly payments, or fifty-two for weekly payments, much as withholding rates are estimated.

This net basis for payment of a support demogrant would appear the better alternative from the standpoint of avoiding large transactions at the end of the tax year. Let us assume such a net payment type of support demogrant in order to inquire whether there are incentive problems. For an unemployed worker receiving both UI and demogrants, how much attraction do earnings present? What is the net change from nonworking to working income?

This can be estimated using Okner's data, if we take some of his assumptions about the demogrant and add some of our own about UI. Let us assume a tax credit schedule of $1250 for each of the first two in a family, $750 for each of the next two, $500 for each of the next two, and $250 each thereafter, that is, Okner's Schedule D.[29] Also, we take the uniform tax rate of 40 percent that goes with it. Let us also assume a UI system that pays benefits of 50 percent of weekly earnings with no dependent benefits, that is, strictly wage insurance.

It is clear at the outset that smaller- and higher-income families will not be net recipients after the end-of-year accounting and would not receive regular demogrant payments during the year. Thus, we need look only to lower-income and larger families for an estimate of incentive effects from the combined demogrant and UI payments.

Table 9.6 Disposable Income on Layoff Relative to Disposable Income While Working, Selected Examples under a Demogrant

	$(UI^a + demo.^b)$	$\div$	$(Earnings + demo.^b)$	$=$	Ratio
Four-person family					
Low earnings ($4000)	(39 + 46)	$\div$	(77 + 46)	=	.69
Higher earnings ($7500)	(72 + 19)	$\div$	(144 + 19)	=	.56
Six-person family					
Low earnings ($4000)	(39 + 65)	$\div$	(77 + 65)	=	.73
Higher earnings ($7500)	(72 + 38)	$\div$	(144 + 38)	=	.60
Eight-person family					
Low earnings ($4000)	(39 + 75)	$\div$	(77 + 75)	=	.75
Higher earnings ($7500)	(72 + 48)	$\div$	(144 + 48)	=	.63

[a] UI (weekly benefit) $= \dfrac{\text{annual earnings} \div 52 \text{ weeks}}{2}$.

[b] Demogrant (weekly payment) $= \dfrac{\text{tax credit} - .4 \text{ annual earnings}}{52 \text{ weeks}}$.

[29] Okner, see Chapter 3.

The estimates are shown in Table 9.6. Before layoff, the recipient receives earnings and the demogrant. After layoff, he receives UI and the demogrant. We look to the ratio of disposable income after layoff to disposable income before layoff as the measure of disincentive. The ratio varies with family size and income level, and for a family of eight with annual earnings of $4000, the ratio reaches 75 percent. Only in extreme cases are the "tax rates" or disincentive effect likely to be of concern, and a simple limit would suffice. Very few persons would be adversely affected by imposing a limitation that reduces UI benefits so that the combined UI and demogrant would not exceed 80 percent of disposable income while employed.

Conclusion: Policy Perspectives

Three kinds of policy questions have been raised in this chapter.

1. How well is UI meeting its income support role? The deficiencies were found to result from the low level of maximum weekly benefits relative to earnings levels, limitations in the duration of benefits, inequities between states, the disincentives in the partial benefits, and from some coverage shortcomings.

2. What policies might improve the antipoverty effectiveness of UI? The most effective changes for this purpose would be lowering wage-qualifying requirements, raising benefits for low-income workers through "weighted" schedules, adding dependent benefits, extending the duration of benefits, and adding a supplemental program (financed through general revenue) for new entrants and reentrants to the labor market. Some of these changes, however, are inconsistent with wage insurance principles.

3. What policies would adapt UI to coexist with broad-based income maintenance programs? UI could coexist with an income-tested plan if UI partial benefit schedules were made similar in rate to the benefit reduction rate (tax rate) of the income-tested plan. Such a plan should also allow some portion of the UI benefits to be ignored (not counted as income), particularly if the guarantee level is uniform over the country. A demogrant or tax credit plan would work best with UI if UI benefits were taxable under the federal personal income tax. Either type of income maintenance plan, but particularly the demogrant, would free UI to focus on a wage insurance role, for example, to tighten wage-qualifying requirements, provide uniform duration of twenty-six or thirty-nine weeks, abolish dependent allowances, and avoid weighted benefit schedules. To prevent disincentive effects under either type, an overall limitation could be adopted that would constrain the UI benefit in any particular case, so

that combined UI and income maintenance payments do not exceed specified limits relative to prelayoff income.

It is beyond our purpose here to inquire into the interrelationship of all these policy changes except to note briefly that each of the three perspectives suggests some changes that are different and some that are the same. An example of a desirable change from all viewpoints is the reconstructing of partial benefit schedules on incentive principles. Another is the raising of maximum weekly benefits to a uniform national standard and the simultaneous inclusion of UI as taxable income in the federal income tax. But there are policy changes that cannot serve both antipoverty and wage insurance objectives, such as dependent allowances, weighted benefit schedules, the previous earnings qualifications, and duration provisions; UI could be relieved of conflicting demands in these matters by the enactment of an income maintenance program with antipoverty objectives.

What changes can be made in the interim, before the enactment of such an income maintenance program? At the least, dependent benefits could be made universal if provided as a flat amount per dependent, supplementing the wage-related benefit. In this form, they could be easily repealed if an income maintenance plan were adopted. (The integrated schedules or variable maximum schemes, such as those in Michigan, Illinois, and Ohio, should be avoided.) Some of the duration provisions (in variable duration plans) that now limit UI beneficiaries to as few as twelve or fifteen weeks of benefits could be liberalized without entering the area of income maintenance, which alone can deal with very long-term unemployment. Finally, a supplementary program for reentrants and new entrants financed from general revenues is needed. If designed as a parallel to the UI program, but structurally separate, it would be easily replaceable by an income maintenance program with antipoverty objectives.

These are only the more obvious suggestions demonstrating how UI can be adapted to some improved antipoverty effectiveness now, and yet be reserved for its wage insurance task whenever an income maintenance plan is enacted.

Acknowledgments

The author wishes to thank Robert Lerman and Saul Blaustein for their valuable suggestions.

10

Public Medical Programs and Cash Assistance: The Problems of Program Integration

Theodore R. Marmor

Introduction

This chapter investigates how the public financing of medical care is and should be combined with income-related cash transfers. It deals with the issues of equity, efficiency, work incentives, and benefit levels which arise when one considers the joint provision of cash and in-kind services such as medical care. Part I addresses these issues in connection with the operation of Medicaid and Medicare, our two largest public medical care programs. Part II addresses these same issues in connection with two income maintenance plans (a demogrant and a negative income tax).

I. Medicare and Medicaid

Medicare and Medicaid have a substantial place in our current public income transfer programs. In 1974, Medicare and Medicaid expenditures amounted to 59 percent of the $37.4 billion government expenditures for health. Medicare separately accounted for $11.1 billion, and Medicaid, with 27 million beneficiaries, accounted for federal, state, and local expenditures of $11.2 billion. Since their enactment in 1965, expenditures for these two programs have increased dramatically, as Table 10.1 demonstrates. Indeed, while the debate over welfare reform concentrated on cash assistance, in practice, government action expanded in-kind services. Because Medicare and Medicaid programs reflect social insurance conceptions on one hand and public welfare conceptions on the other, it is all the more important to integrate these contrasting transfer programs.[1]

The Problem of Eligibility

Practically all aged persons are eligible for Medicare's hospital (Part A) and supplementary medical (Part B) benefits. Hospitalization Insurance (HI) is available without premium charge to all persons over sixty-five with some minor exceptions. The Supplementary Medical Insurance (SMI) is open to all the aged upon payment of monthly premiums of $6.30. In 1970, 96.2 percent of the 20.4 million aged were participating in the SMI program.[2]

Table 10.1 Government Health Expenditures for Medicare and Medicaid, Fiscal 1966–1967 through 1970–1971

Year	Medicare			Medicaid
	Total	HI	SMI	
1966–1967	3.4	2.6	.8	2.2
1967–1968	5.4	3.8	1.5	3.6
1968–1969	6.6	4.8	1.8	4.4
1969–1970	7.1	5.0	2.2	5.0
1970–1971	7.9	5.6	2.3	6.5

Source—Barbara S. Cooper and Dorothy P. Rice, "National Health Expenditures, 1929–70," *Social Security Bulletin* 34, No. 1 (1971).
Howard West, "5 Years of Medicare—A Statistical Review," *Social Security Bulletin* 34, No. 12 (1971).
Note—In billions of dollars.

[1] Among the integration problems are the effects of persons receiving two or more benefits on the total benefit level, the eligibility for and administration of each program, and incentives to work. The incentive to work is strongly influenced by the rate at which the benefits of all programs together are reduced as earnings increase, or the cumulative tax rate.

[2] U.S., Department of Health, Education, and Welfare, Social Security Administration, Office of Research and Statistics, "Medicare: Number of Persons Insured, July 1, 1966–July 1, 1970," *Health Insurance Statistics*, 19 May 1972.

It should be recalled how this nearly universal coverage emerged. Such a pattern would not have occurred had Medicare been restricted to fully insured Social Security beneficiaries. Instead, Part A "blanketed in" the uninsured aged, using as the eligibility condition age sixty-five alone rather than social insurance participation. (This was changed after 1968, reintroducing social insurance participation as a condition of eligibility for people turning sixty-five after that time.) In Part B, for which enrollment and payment of monthly premiums are required, social insurance participation was not a condition at all. This use of an age criterion is in sharp contrast with the more complex eligibility processes of Medicaid.

Medicaid was originally designed as a state-option program to finance health services to a large proportion of America's low-income population. The 1965 legislation required each participating state to cover all persons receiving, or eligible to receive, cash assistance, and it gave states the option of including "medically needy" blind, disabled, and dependent children (as well as the "medically needy" aged).[3] However, its implementation has produced horizontal inequities[4] and substantial regional variation in eligibility and benefits. In roughly half the states as of July 1973, Medicaid benefits were restricted to persons already eligible for one or another of the federally financed assistance categories.[5] As Table 10.2 makes plain, the rest of the states had expanded their Medicaid programs to a "medically needy" population larger than the categorically poor. The medically needy include persons and families who otherwise would have been eligible for one of the categorical programs but whose income exceeded eligibility limits. They can qualify for Medicaid because their income *after* deducting medical expenses is below the AFDC payment standard for families of comparable size or, at the option of the state, below 133 percent of the AFDC payment standard.

Poor people who are not aged, blind, disabled, or with children under twenty-one cannot be treated as medical indigents. This is another anomaly highlighted by the rediscovery of the working poor in connection with recent welfare reform efforts. Equally poor families that are not in the appropriate demographic categories are, thus, not equally eligible for even the medically indigent program under Medicaid. And those eligible for the medical indigent program are not treated equally in the various states. Horizontal equity problems are, thus, central to both the statutory and administrative provisions of Medicaid.

---

[3] U.S., Congress, Senate, Finance Committee, *Medicare and Medicaid: Problems, Issues, and Alternatives*, 91st Cong., 1st sess., February 1970, p. 42.

[4] Horizontal inequity means the unequal treatment of persons in similar circumstances (for example, low income).

[5] Two states, Alaska and Arizona, have never adopted the Medicaid program.

Table 10.2   Federal Medical Assistance Percentage for Medicaid
Financing and Treatment of Medically Indigent, by State

States excluding medically indigent:[a]	Percent	States including medically indigent:[b]	Percent
Alabama	78	California	50
Arkansas	79	Connecticut	50
Colorado	58	District of Columbia	50
Delaware	50	Guam	50
Florida	61	Hawaii	51
Georgia	70	Illinois	50
Idaho	72	Kansas	59
Indiana	55	Kentucky	73
Iowa	58	Maryland	50
Louisiana	73	Massachusetts	50
Maine	69	Michigan	50
Mississippi	83	Minnesota	57
Missouri	60	Nebraska	58
Montana	67	New Hampshire	59
Nevada	50	New York	50
New Jersey	50	North Carolina	73
New Mexico	73	North Dakota	71
Ohio	54	Oklahoma	69
Oregon	57	Pennsylvania	55
South Carolina	78	Puerto Rico	50
South Dakota	70	Rhode Island	50
Tennessee	74	Utah	70
Texas	65	Vermont	65
West Virginia	77	Virgin Islands	50
Wyoming	63	Virginia	64
		Washington	50
		Wisconsin	56

Source—U.S., Department of Health, Education, and Welfare, Social and Rehabilitation Service, Public Information Office, 1971.
Note—Federal medical assistance percentage: rate of federal financial participation in a state's medical vendor payment expenditures on behalf of individuals and families eligible under Title 19 of the Social Security Act.
[a] These states offer basic required Medicaid services for people receiving federally supported financial assistance.
[b] These states also offer Medicaid services for people in Public Assistance categories who are financially eligible for medical but not for financial assistance.

Benefit Scope

What services are covered (and excluded) and what groups bear the cost of excluded services? By considering Medicare and Medicaid together, the interdependence arising from the benefit stringency of the former and the residual role of the latter is made clear.

The original Medicare statute did and still does include the following major benefits: 60 days of hospitalization with a deductible of roughly one daily service charge, $84 in 1974; 100 days of extended-care facilities (following three days of hospitalization, with a $21 deductible and a $10 per day copayment after the twentieth day); home health services; reimbursement of physician services (with a $60 deductible and a 20 percent copayment); and diagnostic services such as X-rays and laboratory costs. Drugs provided outside the hospital were not covered, and nursing home care other than that required for post-hospital convalesence was expressly excluded. This benefit package, never intended to be comprehensive, was in fact copied from the insurance plan available to federal employees.

Medicaid benefits vary substantially by region and type of location. States are required to pay for hospital and nursing home care, physicians and laboratory services, and diagnostic testing of children, but have the option of including dental care, drugs, eyeglasses, and other services. Poorer states provide less generous Medicaid benefits, even though they are more generously reimbursed by the federal government. A 70 percent reimbursement is insufficient to induce some southern states to expand eligibility and benefits. One measure of this pattern, presented in Table 10.2, is the higher rate of federal participation in state medical vendor payments where the Medicaid benefits are restricted to those receiving cash assistance. Note as well that, of the twenty-five states without a medical indigency program, eleven are southern or border states. (Two western states have no program at all.)

The variations in coverage and benefits mean that federal Medicaid expenditures are very unevenly distributed by state and region. As with the predecessor Kerr–Mills legislation, the largest industrial states dominate the Medicaid program despite their lower rate of federal cost sharing. Of the $4.4 billion expended by Medicaid in 1969, more than half was spent in four states: New York, $1.2 billion; Michigan, $174.0 million; California, $871.0 million; Illinois, $169.0 million.[6] Put another way, more than 47 percent of the federal expenditures for Medicaid went to two states—New York and California. In the area of health, transfer programs that depend upon state spending appear to concentrate their benefits in the higher-income states.

[6] U.S., Department of Health, Education, and Welfare, Social and Rehabilitation Service, Office of Program Statistics and Data Systems, National Center for Social Statistics, "Numbers of Recipients and Amounts of Payments under Medicaid and Other Medical Programs Financed from Public Assistance Funds, 1969," 1 March 1972.

The mixture of deductibles, co-insurance, premiums, and exclusions under Medicare virtually assured that Medicare and Medicaid would overlap. For some, the overlap would arise from the aged's inability or unwillingness to pay the monthly premiums for medical insurance (originally $6.00 per month per couple, now $12.60). State Medicaid officials were first encouraged (and later pressured financially) to "buy" Medicare Part B coverage for recipients of Old Age Assistance. By July 1970, there were nearly 2 million Public Assistance recipients enrolled for Medicare's Supplementary Medical Insurance under welfare "buy-in" agreements; only five states (Alaska, Arizona, Louisiana, Oregon, and Wyoming) were then not participating.[7] Participating states alone finance the enrollee premium for aged persons in the medically indigent category. For regular Old Age Assistance recipients, states share the premium cost with the federal government under the usual federal Medicaid matching. The consequence is that the medically indigent aged are more expensive to the state than are Old Age Assistance recipients.

The interaction between Medicaid and Medicare, as a matter of federal policy, is fiscally encouraged. Beginning in January 1970, federal matching was no longer available for any expenditures for Medicaid services that would have been financed by Medicare if the patient had been enrolled in the Supplementary Medical Insurance program. How much fraudulent billing has occurred as a result is difficult to estimate precisely. In its 1970 review of Medicare and Medicaid, the Senate Finance Committee concluded:

> A Medicaid fraud and abuse unit should be established in the Department of Health, Education, and Welfare in order to facilitate and coordinate both State and Federal efforts toward the prevention or discovery and prompt investigation, prosecution, and other followup activities designed to curb and punish fraud and abuse.[8]

The committee cites instances where a Medicare fraud case also involved Medicaid but where there was no investigation to determine the legitimacy of the Medicaid claims. It recommends specific organizational units at the state level for the prevention, detection, and investigation of abuse and fraud in state health care programs.

Interdependence arose as well from the effort to reduce Medicare program costs by excluding or narrowly defining benefits that aged persons could be expected to seek. The most dramatic example is nursing home services. Attempts were made to restrict Medicare's financial responsibility for nursing home care to convalescence of formerly hospi-

---

[7] Social Security Administration, "Medicare: Number of Persons Insured."
[8] Senate Finance Committee, *Medicare and Medicaid*, p. 132.

talized patients in specially organized "extended-care facilities" (ECF). The use of special jargon—distinguishing ECFs from nursing homes—indicated conscious design. Indeed, when explaining this benefit to Congress in 1965, the Secretary of Health, Education, and Welfare explicitly contrasted post-hospital skilled nursing and rehabilitative care with the "long-term custodial care furnished in many nursing homes," which Medicare would not finance.

Predictable difficulties arose from this effort to treat a problem by defining it away. First, ECF expenditures under Medicare were dramatically higher than expected, indicating that physicians, patients, and intermediaries were not complying fully with the narrow definition of benefits. HEW estimated .16 ECF days per Medicare beneficiary in the first full year of operation; 1967 expenditure data revealed utilization rates of approximately one day per enrollee, and average costs of more than $18.00 per day in contrast with the HEW estimate of $11.27.[9] The restrictive definition of benefits, thus, only partially constrained the demand for nursing home services.

Medicaid regulations excluded purely custodial care, but a reference to "skilled nursing homes" opened the way to a transfer of some of the worst-off aged onto its rolls. The aged who required custodial care—those who were chronically ill or senile or incapable of caring for themselves—had either to pay for nursing home services themselves, to get into a hospital and induce a physician to require extended-care facilities, or to become eligible for Medicaid's medical indigency program (where that was available) by spending enough on health care so that their income fell to the state-set eligibility level for the medically needy. Medicaid, thus, is the net under Medicare's aged; its residual role makes overlap between the two programs a continuing issue.

Where overlap does not in fact occur (for example, in the twenty-five states without a medical indigence program), hospitals are forced into a residual financing role. This became a more serious issue as Medicare administrators increased their cost-cutting efforts in the late 1960s. In Illinois, for instance, the Medicare intermediary has begun to reject hospital bills for patients who, according to medical-chart data, could have been cared for in an ECF or custodial nursing home. When the patient is ineligible for Medicaid, or ECF facilities are unavailable, or nursing home spaces are impossible to procure, the hospital must bill a typically low-income, aged patient or accept the rejected bill as a bad debt. In the first six months of 1972, one Illinois hospital had over $500,000 in rejected claims outstanding from some eighty cases of long-stay patients, with prospects of recovering from perhaps 2 percent of them. The

---

[9] Senate Finance Committee, *Medicare and Medicaid*, pp. 34ff.

hospital is caught in the crack. Doctors decide when patients enter and leave the hospital, but are not responsible for the financial consequences of their actions. Medicare excludes services after they have been provided, Medicaid intervenes in some cases, and the hospital or the patient is left to finance what they otherwise assumed Medicare would cover.

Tax Rate Issues

Under Medicare, neither eligibility nor benefits are conditioned on income, and the program, therefore, does not present special problems of integration with income-tested programs. However, difficult issues do arise in Medicaid in dealing with both the cumulative tax rate and notch issues. The notch for cash assistance recipients arises from the sudden termination of Medicaid benefits when their income rises above the eligibility cut-off point for cash assistance. Consider a state where the estimated value of the Medicaid health benefit is $600 per year for a family of four receiving Aid to Families with Dependent Children (AFDC). When this family earns $1 above the AFDC cut-off point, it loses its Medicaid benefit so that total income is $599 lower than if it had not earned the last dollar. At the eligibility margin, such families face a tax rate far in excess of 100 percent. Table 10.3 presents data on average Medicaid costs in eighteen states, showing the potential seriousness of the notch problem.

The notch obviously creates substantial incentives to avoid earnings that would make one ineligible for Medicaid. But a different problem arises for "medically indigent" persons whose incomes are too high for cash assistance standards, but whose medical expenses reduce their disposable income below the state-set eligibility for the medically needy (that is, no more than 133 percent of maximum payments for AFDC families of comparable size). Such families face indirect, 100 percent tax rates on earnings above the eligibility level. Whatever that income level, they must "spend down" to become Medicaid recipients; each dollar of additional earnings thus makes them no better off if they have medical expenses.

A vertical equity issue arises from the differential treatment of the income of cash recipients and the medically indigent. Certain deductions from income are permitted in determining eligibility for the cash programs that are not permitted in determining medical indigency. A family that once becomes eligible for AFDC can continue to claim these deductions and can increase its gross income above 133 percent of the AFDC payment standard and remain eligible for cash and Medicaid. But a family with the same income that is not already eligible for AFDC cannot claim

Table 10.3   Annual Income Limits for Medicaid Benefits and Annual Medicaid Cost Per AFDC Family for Selected States

State	Maximum income for initial eligibility for a medically indigent family of four	Average Medicaid cost per AFDC family, 1970–1971
California	3600	876
Colorado	2820	344
Florida	1606	334
Georgia	1788	394
Illinois	3600	908
Indiana	2100	553
Iowa	2916	692
Massachusetts	4176	738
Michigan	3696	700
Mississippi	a	89
Missouri	a	335
New Jersey	a	491
New York	5000	970
North Carolina	a	503
Pennsylvania	4000	610
Texas	a	640
Vermont	3828	668
Washington	4260	484

Source—Column 1—U.S., Department of Health, Education, and Welfare, Social and Rehabilitation Service, Assistance Payments Administration, Division of Program Evaluation, "Income Levels for Medically Needy in Title XIX Plans in Operation, As of Dec. 31, 1971" (March 1972), and Table 1. Column 2, U.S., Department of Health, Education, and Welfare, Office of Assistant Secretary for Planning and Evaluation, unpublished tabulation, 16 March 1972.
Note—Amounts in dollars.
a State offers Medicaid only to cash assistance recipients.

these deductions and is not eligible for Medicaid until it "spends down" to below 133 percent of the payment standard. Families with equal incomes thus receive very different treatment, depending on whether they first entered the AFDC program and then increased their income or they never entered the program at all. It is this equity problem that often is referred to when contrasts are drawn between the treatment of nonwelfare and welfare families of similar incomes.

The problem of this notch in real income has dominated much recent discussion of Medicaid reform. But it is the cumulative tax rate issue that is central to reform proposals to reduce the value of the Medicaid subsidy as income increases. Taking the previous example once again, one could treat Medicaid as a $600 annual insurance subsidy for a family of four and require graduated premium contributions that increased with income. If it were decided to maintain the existing Medicaid eligibility cut-off points, the result would be a higher marginal tax rate on earnings for all current Medicaid recipients and, of course, reduced benefits for many. For example, if the cut-off point were $6000, the Medicaid subsidy assumed here would require families to pay 10 percent of their incomes for medical insurance. The tax rate on their incomes would be higher, their net income lower, and they would be required to spend a larger share of their modest incomes on medical care. To prevent present recipients from losing benefits would require a gradual reduction of the subsidy beyond the cut-off point; that would increase the number of Medicaid eligibles dramatically, though the subsidy for the new eligibles would be less than $600 per year and would drop farther as income increased.

Some states have tried cost-sharing devices to lighten their financial burden from Medicaid. Deductibles and co-insurance (often 20 percent of certain services) are employed for the medically indigent, thus making the categorical programs more attractive for families facing chronic illness and continuing medical expenses. The 1972 amendments contained in H.R. 1 permit deductibles and co-insurance for cash assistance recipients receiving certain optional Medicaid services, and require premium payments for the medically indigent.

Valuing the Medicaid benefits for purposes of considering work incentives raises some difficult problems. The common procedure is to determine what one would have to pay for the state's Medicaid benefits if an insurance company were selling such a policy. This could be calculated as total costs divided by eligibles: in Michigan, roughly $600 per year for an AFDC family of four; in New York, $1000 per year. The difficulty is that families have very different probabilities of incurring average costs in any one year. For example, the aged have Medicaid's highest average per beneficiary expenditures, and nursing home charges represent a very substantial share of those expenditures. Should AFDC recipients be treated as if they were "buying" policies whose premiums reflect substantial nursing home costs that they would, in all probability, never incur? One solution, perhaps, is to allocate costs to different age groups and estimate premiums for separate demographic groups. The theory of insurance requires spreading costs among enrollees; social insurance requires spreading them among larger groups than private insurance companies would cover. But spreading medical care costs among all Medicaid recipients particularly overestimates the benefits that the non-aged poor receive from their Medicaid "policy."

The argument also is advanced that such premiums overstate the benefits families receive from the "insurance," even when adjustments by age group are permitted. It proceeds from the assumption that poor people value medical insurance less than others because of more pressing claims on their income for food, shelter, clothing, and transportation. Thus, the insurance "premium" estimation procedure involves imposing a social decision about the value of insurance for poor people who might be expected to value income in cash higher than income in kind. One solution proposed by Martin Feldstein is to provide a lump-sum transfer equal to average expenditures and permit poor families to buy their own preferred insurance package. But the problem is that, if they under-insure, face large medical bills, and become destitute, public programs will finance their under-insurance. And that means those who insured themselves more adequately are treated unfairly.

Method of Financing

The present methods of financing Medicare and Medicaid encompass the range of usual possibilities: Social Security payroll taxes, general federal revenues, beneficiary contributions (premiums, deductibles, and co-insurance), and general state and local funds. Medicare's hospital plan is financed by an earmarked portion of the regular Social Security payroll tax (.6 of a percentage point for both employees and employers); those who have been "blanketed in" are financed from general revenue transferred to the Social Security trust funds. The physician program is financed quite differently but does not present special problems of integration, since it is not income-tested. Enrollees pay premiums financing half the costs of the program; general revenues pay the other half, thus transfers take place from non-aged taxpayers to aged Part B beneficiaries. As noted previously, the size of these expenditures is very substantial. In 1974, Part A federal expenditures were $8.0 billion; Part B, $3.2 billion.[10] Medicaid uses almost exclusively general revenue financing from federal, state, and local treasuries, with the federal government contribution proportionately more to states with lower per capita incomes. As indicated in Table 10.2, federal matching percentages range from 83 percent in Mississippi to 50 percent in New York and other high-income states.

Looking at the federal source alone, such financing means that Medicaid is relatively progressive in its financing provisions. The state and local payments arise from a variety of tax sources and may well have a regressive impact. Taken together, however, Medicaid financing is almost certainly more progressive in its distributional impact than is Medicare financing. Medicare hospitalization insurance (Part A) is financed by the general Social Security payroll tax, which is generally viewed as regressive

[10] Nancy L. Worthington, "National Health Expenditures, 1929–74," *Social Security Bulletin* 38, No. 2 (1975).

in character. It has, however, been undergoing change in the 1960s as the wage base on which it is calculated has been increased rather dramatically. It is roughly estimated that the hospital tax is proportional up to about median earnings and takes a decreasing share of income above that level.

The Medicaid financing scheme, while attractive in its distributional aspects, has the vices of its virtues. It is subject to yearly congressional review with its intense criticism, and the program has been cut back from its original benefit and eligibility scope. Whether uncertainties arise from the general revenue financing, or the clientele of the program explains Medicaid's unsteady course, is difficult to tell. The cliché that programs for poor people are poor programs may well be true, although this cliché ignores the far more generous benefits provided by Medicaid than Medicare in most cases. Clientele may determine the political treatment of a program, not the character of the taxes that support it. Some support for this interpretation can be found in the Medicare program: There is no evidence that the separate financing of physician insurance—and the failure to use the payroll tax for it—has made Part B more similar to Medicaid than to the hospital part of the Medicare program.

Equity and tax theory considerations would argue against using payroll taxes in their present form to finance a large public medical care program. This issue will come up again when we discuss the Kennedy–Griffiths health insurance bill; its particular mixture of payroll taxes and general revenue financing has no particular economic rationale. But I would suggest here that one might favor a variation of the payroll tax if its entitlement and political attributes are sought. One could imagine a payroll tax, expressed as a proportion of income tax liability, that would provide the attributes of a separate trust fund but have quite different and desirable progressive distributional features. To avoid "free riders," one could require a minimum payment each year, with a surtax on income tax liability as the main financing mechanism. That surtax, designed to finance current expenditures on a pay-as-you-go basis, would vary with the present expenditures of the system. It would have as much legal force as the present trust funds, which basically are U.S. government promises to pay designated citizens certain sums of transfer payments.

All these remarks stress the burdens entailed by financing forms of government health programs. They do not try to deal simultaneously with the distribution of benefits. In health care, there is a special reason for that—the insurance, not just the health expenditures made on behalf of sick people, is the benefit. Any public insurance for medical care distributes benefits disproportionately to the sick if benefits are measured by expenditure patterns. There is considerable merit in separating the issue of what insurance one wants from how one wants the government to finance that package. And, in that financing choice, one must be explicit about the ideological and political benefits connected with social insurance programs and not be mystified about the causes of those benefits. Most citizens have no precise idea of the relation between contributions and benefits in social insurance; the notion of a separate fund, and the idea that contributions entitle one to benefits within the program, give social insurance its peculiar popularity advantages, rather than the precise wage base, taxing mechanism, or benefit ratios.

Cost Sharing and the Problems of Integration

The rapid growth of Medicaid—particularly in New York and California—has made cost control a dominant theme of the Medicaid and general health insurance debates. Patient premiums, deductibles, and coinsurance copayment all have been suggested as ways to reduce the government costs of Medicaid and, in some instances, to change the incentives facing patients so that a more rational use of expensive services would be encouraged. A similar concern about greater patient payment has emerged with Medicare, though with less intensity and less surprise since it is already using the full range of cost-sharing devices.

Sharing costs obviously conflicts with the goal of removing the financial obstacles to care, though there is no agreement about the precise impact of different devices. Requiring premiums in Medicare probably has meant that the largest proportion of the uninsured (for Part B) are lower-income aged.[11] This group is the potential user of income-tested medical assistance, whether Medicaid, medical assistance to the aged, or charity medicine. For the aged, the pecuniary advantages of Medicaid can be interpreted as being the difference between the Medicare policy and the Medicaid policy value; for a particular aged person with illnesses requiring services Medicare does not cover, the difference can be very large—monthly premiums, the deductibles and copayment, and the total cost of drugs, nursing home, and other uncovered services.

Increasing the cost sharing within Medicaid reduces the financial incentives to enter the program. But the devices themselves present problems for the cumulative tax rates that present recipients face. Cost sharing that does not vary with Medicaid recipients' income retains (although reduces) the notch problem, but presents no special difficulties with increasing marginal tax rates. Varying the cost sharing with income—and thus improving vertical equity among Medicaid beneficiaries—presents both administrative and cumulative tax rate difficulties.

How great these difficulties are depends partly on how the cost

[11] Social Security Administration, "Medicare: Number of Persons Insured."

sharing is calculated. For potential users of Medicaid-covered services, the insurance subsidy is reduced from the full "insurance premium" value. For actual users, there is the incurred financial burden that is not captured by actuarially estimating the declining value of the policy. For recipients with very different propensities to require medical services, the use of averages may not be helpful for estimating the benefits from the policy. One would be interested also in the distribution of losses incurred by increased earnings and, hence, higher deductibles, co-insurance, and co-payments.

A nearly insoluble problem arises from trying simultaneously to introduce cost sharing and to prevent present Medicaid recipients from suffering a drop in benefits. To do so requires a full premium subsidy to the present cut-off point and a declining one (increasing premiums) above that figure. Consider a hypothetical state with a Medicaid benefit value at $500, a cut-off point of $7000 for a family of four, no other income-tested benefits available except cash assistance, and a marginal tax rate of 80 percent. A medical premium reduction rate of 10 percent, increasing the cumulative tax rate to 90 percent, requires a cut-off of $12,000. Thus, roughly half the people in a typical state would become eligible for some Medicaid benefits. To have the premium subsidy disappear at the cash assistance cut-off point would make all present recipients worse off, increasing their cumulative tax rate by about 7 percent. Present suggestions for reforming Medicaid through cost sharing all suffer from this defect. The answer of the Nixon Administration—that welfare reform should simultaneously increase the cash income of many of the poor—would not have been valid for those states whose cash assistance levels would not have been preempted by H.R. 1.

II. Integrating Program Reforms in Welfare and Medical Care

Part I has raised a number of program integration issues in connection with the current operation of Medicare and Medicaid. This section will focus on issues of equity and combined tax rates that arise when welfare reform and medical care reform are considered simultaneously. For purposes of discussion, we will restrict comment to a pair of welfare reform plans and a pair of medical care reform plans. Discussion will proceed by examining the issues raised for each welfare reform plan by each of the medical care proposals.

Before proceeding, a brief characterization of the welfare and medical care plans to be discussed is required. The negative income tax example is the Nixon Administration's welfare reform plan embodied in the House-

passed version of H.R. 1 (Ninety-second Congress). Restricted to families
with children, the plan combines a modest income guarantee ($2400 per
year for a family of four) with a tax rate of 67 percent. The second
welfare reform is a demogrant plan that combines a universal tax credit
of $1200 per year per adult and $600 per child with a general proportional
tax rate of 33 percent. Put differently, we have two income redistribution
plans of a negative income tax type: one guaranteeing $2400 for a family
of four; the other, $3600 for a two-adult family of four. The former is
restricted to families with children; the latter is universal. The former
reduces benefits at a two-thirds rate as income increases; the latter, at a
one-third rate. The former requires additional federal outlays of $5
billion; the latter requires extensive tax reform to finance its greater cost.

The two medical care plans are variants of national health insurance.
The more familiar is the Kennedy–Griffiths proposal (H.R. 22 and S. 3,
Ninety-second Congress). Universal in eligibility, the plan provides comprehensive benefits including almost all medical expenses except "cos-
metic" care. Financed by a combination of federal payroll and income
taxes, the H.R. 22 scheme eschews income testing and any significant use
of cost-sharing devices. In effect, it would direct almost all health care
expenditures through the federal government. The Social Security Administration estimated that the plan would require $91 billion of additional
federal expenditures in 1974, representing at least a 20 percent increase in
total federal taxes at estimated 1974 levels.

The other national health insurance scheme under discussion is the
catastrophic plan proposed by Feldstein.[12] Known as major risk insurance
(MRI), it proposes universal, comprehensive national health insurance
with a large income-related deductible. Feldstein proposes a deductible of
10 percent of annual family earnings, thus protecting all citizens from
extraordinary health expenses but retaining private payment for most
health care use. Feldstein suggests special treatment for families below the
poverty line, which we will ignore here. Such a plan, Feldstein estimates,
would require annual expenditures of $10 billion to $12 billion.

H.R. 1 and H.R. 22

The combination of H.R. 1 and H.R. 22 does not raise difficult
problems of integration. The health insurance scheme's exclusion of
means-tested benefits avoids cascading cumulative tax rates. Universal

[12] Martin S. Feldstein, "A New Approach to National Health Insurance," *The Public Interest* 25 (Spring 1971). Different versions of Feldstein's plan, employing both
deductible and co-insurance features with an upper limit, have appeared. See reports
in Robert Eilers, "National Health Insurance: What Kind and How Much," *New
England Journal of Medicine* 284, No. 16–17 (22 and 29 April 1971): 881–886, 945–954.

coverage in the health plan avoids the horizontal inequities of the present Medicaid–welfare combinations. The comprehensiveness of benefits assures that health expenses will not be a cause of impoverishment. But two problems remain. The first is H.R. 1's high marginal tax rate of 67 percent, a potential problem for work incentives in and of itself. The second is the large tax increase the H.R. 22 health plan would require. Unless that tax increase is received exclusively from non-H.R. 1 beneficiaries, the income tax rates of some welfare families who are working would have to be increased substantially. Of course, any increase in taxes to finance this plan would replace current personal health expenditures, and thus would not mean new payouts for many taxpayers.

H.R. 1 and Major Risk Insurance

The universal eligibility of MRI, as with H.R. 22, avoids horizontal equity issues. MRI's deductible of 10 percent of income means that increases in earnings of H.R. 1 recipients above the poverty line would be subject to an increasing marginal tax rate of a relatively small magnitude. Were H.R. 1's basic tax rate below 50 percent, this increase of no more than 10 percent would not be serious. As it is, any addition to a 67 percent tax rate imposes tax rates on H.R. 1 recipients that are higher than the rates anyone else in the society is required to pay under the positive income tax. The adequacy of MRI's health benefit is, of course, a separate but serious issue.

Demogrant and H.R. 22

The combination of the demogrant and H.R. 22, considered apart from other income-tested programs, does away with the problems of high cumulative tax rates and vertical and horizontal inequities. The universal eligibility, combined with the demogrant's tax rate of 33 percent, and the health plan's exclusion of income testing, produces this result. Yet, one can say this only by looking at the combined administration of benefits. If one turns to the financing of such an expensive combination—requiring tax increases of perhaps $100 billion—the problem of marginal tax rates reappears, shifted from the low-income population to the population at large. These funds can be raised only by levying additional taxes on those above the demogrant's break-even point ($10,800 per year for a family of four). This combination, then, minimizes problems of integration at the price of raising serious difficulties in allocation of very substantial income tax increases. It thus requires substantial tax reform in the treatment of middle- and upper-income families.

Demogrant and Major Risk Insurance

A combination of the demogrant and MRI has most of the features of the preceding one, with two major exceptions. First, MRI has an income-related deductible, which means that a marginal tax rate addition of up to 10 percent applies to increased earnings. But this is less serious for a demogrant with a low proportional tax rate than for an H.R. 1 plan with a high marginal tax rate. Excluding all other considerations, the combined plans would entail tax rates below 50 percent for recipients. The other difference is the lesser expenditures that MRI would entail, perhaps one-sixth the burden of the H.R. 22 plan. MRI would bring about tax reform as well as tax increases. As with H.R. 22, MRI purposes abolishing the present tax deduction of medical expenses above 3 percent of income.

Conclusion

The problems of the MRI and the Kennedy–Griffiths health care plans are not, at bottom, ones of equity, cumulative tax rates, or adequacy. Rather, they concern resource allocation, tax burdens, and efficiency, which fall outside this chapter's scope. MRI removes the financial barrier to very expensive care and, according to critics, subsidizes costly care at the expense of encouraging preventive care. In fact, both plans require a social choice about the distribution of expensive treatment; regulation would have to substitute for the role financial means (including insurance) now plays in deciding who lives when the price of maintaining life is dear. Rationing these health resources under MRI would be public and visible, and, one hopes, fair. The H.R. 22 plan raises similar rationing problems by fixing a national health budget, but the rationing would be required over a larger range of services than MRI. These brief remarks are not meant to foreclose discussion but to suggest that, while program integration problems may be lessened or even eliminated by universal health plans, other critical issues remain to be resolved. Furthermore, even if cash and medical care programs are reformed with respect to marginal tax rates, other programs, like housing and day care subsidies, still add to marginal tax rates when their benefits decrease with family income.

Another important issue not dealt with extensively in this chapter is the complexity of administering cash assistance and health care programs. Of the health care plans considered, H.R. 22 is the most simple to administer, but it is complex in the type and amount of provider regulation it would entail. Its combination with the demogrant would be the least complex arrangement but would entail federal expenditures of more than $100 billion. The MRI–demogrant combination would be less cumbersome to administer than the MRI–H.R. 1 alternative, but at considerably increased federal cost.

Comparing the two health alternatives alone, it appears that MRI is somewhat more complex for beneficiaries but less so for providers of health care. However, this conclusion rests on the assumption that the Treasury would administer MRI as it now administers the deduction for health expenses of more than 3 percent of taxable income, using a credit rather than a deduction device to determine governmental fiscal responsibility. All such administrative assessments are subject to a wide margin of error and are included here to open the issue for further discussion.

11

Day Care and Welfare

Michael Krashinsky

Introduction

The various reforms in the welfare system currently being considered will mean a significant shift in the approach to care for young children. In the past, it has been felt that children require a parent in the home full time, well beyond the first years of life. In single-parent families, Aid to Families with Dependent Children (AFDC) has provided financial support to enable the mother to remain at home with her children until they are well through primary school. Although the mother might work, it has been generally assumed that she will not, and in fact the system has discouraged work.[1] The proposed reforms, however, imply a different approach, one more tolerant to the shifting of child care away from the parent.

A universal demogrant plan (UDP) would reduce the large work disincentive now facing an AFDC mother, by lowering the tax rate on her earnings. Both the "work fare" proposal advanced by the Senate Finance Committee (SFC) and the categorical negative income tax passed by the House of Representatives in 1971 (hereafter referred to as H.R. 1) go even further. They both require work of mothers whose children are

[1] Before 1969, assistance in many states decreased $1 for every $1 earned, while, after 1969, recipients could keep at least one-third of each additional dollar earned.

past a minimum age, under penalty of loss of assistance: The Senate Finance Committee's proposal would enlist all mothers in single-parent households with no children under six years of age; the House bill extends that age limit to three years of age.

Where there are strong incentives for mothers with young children to work, there must be some concern for the alternative arrangements that will be made for care for these children. This is especially the case in H.R. 1, and only slightly less so in the SFC proposal, since the largest group of employable but currently nonworking poor aimed at by both reforms are mothers with young children and no husbands in the home. In particular, it is necessary to decide what allowance is to be made for day care expenses in computing the tax assessed or subsidy provided when the mother works. In this chapter, the three proposals just mentioned are discussed with special attention to the provision of day care. Given the goals of each proposal, various ways to integrate day care into the proposal are discussed and the costs to the public determined. Of course, these costs will depend on the assumptions made about the quality of day care used. An attempt is made to develop a range of costs corresponding to the suitable range in day care quality (although my own views about which part of the range is preferable will be clearly stated).

Part I examines the day care debate. It considers the different motives of those supporting a large expansion in organized day care and then examines some of the justification for public support of day care. Part II attempts to define the costs of day care (both monetary and real). These will depend on both the type of day care being considered and the types of costs taken into account. Part III examines each reform proposal in turn, and considers how day care might be integrated with each one. Should care be subsidized and, if so, how? What will various approaches cost and how might those costs be reduced? Part IV briefly looks at some of the other issues that might be of concern for public policy in day care.

I. The Origins of the Day Care Debate: Rationales for Day Care

The current policy dialogue on day care calls for a major increase in extrafamily day care. Yet there are some real differences among the views of advocates of public involvement in day care. Those who favor day care to free mothers to work wish both to enable mothers to escape from welfare by working and to ensure that their children receive adequate care. Those who favor day care to help poor children wish to reach them with particular services, such as medical care, food, and compensatory education like Head Start that will help them later to break out of the cycle of poverty. And those who favor day care as early education want to reach all children with educational services early in life, regardless of family income, as the natural downward extension of the public school system. The last two groups view poor children as a separate clientele for welfare services that can help them escape from poverty, whatever their parents do.

This section will attempt to deal with these motives for day care and will consider some of the theoretical reasons for public intervention into day care. The treatment is not meant to be exhaustive but merely to point out some of the questions to be answered.

Motives for Day Care

CUSTODIAL MOTIVES

Historically, the AFDC program was developed because it was felt that mothers were needed in the home to look after their children and ought to be supported so that they could remain there. In the last few decades, there has been an increase of labor force participation by women with children. This increase has led those making public policy to be less willing to justify keeping at home all poor women with as few as one schoolchild, and discouraging those women from working. But it would seem strange to move directly from one extreme to the other—from paying mothers to stay home to requiring them to leave home and work.

This chapter will advocate a middle position, which encourages work through low benefit-reduction ("tax") rates and by day care deductibility. It is argued that any requirement that welfare recipients work ought to be limited to certain types of families for whom day care is relatively inexpensive, for example, those with no preschoolers and only a few schoolchildren.

When a mother with young children is required to work in order to receive welfare support, the cost of good-quality day care will usually be very high. Unless that cost is at least partially borne by the government (through publicly provided or financed day care), there is the danger that she may find it necessary to use very low-cost day care of inferior quality. Such an arrangement may endanger the development of her children and would represent a shortsighted approach to the problems of poverty.

AFFECTIVE MOTIVES

Formerly, child psychologists felt that maternal deprivation was extremely dangerous; now they take the position that extrafamily child care, although potentially dangerous for young children, can be useful in many cases. For neglected children in poor families, government-sponsored day care can be invaluable. Yet it would cost a great deal to replace the care of most young children looked after by parents who are poor but otherwise capable of raising their children. This applies especially to young children (certainly those below age three). It may make more economic sense to pay parents enough to be good child-rearers rather than to ask them to surrender the care of their children to others. The burden rests on those favoring affective day care to show that children are made better off by being placed in high-quality, high-cost, developmental day care, rather than being left at home with parents *to whom are transferred* the resources that otherwise would be used in that day care.[2] Parental love is hard to buy.

It may be felt that poor parents, especially those in one-parent homes, will bring up children who will be poor in turn. This statement, implying that many poor parents cannot properly rear their children for reasons not directly related to their poverty (for example, alcoholism, poor attitudes), is politically explosive. It seems to have been contradicted in the past by the upward mobility of the children of the poor, and its acceptance today would require much hard evidence.

COGNITIVE MOTIVES

Poor children seem to start off behind middle-class and rich ones when they enter grade one. There is a real debate over what effect early educational intervention can have in raising their permanent performance. One view, the "critical period" thesis, holds that early enough intervention can be permanently effective. The other view, the "fade-out" effect, holds that such intervention can result only in a temporary spurt that fades out after a length of time. Recently the debate has centered on Head Start, with unclear results. What may be needed is an increase in available resources for educating children throughout their school years. But we need not place children in child care for ten hours per day to achieve our educational objectives. Achieving these objectives would not require extensive day care but a wider use of subsidized nursery schools (year-round Head Start). But if we provide extensive day care from other motives, the opportunity could be used to deliver educational services to the poor at relatively lower cost.

Some precise idea of what can be achieved in early education is

---

[2] The argument is developed in depth by William Shannon, "A Radical, Direct, Simple, Utopian Alternative to Day-Care Centers" (*New York Times Magazine*, 30 April 1972). For other treatments on the effect of maternal deprivation, see Gilbert Steiner, *The State of Welfare* (Washington, D.C.: Brookings Institution, 1971), or Sheila Coles in *New York Times Magazine*, 12 December 1971.

needed before it is made a major justification for day care. If parents are doing a poor job, we might seek to make them better parents rather than place their children in day care centers.

These rationales for day care, while not entirely contradictory, imply different qualities of child care. Custodial motives would favor standard day care, educational and affective motives a more extensive and more fully and generally subsidized form of care. On the other hand, if we accept one motive for day care, achieving the others becomes cheaper. If children are in nursery schools three or four hours per day, it would cost less to free mothers for the entire day.

There is a danger that the very poor will be used as "showcase" consumers, that limited resources will be used to purchase extremely good care for a small number of poor children while the majority of poor and near-poor children with working parents remain in inadequate day care. This approach would fail to deal with the real problems posed by a system based on generally poor care for children.

Economic Rationales for Government Financing of Day Care

But why should the government intervene economically in the provision of day care? Some traditional arguments suggest themselves, but most, while they point out inadequacies in the present setup, do not indicate a clear need for extensive day care as the only or best answer.

EXTERNAL ECONOMIES

It can be argued that the lack of good preschool day care prevents a number of poor children from developing to their full potential, and that this makes society as a whole worse off. If antisocial behavior could be traced to inadequate early child care, there might be a strong argument for public intervention. But this intervention need not occur through heavy public support of day care. It might more efficiently come from raising the income levels of the parents.

CAPITAL MARKET FAILURE

A more convincing argument is that the private capital market fails to provide sufficient funds for day care. College students with access to the capital market can borrow for their education against future earnings (or at least the government now makes it possible for them to do so). Children have no such option. Parents make the decision for them, with the child's welfare as only one of many considerations; nor could the parent finance the day care from the child's future income, even if he wanted to. Nor can the adult in later years go back and spend money on early education for himself. In effect, society alone can make that decision for the child. The parent's time horizon tends to be much shorter than society's.

HORIZONTAL EQUITY: A FAILURE OF NONMARKET INSTITUTIONS

Society is set up for two-parent families who take the responsibility for raising children. If one parent is absent, society must step in to correct this failure in its institutions and help to raise the child. Again, both this argument and the previous one, even if we accept them, do not necessarily argue for day care. They might argue equally for supporting the single parent in the home and perhaps aiming programs like Head Start at the child. The real issue is noneconomic: What makes children into better adults, and what makes them happier while they are children?

VERTICAL EQUITY

As part of income redistribution, we often transfer specific goods to the poor. Why not support day care for them, enabling them to work outside the household and earn more? As we argue later, this may well be a very inefficient way to help either poor parents or their children, both of whom might be substantially better off receiving their help in another form.

MERIT WANTS AND EXTERNALITIES OF CONSUMPTION

This argument states that work outside the family is a virtue in and of itself and ought to be encouraged. Those who work are better citizens. Work inside the household is not considered to be of such merit. This argument is partially normative, but to the extent that we all agree on some definition of the term "better citizen," the argument ought to be empirically testable. If we do accept this argument, it calls for custodial care and views children largely as a hindrance to the goal of labor force participation.

On the other hand, labor force participation by parents may be seen as essential in helping the children develop positive attitudes toward work, and teaching them to become productive workers. This would argue for tolerating possible present losses in the parents' working in order to help the children eventually to escape poverty.

WOMEN'S RIGHTS

The current arrangements discriminate against women who are forced to take care of children, according to this argument. A larger supply of day care will enable women to choose rationally what kind of work (in the home or in the marketplace) best suits them. While this is a persuasive argument for allowing deduction of day care expenses from income, it hardly argues for a subsidy of day care beyond that, which would skew the decision the other way and make the alternate care of children seem free. At issue here is the question, Who is primarily responsible for child care, the parents who bear them or society at large? Is society to step in only when parents cannot fulfill their obligations, or should it remove those obligations altogether? The tendency to date has been very much against the latter view.

Most of the arguments in this section have finally focused on the issue of what effect on children preschool care of various qualities can have. Until we know exactly what results an extra dollar of day care buys us, the discussion can remain at best intuitive, while talk about externalities just points out our inability to measure the true results of widespread expansion of extrafamily day care.

II. The Costs of Day Care

As much as possible, it is desirable to avoid economically inefficient programs. An income maintenance program is inefficient if another program with the same level of expenditures can make some recipients better off and none worse off. For example, it would be inefficient to induce mothers to work and use state-provided (or financed) day care if the value of the extra production generated by their working were less than the cost of day care for their children.[3] By giving this money to the mother and allowing her to stay home, the family would receive more income and be better off, assuming, of course, that the children are not substantially better off in the day care facility.[4]

---

[3] The value of work should include any later productivity gains (properly discounted) owing to the present attachment to the labor force.

[4] While some taxpayers may feel better off when welfare mothers are forced to work, we do not discuss this because it is not measurable. Some taxpayers who value care for children by mothers may feel the reverse, and, more importantly, we suspect that opinions are not so easily vocalized by taxpayers. To consider such an effect, we would have to find taxpayers who would answer "yes" to the following question: "Would you agree to forcing welfare mothers to work if it did not lower your tax bill and it made the poor families involved worse off?" Taxpayers may now say they favor forcing mothers to work because they feel this would lower their taxes (thus indicating their preference for lower taxes).

Defining the Level of Day Care

Before we can evaluate the various child care programs and estimate their costs, it is necessary to specify the type of day care used, since the cost per child can vary substantially. The terms "minimum," "acceptable," "desirable," "custodial," and "developmental" all are used to describe day care. While it is clear that the projected costs of care will depend on who is setting the standard, the following criteria might be used. "Standard care" means the level of care necessary to replace the care given to the child by a mother present in the home full time. Standard care should include the physical and supervisory care provided by the mother, but it also should include the emotional and developmental care available at home that is necessary to insure the child's proper development. The child should be neither better nor worse off under standard care than he would be at home, especially as concerns his mental and physical growth. With this approach, care beyond this level is treated as a deliberate transfer of resources to the child, not as an expense of child care incurred in order to free the mother to work. Even accepting this, some problems still remain, such as defining "the level of care necessary to replace the care given to the child by a mother present in the home full time." Even allowing for personal differences among parents with the same income, children in poor homes often receive poor physical care, because the money is just not available to purchase decent food, clothing, or shelter.[5] This being the case, we might set standard care equal to the average care given to children in homes just above the poverty line (or wherever the minimum income line is set), since, in some sense, we have determined that the physical quality of life among families below this income is inadequate.

The definition of standard care permits a comparison of one situation in which a mother stays home and receives welfare with another in

---

We might also be concerned about possible bad effects on the children of having no adult in the family working. It may be that children learn how to participate in the labor market by observing their parents, or that they see work as a normal and important part of their lives only if they see adults around them working. In that case, there would be a real gain in the long run in inducing the parent to work (even if it were very costly) so as to reduce the probability that the children will themselves require welfare.

[5] The poor mother forced to work by inadequate public income, who places her children in low-cost, low-quality day care, is not abusing them. Rather, she is deciding that the level of physical care she can give them while not earning money is so low as to make them better off in bad day care, with enough additional income for food and shelter, than they would be either with her or in high-quality day care that costs too much.

which she goes to work and uses day care. Usually three variables are evaluated: the change in the mother's spendable income; the change in the total government expenditure on the family; and the change in the welfare of the child. Using the concept of standard care, we would assume that the child is as well off in either case. This limits the discussion to the other two variables, both of which can be stated more easily in monetary terms.

The Cost of Standard Care

Much of the discussion in the literature regarding the cost of child care has been confusing. In this section, I shall attempt to identify exactly what items should be included in a measure of cost. But the cost per child still will depend on the critical staff-to-child ratio. Between 75 and 80 percent of day care center costs are salaries, so the costs of standard care will depend on what staff level fulfills our criterion of replacing the mother's care. In the numbers developed here, a range will be given for standard care, with the staff-to-child ratios identified and the costs calculated at each end of the range. The reader can then decide just what costs best suit our notion of standard care. While I favor the upper end, and later will support this bias, there is room for disagreement. Most experts would agree that poor day care can damage a child's development, but the gradations from poor to adequate and above are difficult to determine objectively. Just what "adequate" day care means is unclear. The debate over the evaluation of Head Start indicates how hard it is to show that a developmental program is essential for a child's welfare.

In determining the cost of standard care, we shall use the per-child cost estimates published by HEW in 1968. Tables 11.1 and 11.2 reproduce two of the cost tables. One is for children between the ages of three and five in a day care center for a full day and the other for children of school age (up to fourteen) cared for before and after school and during the summer. Costs are provided for three different qualities of day care in each case: "minimum" defined as "the level essential to maintain the health and safety of the child, but with relatively little attention to his developmental needs"; "acceptable" defined as "to include a basic program of developmental activities as well as providing minimum custodial care"; and "desirable" defined as "to include the full range of general and specialized developmental activities suitable to *individualized* development."[6]

---

[6] U.S., Department of Health, Education, and Welfare, Office of Child Development, *Standards and Costs for Day Care*, 1967.

Table 11.1 Estimates by HEW of the Annual Cost of Full-time Day Care for Children Age Three to Five

Program element	Minimum		Acceptable		Desirable	
	Description	Cost	Description	Cost	Description	Cost
1. Food (meals and snacks)	1 meal, snacks	$140	2 meals, snacks	$210	2 meals, snacks	$210
2. Transportation	By parents	0	By center	60	By center	60
3. Medical and dental	Examinations and referral	20	Examinations and referral	20	Examinations and treatment	60
4. Work with parents	Little or none except problem cases	10	General activities and limited counseling	30	Parent education and full counseling	70
5. Facilities and utilities (rental)	State requirements	90	State requirements	90	More generous	110
6. Clothing, other emergency needs	As necessary	20	As necessary	20	As necessary	20
7. Supplies and materials	Custodial program	40	General developmental program	50	Individualized developmental program	75
8. Equipment (replacement costs)	Custodial program	10	General developmental program	12	Individualized developmental program	15
9. Staff:						
(a) Classroom professional (at $6600)	1 per 20 children	275	1 per 15 children	405	1 per 15 children	405
(b) Classroom nonprofessional (at $4400)	2 per 20 children	320	2 per 15 children	420	3 per 15 children	640
(c) Social service professional (at $6600)	1 per 150 children	65	1 per 100 children	65	1 per 100 children	65
(d) Community, parent, health aides ($4400)	None	0	1 per 100 children	20	2 per 100 children	45
(e) Business and maintenance (at $4400)	2 per 100 children	80	3 per 100 children	120	3 per 100 children	120
(f) Special resource personnel (at $4400)	Urgent need only	20	1 per 100 children	60	2 per 100 children	120
(g) Supervision (at $8000)	1 per 100 children	80	2 per 100 children	160	2 per 100 children	160
10. Training	10 percent of salaries	75	10 percent of salaries	120	10 percent of salaries	145
Total per child		$1245		$1862		$2320

Source—U.S. Department of Health, Education, and Welfare, Office of Child Development, *Standards and Costs for Day Care,*

In the notes to the figures, the report states:

> Individual experts will differ as to the elements required for each level of quality. Most experts feel that the disadvantages to children of a "minimum" level program far outweigh the advantages of having the mother work. Some will feel that for children from "disadvantaged" homes only the "desirable" level is appropriate. The figures shown represent a consensus among a number of experts of what would be required at each level of quality.

The HEW numbers do not appear to be out of line with those of other recent studies (although, of course, they may have been influenced by the earlier HEW results). Rowe examines some of these other studies and finds that their cost estimates are compatible with those of HEW.[7]

In refining HEW's cost to yield those of standard care, an attempt is made to exclude those items in the HEW estimates that do not replace services rendered *directly* by the parent but, instead, replace items normally *purchased* by the parent for the child. Since the latter represents expenses to the parent that must be borne whether or not the child is cared for outside the home, they cannot be counted as "day care," that is, as a new cost to parents resulting from having the child cared for by someone else. The intent is to measure the cost of replacing the parent's time when the parent enters the labor force. For example, suppose the center arranged for the purchase of children's shoes through the center. The parents would then be billed by the center, but no one would pretend that the cost of shoes is "day care." The costs that more usually come into question, discussed later, are to be treated by similar principles. We also do not include the cost of extra services not necessarily bought by the parent but deemed necessary for poor children by public policy (for example, preventive medical and dental care). These can be regarded as resources transferred directly to the child. Since they do not really replace what the parent normally does for the child, they cannot be included in the cost of "day care" (in the sense of replacing the parent's *care*).

[7] U.S., Congress, Senate, Committee on Finance, "The Economics of Child Care," by Mary P. Rowe, hearings on S. 2003, Child Care Provisions of H.R. 1 and title VI of printed amendment 318 to H.R. 1, 92d Cong., 1st sess., 22, 23, 24 September 1971 (Washington, D.C.: U.S. Government Printing Office, 1971), pp. 235–313; see especially pp. 272–292. She examines estimates done by Abt Associates, Inc., and the Westinghouse Learning Corp. and finds that, by adjusting for differences in data and how they treat imputations, part-time attendance, interest, start-up costs, and so on, the numbers can be shown to be rather similar. Abt Associates, Inc., *A Study in Child Care 1970–71* (OEO contract No. OEO–BOO–5213), 55 Wheeler Street, Cambridge, Mass., April 1971, and Westinghouse Learning Corp. (Westat Research), *Day Care Survey 1970* (OEO contract No. 800–5160), April 1971.

Table 11.2 Estimates by HEW of the Annual Cost of Day Care for School-Age Children before and after School and during the Summer

Program element	Minimum		Acceptable		Desirable	
	Description	Cost	Description	Cost	Description	Cost
A. School year (40 weeks)						
1. Food (meals and snacks)	Snack	$30	Snack and breakfast	$70	Snack and breakfast	$70
2. Work with parents	Urgent only	10	Supplementary to school services	20	Supplementary to school services	20
3. Facilities	School, other no rent	10	Same	10	Same	10
4. Supplies and materials	Custodial	20	Developmental	40	Developmental	40
5. Equipment (replacement cost)	Custodial	10	Developmental	15	Developmental	15
6. Personnel:						
(a) Day care workers (at $4400)	1 per 25 children for 3 hours	53	1 per 15 children for 3 hours	88	1 per 15 children for 3 hours	88
(b) Special resource personnel (at $6600)	None	0	1 per 45 children	66	1 per 45 children	66
(c) Business (at $4000)	1 per 250 children	12	1 per 250 children	12	1 per 250 children	12
(d) Supervision (at $8000)	1 per 250 children	24	2 per 250 children	24	2 per 250 children	24
7. Training		9		28		28
B. Summer period (12 weeks)						
1. Food (meals and snacks)	1 meal, snacks	35	2 meals, snacks	50	2 meals, snacks	50
2. Work with parents	Urgent only	5	Supplementary to school services	15	Supplementary to school services	15
3. Facilities	School, other no rent	20	Same	20	Same	20
4. Supplies and materials	Custodial	10	Developmental	15	Developmental	15
5. Equipment (replacement cost)	Custodial	5	Developmental	10	Developmental	10

6. Personnel:

(a) Recreation supervisors (at $4400)	1 per 25 children for 8 hours	40	1 per 15 children for 8 hours	65	1 per 15 children for 8 hours	65
(b) Special resource personnel (at $6600)	None	0	1 per 30 children	55	1 per 30 children	55
(c) Business (at $4000)	1 per 250 children	4	1 per 250 children	4	1 per 250 children	4
(d) Supervision (at $8000)	1 per 250 children	8	3 per 250 children	24	3 per 250 children	24
7. Training	10 percent of salaries	5	15 percent of salaries	22	15 percent of salaries	22
Total per child		$310		$653		$653

Source—U.S., Department of Health, Education, and Welfare, Office of Child Development, *Standards and Costs for Day Care*, 1967.

Turn to the specific costs in Tables 11.1 and 11.2. Transportation costs must be included in the cost of standard care because they are real costs incurred by the working parent whose child must be brought to the center. Day care staff are counted to the extent that they replace the mothers' services. Food costs are harder to break down, however. Some of the costs replace those normally incurred by the parent (the child must be fed at home, too); some of the costs are for preparation, a service rendered directly by the parent; and some of the costs in the higher estimates are for more food. (The minimum provides one meal and two snacks; others provide two meals and two snacks.) Our estimate of standard care uses as a compromise the cost of food in the "minimum" HEW estimates. Although some food costs might be counted as a normal out-of-pocket cost to parents, preparation would have been provided directly. Thus, minimum food costs appear in the total.

In an industry like day care, a fairly regular staff turnover might be expected. At least some of the training costs must be seen as ongoing and normal costs of doing business (as they are in private industry). Some of the work with parents and social services are essential for day care since they help the parent adjust to not seeing the child for nearly three-quarters of the child's waking hours. We should not be surprised that some coordination costs result from splitting child care between two entirely different agents. And special resource personnel (computed as one for 300 children for "minimum" care and one for 100 children for "acceptable" care) may be needed to compensate for having an unusually large number of children in one place.

If we subtract from "acceptable" care costs ($1862) in Table 11.1 the extra costs for better food, all medical and dental expenses, and half the training costs, costs can be reduced by $150. But it is difficult to cut much more without lowering the level of what is defined as "acceptable" care (to include "a basic program of developmental activities as well as providing minimum custodial care") below what we have defined as standard. This produces a figure of $1710 ($1860 minus $150).

However, some people would feel that this cost is very high for our definition of standard day care, and that much more could be cut. In a recent report, Bernstein and Giacchino claim that "using HEW standards for cost, about 40 percent of the operating budget of a day care center providing acceptable care can, at a conservative estimate, be ascribed to education, special services, and training."[8] Examine the HEW costs for preschool full-time day care in Table 11.1. "Acceptable" care costs $1862

[8] B. Bernstein and P. Giacchino, "Costs of Day Care: Implications for Public Policy," in *City Almanac*, a bulletin of the Metropolitan Information Service, August 1971, p. 12.

per child per year in 1967. Subtracting 40 percent reduces this to $1117, which is $128 below the cost of HEW "minimum" care. This is not surprising, since the 40 percent figure assumes removing all costs related to training, medical and dental services, work with parents, social service, special resources personnel, and parent and community aides, as well as the cost of one classroom professional. This looks very much like what HEW calls "minimum" care. From the HEW figures for minimum care, subtract all medical costs, parental work, social service, aides, resource personnel, and training, and add back the transportation omitted by HEW in this estimate. This reduces the HEW total by $130. So the Bernstein number resembles the cost of stripped minimum care. I judge the level of this care to be unacceptably low for standard care. Lacking hard evidence, my preference is for "acceptable" care, which seems to resemble more closely the care provided, it is hoped, by a parent in the home full time.

We are now able to establish a range for the cost of standard care, between the Bernstein number and the higher figure for "acceptable" care: $1120 to $1710, with the bias of this chapter toward the higher number. "Minimum" care already has a ratio of 3:20 for staff in direct contact with the child, or, more exactly, $1:6\frac{1}{6}$ (or $6\frac{2}{3}$, omitting social service staff). The staff-to-child ratio of "acceptable" care is $1:4\frac{1}{3}$ (or $4\frac{3}{4}$). By contrast, the recent recommendation reported by the Senate Finance Committee requires only one adult for up to eight preschool children, or two for up to fifteen, well outside this range.[9] The results are summarized in Table 11.3.

Table 11.3   Estimates for Standard Day Care for One Child
between the Ages of Three and Five

	1967 prices	Add 20 percent inflation	Add 30 percent inflation
Minimum (Bernstein)	1120	1344	1456
Maximum (acceptable)	1710	2052	2223
Amount included for food in the above two estimates	140	168	182

Note—In dollars.

[9] U.S., Department of Health, Education, and Welfare, "Proposed Revised Federal Day Care Requirements," in *Additional Material Related to Child Care Legislation*, U.S., Congress, Senate, Committee on Finance (Washington, D.C.: U.S. Government Printing Office, 1971), p. 41.

304 / Michael Krashinsky

It is necessary to correct for inflation over the past six years (up to 1973). Using inflation of 20 percent, the range of day care costs becomes $1344 to $2052, while with inflation of 30 percent, it is $1456 to $2223. These estimates of inflation are not unrealistic. Using the middle of 1967 as a base, the Bureau of Labor Statistics reports that the cost of licensed day care for preschool children had risen 25.8 percent by January 1973. In the same period, the cost of babysitting services (a very important component of child care today) rose by 39.2 percent.[10] We shall generally use the 20 percent figure for inflation.

Taking the top estimate of $2052, standard day care would cost about $40 per child per week. The lower estimate is still over $26 per child per week. Yet, in a Massachusetts early education project study, only 9 percent of all mothers (all incomes) said that they would be able to pay more than $20 for child care of their choice for one child under six years old.[11] Rowe states: "In general, families earning less than median incomes do not, and say they cannot, pay more than $6–$12 per week per child."[12]

The 1968 HEW figures for child care are dramatically lower for school-age children. They require part-time day care only, before and after school and in the summer—only $310 annually for "minimum" care and $653 for "acceptable" or "desirable" care (Table 11.2). Using available school buildings, of course, saves the cost of rent for day care. But the real cost reductions result from the sizable drop in supervision needed. Older children need substantially less supervision than preschool children, and during the school year, that supervision is needed for only three hours per day. Food becomes a more important component in the cost: $65 for "minimum" care and $120 for "acceptable" care. Salaries account for 57.5 percent ("minimum") or 65.5 percent ("acceptable") of what remains. The costs may be somewhat higher for younger schoolchildren and lower for older ones. Using a notion of standard care is somewhat more difficult here, but in 1967, parents would have faced costs of between

[10] The figures were supplied to me in computer printouts from the Bureau of Labor Statistics, Washington, D.C. 20212. These figures would be biased if there were any systematic change in day care quality over the period.
[11] Rowe, "Economics of Child Care," p. 7.
[12] Rowe, "Economics of Child Care," p. 6. One should be careful about reading too much into this statement as a measure of standard care. Some of those women might not particularly want to work and might see day care as a convenient babysitting service (at the right price). Others might simply prefer to use cheaper, inferior day care.

$310 and $598 for a complete year per child. Inflation at 20 percent brings this to $372 and $718. And these figures include food, which parents would have to purchase in any case. Work would appear more attractive to such families, although if there are more than four such children in a family, part-time work during school hours might be more attractive. The results for standard care are summarized in Table 11.4.

The Real Cost of Working to Mothers and Society

Although one mother is needed to care for one child in the home, substantially fewer than four mothers are needed to care for four children in a center. However, this apparent economy of scale occurs largely because caring for a child in the home does not require full-time work, just full-time availability. While she is watching over her child (giving him child care), a mother can also cook, clean house, wash dishes and clothes, shop, and so forth. Seen as a whole, these are the "joint outputs" of housework. For the price, or work, of one, you get both child care and housework.

Thus, when a mother arranges for day care for her child and goes out to work, she also loses all those other outputs and still must find a way to shop, clean, cook, and wash. Little wonder that a mother not in desperate need of income is reluctant to pay a substantial part of her wage for child care. Working involves substantial costs beyond the loss of child care. Her reluctance increases if the mother enjoys taking care of her children, if she dislikes the type of work she is offered (which is

Table 11.4 Estimates for Standard Day Care for One Child between the Ages of Six and Fourteen

	1967 prices	Add 20 percent inflation	Add 30 percent inflation
Minimum	310.00	372.00	403.00
Maximum	598.00	717.60	778.40
Amount included for food in the above two estimates	65.00	78.00	82.00

Note—In dollars.

likely when it is low-skill, low-productivity work), and if she distrusts (or has some uncertainty about) the child care she is buying.[13]

What a mother does at home is generally not considered "production." It is not imputed and added into calculations of the Gross National Product. But ignoring it leads to the conviction that a major gain in efficiency is possible by putting welfare mothers to work. It is thought that, if two mothers have two youngsters each, we ought to be able to assign the child care to one, put the other mother to work, and come out ahead. Yet, given the value of the other things a mother does during the day, the costs of transportation to and from day care and work, the unpleasantness and low pay of low-skill work, and the risks and loss of pleasure in having one's children raised by others, the gain is not at all clear.

Work for women with preschoolers is a clear gain only when low-cost, reliable day care is easily available or when the mother is extremely productive in a marketable job, a situation that usually is found among well-educated women, who in general are not poor. Among middle-class families, a working mother generally pays for the heavy housework as well as for child care. Work is also more clearly a gain when the children are not present most of the day (when they are of school age); during school hours, the mother no longer produces child care as she works in the home, so that the cost of going to work is reduced. It would seem, then, that requiring welfare mothers to work is inefficient when the cost of day care begins to approach the value of their work outside the home (see the earlier discussion), since they also lose the value of their own housekeeping services. (A more precise criterion for inefficiency would depend upon being able to accurately measure the value of non-child care services in the home.)

III. Integrating Day Care with Welfare

Three plans will be examined separately, although we shall spend more time on H.R. 1 since, of the three, it would require by far the largest expansion of extrafamily day care. In some sense, both a demogrant and H.R. 1 are negative income taxes, since both guarantee a basic income level and impose a positive marginal tax on all earnings. The most important characteristic of these programs, as far as day care is concerned, is whether or not there is a work requirement as a condition of eligibility.

[13] For a sophisticated treatment of labor market participation by married women, see Glen G. Cain, *Married Women in the Labor Force: An Economic Analysis* (Chicago: University of Chicago Press, 1966).

If there is a work requirement, our concern for the welfare of children implies a special concern for the arrangements that will be made for day care. Without a work requirement, we may rely somewhat more on parents to forgo work if they cannot make adequate day care arrangements. Of course, even without a formal work requirement, a low basic guarantee level will induce women who might not work at a higher guarantee to enter the labor market.

One of the problems in any cost estimate is that we do not know how mothers will react to a given scheme of incentives. Since work is required in some of the plans, we can identify at least partially who will be working. But the day care arrangements that will result may be harder to estimate.

The Issue of Deductibility and Subsidy

Before examining the three alternatives in detail, it will be useful to consider the various ways of treating the day care expenses of those receiving welfare. The discussion of deductibility and subsidy will focus on a negative income tax with a positive implicit tax rate on earned income. (With the Senate Finance Committee's workfare proposal, which involves a negative marginal tax rate,[14] the issue of deductibility is meaningless.)

Consider a negative income tax scheme with a marginal tax rate of two-thirds (which is the H.R. 1 rate). Allowing the deduction of day care expenses implies that, for each extra dollar spent on day care (up to the limit of deductibility), the government pays $.67 more in benefits to the family. Families with low incomes and high day care expenses could be allowed to deduct more than 100 percent of their day care expenses: A deduction of 150 percent of day care at the two-thirds tax rate would permit the government to absorb fully each extra dollar spent on day care. Or we could choose a percentage in between, for example, a 125 percent deduction. This is exactly equivalent to the following arrangement: For given day care expenses and income, the government pays directly for a certain part of day care; the rest is paid for by the family and is deductible.[15]

[14] See the later discussion of the second alternative.

[15] This may be seen analytically. Imagine a family with a guarantee level of $2800 and an income disregard of $720 (H.R. 1 applied to a family of five). Say the family uses child care costing C, of which the government directly pays a fraction a. The family thus pays $(1 - a)C$ for child care. If there is no limit on child care deductibility (although there would be a limit in H.R. 1), then the benefit level becomes (where earnings are W)

(1) $$B = \$2800 - \tfrac{2}{3}[W - \$720 - (1 - a)C]$$

Two questions arise with respect to such a subsidy. First, how will the size of the subsidy fall as income rises (given the total cost of day care as fixed)? The faster the subsidy falls, the less its overall cost will be and the greater its effect in increasing the marginal tax rate on earnings. One dollar more in earnings not only reduces income supplement benefits by $.67, but also reduces the day care subsidy. This is a serious consideration with the income supplement tax rate already at two-thirds.[16]

Second, how will the subsidy increase with the cost of day care to a family with a given income? The government might determine that it wants no family with earned income W to have to pay more than $f(W)$—some amount dependent on W—for standard day care (although, of course, the family would bear any day care expenses beyond the cost of standard care). Thus, a person who pays C_s to purchase standard day care (and for whom $f(W)$ is less than C_s) will receive a direct government subsidy of $C_s - f(W)$. In that case, $f(W)$ will be the household spending for day care and will be deductible. Note that the effective marginal tax rate discussed earlier will be influenced by how $f(W)$ is set. However, the consumer may find care costing less than C_s. Just how the saving is divided between him and the government will depend on how the subsidy declines as the cost of care falls below C_s (when care costs C_s, the subsidy is always $C_s - f(W)$ when $f(W) \leqslant C_s$). This question is equivalent to asking *which* dollars of care (up to C_s) are to be subsidized.

---

and the total family income after taxes (benefits) and day care is

(2) $\qquad Y^d = W - (1-a)C + \$2800 - \tfrac{2}{3}[W - \$720 - (1-a)C],$

which can also be written as

(3) $\qquad\qquad Y^d = \$3280 + \tfrac{1}{3}W - \tfrac{1}{3}(1-a)C.$

This is exactly equivalent to allowing this family to deduct $100 + 50a$ percent of day care after paying for all of it (clearly $100 + 50a$ lies between 100 and 150 for a between 0 and 1). To see this, we may rewrite the expression for family income after benefits and day care as

(4) $\qquad Y^d = W - C + \$2800 - \tfrac{2}{3}[W - \$720 - (1 + a/2)C].$

When simplified, this expression becomes exactly the same as (3).

[16] This may be seen analytically by partially differentiating expression (3) in footnote 15 with respect to W:

(5) $\qquad\qquad \partial Y^d/\partial W = \tfrac{1}{3} + (\tfrac{1}{3}C)\partial a/\partial W$

where $\partial a/\partial W < 0$.

The marginal tax rate is thus

(6) $\qquad\qquad t_e = \tfrac{2}{3} - (\tfrac{1}{3}C)\partial a/\partial W.$

Under this scheme, the government can then subsidize the last dollars of care, either by allowing anyone who spends more than $f(W)$ to claim the difference as a tax credit, or by providing standard care for the price of $f(W)$. These methods, while they definitely encourage parents to purchase quality day care, also provide a very minimal incentive to economize by using whatever low-cost reliable care is available. On the other hand, the government can subsidize the first dollars of care, by crediting (toward higher benefits) the first $C_s - f(W)$ dollars spent, where C_s is the cost of standard care. Thus, the government would pay for all day care costs up to $C_s - f(W)$, and the parents would pay for any additional costs beyond that amount. This second plan involves higher costs than the first one to the government for all individuals who pay less than C_s for day care. It also unfortunately provides no incentive to economize on day care expenditures up to $C_s - f(W)$, the marginal cost to the parent of an additional \$1 of day care being zero, and no incentive to improve the child's day care arrangements beyond $C_s - f(W)$ (with the exception of the income effect), the marginal cost being 1 (all compared to the no-subsidy case). To those parents already spending more than $C_s - f(W)$ on care, it amounts to a flat grant. Finally, the government might choose a plan somewhere in the middle and subsidize a part of each dollar spent on care, say by crediting a fraction $[C_s - f(W)]/C_s$ of every dollar up to C_s spent on care. This reduces (as against no subsidy) the marginal cost of every dollar of day care to the parent, but still maintains some incentive to keep the cost of day care below the cost of standard care. This is the proportional scheme that I shall use later in computing some of the day care costs under H.R. 1. Obviously, many other subsidy schemes are possible.

Of course, the real operation of any of these schemes depends crucially both on how the subsidy is related to earnings (the function $f(W)$) and, above all, on the estimates of the cost of standard care (C_s). In our calculations, we will arbitrarily use $f(W) = .6W$. For those spending all of C_s on day care, this raises a marginal tax rate of .67 up to an effective rate of .87. As in the cash supplement program, there is a trade-off between the amount of the subsidy for persons with low incomes, the work incentive effects of high benefit reduction rates, and high program costs. And in determining the level at which to set C_s, we must also trade off higher program costs with higher-quality day care for children. As we shall see below, the low levels of day care deductibility recommended by H.R. 1 would indicate a preference in the bill for lower estimates of C_s.

Some controls will be needed under the proportional subsidy scheme (as well as under others) to prevent obvious abuses. To see this, suppose that standard care for a given family costs $3000 and that the government pays 75 percent of every dollar spent on day care (up to $3000) by this family. If the family could find a relative or a neighbor who would be willing to take good care of the children, they might be able to pay $1200 for this service (instead of $3000 for standard day care). The family's share of this would be $300. But if the family were to claim that they were paying $2400 for care, while really paying $1400, then the family would gain $700 (the government pays them $1800 for care, so that they end up $400 ahead instead of $300 behind), while the relative or neighbor gains $200. This might also be exploited by local low-cost day care firms. The fact that the relative would have to pay tax on the *full* $2400 would somewhat mitigate this incentive to misrepresent expenses, but it might still be necessary to limit the amounts declarable as day care expenses for various *types* of care (for example, by a relative in the parent's home, by a relative in the relative's home, and so on). This type of abuse would occur in any scheme having some form of deductibility, and resembles the normal problems encountered in enforcing tax law against anyone who tries to inflate illegitimately his income tax deductions.

The various plans that we have discussed are summarized algebraically in Table 11.5. Several special cases arise. In Table 11.5, we assume that earned income exceeds the disregard.[17] If day care expenses are so high as to make declared taxable income negative, then we assume that the benefit is increased over the guarantee level (for the negative income tax) by the taxable income multiplied by the marginal tax rate. This special treatment may not be allowed, however. The amounts under H.R. 1 for a single-parent family of five are indicated in parentheses in the notes to Table 11.5.[18] The derivations are shown in Appendix 1 of this chapter. The case in which earned income is less than the disregard generates a new table (Appendix 2 of this chapter).

Now examine Table 11.5. If working women cannot deduct their day care expenses, they will frequently end up with less than the minimum guarantee level, even when their wages more than cover day care. In our example (a family of five under H.R. 1, facing a marginal tax rate of two-thirds), if care costs $3000, the mother must earn more than $7560 before her disposable income (after day care is paid for) again tops $2800. Besides encouraging low-quality care, this situation also seems to contra-

---

[17] The disregard refers to those initial earnings that are not considered—"disregarded" —in computing total benefits. In H.R. 1, the disregard is $720. Thus, a man who earns $2000 is taxed the implicit rate of two-thirds only on $1280.

[18] This family has a guarantee level of $2800 and a disregard of $720. In addition, under H.R. 1, there would be a limit on the deductibility of day care of $2200.

dict the notion of rewarding work effort, as well as running counter to the
real meaning of the guarantee.[19] The other schemes all provide that the
mother will not lose so long as she can cover day care out of her earnings.[20] But when some form of subsidy is being offered (say to protect the
woman who cannot cover the cost of care), then it is the government that
may lose when she works. This can be seen clearly by noting that, if we
imagine the mother paying for day care, with the subsidy and deduction
rebate being paid as part of her benefit, then

$$(7) \qquad Y^d = G + W - C,$$

where Y^d is her disposable income after benefits and day care, and G is
the total cost to the government. In a situation in which the mother stays
home, $Y^d = G_0 =$ minimum guarantee, and W and C are zero; if, when
she goes to work, the government wants to make sure that Y^d does not
fall, then G must rise if $W - C$ is less than zero (that is, if her earnings do
not cover the cost of care). If the government does not let G rise, then
the mother is forced to face the choice discussed earlier: inadequate income
or poor care.

If the mother's yearly earnings, augmented by the present discounted
value of her extra future earnings due to working, do not exceed the cost
of purchasing standard care, then there is a *real* loss in output to society
in her working, even neglecting the value of her housework and leisure.
So someone must be worse off—either the government in higher overall
cost, or the mother in lower net income, or the child in below-standard
day care, or all three (in comparison with a situation in which the mother
is given the basic guarantee and left at home). We might question the
gains from requiring mothers with many children to work or accept
training, no matter how we pay for the care these children receive.

[19] It is felt by some that the other schemes are very expensive, since the government
would essentially pay for a major part of the costs of day care. In the case of simple
deductibility, the government's share would be equal to t (here two-thirds). This
characterization is somewhat misleading. In comparison with a system not allowing
this deductibility, the government costs indeed rise by two-thirds of the day care
used. Yet, in comparison with a system in which the mother does not work and receives the guarantee, the government also saves on the welfare payment. We might
better characterize deductibility as follows. The mother pays for all of day care
herself out of her earnings. What is left is then used to compute the supplement. This
more properly pictures day care as a work expense, not as consumption.
[20] This loss, if she cannot cover day care out of her earnings, is only again in comparison with a system in which she stays at home and receives the minimum guarantee. In states where the current welfare levels are very low, she will be better off
under H.R. 1 regardless of how we treat day care expenses.

Table 11.5 Day Care, Government Costs, Family Income, and the Tax Rate

	Y^d	TC_g	t_e	MC_o
1. No work	G	G	—	—
2. Work, no deduction for day care	$G + tD + W(1-t) - C$	$G - t(W-D)$	t	1
3. Work, deduction limited to C_o (C_o could be C_s)	$G + tD + (1-t)(W-C)$ for $C \le C_o$	$G - t(W-D-C)$	t	$1-t$
	$G + tD + (1-t)W - (C - tC_o)$ for $C > C_o$	$G - t(W-D-C_o)$	t	1
4. Work, full subsidy on first $C_s - f(W)$ dollars, $C - [C_s - f(W)]$ deductible	$G + tD + (1-t)W$ for $C_s - C \ge f(W)$	$G - t(W-D) + C$	t	0
	$G + tD + (1-t)\{W - [C - (C_s - f(W))]\}$ for $C_s \ge f(W) > C_s - C$	$G - t(W-D-C) + (1-t)[C_s - f(W)]$	$t + f' - tf'$	$1-t$
	$G + tD + (1-t)(W-C)$ for $f(W) \ge C_s$	$G - t(W-D-C)$	t	$1-t$
5. Work, full subsidy on last dollars, first dollars deductible	$G + tD(1-t)[W - f(W)]$ for $f(W) \le C$	$G - t(W-D) + C - (1-t)f(W)$	$t + f' - tf'$	0
	$G + tD + (1-t)(W-C)$ for $f(W) > C$	$G - t(W-D-C)$	t	$1-t$

6. Work, proportional subsidy up to C_s, payments by family deductible

$$G + tD + (1-t)\left[W - \frac{f(W)}{C_s}C\right] \qquad G - t(W - D) + \qquad t + (1-t)\frac{fC}{C_s} \qquad (1-t)\frac{f(W)}{C_s}$$

$$\text{for } f(W) \le C_s \qquad\qquad C\left[1 - \frac{(1-t)f(W)}{C_s}\right]$$

$$G + tD + (1-t)(W - C)$$

$$\text{for } f(W) > C_s \qquad\qquad G - t(W - D - C) \qquad\qquad t \qquad\qquad\qquad 1 - t$$

Note—Y^d = parent's net income after paying day care and receiving net benefits; TC_g = total cost to government including day care and net benefits; t_e = effective marginal tax rate $(1 -$ the increase in Y^d given a \$1 increase in W); MC_g = the marginal cost to the parents of using \$1 more worth of day care; G = guarantee level (\$2800); D = disregard (\$720); t = tax rate or benefit reduction rate ($\frac{4}{9}$); C_s = cost of standard care (\$2460 to \$405); C = cost of day care used; W = family earnings, assumed more than D; $f(W)$ = maximum payment for standard day care.

The formulas that appear above are derived in Appendix 1 of this chapter. If the government allows no deduction of day care beyond C_s, then each extra dollar of care beyond C_s will lower income by \$1; if deduction is allowed, then that dollar will lower income only $1 - t$; any subsidy tied to income will further that cost drop, and also will extend the increase of the effective tax rate to higher incomes.

Alternative 1: H.R. 1 as Passed by the House of Representatives

Now turn to the specific provisions of H.R. 1 regarding child care.[21] Female heads of households in which there are no children under three years of age are required to register for job training and work. This requirement does not apply to mothers whose husbands are registered under H.R. 1.[22] Failure to register by the head of the family would reduce the welfare payments by $800, so that most people required to register probably would do so. During training, child care would be financed by the government. After training, the mother would be expected to pay for child care if her earnings were substantial enough, but would be allowed to deduct its cost from her earnings before calculating her welfare benefits (subject to certain limitations on the size of the deduction). In the first year, $750 million is assigned to child care, $50 million of that to fund the creation of new facilities; the remaining $700 million is expected to finance day care for mothers in training. This $700 million is expected to pay for 875,000 child care slots, 291,000 of them for preschool children.

FIRST-YEAR TRAINING COSTS

The $700 million is meant to cover the explicit cost of providing day care slots to parents taking training in the first year, and does not include the costs of deductibility for those already working. Using the costs estimated earlier for standard care, it is possible to calculate whether the $700 million allocated for day care would be sufficient to pay for the 875,000 day care slots. The results are summarized in Tables 11.6 and 11.7. Including food (in the amount allotted in the "minimum" HEW figures), those day care slots would cost between $1.016 billion and $1.101 billion (depending on inflation) based on the upper estimate for standard care (favored by this chapter). The range drops to between $608 million and $659 million if the lower estimates of costs for standard care are used.

It appears, then, that the 875,000 day care slots can be delivered for

---

[21] U.S., Congress, House, Committee on Ways and Means, *Social Security Amendments of 1971*, H. Rept. 92–231 (Washington, D.C.: U.S. Government Printing Office 1971); see especially pp. 158–172.

[22] This provision seems highly arbitrary. If the desire of H.R. 1 is to ask adults who receive welfare to show some work effort, then it would seem that two-parent families are as able to supply two workers as one-parent families are to supply one. In fact, one would suspect that a child with two parents in the home is emotionally better prepared for day care than the child with one parent, and that the parent in a one-parent home already bears a much larger burden than the individual parents in the two-parent home with the same number of children.

Table 11.6   Minimum Range Costs for Standard Day Care (HEW "Minimum" Modified)

	1967 prices per child	Total using 1967 prices	Total with 20 percent inflation	Total with 30 percent inflation
291,000 preschoolers in day care:				
Total cost	1120	325,920,000	391,104,000	423,696,000
Food cost in above total	140	40,740,000	48,888,000	52,962,000
584,000 school-age children in day care:				
Total cost	310	181,040,000	217,248,000	235,352,000
Food cost in above total	65	37,960,000	45,552,000	49,348,000
Total cost for 875,000 children	—	506,960,000	608,352,000	659,048,000
Total food cost in above total	—	78,700,000	94,440,000	102,310,000
Total cost without food	—	428,260,000	513,912,000	556,738,000

Note—Amounts in dollars.

Table 11.7 Maximum Range Costs for Standard Day Care (HEW "Acceptable" Modified)

	1967 prices per child	Total using 1967 prices	Total with 20 percent inflation	Total with 30 percent inflation
291,000 preschoolers in day care:				
Total cost	1710	497,610,000	597,132,000	646,893,000
Food cost in above total	140	40,740,000	48,888,000	52,962,000
584,000 school-age children in day care:				
Total cost	598	349,232,000	419,078,400	454,001,600
Food cost in above total	65	37,960,000	45,552,000	49,348,000
Total cost for 875,000 children	—	846,842,000	1,016,210,400	1,100,894,600
Total food cost in above total	—	78,700,000	94,440,000	102,310,000
Total cost without food	—	768,142,000	921,770,400	998,584,600

Note—Amounts in dollars.

$700 million only if standards for day care are set barely above the "minimum" care level that we have discussed. On the other hand, the estimated cost of providing 875,000 slots is not ridiculously high. Using 20 percent inflation and not including food (which could either be billed to the mothers, subtracted from their welfare benefit, or covered by a separate appropriation for "food for children"), the maximum cost for the 875,000 children is $922 million, about 32 percent above the allotment. Including food, the $1.016 billion figure is 45 percent above the allotment.

A much more serious problem results from the $50 million allotment for the expansion of day care facilities. There has been rapid expansion in day care centers over the past decade. Steiner reports that their number tripled between 1960 and 1969.[23] Using a somewhat different definition, the Westinghouse study found that 17,500 centers in 1970 offered full-time care for seven or more preschool children, caring in all for 575,000 children for a full day (and caring for additional children part time).[24] But we are now talking about providing 291,000 new full-time day care slots for preschoolers, an expansion of the industry by over 50 percent in one year. It is not so much a question of whether or not $50 million will be enough,[25] but whether or not such an expansion is even possible in one year.

If we were serious about immediately training all those mothers who would come under the bill, we might need more slots and/or money. Using current population data extrapolated from previous figures, slightly more than 750,000 mothers with almost 1.75 million children aged six to fourteen would register for work under the bill in 1973.[26] Only about 200,000 of those mothers (with 450,000 of the children) now work a half year or more. If we were to train the rest, 1.3 million slots for school-children would be needed the first year. This is more than double the number of slots for schoolchildren included in the 875,000 figure by H.R. 1. Some slots might be provided by babysitters, but only if parents were given some incentive to use such less expensive (and possibly less reliable) arrangements. In any case, since it is unlikely that the training facilities could be expanded so quickly to handle so many individuals, the problem

---

[23] Steiner, *State of Welfare.*

[24] Westinghouse Learning Corp., *Day Care 1970.*

[25] If the government had to help all the centers set up, and each center could handle twenty-five preschool children, there would be available just under $4300 to help fund each center. This might well be enough to finance the needed capital expansion, if the centers could have access to existing facilities—churches and so forth—that would not need major alterations.

[26] This estimate and those that follow were made by Carolyn Lawall in a document for the U.S. Department of Health, Education, and Welfare, Welfare Reform Planning Staff, entitled *Population and Cost Estimates for H.R. 1 Child Care.*

of sufficient funding for day care slots may not be acute (although the problem of rapidly expanding the capacity of the industry would still remain). Exactly how the federally provided day care slots would be apportioned is not discussed in committee documents.

Some mothers with children under six might also be expected to volunteer in the first year. Even if volunteers were only those mothers who are already working (and who probably will not require training), some financing of their day care might be required (probably through deductibility). If they needed training, day care would be required, but it is not likely that there would be an immediate need for the 291,000 new preschool slots budgeted for the first year. The real pressure for preschool day care would come after July 1974, when the mothers with children older than three would be required to work.

The estimates for day care during training in the first year of H.R. 1, thus, seem to overestimate the number of preschool slots needed. The need for day care for school-age children would depend on how many of the eligible mothers could be accepted for training.

PERMANENT COSTS: DAY CARE FOR WORKING MOTHERS

In the first year of H.R. 1, when mothers with children under age six would not be required to register for work, the explicit cost of supporting day care for working mothers (as opposed to those in training) would be relatively low. But, in later years, when women with preschool children would be required to register for work, the situation would change. Table 11.8 shows the range of costs for standard day care between our maximum and minimum estimates for various family sizes. Clearly, a woman with four children, one of them of preschool age, would have to pay between $2460 and $4205 for standard day care in a day care center (including food). Would we require that a woman's entire paycheck go to cover day care?[27] The answer depends on how we interpret the Ways and Means Committee's phrase, "the mother would be required to pay for the care out of her earnings, *if her earnings were substantial enough*" (emphasis supplied).

As proposed, the bill limits the deduction for child care from earnings (in order to determine the size of the benefit payment) to $2000 for a family of four, raising it by $200 per additional child up to a limit of $3000. However, for a family of five, standard care might cost substantially more than the $2200 allowed as a deduction. Suppose the previously

---

[27] Perhaps more importantly, could we even force such a woman to work when it is so much against her best interest? Experience with Unemployment Insurance would suggest that, when an individual decides that it is in his best interests to be unable to obtain or hold a job, then he will be most successful in doing just that.

Table 11.8 The Cost of Standard Day Care for Various Family Sizes

	Number of children of school age							
	0	1	2	3	4	5	6	7
Number of children ages three to five:								
0	0–0 (0)	372–718 (78)	744–1435 (156)	1116–2153 (234)	1488–2870 (312)	1860–3588 (390)	2232–4306 (468)	2604–5024 (546)
1	1344–2052 (168)	1716–2770 (246)	2088–3487 (324)	2460–4205 (402)	2832–4922 (480)	3204–5640 (558)	3576–6358 (636)	3948–7076 (714)
2	2688–4104 (336)	3060–4822 (414)	3432–5539 (492)	3804–6257 (570)	4176–6974 (648)	4548–7692 (726)	4920–8410 (804)	5292–9128 (882)
3	4032–6156 (504)	4404–6874 (582)	4776–7591 (660)	5148–8309 (738)	5520–9026 (816)	5892–9744 (894)	6264–10,462 (972)	6636–11,180 (1050)

Note—Amounts in dollars. The two numbers given for each family type represent the minimum and maximum estimates to the nearest dollar developed in Tables 11.3 and 11.4. Both numbers include food, which is then separated out in brackets for each family size. All the numbers assume 20 percent inflation over 1968 prices.

discussed mother earns $3300 and pays $3100 for day care (well below the top cost for standard care). Her income after receiving benefits and paying for day care (of which $2200 is deductible before calculating the supplement) is $2747. This is below the guarantee level of $2800.[28] If she has two preschoolers among her four children, the range for standard day care rises to $3432–$5539. But she must keep her day care costs below $3000 to keep much out of her earnings. Unless there is cheap reliable day care available, this mother faces a crisis: Good day care for her children means a drop in her income below the guarantee. She would be better off opening up her own day care center and employing herself for $2900 to care for her own children.[29]

The committee's statement on paying for day care, quoted earlier, would seem to imply some form of subsidy to women with lower income and high standard day care costs. But as we have seen, this might well be economically inefficient for many families, besides being very expensive for the government (a question we explore later). Rather, it would seem that the Ways and Means Committee suspects that standard care would be very cheap for the families under H.R. 1. At the center of this is the suspicion that mothers in the home are not particularly productive and do not work hard. The committee states:

> More than half of all mothers with children age 6 to 17 are now in the labor force . . . about one-third of mothers with children under 6 are now in the labor force. . . . To require such women to support out of taxes on their earnings those mothers who choose not to work but to live on public monies would be inequitable in the extreme.[30]

But the view that welfare mothers "choose not to work but to live on public monies" implies that running a home and caring for one's own children is not "work" (it is nonmonetized). Yet, working in a day care center taking care of children, or as a housekeeper in a wealthy neighborhood, is considered work. In a day care center, a mother can care for more children than at home, but she also requires materials, space, super-

[28] The figure of $2747 can be easily calculated. Her "taxable" income, for purposes of obtaining the benefit level, is her earnings of $3300 minus the $2200 child care deduction and the $720 disregard. This comes to $380. The benefit level thus is reduced below the guarantee of $2800 by two-thirds of $380. Thus, the mother receives $2547 in benefits, $3300 in wages, and pays $3100 in day care costs, for a net of $2747.

[29] Under the law, caring for someone else's children is work, caring for one's own is not.

[30] House Committee on Ways and Means, *Social Security Amendments of 1971*, p. 163.

vision, as well as the aid of a trained person. Furthermore, she cannot perform her normal household tasks while caring for children.

The economic efficiency of a full-time work requirement will obviously depend upon the relative productivities of the welfare mothers in and out of the home, that is, upon the relative sizes of the estimate for standard care and the expected value of the mothers' wage in the labor force. To save costs and prevent inefficiency, the government might relieve from the full-time work requirement those single-parent households in which the number and ages of children make the cost of standard care too high in relation to the parents' earnings. (This break-off point need not be at the point where the two are equal, so as to allow for other losses—housework, commuting, and so on—borne by a working mother.)[31] Some kind of part-time work in the home might be provided for those mothers not required to work. Of course, such a mother would be free to work full time if she could make substantially cheaper day care arrangements (in which case she would qualify for a day care deduction but not a subsidy). We discuss later the potential gains available in such an approach.

The committee quote appearing earlier also seems to be making a statement on horizontal equity. If we accept the notion that a natural outcome of income supplement programs is some amount of income redistribution, then taxing working mothers in high-income families to support low-income mothers should not be viewed any differently from the income redistribution from high- to low-income, male-headed families, which also results from H.R. 1. However, we do want women who work part time to be better off financially (given that they can more than cover child care cost) than those who do not work. This is what the work incentive is all about.

THE COST OF DAY CARE UNDER H.R. 1

The cost of providing day care for single-parent families during training would be very substantial in the early years of the program, due to the large number of untrained women. But, after these mothers are all trained, government day care payments for trainees should fall abruptly. There would be some new mothers entering H.R. 1 each year, but the number of trainees would be very low.[32]

[31] This would appear to create some strong incentives to have children, an issue dealt with later in Part IV.
[32] Estimating the number of new mothers who would need training each year is very difficult, since many of them might have received training before; and, in any case, we are trying to estimate children who are not yet born. But if we imagine a generation to last twenty-five years, and assume that our total training costs would be spread

In contrast, the cost of providing day care for single-parent families during work would be a continuing one. The "costs" associated with a scheme of support for day care through deductibility, and those associated with a direct subsidy, depend on the alternative with which the scheme is compared. Of course, in comparison with a system with a general work requirement and no deductibility, allowing the deduction of day care expenses would be very expensive. Not only would the potential payments to those working and on welfare rise, but payments would also be made to eligible families who otherwise would not qualify. But some support for child care expenses is an integral part of a work requirement, a requirement that is politically unacceptable without some consideration for child care (a position with which the Ways and Means Committee seems to agree). Would the work requirement generate a real gain to the government? To determine this, we compare total expenditures under the following two alternatives. In one, work is required and some subsidy-deductibility scheme is adopted for day care expenses. In the second, single parents do not work but receive the minimum guarantee under the Family Assistance Plan (FAP). The total cost or saving of requiring work of adults in single-parent families can then be seen clearly.

This cost can be calculated using a breakdown of current AFDC families by age and number of children.[33] Assume the adoption of a proportional subsidy plan like that developed earlier (with $f(W) = .6W$) and also assume that every family will use standard care (that none will find cheaper care, despite the incentives).[34] Compared to a system of just paying out the guarantee with no work by the parents, the total difference

---

out rather than concentrated over that period, once the program becomes ongoing, we are clearly talking about an abrupt decline in costs, from $4.6 billion over three years to under $200.0 million per year (using the top figure).

Another factor might, however, increase the day care costs during training in the future. Thus far, we have assumed that each adult need be trained only once before participating in the labor force. It might develop, however, that we would need to retrain these workers periodically as jobs disappeared and new ones appeared. This would substantially increase all training costs.

[33] Standard care costs from Tables 11.3 and 11.4 are used, adding 20 percent for inflation. Data on AFDC families by age and number of children are from the 1971 AFDC Characteristics Survey. There were 1,511,300 AFDC families with seven or fewer children, which provided the basis for the calculations made here.

[34] Since this is obviously not the case, the potential gains to a work requirement will be understated. With a reliable distribution of day care expenses, new calculations could easily be done. However, it is important to note that this subsidy encourages, relative to the no-subsidy case, the purchase of better care by new workers and by those women now using cheap care. Just what the final day care distribution would look like is unclear.

in costs to the government for all current AFDC families can be derived using two different possible average yearly earnings ($3000 and $4200)[35] and the two ends of our range for standard care. We assume that day care for each child aged thirteen to eighteen would cost one-half that for a child aged six to twelve.[36] Some families, under these assumptions, would cost the government more under the work requirement, and some less. The totals for these two groups (gains and losses), and the sums, are shown in Tables 11.9 and 11.10 (the calculation for a sample family is in Table 11.11). We divide the gains and losses to suggest the gains possible in making the work requirement more selective. Most of the losses, in fact, occur in families with at least one preschool child.

The numbers in Tables 11.9 and 11.10 can be placed in perspective by comparing them to the cost of supporting all those families at the FAP guarantee, which would cost a total of $3,391,250,000. So, using the low estimate for day care and assuming all mothers can earn an average of $4200, we can save 65 percent of the FAP costs by requiring them all to work. But the savings can even be increased by giving the FAP guarantee to those families who would cost the government more under the subsidy

Table 11.9 Gains and Losses to the Government, Using a Proportional Subsidy and Work Requirement, As against FAP with No Work by Parents in These Families

| | Wage level | |
Cost of standard care	3000	4200
Low estimates	+1,138,764,400 −206,248,600 +932,515,800	+2,247,038,400 −41,496,300 +2,205,542,100
High estimates	+640,514,700 −956,585,000 −316,030,300	+1,549,546,700 −458,933,900 +1,090,612,800

Note—Amounts in dollars.

[35] The two numbers are arbitrarily chosen, although they might serve as a range for possible average earnings. The calculations are easily redone for other average incomes.
[36] This may be projecting costs too high, especially for children between the ages of fifteen and eighteen. In many homes, these children currently dispense day care to their younger brothers and sisters while their parents work. On the other hand, children at the lower end (thirteen to fourteen) may need more care than this.

Table 11.10   Gains and Losses from Table 11.8, by Family Size

Number of children	Low estimate standard care costs		High estimate standard care costs	
	3000 wages	4200 wages	3000 wages	4200 wages
1	+494,824,000	+842,184,000	+357,244,100	+754,810,100
	0	0	0	0
2	+321,342,400	+610,134,400	+199,365,600	+437,716,800
	−22,152,000	0	−128,762,400	−36,816,000
3	+185,453,200	+406,638,000	+71,944,200	+230,720,400
	−31,303,600	−4,098,400	−180,049,300	−72,056,700
4	+91,211,600	+227,363,200	+11,863,600	+98,599,200
	−43,858,400	−8,908,000	−202,376,900	−98,600,600
5	+33,377,600	+103,054,200	+97,200	+25,465,200
	−41,492,600	−9,400,200	−187,130,700	−94,651,400
6	+10,861,600	+43,760,400	0	+2,177,000
	−38,110,000	−9,537,300	−155,179,000	−87,778,900
7	+1,694,000	+13,904,200	0	+58,000
	−29,332,000	−9,552,400	−103,086,700	+69,030,300

Note—Amounts in dollars.

plan. The potential gains in such a move are more substantial using higher day care costs and lower wage estimates. Using wages of $3000 and the high estimates for standard care, the subsidy will add 9.3 percent onto the FAP-level costs; eliminating the families that cost more can lower potential costs by 18.9 percent. The gains and losses developed here omit all families with more than seven children, where a work requirement is likely to prove even more inefficient (there are almost 60,000 such families).

How would the families forced to work fare under the proportional subsidy scheme? No family's income can fall below the guarantee level. The total increase in net income to these families after paying for day care and receiving the benefit is the sum of three quantities: the increase

Table 11.11   Sample Calculation for Family with One Preschool Child and One School-Age Child—Net Government Gain or Loss

	Wage level	
	3000	4200
Low-cost standard care (2088)	+ 834	+928
High-cost standard care (3487)	−1367	−327

Note—Amounts in dollars. For calculation, see Table 11.5. Minimum guarantee is $2400.

in government expenditures (calculated in Table 11.9), the total wages earned, and the negative of the total child care expenditures. Total wages are obtained by multiplying the 1,511,300 AFDC families by the average yearly wage; total child care costs are easily derived from the distribution of AFDC families by age and number of children. The results are shown in Table 11.12.

In some sense, this has overstated the gains possible through a work requirement, since those families for which we show the largest gains (primarily families with one or two school-age children) are exactly those families who would work in the absence of a work requirement (and who do work now). In addition, single-parent families who now work and who would qualify for the day care subsidy might cost the government a fair amount.

In summary, if we guarantee that no family would be worse off financially under a work requirement than if they received only the minimum guarantee, then, depending crucially on what estimates we choose for day care and earnings, a large number of families would end up costing the government more under a work requirement.

Alternative 2: Guaranteed Job Opportunity

This alternative, proposed by the Senate Finance Committee, requires work by eliminating entirely the minimum income for "employables." For all families other than single-parent families with children under six years old, welfare will no longer exist. For those who cannot find jobs, public employment will be provided at $1.50 per hour for up to thirty-two hours per week. No other support will be provided. In order to give low-wage workers an incentive to work in the private labor market, all private work at between $1.50 and $2.00 per hour will be subsidized at 75 percent of the difference between the wage and $2.00. An additional 10 percent

Table 11.12   Average Gain Per Family in Net Income (after Day Care and Benefits) Using a Proportional Subsidy and a Work Requirement, As against FAP with No Work by Parents in These Families

	Wage level	
Cost of standard care	*3000*	*4200*
Low estimates	1130	1488
High estimates	1029	1298

Note—Amounts in dollars.

bonus will be paid on all incomes up to $4000 per year, the bonus falling to zero as income raises to $5600.[37]

The program assumes that, for the poor who desire work, poverty is due both to low wages and to the difficulty in finding a job. The proposal directly attacks both these problems. It should be noted that the wage subsidy is not related in any way to family size.

Day care is less important in this proposal, since all one-parent families with preschool children are exempt from the work requirement. For women with children over six in single-parent households, who take federally funded jobs, the Senate Committee states:

> However, a woman with school-age children would not be required to be away from home during hours that the children are not in school (unless child care is provided), although she may be asked, in order to earn her wage, to provide after-school care to children other than her own during these hours.[38]

This still leaves day care to be provided during the summer. The spirit of the report indicates that some of the women would be employed to supervise their own and other children. This amounts to a 100 percent subsidy for day care for all women working at the federally provided jobs, since they all take home the government salary of $2500 and pay nothing for day care, whether they are being paid to supervise their own and other children or are receiving the services of other mothers.

But how are the mothers who do not take federally funded jobs to be treated? The report states:

> Subsidization of child care for low-income working mothers will depend on the availability of appropriations. Mothers able to pay will be charged the full cost of services.[39]

What is meant by "able to pay"?[40] If day care for mothers earning $2500 is fully subsidized, the subsidy would have to be reduced gradually with

[37] U.S., Congress, Senate, Committee on Finance, *Social Security and Welfare Reform, Summary of the Principal Provisions of H.R. 1 As Determined by the Committee on Finance* (Washington, D.C.: U.S. Government Printing Office, 1972); see especially p. 63 onward.

[38] Ibid., p. 73.

[39] Ibid., p. 92.

[40] This rather resembles the phrase "the mother would be required to pay for the care out of her earnings, if her earnings were substantial enough," quoted earlier from the House-passed version of H.R. 1. The same sort of implied subsidy seems to exist here.

increased income to keep the effective marginal tax rate fairly low (and maintain the incentive to secure private employment). For each extra dollar of annual take-home income, we might require that some fraction go toward day care, until the mother has assumed the whole cost. The actual effect on the effective tax rate will depend on which tax rate is being considered. As it turns out, this scheme has two tax rates, because the plan treats differently an increase in income resulting from more hours worked and one resulting from a rise in the wage rate. Within the range of the plan, the first is treated much more favorably than the second. If income rises because of an increase in hours worked, the take-home pay rises by the market wage plus the subsidy. But if income rises because of an increase in the market wage, then take-home pay rises by a fraction of the wage increase, since the subsidy per hour falls.

If the worker earns less than $4000 per year (and, hence, earns the full 10 percent bonus) at a private wage of $1.80 per hour, then working an extra hour gains him an extra $2.13 ($1.80 plus 10 percent of $1.80 plus three-quarters of the difference between $1.80 and $2.00). This represents an effective marginal tax rate of -18 percent (an added benefit of 18 percent per extra hour worked). Requiring him to pay a fraction, g', of his take-home increment[41] toward day care will make the tax rate $1 - 1.18$ $(1 - g')$.[42] If $g' = .4$, the effective tax rate on the original earned income becomes 29 percent; if $g' = .6$, it becomes 53 percent.[43] If, on the other hand, the worker takes a higher-paying private job with a wage of $1.90, his take-home pay rises to $2.165 ($1.90 plus 10 percent of $1.90 plus three-quarters of the difference between $1.90 and $2.00), making for an effective marginal tax rate on wage rate increases of 65 percent. Paying g' of the increment toward day care makes the effective tax rate $1 - .35$ $(1 - g')$. If $g' = .4$, the effective marginal tax rate becomes 79 percent;

[41] By "take-home increment," I mean the total increase in his income from work resulting from the extra hours worked. This increase includes the government wage subsidy and the bonus.

[42] If he works one more hour, he earns $1.80 more and receives an additional $.33 from the government. But if he is obliged to pay an extra $2.13g' for day care, he gains only $1.80 + $.33 − $2.13g' = $2.13(1 − g'). As a fraction of his original extra earnings, this is $2.13(1 − g')/$1.80. The effective marginal tax rate is thus $1 - ($2.13 [1 − g']/$1.80) or $1 - 1.18(1 - g')$.

[43] However, once the worker is earning above $2 per hour, he is also earning more than $4000 annually (if he is able to work full time), and so he has the $400 bonus at $4000 reduced by $.25 for every extra dollar earned. The negative marginal tax rate he enjoyed at a lower wage has become a positive rate of 25 percent. There will be many families still receiving day care subsidies at this point, and reduction of this subsidy as income rises will make this tax rate much higher. If $g' = .5$, then, at the annual income of $4400 after the subsidy, the family must pay the first $950 of day care expenses and the effective marginal tax rate is $62\frac{1}{2}$ percent.

if $g' = .6$, it becomes 86 percent. These rates are rather high, but inevitable, given the plan's high rate of effective tax on wage rate increments in this range. This may be of less concern than tax rates on the extra hours worked.[44] But the earlier transformation of the negative tax rate on extra hours of work to a substantial positive rate points out the basic problem: Any attempt to reduce a subsidy fairly rapidly as income rises would make for a high positive tax rate, no matter what the original features of the plan.

Of course, we would want to encourage parents to use cheaper care if it were available. To do this, parents who use cheaper care might be paid a bonus of some fraction of every dollar saved the government in subsidies. This fraction might be .3 or .5. If, however, the government were to employ mothers in federal jobs to care for other women's children, then day care costs would be part of the federal wage bill for the plan. It might be undesirable to pay a partial subsidy for private day care arrangements when the mothers providing it are not easily employable elsewhere in the government. The bonus might be cut to .1 or even zero, since parents using cheaper care would then not save the government much.

Some limit might be set on the size of the family whose single parent would be employable in order to reduce some of the inefficiencies discussed earlier. Without a limit, cases will arise in which child care costs more money than is earned by the parent. However, the lower cost of care for children in school compared with the cost for preschool children makes this issue somewhat less powerful.

The cost of child care could be reduced by using some of the public employees as day care workers, since their wage of $2500 per year is well below the cost used in the HEW calculation ($4400 per year). Even at the "acceptable" supervision level of one adult to fifteen children, this comes to only $173 per child in immediate labor costs. Unfortunately, this work would be only part time (even less than the thirty-two hours per week of guaranteed employment), so something else would have to be found for the employees at other hours. These workers might also work in day care centers for mothers of preschoolers who want to work. Here we see the difficulty in calculating government costs for day care under such a plan, if many of the resources used to provide day care cost the government relatively little. The alternate "uses" for day care mothers may not be very productive.

[44] However, this feature is vulnerable to attempts by part-time workers to conceal their true wage rate if it is high, and to both inflate the number of hours worked and deflate the reported wage rate. There is also a serious reduction in the incentive to leave government employment and seek private work if g' is too high.

The specific day care cost in the workfare program would depend critically on how much mothers could earn and on what day care arrangements they could make. If parents do pay for food in all cases, day care can cost, at most, $640 (see Table 11.4). Since the minimum income of $2500 in federal jobs is low, we might want to separately fund food for children. Applying the $640 to the 777,000 families with 1,729,000 children, which would come under H.R. 1,[45] the potential costs are $1.1 billion. If we pay for day care only during the summer,[46] the number drops to $630.0 million. But 26 percent of these children are in families whose mothers now work at least half the year, and half of them use low-cost care. Assuming that half as many of the nonworking families (that is, 24 percent of them) also would have access to low-cost care, we have 524,000 children in lower-cost care. Averaging the lower-cost care to $200 per child per full year, and paying one-quarter of the savings to parents as a bonus ($110), the bill for day care drops by 15 percent. Since many mothers will earn above the minimum, even if the average is only $3328 (the minimum wage of $1.60), families will be expected to pay for part of the day care. This will reduce the cost further, depending on the effective tax rate chosen. But separating out the cost we can call "day care" is difficult, especially if we use day care as a way to employ the working mothers in government jobs. Exact figures will depend upon estimating accurately the number of mothers who will secure private employment, and the size of their earnings.

It is certainly possible to extend workfare to include mothers with preschool children. In that case, the program would begin to resemble H.R. 1, since the high cost of day care when the mother was publicly employed would require a high rate of benefit reduction as the mother's earnings rose (and, thus, a high implicit tax rate). Otherwise, the costs for day care would be very large.

The Senate Committee seems to have accepted what the Ways and Means Committee would not: that mothers with preschool children are extremely productive within their own homes.

Alternative 3: Universal Demogrant Plan (UDP)

The universal demogrant analyzed here would grant $1200 per adult and $600 per child, then tax any income earned by an individual at a flat rate of 33 percent, with very limited deductions. There are no work requirements at all. This provides the best opportunity to deal rationally

[45] Department of Health, Education, and Welfare, *Population and Cost Estimates.*
[46] Since public work is provided only 32.0 hours per week (6.4 hours per day), day care might not be needed while school is in session.

with the issue of child care. Since the UDP distorts as little as possible the individual's incentives to work rather than requiring him to work, no federal provisions for financing day care need be made. If there is a work requirement, then the issues are the same as those dealt with in Alternative 1, but with a higher guarantee level.

Since standard day care is clearly a legitimate work-related expense, it ought to be fully deductible. This would be necessary to ensure some horizontal equity between working and nonworking mothers (and, thus, retain the work incentive for mothers implicit in the UDP). Day care expenditures beyond the cost of standard care ought to be viewed as consumption, and nondeductible. While wealthy working parents might consider higher-quality care as essential before they work, any other arrangement would tend to overcomplicate the tax structure. This higher-quality care would represent consumption rather than a single replacement of the mother's supervisory and developmental care. The standard for care should be set at the legitimately high level of $2052 for preschool children. While parents can spend less than this, we would hope they would act in the best interests of their children. In extreme cases of inadequate care, the parent correctly might be accused of misusing the $600 grant to his child and be instructed to either improve the child's lot or face outside control of the grant. But this would be a rarity. And, in any case, this would be an issue whether the parent is working or nonworking, rich or poor.[47]

This approach forces the parent to face the true social cost of working. If the economic gains and possible utility of working are not sufficiently above the standard child care costs to justify the loss of leisure and productivity in the home, then the individual will not work and probably should not. The marginal tax rate will distort this somewhat, but this is an unavoidable result of all practical taxes.

The cost of day care to the government would be in its deductibility. Although eliminating the full deductibility of standard day care might reduce substantially the overall tax rate (holding government revenue constant), even this is not certain. While some working mothers would then have to declare more income, some others might cease working altogether and depend on the grant, increasing government expenditures. The full cost of deductibility is not easily estimated, but it probably would be high. Nevertheless, allowing deductions for day care is appropriate in enabling rational work decisions and encouraging workers to purchase high-quality day care, as well as for horizontal equity.

---

[47] To collect the $600 per child, a working parent might be required to prove that adequate care was being provided, but such a requirement would be costly, tedious, insulting, and very much counter to the general aims of a UDP.

IV. Other Issues

In this section, some other issues related to day care will be sketched briefly.

FAMILY SIZE

There is some concern about the state assuming too many of the costs of children. Since unsupported children in poor families represent a very real cost to society, one might argue that society ought to give parents some disincentive to having children they cannot afford.[48] Subsidized day care, especially as proposed for the first two income plans above-mentioned, substantially reduces the cost of extra children to the working poor; and the UDP at least partially absorbs the costs of children. And currently, AFDC increases family benefits for each new child.

Unfortunately, there is no resolution to this problem. Although we might like to pose serious disincentives for conceiving an additional child, actually imposing penalties once the deed is done can only reduce the welfare of the whole family, not incidentally including the children.

Furthermore, even the theoretical impact of day care subsidies on family size is ambiguous. The subsidy not only reduces the cost of an additional child, it also makes work more attractive, which in turn would tend to reduce the free time available for child care. This might lead the family to have fewer children, but children of "higher quality."[49]

TRANSFERS TO CHILDREN

Quite aside from day care, we may want to try to help poor children directly rather than through their families. This might be based on a feeling that public dollars spent to alleviate poverty are more effective when channeled to children at a young age (to an extent not taken into account by the children's parents). But reaching these children with those resources should not be tied to the parents' decisions on work. The children in day care centers can be reached easily with better medical care, food, special education, and social work. But these aids should not be denied to

[48] Glen G. Cain has treated the effects of income maintenance plans and particularly day care arrangements on the birth rate in "The Effect of Income Maintenance Laws on Fertility in the United States," in United States Commission on Population Growth and the American Future, *Aspects of Population Growth Policy*, edited by Robert Parke, Jr., and Charles F. Westoff, Volume 6, Commission's Research Report (Washington, D.C.: U.S. Government Printing Office, 1972) (see especially pp. 19–31).
[49] For a development of this point, see M. Krashinsky, "Day Care and Public Policy" (Ph.D. diss., Yale University, New Haven, Conn., 1973), pp. 226–231.

children whose mothers do not work. Vouchers for medical care, food, and education could be issued to poor parents as part of their supplement. If the child is in day care, these vouchers could be used through the center. But if the parent does not work, clinics, nursery schools, and other facilities might serve the children.

HORIZONTAL EQUITY

Many of the arguments raised in this chapter have concentrated on horizontal equity among families with different numbers of children. Mothers with large numbers of children with no second parent present are at a real disadvantage as against two-parent families, where one parent can work outside the home to support the other working within the home. Therefore, we treat them differently. This view treats children as a general responsibility and investment of society, which must intervene in case of breakdown of the normal mechanism for protecting children, the two-parent family.

It is possible to take another view, that children represent a consumption decision made by parents, and that any subsidies toward child-rearing for parents with large families is an unfair burden on other adults, most particularly those who have chosen to have few children or none at all.[50] Yet, the entire tax structure testifies that Americans have chosen not to consider expenses for children as pure consumption. More to the point, children, while they may be partially a consumption decision by their parents, also are citizens in their own right. Reaching poor children with aid, by increasing the incomes of their parents (or by subsidizing their day care), is as important a goal in welfare policy as reaching the poor parents themselves with aid.

WHAT ARE THE LONG-RUN EFFECTS?

Is it really desirable to replace a parent with day care in a center? Do children reared in day care centers grow up to be different from those reared at home? At what age can a child realistically be placed in a day care center? Day care would last for longer hours than public school now does for most children, and would start at a much earlier age. Does it represent a promising new way to improve the lot of children and their parents, or a trap for those who want to separate mothers from their children for whatever reason?

[50] Do all parents consciously decide on family size? The question of what is an unfair burden might also be turned around. Since society desires to reproduce itself, it may be fair to ask those families that choose not to have children to share in the cost of raising the next generation.

Acknowledgments

The author is much indebted to Richard R. Nelson for his encouragement and comments during the development and rewriting of this chapter, and to Robert S. Goldfarb for his comments during the final revision. The author, of course, bears all responsibility for all statements and numbers. The author also appreciates the help he received from numerous sources during the conference at Wisconsin, and the useful comments and suggestions he received from the subcommittee staff.

Appendix 1: Descriptive Extension of Table 11.5

1. This is the case of no day care and no labor force participation.

2. If there is no deduction for day care, then the net benefits are $G - t(W - D)$, providing $W \geqslant D$ (which we assume here). Therefore,

$$Y^d = G - t(W - D) + W - C$$
$$= G + tD + (1 - t)W - C.$$

To obtain t_e and MC_c we need simply note that

$$1 - t_e = \partial Y^d / \partial W$$

and

$$MC_c = \partial Y / \partial C$$

3. If there is deduction allowed up to C_0, then if $C \leqslant C_0$, the net benefit is $G - t(W - D - C)$ and

$$Y^d = G - t(W - D - C) + W - C$$
$$= G + tD + (1 - t)(W - C).$$

If $C \geqslant C_0$, the total deduction is limited to C_0, and the net benefit is $G - t(W - D - C_0)$ and

$$Y^d = G - t(W - D - C_0) + W - C$$
$$= G + tD + (1 - t)W - (C - tC_0).$$

4. If there is a full subsidy on the *first* $C_s - f(W)$ dollars of day care, then as long as $C \leqslant C_s - f(W)$, there will be no day care cost to the family and

$$Y^d = G - t(W - D) + W$$
$$= G + tD + (1 - t)W.$$

(Note that $C \leqslant C_s - f(W)$ is the same as $f(W) \leqslant C_s - C$.) When $C > C_s - f(W)$, that is, $f(W) > C_s - C$, then the family still receives the subsidy for day care of $C_s - f(W)$, if $C_s < f(W)$, but must pay the remainder (deductible) for day care of $C - [C_s - f(W)]$ and the benefit is

$$G - t\{W - D - [C - C_s + f(W)]\}.$$

Thus,

$$Y^d = G - t\{W - D - [C - C_s + f(W)]\} + W - [C - C_s + f(W)]$$
$$= G + tD + (1 - t)\{W - [C - C_s + f(W)]\}.$$

Finally, when $f(W) > C_s$, there is no subsidy, and

$$Y^d = G + tD + (1 - t)(W - C)$$

as in (3).

5. If there is a full subsidy on the last $C_s - f(W)$ of day care, up to the total of C_s on day care, and if $f(W) \geqslant C$, then there will be no subsidy, and $Y^d = G + tD + (1 - t)(W - C)$ as in (3).

If $f(W) < C(C_s > C)$, the subsidy is $C - f(W)$, and the parent pays $f(W)$ for care; therefore, the benefit is $G - t[W - D - f(W)]$, and

$$Y^d = G - t[W - D - f(W)] + W - f(W)$$
$$= G + tD + (1 - t)[W - f(W)].$$

6. If there is a proportional subsidy of $C_s - [f(W)]/C_s$ on each dollar spent on day care up to C_s, then the parents pay $Cf(W)/C_s$ for day care as long as $f(W) \leqslant C_s$. Thus, the benefit is

$$G - t[W - D - Cf(W)/C_s]$$

and

$$Y^d = G - t[W - D - Cf(W)/C_s] + W - Cf(W)/C_s$$
$$= G + tD + (1 - t)[W - Cf(W)/C_s].$$

If $f(W) > C_s$, there is no subsidy, so $Y^d = G + tD + (1 - t)(W - C)$, as in (3).

Appendix 2: Day Care Costs in Table 11.5 if $W < D$

	Y^d	Government cost	t_e	MC_c
2.	$G + W - C$	G	0	1
3.	$G + W - (1 - t)C$ for $C \leqslant C_0$	$G + tC$	0	$1 - t$
	$G + W - (C - tC_0)$ for $C > C_0$	$G + tC_0$	0	1
4.	$G + W$ for $f(W) \leqslant C_s - C$	$G + C$	0	0
	$G + W - (1 - t)\{C - [C_0 - f(W)]\}$ for $C_s - C < f(W) \leqslant C_s$	$G + [C_0 - f(W)] + t\{C - [C_0 - f(W)]\}$	$(1 - t)f'$	$1 - t$
	$G + W - (1 - t)C$ for $f(W) > C_s*$	$G + tC$	0	$1 - t$
5.	$G + W - (1 - t)f(W)$ for $f(W) \leqslant C$	$G + C - (1 - t)f(W)$	$(1 - t)f'$	0
	$G + W - (1 - t)C$ for $f(W) > C$	$G + tC$	0	$1 - t$
6.	$G + W - (1 - t)Cf(W)/C_s$ for $f(W) \leqslant C_s$	$G + C[1 - (1 - t)f(W)/C_s]$	$(1 - t)Cf'/C_s$	$(1 - t)f'/C$
	$G + W - (1 - t)C$ for $f(W) > C_s*$	$G + tC$	0	$1 - t$

Note—Asterisk (*) implies that the case is unlikely.

12

Rationales for Interstate Differentials in Assistance Benefits and for State Supplementation

Irene Lurie

Public assistance (PA) has traditionally been a function of state and local governments and the Social Security Act of 1935 provided that welfare would continue to be a state program. While the states were required to conform to federal rules and regulations as a condition of federal financial support for PA, they were given authority to determine many critical features of their assistance programs. Most important, they were given complete responsibility for setting the level of benefits paid under their programs. No federal statutes imposed or even suggested a minimum or maximum dollar amount for the payments given recipients, and payments to persons in similar circumstances varied considerably from state to state.

The inequity of these interstate differentials, and widespread dissatisfaction with other features of the welfare system, have created pressure for welfare reform. A federal system paying uniform benefits now has wide appeal as a way to end the inequity of differentials and to relieve the states of the financial burden imposed by the current system. A number of alternative programs that would provide uniform federal benefits have been proposed, and one has been enacted. The new Supplemental Security Income (SSI) program, which became effective in 1974, is a federally administered and financed program providing uniform income-conditioned benefits to the aged, blind, and disabled. None of the proposals to

336 / *Irene Lurie*

replace Aid to Families with Dependent Children (AFDC) has been passed, and it continues as a state program.

While the wide variation in benefits paid by the states has been a prime source of dissatisfaction with Public Assistance, it has also been one of the major impediments to the passage of federal programs to replace it. The existing variation in benefits complicates the choice of a uniform federal benefit and makes congressional compromise difficult. A federal benefit equal to the highest payment now made by any state would not only be very costly but could have labor market implications for the states with lower wage levels. For example, Lester Maddox criticized the Family Assistance Plan (FAP) because "You're not going to be able to find anyone willing to work as maids or janitors or housekeepers."[1] A lower federal payment could avoid this problem, but it could leave some recipients worse off than they are now. The prospect of welfare recipients experiencing a cut in benefits with the introduction of a new federal program is not appealing, particularly to congressmen from high-benefit states.

The solution adopted by the SSI program is to require the states to supplement the federal payment so that no recipient suffers a drop in benefits. H.R. 1, as passed by the House of Representatives in June 1971, and the Senate Finance Committee's version of H.R. 1 of June 1972 would not have required state supplementation but would have permitted it. While supplementation avoids the above-mentioned problems, it also would preserve many of the interstate differentials, whose reduction or elimination is a primary objective of welfare reform. Supplementation provisions also reintroduce other undesirable features of the present welfare system, such as the incentive for families to break up, or to migrate, and the potential for inequities resulting from administrative discretion.

The questions to be discussed in this chapter are whether or not interstate differentials in welfare benefits are justified on other than political grounds, and whether or not and how the federal government should provide for them.

The first section begins with a description of payment levels under the PA programs as they were operating prior to 1974. These payment levels are compared with those under the version of the Family Assistance Plan passed as H.R. 1 by the House in June 1971, the SSI program, the Senate Finance Committee plan of June 1972, and a universal demogrant plan paying $1200 per year to adults and $600 to children. This comparison gives an idea of the supplementation that would be required to keep welfare recipients as well off under these programs as they are now.

---

[1] *Wall Street Journal*, 15 December 1970.

The second section presents the arguments for and against interstate differentials in welfare benefits, and discusses how these differentials might be provided to meet various objectives.

I. Payments under the Current and Proposed Programs

The process of computing payments under AFDC, and the process that was used prior to 1974 under Old Age Assistance (OAA), Aid to the Blind (AB), and Aid to the Permanently and Totally Disabled (APTD), are complex and vary considerably from state to state. States establish "payment standards for basic needs," which vary according to the size of the family and, in some states, the age and sex of its members. Basic needs are items that all families require—food, clothing, shelter, and utilities. Many states also recognize "special needs," such as special diets and transportation expenses, that arise for people in specified circumstances. The payment to which a family is entitled, although not always the payment it actually receives, is computed by adding the relevant payment standard and any special needs that are recognized and then subtracting its "countable income." Countable income includes earnings and property income from all sources and some sources of transfer income,[2] less specified amounts of "disregarded income." The amount of disregarded, or deducted, income varies from one program to another and will be described in more detail later.

Most states pay recipients the entire difference between their countable income and the sum of the payment standard and special needs. Some limit the payment by paying only a maximum amount regardless of the payment to which the family is entitled. Others limit payments by applying a "percentage reduction," that is, they pay a percentage of the difference between countable income and the sum of the payment standard and special needs.

Public Assistance Payments to Recipients with No Income

The Department of Health, Education, and Welfare regularly collects and publishes data on payment standards for basic needs, but reliable

---

[2] Many recipients of Public Assistance receive Food Stamps, commodities, Medicaid, and public housing. The bonus value of these in-kind transfers, that is, the difference between their face value and the price paid for them, is not counted as income in determining Public Assistance benefits.

data on special needs are, unfortunately, not collected.[3] The payment standards for basic needs for the four Public Assistance programs in July 1971 are shown in Table 12.1. In states that do not limit payments by maximums or a percentage reduction, the payment standard represents the payment that would be given to a family with no countable income. In states that do limit payments, families with no countable income would receive the amount in the column, "largest amount paid." In states that recognize special needs, some families would receive more than the amount shown in the table. Families paying rents below the maximum permitted would receive less.

The welfare payments made to persons with no income varied widely from one state to another. In the adult categories, monthly payments to a single person ranged from about $66 to $250. For an AFDC family of four, they varied between $60 and $372.

Public Assistance Payments to Recipients with Income

The computation of benefits received under the four Public Assistance programs becomes more complicated when recipients have income. Benefits are reduced as earned income increases, and the rate at which benefits are reduced, the implicit tax rate, depends on many characteristics of the state programs. In large part, the tax rate depends on the amount of income that is disregarded in determining the size of the payment.

Under the AFDC program, states are required to disregard the first $30 of monthly earnings plus one-third of the remainder to provide an incentive for recipients to work. A state with no maximum or percentage reduction would give recipients the following amount:

(1) Monthly payment = payment standard for basic needs
       + special needs
       $- [(Y_E - \$30) - \frac{1}{3}(Y_E - \$30) + Y_U - Y_D]$,

[3] Most states do not establish standards for shelter costs, but, rather, pay a person or family according to the shelter costs actually incurred, up to a maximum. The payment standards published by HEW and used in Table 12.1 are, in general, for persons or families living alone in rented quarters and paying the maximum rent. Payment standards are lower for families paying less than the maximum, for those sharing quarters with other persons, for most homeowners, and for those with free housing. Standards for basic needs do not usually apply to aged, blind, or disabled recipients who are unable to live alone or with relatives and require care in boarding homes or other nonmedical residential facilities. Payments for such care are often higher than reported standards, which are based on ordinary personal and household expenses.

where

$$Y_E = \text{income from earnings,}$$
$$Y_U = \text{unearned income, and}$$
$$Y_D = \text{deductions other than the disregard of \$30}$$
of earnings and one-third of the remainder.

In addition to the $30 and one-third disregard of earnings, states are required to deduct *(1)* expenses of earning income, including day care expenses, *(2)* earnings of children who are in school, and *(3)* incentive payments from the work incentive program. States have the option of deducting *(4)* $5 of income, *(5)* income set aside for the future needs of a child, *(6)* income allocated to expenses not included in the assistance budget, and *(7)* income assigned to support dependents outside the assistance unit. In all four PA programs, deductions in excess of income are ignored. That is, a family with deductions greater than income receives a payment equal to the payment standard plus their special needs, and is not reimbursed for its excess deductions.

Under AB, states were required to disregard the first $85 of monthly earnings plus one-half of the remainder. A state with no maximum or percentage reduction determined payments using the following rule:

(2)   Monthly payment = payment standard for basic needs
+ special needs
$$- [(Y_E - \$85) - \tfrac{1}{2}(Y_E - \$85) + Y_U - Y_D],$$

where

$$Y_D = \text{deductions other than the disregard}$$
of $85 of earnings and one-half of
the remainder.

In addition to this earnings disregard, states were required to deduct *(1)* expenses of earning income, *(2)* $4.00 of Social Security benefits, and *(3)* additional income of persons with a plan for achieving self-support, for up to one year. A state had the option of deducting *(4)* additional income of such a person for another two years, and *(5)* $7.50 of income.

Under OAA and APTD, states were given the option of deducting up to $50 of earnings: the first $20 and half of the next $60. A state with no maximum or percentage reduction which did not choose the optional earnings disregard determined the payment in this way:

(3)   Monthly payment = payment standard for basic needs
+ special needs
$$- (Y_E + Y_U - Y_D).$$

Table 12.1 Monthly Income Guarantees and Break-Even Points in Public Assistance, July 1971, Compared to the SSI Program, FAP, and a Demogrant Plan

	Old Age Assistance (1 person)			Aid to the Blind (1 person)			Aid to the Permanently and Totally Disabled (1 person)			Aid to Families with Dependent Children (family of 4)		
	Payment standard	Largest amount paid	Break-even point[a]	Payment standard	Largest amount paid	Break-even point[a]	Payment standard	Largest amount paid	Break-even point[a]	Payment standard	Largest amount paid	Break-even point[a]
SSI program	130		345	130		385	130		345	200		360
Family Assistance Plan												
Demogrant plan, ⅓ tax rate, $100 per adult, $50 per child	100		300	100		300	100		300	250		750
Present Public Assistance programs:												
Alabama	146	103	166	105	85	350[b,h]	71		91	81		242
Alaska	250		270	250		625	250		270	400	372	720[j]
Arizona	118		146[b]	118		376[b]	118		138	256	167	512[c,j]
Arkansas	109	105	179[d]	109	105	343	109		179[d]	229	111	464
California	178		248[d]	192		524[b,h]	172	105	242[d]	274	261	531
Colorado	140		210[d]	105		335	123		193[d]	242		483
Connecticut	169		239[d]	169		463	169		239[d]	327		610[j]
Delaware	140		215[c,d]	189		518[b]	117		192[c,d]	287	172	558[c]
District of Columbia	153		230[b,d]	153		231[b,h]	153		231[b,d,h]	239		486[c,j]
Florida	114		184[d]	114		353	114		134[i]	223	134	454
Georgia	105	91	180[c,d]	105	91	445[c,h]	105	91	180[c,d,h]	227	149	460
Hawaii	132		210[b,d]	132		404[b]	132		210[b,d,h]	271		534[c]
Idaho	163		191[b]	163		466[b]	163		191[b]	241		489[c]
Illinois	169		239[d]	169		463	169		239[d]	272		528

State												
Indiana	185	100	213^b	185	125	510^b	185	80	213^b	363	205	673^e,j
Iowa	117		187^d	144		423^c	117		187^d	300	243	570
Kansas	203		273^d	203		531	203		273^d	321		602^j
Kentucky	96		174^b,d	96		332^b	96		174^b,d	234	171	471^j
Louisiana	143	100	213^d	106	101	337^h	95	66	165^d,h	104		276
Maine	123	115	200^b,d	123	115	386^b	123	115	200^b,d	349	168	644^j
Maryland	96		146^f	96		317	96		116	200		420^j
Massachusetts	189		259^d	180		500^b,h	178		248^d	349		644^j
Michigan	224		244	224		573^h	224		244	350		645
Minnesota	183		253^d	183		491^h	183		253^d,h	334		621^j
Mississippi	150	75	178^b	150	75	440^b	150	75	178^b	277	60	536
Missouri	181	85	236^c,f	250	90	635^c	170	80	195^c	303	130	582^c
Montana	111		178^b,e	111		362^b	111		188^b,a	206		429^j
Nebraska	182		260^b,d	182		504^b	182		260^b,d	347	226	648^c
Nevada	170		225^c,f	155		450^b	0		0	176		392^c
New Hampshire	173		248^c,d	173		481^c	173		248^c,d	294		561
New Jersey	142		162	142		409	142		162	324		606^j
New Mexico	116		136	116		357^h	116		136	203	179	424
New York	159		186^b	159		458^b	159		186^b	336	313	624
North Carolina	112		132	120		365	112		132	159		358^j
North Dakota	125		195^d	125		375	125		195^d	300		570^j
Ohio	126		204^b,d	126		392^b	116		194^b,d,h	200		420
Oklahoma	130		200^d	130		385^h	130		200^d,h	189		404
Oregon	122		180^b,f	163	105	466^b	122		150^b	279		538^j
Pennsylvania	146		196^f	150		435^c,h	146		166	313		590
Rhode Island	163		233^d	163		451^h	163		233^d,h	263		514^j
South Carolina	87	80	162^c,d	103	95	331	87	80	157^d	198	103	417
South Dakota	180		205^c	180		495^c	180		205^c	270		525
Tennessee	102	97	122	102	97	329	102	97	122	217	129	446
Texas	119		146^b	110		345	110	105	130	148		342
Utah	103		173^d	113		351	103		173^d,i	218		447

Table 12.1 (cont.)

Vermont	177	177	227f		479g	177	227f, h	327		610
Virginia	152	153	182g		431	152	172	261		512
Washington	143	143	213d		411h	143	213d	286	274	549j
West Virginia	76	76	104b		277	76	96i	138		327
Wisconsin	158	158	228d		441	158	228d	274		531j
Wyoming	139	139	166b	104	418b, h	127	154b	260	227	510

Sources—U.S., Department of Health, Education, and Welfare, Social and Rehabilitation Service, *Public Assistance Programs: Standards for Basic Needs, July 1971,* Report No. 72–03200, 20 March 1972. U.S., Department of Health, Education, and Welfare, *Characteristics of State Public Assistance Plans under the Social Security Act: General Provisions,* Public Assistance Report No. 50 (1970) (Washington, D.C.: U.S. Government Printing Office, 1970).

[a] All amounts in dollars. All income is assumed to be earned income; families with unearned income will have lower break-even points. In computing the break-even points, work expenses were deducted from income. They were assumed to be $20 for recipients in the adult categories and $60 for AFDC recipients.
The following amounts, chosen at the option of the states, were deducted from income in computing the break-even point:
[b] $7.50 of income.
[c] $5.00 of income.
[d] $20 of earnings plus ½ of the next $60 of earnings.
[e] $20 of earnings plus ½ of the next $40 of earnings.
[f] $10 of earnings plus ¼ of the next $40 of earnings.
[g] $10 of earnings.

In addition to the amounts disregarded in calculating the break-even points, states report disregarding:
[h] Income of an individual who has a plan for achieving self-support approved by the state welfare agency, for up to three years.
[i] Income of an individual who has a plan for achieving self-support approved by the state welfare agency, for up to one year.
[j] Income deducted for the future identifiable needs of a child, with each state stipulating the particular conditions under which income can be deducted.

States were required to deduct (*1*) expenses of earning income and (*2*) $4.00 of Social Security benefits. In addition to the earnings disregard, states had the option of deducting (*3*) $7.50 of income and, (*4*) for recipients of APTD, additional income of persons with a plan for achieving self-support, for a period of up to three years.

It is difficult to generalize about the payments made to families at various income levels. As noted before, reliable information about special needs is not available. While the federal statutes and regulations give all states the same opportunity to disregard recipient's income, the deductions permitted vary considerably from state to state, from one welfare department to another, and undoubtedly from one caseworker to another. Work expenses, which states are required to deduct, can be defined in many different ways, from the relatively strict definition used in the federal income tax, to one that includes lunch and street clothes. According to one expert, "some proclient caseworkers take pride in generating enough expenses so that available income falls to zero."[4] Federal law puts no limit on the income that can be set aside for the future identifiable needs of the child, and the amounts vary greatly. Similarly, deductions for other purposes can be made small or large, depending on the state, the caseworker, and the particular circumstances of the recipient. This is one of the main sources of horizontal inequity in the Public Assistance system.

One measure of how payments vary with income is provided by the "break-even point," the income level at which a recipient's payment falls to zero. Break-even points were calculated under specific assumptions concerning sources of income and amount of disregards.[5] In computing the break-evens, special needs were ignored. All income was assumed to be

---

[4] W. Joseph Heffernan, Jr., "Variations in Negative Tax Rates in Current Public Assistance Programs: An Example of Administrative Discretion," *Journal of Human Resources* 8, supp., 1973.

[5] In the adult categories, the payment standard is used to determine both eligibility of applicants and payments of recipients. The break-even points shown in Table 12.1 are, therefore. the levels at which people enter and leave the program. In AFDC, however, eligibility of people who are not receiving assistance or have not received it within the past four months is determined by comparing income *before* the $30 and one-third disregard to the *cost* standard. (The cost standard is the amount of money that states decide a recipient needs, and it is greater than the payment standard in twenty states.) Only if they are eligible by this standard can their income, less *all* permitted disregards, be compared to the *payment* standard to compute the payment. Even though the cost standard is greater than the payment standard in many states, the inability to claim the $30 and one-third disregard in determining initial eligibility means that the income at which a family can initially become eligible for AFDC is lower than the income at which the benefit falls to zero.

344 / Irene Lurie

earned, and all of the required disregards were taken into account.[6] Work expenses were assumed to equal $60 for AFDC families and $20 for adult recipients. Optional disregards were taken into account only if they were reported by HEW in its publication, *Characteristics of State Public Assistance Plans*.[7] The estimated break-even points are presented in Table 12.1.

The break-even points facing families with unearned income only or with a combination of earned and unearned income will be lower than those shown in Table 12.1. Families who pay less rent than is assumed in the payment levels published by HEW will also face lower break-even points. On the other hand, families with special needs will have higher break-evens, as will families with greater disregards than were assumed in preparing the table.

The variation in break-even points is quite large. For a family of four, AFDC break-even points ranged from $242 per month in Alabama to $720 per month in Alaska. There is less variation in the adult categories. In OAA, the break-even points for a single recipient ranged from $104 in West Virginia to $273 in Kansas; in APTD, from $91 in Alabama to $273 in Kansas; and, in AB, from $277 in West Virginia to $635 in Missouri.

Payments and Break-even Points under FAP and SSI

H.R. 1, as passed by the House of Representatives in June 1971, would have substituted the Family Assistance Plan for AFDC and a single federal program for the three adult Public Assistance categories. The Senate never approved FAP but the program for adults finally emerged as the SSI program. The common origin of FAP and the SSI program

[6] Earnings of children in school and incentive payments from the Work Incentive program (WIN) were assumed to be zero. Additional income of an AB recipient who has a plan for achieving self-support was also assumed to be zero.
[7] U.S., Department of Health, Education, and Welfare, Social and Rehabilitation Service, Assistance Payments Administration, *Characteristics of State Public Assistance Plans under the Social Security Act*, Public Assistance Report No. 50 (Washington, D.C.: U.S. Government Printing Office, 1970). Some states permit disregards that are not reported in this publication. For example, the only optional disregards reported for AFDC families are the disregard of $5 of income and the disregard of income set aside for the future identifiable needs of a child. But a survey of AFDC recipients in 1971 reported that about 3 percent of families claimed disregards for "expenses not included in the assistance budget" and "income assigned to support of other dependents." "Additional disregarded income," reported by 17 percent of the families in the survey, includes the $5 disregard and the $30 and one-third disregard taken into account in Table 12.1, but also appears to include some other items that are not taken into account. U.S., Department of Health, Education, and Welfare, National Center for Social Statistics, *Findings of the 1971 AFDC Study, Part II. Financial Circumstances*, Report AFDC-2, 1971, Table 71.

gives them many similar features and they are analyzed together here.
Under FAP, a family of four would receive

(4) Yearly payment = $2400 - [Y_E - Y_{DE} - \$720 -$
$\qquad \frac{1}{3}(Y_E - Y_{DE} - \$720) + Y_U - Y_X],$

where

$\qquad Y_{DE}$ = deductions that must be taken from earnings
before the deduction of \$720 of earnings and
one-third of the remainder, and

$\qquad Y_X$ = other disregarded income.

Y_{DE} includes (1) child care expenses, but with upper limits set by HEW,
(2) earnings of children in school, with upper limits set by HEW, and
(3) irregular earned income of $30 or less per quarter and irregular un-
earned income of $60 or less per quarter. Included in Y_X are one-third of
child support and alimony payments, training allowances of up to $60 per
month, assistance based on need (except veterans' pensions), and some
additional less important amounts.

Some families would receive greater payments under FAP than under
AFDC, while others would experience a loss.[8] Generalizing about the
difference in payments under AFDC and FAP is difficult: It depends on
many factors, including the state in which a family is living, its size and
composition, the amount and sources of its income, its special needs, and
the disregards it has been permitted to claim. The procedure used here
will be to compare payments made to families with no income, then compare the permitted disregards, and finally compare the programs' break-
even points calculated under certain assumptions. This will give some idea
of the ranges of difference between payments made under the existing
programs and under FAP, assuming no state supplementation.

The AFDC payment to a family of four with no countable income
is either the "payment standard" in Table 12.1 or, in states with maximums
or percentage reductions, the "largest amount paid." FAP would provide
such a family with $2400 per year. The AFDC payment is higher than the
$200 per month which would be paid under FAP in thirty states. The
importance of the difference depends, of course, on how many families
have no income other than welfare: In 1971, 60 percent of AFDC families
had no other income than welfare.

For many families with income, the provisions in FAP relating to
deductions would have a greater effect in reducing payments below the

---

[8] The major extension in coverage would be to families headed by a working male,
which are now ineligible for Public Assistance. Without intending to minimize this
important liberalization, the focus here will be on the change in payments to families
which are now eligible for Public Assistance.

current AFDC level than would the reduction in the basic benefit given to a family with no income. First, FAP allows fewer types of deductions than can be claimed by AFDC recipients. Most important, work expenses could not be deducted by these families. The increase in the 100 percent disregard from $30 per month under AFDC to $720 per year ($60 per month) under FAP is designed to compensate recipients for the loss of the work expense deduction. But this minor liberalization would leave many working recipients worse off because the increase in the amount disregarded would be less than average work expenses. Second, FAP requires HEW to set limits on the deduction of day care expenses and children's earnings, thereby reducing the amount and variability in deductions claimed by recipients. Third, it changes the order in which items must be deducted. It is now required by HEW that the $30 and one-third disregard be deducted from earnings before any other items, including work expenses,[9] are deducted. The effect of this procedure is to reimburse recipients fully by an amount equal to the earnings that are disregarded. It also has the effect of increasing the break-even by $1.50 for every dollar increase in disregarded earnings. Under FAP, certain items must be deducted from earnings before $720 and one-third of the remainder are deducted. The most important effect of this change would be that recipients would no longer be fully reimbursed for their entire day care expenditure but would be reimbursed for only two-thirds.

As a consequence of the fewer disregards permitted by FAP, the tax rate for many AFDC recipients would increase and the break-even level would fall. If unearned income, Y_X and Y_{DE} are assumed to be zero, the break-even point for a family of four under FAP would be $4320, or $360 per month. This is less than the AFDC break-even points shown in Table 12.1 in forty-six states. Families headed by men and female-headed families in the less generous states would, of course, be better off under FAP. But a considerable number of AFDC families with nonwelfare income would incur a loss if states did not supplement the federal program.

The SSI program means fewer changes in payments and break-even points for recipients of OAA, AB, and APTD than FAP would have meant for AFDC recipients. The most important change is the replacement of the widely varying state benefits by a uniform benefit of $130 per month for a single person and $195 for a couple. As shown in Table 12.1, the Public Assistance payments made to adult recipients with no countable income were higher than the $130 monthly payment under SSI in almost half of the states. The permitted deductions under SSI are similar, al-

[9] This means that the $30 and one-third disregard of earnings is applied to gross, rather than net, income. In contrast, a personal income tax applies the tax rate to income net of work expenses.

though not identical, to those under Public Assistance. All recipients can deduct $65 of earnings each month and one-half of the remainder. The deduction of $4.00 of Social Security benefits and the optional deduction of $7.50 of other income is replaced by a deduction of $20.00 of unearned or earned income. Specified amounts of infrequently or irregularly received income also are disregarded. Only the blind are permitted to deduct work expenses.

The break-even points under SSI, calculated under the same assumptions just used, are $345 for the aged and disabled and $385 for the blind. This means that the break-evens under SSI are higher than the break-evens under OAA and APTD in all states. But the break-evens under AB are higher than the SSI break-even in thirty-one states, implying that federal payments to blind people with significant amounts of earnings are considerably lower than former AB benefits.

The SSI legislation originally prohibited recipients from participating in the Food Stamp or commodity distribution programs; FAP would have excluded recipients from Food Stamps only. The loss in benefits resulting from this exclusion would have varied considerably among recipients, depending on their income and family size and, of course, whether they were participating in a food program. In 1970–1971, about 15 percent of Public Assistance recipients received commodities, worth an average of $13 per person per month. About 20 percent of recipients in the adult categories participated in the Food Stamp program, and more than 50 percent of AFDC families participated. The "bonus value" of the stamps, that is, the difference between their face value and the price paid for them, decreases with income. The bonus value for a single person with no income is $32 per month, decreasing to zero when income reaches $190. The bonus value for a family of four with no income is $108, falling to zero when income exceeds $390.

A single person whose only income was the SSI payment of $130 per month would have lost $10 by the denial of Food Stamp benefits. Before SSI became effective, the law was amended to permit SSI recipients to receive stamps, indicating the political unpopularity of program changes that make the poor worse off.

Payments and Break-even Points under a Universal Demogrant Plan

Under a universal demogrant, everyone would receive a payment from the federal government regardless of his income. The payment could be the same for all persons or could vary by age and/or size of the family. The demogrant would be accompanied by a tax on income other than the

348 / Irene Lurie

grant. While the payment would not vary with income, the *net* payment after tax would decline as income became greater.

The demogrant considered here would pay adults $1200 per year and children $600, and would tax income at a rate of one-third. The demogrant would replace Public Assistance, but could replace other income-related programs. Food Stamps could be eliminated, while Social Security, veterans' programs, and housing programs need no longer have an anti-poverty component, that is, need no longer be structured to provide special aid to the poor. These changes, of course, would have a major impact on low-income people other than welfare recipients and would raise problems besides the issue of the reduction in welfare benefits.

Under the demogrant, the typical AFDC family of four, a family of one adult and three children, would receive

(5) Yearly payment = $3000 − $\frac{1}{3}$(all income except the demogrant).

The demogrant would replace current personal exemptions and deductions and the special low-income allowance in the federal income tax. The break-even point would be at total income of $9000. A single adult would receive $1200 per year and would receive no net gain after taxes when his income reached $3600.

Among those whose sole source of income is Public Assistance, recipients of Aid to the Blind would suffer the largest drop in income under this demogrant. The demogrant would be lower than the largest amount paid by AB in forty-two states, and the demogrant break-even lower than the AB break-even in every state except West Virginia. Many recipients of OAA and APTD would receive less if they had no other income, but the demogrant's break-even would be greater than under OAA and APTD in all states. Recipients with relatively large amounts of other income would be better off under a demogrant. For example, many recipients of aid to the aged, blind, and disabled have Social Security income, and this income would be "taxed" only at a 33 percent rate rather than at 100 percent as is generally the case now. Recipients of AFDC would tend to be the best off under a demogrant. The largest amount paid by AFDC is greater than the demogrant in only twenty-one states, and the break-even point for a family of four under AFDC is always lower than under the demogrant.

Benefits under a Wage Subsidy–Public Employment Approach

The Public Assistance programs, FAP, SSI, and a universal demogrant plan have a similar benefit structure: A payment is made to people who have no income, and the net benefit declines at a specified rate as income increases. In contrast, a wage subsidy or public employment program would condition payments on the amount of work performed; the benefit from the program would generally increase with the amount of work effort or earnings. Wage subsidy payments would be calculated as some fraction of a person's earnings or some fraction of his wage rate multiplied by the number of hours he worked. A public employment program would provide people with jobs and, therefore, earnings.

The wage subsidy and public employment program considered here is the program for families with children contained in the welfare reform bill proposed by the Senate Finance Committee in June 1972. The committee's proposals concerning the adult Public Assistance categories have a similar benefit structure as the types of programs already analyzed—Public Assistance, FAP, SSI, and the demogrant—and will not be discussed.

Under the committee's proposal, families with children would be divided into two groups according to their head's employability. The less employable group includes families headed by mothers with children under age six or by mothers who are ill, incapacitated, living in a geographically remote area, or attending school full time. They would continue to receive AFDC in much its current form. The major change for them would be a reduction in permitted disregards to a flat monthly exemption of $20 per month and an additional disregard of $20 of child support payments. While this is a significant change from the AFDC benefit structure, it would not cause a sharp decrease in payments for most of the families placed in this category. They are unlikely to work and so take advantage of the current disregards under AFDC, and, if they did work, they would be likely to place themselves voluntarily in the second category created by the committee's program.

The second category of families would be those with heads considered by the committee to be employable. This group would include families with children not eligible for AFDC under the new requirements: male-headed families and about 40 percent of current AFDC families. Three types of benefits would be offered to them, and all would be conditioned on employment: (1) The family head could take a public employment job paying $1.50 per hour for up to thirty-two hours per week;[10] (2) if the head takes a regular job paying between $1.50 and $2.00 per hour, he or she would be paid a subsidy equal to three-quarters of the difference between the wage paid and $2.00 per hour; and (3) workers in regular employment would receive an earnings bonus of 10 percent of

---

[10] The committee's proposal provides for public employment wages at three-quarters of the federal minimum wage and for supplementation of regular wages that are at least three-quarters of the minimum wage but are below the minimum wage. The illustration used by the committee is based on the assumption that the federal minimum wage is $2 per hour.

the husband's and wife's combined earnings up to an earnings level of $4000, which would decline by $.25 for each dollar of earnings above $4000.

How a family's benefit under this plan would compare with payments under AFDC depends, of course, on its earnings and which combination of these benefits it chooses. A family head working the maximum of thirty-two hours in public employment would obtain a total income of $2400 per year, or $200 per month. A family head working full time in a regular job at $1.50 per hour, and receiving both the wage subsidy and the earnings bonus, would obtain a total income of $4050 per year, or $338 per month. If the job paid $2.00 per hour, he would obtain a total income of $4400 per year, or $367 per month. Table 12.1 can be used to compare these income levels to the AFDC payments given to families with no income. In thirty states, public employment earnings of $200 per month would be less than AFDC payments to a family of four with no income. Total monthly income of a family whose head worked full time at $1.50 per hour would be less than AFDC payments in three states, and, at $2.00 per hour, would be less income than AFDC in only one state.

Comparisons with AFDC payments to families with earnings are more complicated, and only one example will be given here. Assume that the cost standard for a family of four is $270 per month, the median in 1971, and that a family has $60 of work expenses. If the family head worked full time at $1.50 per hour, he would earn $250 per month and receive $183 in AFDC, for a total income of $433. Under the committee plan, in comparison, the family would receive $88 in subsidies for a total income of $338. If the family head worked full time at $2.00 per hour, it would receive $128 in AFDC, compared to subsidies of $33 under the committee plan.[11] In states with low AFDC benefits, however, an AFDC family with earnings would benefit under the committee plan.

One characteristic of the committee's proposal would cause some AFDC families to experience a particularly large drop in benefits: neither public employment earnings, the wage subsidy, nor the earnings bonus would be adjusted for family size. While it is possible that the benefits of an employment-conditioned transfer program could vary by family size, phasing out the variable benefits as earnings rise would increase the tax rate if the break-even level is held constant. Because the committee

[11] Here, as in comparisons of AFDC with FAP, the impression should not be left that the benefits of these plans can be compared with precision. For example, child care would be subsidized to some extent under the committee plan. To the extent that working women required child care, their benefits under the committee's plan would be higher than those shown here and, therefore, would be closer to AFDC benefits.

wanted to keep the break-even level and the tax on earnings as low as possible, because it wanted payments to be related to work effort rather than need, and because it did not want to encourage families to have more children, it was willing to sacrifice the well-being of large families.[12]

II. Considerations for and against Interstate Differentials in Benefits

The broader issue, which is the main focus of this chapter, concerns the economic justifications for *any* interstate variation in welfare benefits. States are required to supplement SSI payments to prevent recipients from suffering a drop in benefits. Most other welfare reform proposals before Congress have permitted states to supplement the federal benefit; some bills have even provided federal financial assistance to the states for such supplementation. But these provisions have been the result of political compromise, not of reasoned analysis of their equity and economic efficiency. Supplements resolve the conflict between high-benefit states whose recipients would receive less under the proposed alternatives discussed earlier and low-benefit states that are reluctant to have a still higher level of federal benefits than in these alternatives. Can such supplementation be justified on economic grounds?

The economic reasons why benefits should or should not vary from one plan to another will be discussed here, as well as the appropriate federal policy toward such variation. Three arguments in favor of interarea differentials will be examined: differentials to adjust to area cost-of-living differences; state supplements to allow for varying income redistribution preferences; and supplements to provide for individuals' special needs. The rationale for federal financing will be considered in each case. The major argument against these three types of differentials is that they will create incentives for people to migrate. Unless this migration is desirable, it is a cost that must be balanced against the benefits resulting from the differentials.

Migration

Whether or not interarea differentials in welfare benefits stimulate migration to places where benefits are high is an empirical question. Circumstantial evidence suggests that interstate differentials in benefit levels do stimulate migration. The large-scale, postwar migration of blacks has been from low-benefit states to more generous ones, and the high-benefit

[12] The committee would permit state supplements to be related to family size.

states have experienced a large increase in their AFDC caseload. But, apart from this sort of argument, little is known about the effect of differentials on migration. How much do welfare differentials influence the decision to migrate? How important has migration, so motivated, been in increasing the caseload?

Economists now generally view migration as an investment in human capital. The decision to migrate is made by comparing the costs of migrating, both monetary and psychic, to the return obtained by migrating. The return is the change in a family's real income, where income includes not only earnings and income from property but transfer income, public services, climate, presence of friends, and other characteristics of a place that have positive value to a person or family. The return accrues over the future and, therefore, depends on the probability of receiving the various types of real income. The level of welfare benefits at a person's current and potential locations affects the return if he thinks that there is a probability of needing welfare at any time in the future. While some people may move with the explicit purpose of getting higher welfare benefits, knowing that there is a relatively good welfare program to fall back on can also affect the decision of a person who migrates with the intention of being self-supporting.

Empirical studies have shown the importance of total money income, which includes labor, property, and transfer income, in influencing migration. In only a few instances, however, has transfer income been included as a separate variable. Robert Reischauer, in explaining black migration from southern states to urban centers in the North and West, found that welfare opportunities in the South are not strong determinants of the volume of blacks leaving the region.[13] On the other hand, welfare opportunities in the northern and western urban areas are significant in explaining migration to these areas. He concludes that factors other than welfare are responsible for blacks fleeing the South, but that the choice of destination and the level of migration are related to welfare opportunities in the North and West.

Reischauer also examines whether or not welfare encourages people to stay in urban areas even though jobs there are scarce. Does welfare become an acceptable alternative to the low-wage jobs that have moved away? He finds that welfare does not hold blacks in central cities. This conclusion is supported by Lansing and Mueller, who find that welfare does not reduce mobility.[14]

---

[13] Robert D. Reischauer, "The Impact of the Welfare System on Black Migration and Marital Stability" (Ph.D. diss., Columbia University, New York, 1971).
[14] John B. Lansing and Eva Mueller, *The Geographic Mobility of Labor* (Ann Arbor, Mich.: Survey Research Center, Institute for Social Research, University of Michigan, 1967), pp. 323–332.

With inconclusive findings such as these, the burden of proof is on those who believe that welfare has no effect on the decision to migrate. Labor market conditions clearly influence migration. If earnings are important, the availability of transfer income should also enter the decision. Welfare income is discounted by the probability of needing it and the stigma of receiving it, but it should have some influence. Even if welfare benefits were equal in all areas, the availability of welfare income could increase migration by providing insurance against zero income should job opportunities in the new location be insufficient.

The conclusion to be drawn is that provisions for supplementing a uniform federal benefit should be designed with some regard for their effect on migration. There is a limit to the differentials by area that can be tolerated if a neutral effect on migration is sought. This is particularly important if a new program provides information on eligibility and payment levels, and recruits people who are eligible. If the government desired a nonneutral effect on migration, that is, if it were following an explicit policy of population redistribution, welfare benefits could be set to further such a policy.

Area Price and Cost Differentials

Because prices and the cost of living vary from one area of the country to another, a uniform cash benefit would enable recipients in some areas to achieve a higher standard of living than in others. Current federal income maintenance programs make no distinctions based on area price or cost differentials, nor do federal taxes. The uniformity of these programs is not generally considered an inequity, at least not relative to the other inequities of the programs. The reasoning behind this position is that people freely choose where they live, and do not have to tolerate relatively high prices and costs unless they choose to do so.

However, the objectives of the federal antipoverty programs do provide a justification for area differentials. In these programs, poor education, sickness, and large family size are considered factors over which people have little or no control, and they are not expected to change them as a condition of receiving benefits. The location of a person or family seems to be considered in a similar light: Someone living in an area with high costs or few job opportunities is not expected to migrate as a condition of receiving assistance. If the government considers a family's location to be fixed, then it should make cost-of-living adjustments if its objective is to guarantee a minimum real income.

A program that gives families in all locations enough income to attain the same standard of living or welfare would adjust benefits to reflect differences both in prices and in other factors affecting the cost of living.

These include climate, which influences shelter costs and clothing needs, transportation facilities relative to need, the quantity and quality of public services, the type and level of taxation, and recreational opportunities. They vary among warm and cold areas; inner city, suburb, small town, and farm; cities and states with high and low levels of services for the poor; cities and states with income taxes and sales taxes; and other factors.

The Bureau of Labor Statistics (BLS) has developed measures of living costs for forty metropolitan areas, and for nonmetropolitan areas as a group in the four census regions. Using information from a variety of sources, the BLS estimated the amount and quality of the items needed for a family of a certain size and composition to attain a given standard of living. Food, shelter, transportation, and clothing requirements vary from city to city and among regions. By pricing the set of items in each city, an estimate of the cost of living is obtained.

Unfortunately, use of a cost-of-living index like the one developed by the BLS to adjust income maintenance benefits is not entirely appropriate. The index would be appropriate only if it measured not just the cost of living but the benefits associated with the costs. People living in areas with high state and local taxes receive more public services. High rents may also reflect a greater level of public services. The index would also have to adjust accurately for the varying tastes of people who prefer certain life styles over others. For example, cold climates require higher fuel bills, but someone who enjoys winter sports receives a concomitant benefit.

The BLS assumptions about food preferences are particularly open to question. They assumed that preferences for food vary among regions, and found that food costs in southern cities were 92 to 95 percent of those for the country as a whole.[15] But it is likely that these preferences reflect only the low incomes of people in the South. When food preferences were assumed to be the same for all cities, food costs in southern cities were very close to the average.[16]

[15] U.S., Department of Labor, Bureau of Labor Statistics, *City Worker's Family Budget: Pricing, Procedure, Specifications, and Average Prices*, Bulletin No. 1570-3, Autumn 1966.
[16] Harold W. Watts uses the observed behavior of families rather than the judgment of government technicians to estimate area cost-of-living differentials. His Iso-Prop Index is based on the notion that families that are equally well off will spend the same proportions of their income on basic necessities. To determine the incomes in varying locations that provide the same level of well-being, he finds those incomes at which people spend the same proportion of their income on necessities. Although this procedure is appropriate under certain assumptions for adjusting for family size differentials, it is not an appropriate way to adjust for area differentials. If a person in a cold climate needs to spend more in order to keep his house at a given temperature, he would not also need to spend more on all other items than someone

Given that the technical judgments used to develop a BLS-type index cannot take differing tastes into account, it might be better to adjust benefits only for differences in prices. Price levels can be estimated with considerably more objectivity. The choice of which bundle of commodities to use as weights in the index requires some assumptions concerning tastes, but not as many as needed for the BLS cost-of-living index. An index calculated by pricing the same bundle of goods in various regions is shown in Table 12.2. As would be expected, the variation in this price index is smaller than the variation in the cost-of-living index.

These price indexes reveal another difficulty that must be faced in adjusting cash benefits. The price variation within regions is larger than the variation among them. Price-level adjustments between closely situated areas would adjust for a great deal of the total variation, but it is precisely these adjustments that could most easily influence migration. In dividing the country into the price-level areas, therefore, there is a trade-off between the accuracy of price-level adjustment and the minimization of its effect on migration. Because prices vary within regions, the smaller the area adjusted for, the more accurate the measurement. On the

Table 12.2 Price Index Based on the Bureau of Labor Statistics Lower Budget for a Four-Person Family, Spring 1970

	Non-metropolitan areas	Metropolitan areas			Total all urban areas
		Population 50,000 to 1,000.000	Population 1,000,000 and over	All metropolitan areas	
South	93	99	100	99	97
Northeast	92	98	100	100	99
North Central	95	99	102	101	100
West	98	99	108	106	105
Urban United States	94	99	102	101	100

Source—Unpublished table received from the Bureau of Labor Statistics.
Note—The price index was calculated using metropolitan area average quantity weights for all locations.

in a warm climate. If he spent more money on heat and also spent the same proportion of his income on heat as someone in a warm climate, his expenditures on other items and, consequently, his total standard of living would be higher than someone in a warm climate. Harold W. Watts, "The Iso-Prop Index: An Approach to the Determination of Different Poverty Income Thresholds," *Journal of Human Resources* 2 (Winter 1967).

other hand, the smaller the area, the smaller the cost of moving from one to another.

If the federal government decides that price-level differences are large enough to warrant the costs of surveys to measure the differences and the migration that might result from varying benefit levels, the federal benefit could be adjusted to take the differential into account. Payments made to families with no income could vary in direct proportion to the price index for the area. The 100 percent disregard under FAP and SSI could be varied accordingly, although it might not be worth sacrificing the simplicity of the program for such a small amount. The tax rate on earnings under FAP, SSI, and the demogrant would be the same for all areas. Public employment wages also could be varied in proportion to the price index.

Structuring State Supplements to Be Consistent with Federal Programs

Many people would receive less under the three proposed alternative programs than under the four Public Assistance programs, as was shown in the first section of this chapter. Even if the federal benefits were adjusted for differences in the cost of living, people in many states would continue to be worse off. It is, therefore, likely that some states would desire to supplement the federal benefit. Regardless of whether or not it is economically efficient for states to supplement,[17] a federal law prohibiting supplementation would probably be unconstitutional. Assuming that states will supplement, what should be the policy of the federal government toward supplementation?

[17] For a more complete discussion of this, see James M. Buchanan and Richard E. Wagner, "An Efficiency Basis for Federal Fiscal Equalization," in *The Analysis of Public Output*, ed. Julius Margolis (New York: National Bureau of Economic Research, 1970). If the residents of a state prefer a greater degree of income redistribution than the country as a whole, their well-being is greater if the additional redistribution is permitted. Whether or not supplementation leads to economic efficiency in the economy as a whole cannot be determined a priori. A supplement will tend to reduce outmigration of low-skilled people and to increase immigration of low-skilled people from other states. Whether or not this is efficient depends on the productivity of labor in the supplementing states relative to productivity of labor in other states and the externalities resulting from population levels and shifts. It is likely that states that supplement will have higher incomes than those that do not. This means that the supplementation will attract unskilled labor into areas where their productivity is greater, thereby increasing total output. It is difficult to generalize about whether these higher-income states would experience positive or negative externalities owing to a larger population.

The federal role in financing state supplements will be discussed in the next section. The concern here is with the constraints that the federal government should place on the states so that the supplements are consistent with the objectives of the federal program. State supplements can easily destroy the desirable features of a federal program. The greatest danger is that they will reduce the incentive to work and reintroduce the incentive for family break-up.

To maintain work incentives, the state supplement should not increase the tax rate implicit in the federal benefit. An example illustrates how this could be done. If the federal government paid benefits according to the schedule in FAP, and a state had an AFDC payment standard of $3000, the state would have to disregard all income below $4320 and tax the remainder at 67 percent. This is shown in Table 12.3. In order to preserve the work incentives of the federal program, the states must also give supplements to people with earnings between the federal break-even of $4320 and the state break-even of $5220. If they do not, these people could obtain higher total incomes by reducing their earnings to below $4320.

The SSI program does not constrain the tax rate imposed by the state supplement. Considering the low employability of most recipients, this is not a serious drawback. FAP requires that state supplements given to families who receive federal benefits do not increase the tax rate of the federal program: A family of four with income below $4320 could not have its income taxed at a rate above two-thirds. This means that the state supplement could not decline as earnings rise from $0 to $4320. But if the

Table 12.3   State Supplement Required to Keep Tax Rate of Federal Program Unchanged

Earnings[a]	Federal benefit under FAP[a]	State supplement[a]	Total income[a]	Marginal tax rate
0	2400	600	3000	0
720	2400	600	3720	$\frac{2}{3}$
1000	2213	600	3813	$\frac{2}{3}$
2000	1546	600	4146	$\frac{2}{3}$
3000	879	600	4479	$\frac{2}{3}$
4320	0	600	4920	$\frac{2}{3}$
4620	0	400	5020	$\frac{2}{3}$
4920	0	200	5120	$\frac{2}{3}$
5220	0	0	5220	$\frac{2}{3}$

[a] In dollars.

family's income were above $4320, the state could tax it at 100 percent.[18] This would permit the states to tax AFDC recipients at a considerably higher rate than they do now.

The Senate Finance Committee proposal would also prevent the state supplements from undermining the work incentives of the federal program. State benefits would have to be computed under the assumption that individuals eligible to participate in the federal employment program are actually participating and receiving $200 per month. That is, someone who is eligible to work but not actually working would receive the same supplement as someone earning $200. The state would also have to disregard completely all earnings between $200 and $367 of someone employed full time at $2 per hour. Beyond this income, the states are free to use any tax rate they choose.

The incentives for family stability provided by the federal program can be preserved by paying supplements to all people eligible for the federal benefits. If families headed by men are eligible for federal benefits but not for the state supplement, the federal program would be undermined. The state supplement should also adjust payments for family size in a similar, although not necessarily identical, way as the federal program. For example, if a demogrant bases payments solely on the ages of the family members, the supplement should not introduce incentives for family splitting by making payments for each child decline with the number of children in the family.

The provisions for state supplementation in FAP and the Senate Finance Committee plan counter the incentives for family stability embodied in the federal payment structures. They would permit the states virtually to reestablish the AFDC program on top of the uniform federal benefit structure. Under FAP, states could exclude families with both parents present and able to work, regardless of whether or not they are actually employed, or they could exclude families where the father is actually employed full time. The Senate Finance Committee proposal also would permit states to restrict supplements to families headed by women.

---

[18] The bill is ambiguous about the tax rate the states may impose on families with incomes above the federal break-even point. Section 2156(b)(1)(B) was intended to mean that the states could not impose a tax rate of more than 100 percent on families with incomes above the federal break-even. However, the language of the section is not precise and has been interpreted by some to mean that the states could cease supplementing a family as soon as that family's income rose above the federal break-even point. That is, the state supplement could stay constant as earnings rose from $0 to $4320, and could fall to zero as earnings rose to $4321. This would imply a tax rate of well over 100 percent and would provide an incentive for families to keep their income below $4320 and continue to receive the supplement.

That is, states would have the option of extending aid to all families or maintaining the existing Public Assistance categories.

In these provisions regarding the tax rate and coverage of the state supplements, Congress was being sensitive to the pressures on the states. They realized that welfare recipients whose new federal benefits would be less than under AFDC would come to the states asking for supplementation. For the states to deny them would be politically unpopular, but to supplement all recipients under FAP or the committee plan would be costly. Permitting states to perpetuate the categories and raise the tax rate relieves states of this predicament. However, it makes a mockery of FAP or the committee plan as a "welfare reform" bill.

Federal Financing of State Supplements: Adjustment to the New Benefit Level

If the federal government pays a uniform benefit to people in all states, adjusted perhaps for differences in price levels, is there any reason it should also help finance state supplements? It can be argued that using federal funds to encourage state supplementation would result in more total funds being given to the poor. On the other hand, it can also be argued that the federal government's desire to give money to the poor is satisfied by the uniform federal benefit and that the people of states that choose not to supplement should not be made to share in the cost of the other states' supplements. There is no unequivocal answer to this question; it depends on which states choose to supplement and by how much.[19]

---

[19] The desirability of federal grants to states for this purpose depends upon whether or not the grants increase economic efficiency and interpersonal equity. A grant will be accompanied by some combination of an increase in state supplements and a decrease in state taxes. This will tend to encourage migration into the state. The grant increases efficiency if the induced migration is from states where labor productivity is low to those where it is high, and if it provides incentives that reduce undesirable externalities. The equity of the grant depends on whether it equalizes the welfare of individuals in similar circumstances living in different states.

The richer states are more likely to supplement the federal benefits than are the lower-income states. Grants to higher-income states will be efficient if they encourage migration to these states and if this is not offset by externalities resulting from crowding. However, grants to high-income states will tend to be inequitable by increasing the disparity in income levels between people in high- and low-income states. This will be offset, to some degree, if people in the lower-income states desire that the higher-income states supplement. They will then experience an increase in well-being that will compensate them for the higher taxes required to finance the grant made to the higher-income states.

There is a more clear-cut justification for temporary federal aid to the states following the introduction of a program like FAP or the demogrant. If neither the states nor the federal government supplemented the uniform federal payment under a new program, many recipients would be worse off than before. They could object validly that they have become accustomed to a certain level of income and that a sudden drop would cause temporary difficulties as they adjusted to the lower level.

Welfare recipients would look to the states to supplement the federal benefits. If the states were to do so, and prevent recipients from being worse off, the states themselves might be worse off. That is, the cost of supplementing the federal benefit might be greater than present state and local expenditures for Public Assistance. States could argue, justifiably, that the federal government suddenly reduced its support, and that they should be compensated for such a change in policy.

The federal government, rather than the states, could assume responsibility for temporary supplementation while recipients adjust to a lower benefit level. This would have the advantage of putting no added financial pressure on those states where the cost of supplementation would be greater than previous state and local expenditures for Public Assistance. On the other hand, the federal government might be amenable to pressures to continue paying the supplements after the adjustment period. Furthermore, because Public Assistance benefits are determined by a complex procedure, with a high degree of administrative discretion, the federal government would have difficulty in paying recipients an amount that would leave them as well off as under Public Assistance. The federal government could most easily provide supplements equal to some *average* difference between the Public Assistance payments and the new program. But this would mean a significant change in benefits for individual families, and would make the supplement less effective in helping recipients adjust gradually to the lower benefit levels.

Assuming, then, that the states administer the temporary supplement, how should the federal government help finance it? Matching grants could be given that would depend on the amount of supplementation and thereby reduce the cost to the states of giving an additional dollar of welfare—as do the current matching formulas used in Public Assistance. The reduced price would provide an incentive for the states to supplement the federal benefits, and the greater the price reduction, the greater the incentive. There is no guarantee that the states would supplement up to the current level of Public Assistance payments, even if the price to the states were reduced to zero. But it is difficult to see why states would refuse to supplement if the price to them is no more than the price of Public Assistance now.

The danger in reducing the price to the states is probably not that they would supplement inadequately, but that they would supplement beyond the present level of welfare benefits.[20] In order to prevent this, it would be necessary to impose a limit on the amount of federal matching. This limit, of course, would have to vary from state to state. Defining such a limit would require either that the federal government determine what the states' Public Assistance payment levels would have been (which would be a large task), or that the limit be based on criteria other than Public Assistance payment levels.

Another approach would be to give grants to the states that would not depend on the amount of supplementation and, therefore, would not reduce the price to the states of paying an additional dollar. These flat grants would be based on some other criteria such as (1) the difference between the federal grants under Public Assistance and the new federal benefits to recipients in the former welfare categories or (2) the state's ability to pay the supplements. The grants would encourage states to pay supplements because of the increased revenues available to them. But because the grant would be fixed and would not increase with the amount of supplementation, states would not be encouraged to supplement far beyond the present level of welfare benefits. The drawback to this approach is that states might not supplement enough to prevent welfare recipients from being worse off than under Public Assistance. States could be required to supplement a certain amount as a condition of receiving the grant, but it would be difficult for the federal government to insure that they supplement just enough to leave no one worse off.

The choice between a matching grant and a flat grant depends, in large part, on the extent to which the purpose of federal financial support is to protect welfare recipients against lower incomes, or to protect the states against higher costs. A matching grant, if the federal share were large enough, would be likely to induce the states to maintain the incomes of welfare recipients at their previous levels. The cost of this approach is the possibility that states would make higher payments than before. A flat grant would not provide as strong an incentive to maintain the income of recipients, but would also not create the possibility of increasing state supplements.

The choice between a matching and flat grant requires an estimation of the political power of welfare recipients. Assume the federal govern-

---

[20] This may or may not be desirable, as discussed earlier in footnote 17. If the objective of the grant is to encourage the states to supplement so that recipients can adjust gradually to a lower level of benefits, then the states should be discouraged from supplementing beyond the present level of welfare benefits.

ment made flat grants that equaled the excess of previous federal grants for Public Assistance over the new federal benefits to recipients in the former welfare categories. These grants would be appropriate if welfare recipients had enough power to pressure the states to maintain their incomes at the former level, given that this would impose no additional cost to the states. If, on the other hand, one believes that the states would not use the flat grant to help recipients to adjust to a lower level of benefits, a matching grant would be more appropriate.

A third approach is used by the SSI program, similar to that contained in H.R. 1 as passed by the House. States are required to supplement SSI so that no one receiving Public Assistance when SSI became effective would suffer a drop in benefits. The federal government provides financial support for the states, but only on a limited basis and only on the condition that the federal government administer the supplement.

The amount of the supplement the federal government pays depends on a complicated set of rules involving the previous level of a state's welfare benefits and the state's total welfare expenditures. If a state supplements the federal benefit below or up to a certain level, called the "adjusted payment level," the state is guaranteed that it will not have to spend more for welfare than it did in 1972. The adjusted payment level is the amount of money an individual or family (of a given size) with no other income would have received in January 1972. The state pays 100 percent of the cost of the supplements until its expenditures reach the 1972 level, and the federal government pays all the remainder. But the federal government will not absorb any of the costs of the supplements above the adjusted payment level. Nor will it pay the cost of extending the supplements to families outside the state's previous Public Assistance categories.

This approach has the advantage of guaranteeing that the former Public Assistance recipients will receive adequate supplementation and that the states will not experience a sudden increase in welfare costs. However, it may be a complex system to administer. Controversy could arise over the computation of the adjusted payment level, and conflicts between the states and the federal government are likely to develop over the federal government's administration of the states' supplements.

According to congressional estimates, federal benefits under the SSI program would be greater than the combined value of Public Assistance and the bonus value of Food Stamps in twenty states. In ten states, federal benefits would be less than the combined value of Public Assistance and the Food Stamp bonus, but the cost of a supplement to bring total benefits up to this level would be less than the states' 1972 expenditures. The remaining twenty-one states qualify for federal grants if they wish to supplement to maintain past benefit levels, provided that the supplements are administered by the federal government.

The Senate Finance Committee plan would not require the federal government to administer state supplements as a condition for financial support. However, it would put strict limits on the amount of federal grants to the states. Federal financial support for AFDC would be a block grant adjusted over time only for changes in a state's population. The grant would equal the federal grant for AFDC in 1972 plus one-half of the state costs in 1972 or, if less, the amount needed in 1972 to bring welfare families' income up to $1600 for a family of two, $2000 for a family of three, and $2400 for a family of four or more. The grant would be reduced by an unspecified amount after the employment program became effective in 1974, to reflect the fact that families with children aged six or more would be ineligible for AFDC. After that time, the grant would be changed only to reflect changes in the state's total population.

Compared with the SSI approach, the committee's grant formulas have the advantage of being unambiguous about the level of state payments that the federal government would support, and the federal government would be relieved of the administrative burden of making complicated calculations regarding how much of the state payments would be subject to federal support. Compared with SSI, where the federal government will pay the full cost in twenty-one states of supplements between the states' expenditures in 1972 and the "adjusted payment level," the committee plan would provide less incentive for the states to supplement recipients to keep them from becoming worse off than they currently are.

Special Needs

Under the state Public Assistance programs, caseworkers have been given a certain amount of discretion to give recipients additional money if they have unusual demands on their income. In contrast, federal benefits under SSI, FAP, a demogrant, and the Senate Finance Committee plan would be uniform, based on the presumed need of an average person. While the elimination of administrative discretion in the proposed programs reduces the potential for inequitable treatment, it also removes some desirable flexibility. What would someone do if his house burned down? What would a blind person do who could not manage for himself and required an attendant or boarding home care?

It seems clear that the income maintenance system should retain the flexibility to help people with unusual needs and that this requires administrative discretion exercised at the local level. State supplements for special needs are an appropriate method of providing this flexibility. The question remains whether or not federal financing is appropriate and, if so, how financing can be limited so that payments for special needs do not become a general supplement to the federal benefit.

Federal financing is appropriate if the objective of a federally provided minimum income is to guarantee people a minimum level of well-being. Attaining such a level depends on having enough income relative to the demands on it. We recognize that income relative to demands is the relevant criterion when we adjust benefits for age or family size. In much the same way, extraordinarily large needs over which people have no control increase the income required to attain a given level of well-being.

The problem is that special needs cannot be defined as clearly as can age or family size. What may appear to one administrator as an uncontrollable demand on a family's income may not be considered so by another. But the fact that administrators may not agree on what constitutes a special need should not end all federal efforts to help persons in unfortunate situations.

While federal offices could be set up in the localities, it would be more efficient for state or local agencies to provide such assistance. Federal grants could be made to the states based on the number of low-income persons in the state, the assumption being that each person has the same chance of having a special need. The choice between flat or matching grants up to some amount depends on whether it is considered desirable to use federal funds to encourage some states to spend more on the poor or to spread the funds evenly among the poor in all states.

III. Conclusions

A federal program providing benefits in the range discussed here—$1200 to $1560 for an adult and $2400 to $3000 for a family of four—leaves many people worse off than they are under the state Public Assistance programs (of course, many people will be better off, but that is not the focus here). The changes are large in some cases, and vary enormously from one family to another, depending on the family's sources of income, types of expenditures, special needs, the area it lives in, and, to some extent, on its caseworker. Over time, federal benefits may grow to be as large as Public Assistance benefits in the high-benefit states. And, certainly, normal caseload turnover will minimize long-term losses for individual families. But, in the interim, states are and will be under great pressure to supplement the federal payments.

Whether or not the federal government should build interstate differentials into the federal benefit structure, or help finance state supplements, depends on several factors. Adjusting the federal benefits for area differences in price level is justified by the goals of a federal transfer program to reduce poverty and would, as a by-product, cushion some recipients against a drop in benefits. However, because prices vary among closely situated areas, accurate price adjustments would create incentives to migrate that might be undesirable. It is also questionable whether or not the magnitude of the price differentials warrants the administrative cost of adjusting for them.

In the relatively short run, until recipients have adjusted to lower benefit levels, or the states that desire to supplement have adjusted to higher welfare costs, federal grants to the states for supplementation appear appropriate. However, federal grants for the purpose of helping the states through a transitional period should not be allowed to encourage them to make greater supplements. This means that funds given to the states should be in the form of block, rather than matching, grants.

Whether federal grants to the states for supplementation should be made a permanent feature of the system has not been resolved here. Grants to the states for the types of special needs discussed in the last section seem appropriate. The system should retain flexibility to help people in unusual circumstances and this can best be done at the local level. However, it is less certain that grants should be made to states for general supplementation of the uniform federal benefit. If the country had an explicit policy for redistributing the population, grants would be an appropriate tool for encouraging migration. But a strong case cannot be made for grants to the states for supplementation solely to improve the distribution of income among individuals.

Appendix

Excerpts from *Report*
of the Committee on
Ways and Means on H.R. 1[1]

. . . .

D. Provisions Relating to Family Programs

The present program of Aid to Families with Dependent Children (AFDC) would be repealed effective July 1, 1972, and two new totally federal programs would take effect on that day. The new programs would be adopted for a period of five years (through fiscal year 1977) in order to give Congress an opportunity to review their operation before continuing them in subsequent years. The new programs would be established by a new Title XXI in the Social Security Act. A description of the two new programs follows:

Families in which at least one person is employable would be enrolled in the Opportunities for Families program, administered by the Department of Labor. Families with no employable person would be enrolled in the Family Assistance Plan administered by the Department of Health, Education, and Welfare.

1. Opportunities for Families Program

REGISTRATION FOR EMPLOYMENT AND TRAINING

Every member of a family who is found to be available for work by the Secretary of Health, Education, and Welfare would be required to register for manpower services, training and employment.

[1] U.S., 92d Cong., 1st sess., 26 May 1971, pp. 28–36. Minor changes have been made in capitalization and punctuation, to bring this section into conformity with other chapters in this volume. These changes in no way affect the sense of these excerpts.

An individual would be considered available for work unless such person—

1. is unable to work or be trained because of illness, incapacity, or age;
2. is a mother or other relative caring for a child under age three (age six until July 1974);
3. is the mother or other female caretaker of a child, if the father or another adult male relative is in the home and is registered;
4. is a child under the age of sixteen (or a student up to age twenty-two);
5. is needed in the home on a continuous basis because of illness or incapacity of another family member.

Nevertheless, any person (except one who is ill, incapacitated, or aged) who would be exempted from registering by the above provisions could voluntarily register.

Every person who registered (other than a volunteer) would be required to participate in manpower services or training and to accept available employment. An individual could not be required to accept employment, however—

1. if the position offered is vacant due to a strike, lockout, or other labor dispute;
2. if the wages and other employment conditions are contrary to those prescribed by applicable federal, state, or local law, or less favorable than those prevailing for similar work in the locality, or the wages are less than an hourly rate of $\frac{3}{4}$ of the highest federal minimum wage ($1.20 per hour under present law);
3. if membership in a company union or nonmembership in a bona fide union is required;
4. if he has demonstrated the capacity to obtain work that would better enable him to achieve self-sufficiency, and such work is available.

CHILD CARE AND OTHER SUPPORTIVE SERVICES

The Secretary of Labor directly or by using child care projects under the jurisdiction of the Department of Health, Education, and Welfare, would provide for child care services for registrants who require them in order to accept or continue to participate in manpower services, training, employment, or vocational rehabilitation.

The Secretary of Labor would be authorized funds to provide child care by grant or contract. Families receiving such services might also be required to pay all or part of the costs involved.

Health, vocational rehabilitation, family planning, counseling, social, and other supportive services (including physical examinations and minor medical services) would also be made available by the Secretary of Labor to registrants as needed.

OPERATION OF MANPOWER SERVICES, TRAINING AND
EMPLOYMENT PROGRAMS

The Secretary of Labor would develop an employability plan designed to prepare registrants to be self-supporting. The secretary would then provide the necessary services, training, counseling, testing, coaching, program orientation, job training, and followup services to assist the registrant in securing employment, retaining employment, and obtaining opportunities for advancement.

Provision would also be made for voluntary relocation assistance to enable a registrant and his family to be self-supporting.

Public service employment programs would also be used to provide needed jobs. Public service projects would be related to the fields of health, social service, environmental protection, education, urban and rural development and redevelopment, welfare, recreation, public facility and similar activities. The Secretary of Labor would establish these programs through grants or by contract with public or nonprofit agencies or organizations. The law would provide safeguards for workers on such jobs, and wages could not be less than the higher of the prevailing or applicable minimum wage or the federal minimum wage.

Federal participation in the costs of an individual's participation in a public service employment program would be 100 percent for the first year of his employment, 75 percent for the second year, and 50 percent for the third year.

States and their subdivisions that receive federal grants would be required to provide the Secretary of Labor with up-to-date listings of job vacancies. The secretary would also agree with certain federal agencies to establish annual or other goals for employment of members of families receiving assistance.

ALLOWANCES OF INDIVIDUALS PARTICIPATING IN TRAINING

An incentive allowance of $30 per month would be paid to each registrant who participates in manpower training (states would have the option of providing an additional allowance of up to $30). Necessary costs for transportation and similar expenses would also be paid.

UTILIZATION OF OTHER PROGRAMS

The Secretary of Labor would be required to integrate this program as needed with all other manpower training programs involving all sectors of the economy and all levels of government.

REHABILITATION SERVICES FOR INCAPACITATED FAMILY
MEMBERS

Family members who are incapacitated would be referred to the state vocational rehabilitation service. A quarterly review of their incapacities would usually be made.

Each such incapacitated individual would be required to accept rehabilitation services that are made available to him, and an allowance of $30 would be paid him while he receives such services. (States would have the option of providing an additional allowance of up to $30.) Necessary costs for transportation and similar expenses would also be paid.

. . . .

2. *Family Assistance Plan*

PAYMENT OF BENEFITS

All eligible families with no member available for employment would be enrolled and paid benefits by the Secretary of Health, Education, and Welfare.

REHABILITATION SERVICES AND CHILD CARE FOR INCAPACITATED FAMILY MEMBERS

Family members who are unemployable because of incapacity would be referred to state vocational rehabilitation agencies for services. A quarterly review of their incapacities would usually be made. Such persons would be required to accept services made available, and would be paid a $30 per month incentive allowance plus transportation and other related costs. (States would have the option of providing an additional allowance of up to $30.)

Child care services would also be provided if needed to enable individuals to take vocational rehabilitation services.

Women of child-bearing age would be offered family planning services and the services would be provided if accepted.

. . . .

3. *Determination of Benefits*

UNIFORM DETERMINATIONS

Both secretaries would be required to apply the same interpretations and applications of fact to arrive at uniform determinations of eligibility and assistance payment amounts under the two family programs.

ELIGIBILITY FOR AND AMOUNT OF BENEFITS

Family benefits would be computed at the rate of $800 per year for the first two members, $400 for the next three members, $300 for the next two members and $200 for the next member. This would provide $2400 for a family of four, and the maximum amount which any family could receive would be $3600. A family would not be eligible if it had countable resources in excess of $1500 or less.

If any member of the family fails to register, take required employment or training, or accept vocational rehabilitation services, the family benefits would be reduced by $800 per year.

Benefits would be determined on the basis of the family's income for the current quarter and the three preceding quarters.

After a family has been paid benefits for twenty-four consecutive months, a new application would be required which would be processed as if it were an initial application.

The secretary would establish the circumstances under which gross income from a trade or business, including farming, is large enough to preclude eligibility (net income notwithstanding).

Families would have to apply for all other benefits available to them in order to be eligible.

A family headed by a regular, full-time college student would not be eligible.

DEFINITION OF INCOME

Earned income would follow generally the definition of earnings used in applying the earnings limitation of the Social Security program. Unearned income means all other forms of income among which are benefits from other public and private programs, prizes and awards, proceeds of life insurance not needed for last illness and burial (with a maximum of $1500), gifts, support, inheritances, grants, dividends, interests and so forth.

All income except that excluded would be used to reduce the benefits otherwise payable.

The following items would be excluded from the income of a family:

1. Earnings of a student regularly attending school, with limits set by the Secretary.
2. Irregular earned income of an individual of $30 or less in a quarter and irregular unearned income of $60 or less in a quarter.
3. Earned income used to pay the cost of child care under a schedule prescribed by the Secretary.
4. The first $720 per year of other earned income plus one-third of the remainder.
5. Assistance based on need received from public or private agencies, except veterans' pensions.
6. Training allowances.
7. The tuition part of scholarships and fellowships.
8. Home produce.
9. One-third of child support and alimony.
10. Foster care payments for a child placed in the family by a child placement agency.

The total of the exclusions under (1), (2), and (3) above could not exceed $2000 for a family of four rising by $200 for each additional member to an overall maximum of $3000.

EXCLUSIONS FROM RESOURCES

A family cannot be eligible for payments if it has resources in excess of $1500. In determining what is included in the $1500 amount, the following items are excluded:

1. The home to the extent that its value does not exceed a reasonable amount.
2. Household goods and personal effects not in excess of a reasonable amount.
3. Other property which is essential to the family's self-support.

An insurance policy would be counted only to the extent of its cash surrender value except that if the total face value of all such policies with respect to an individual is $1500 or less, no cash surrender value would be counted.

The secretary would prescribe periods of time, and manners in which, property must be disposed of in order that it would not be included as resources.

MEANING OF FAMILY AND CHILD

A family would be defined as two or more related people living together in the United States where at least one of the members is a citizen or a lawfully admitted alien and where at least one of them is a child dependent on someone else in the family.

No family will be eligible if the head of the household is an undergraduate or graduate student regularly attending a college or university full time. Benefits would not be payable to an individual for any month in which he is outside the United States.

The term "child" means an unmarried person who is not the head of the household, and who is either under the age of eighteen or under the age of twenty-two if attending school regularly.

Appropriate state law would be used in determining relationships.

The income and resources of an adult (other than a parent or the spouse of a parent) living with the family but not contributing to the family would be disregarded and the adult will not be considered a family member.

If an individual takes benefits under adult assistance, he could not be eligible for family benefits.

OPTIONAL STATE SUPPLEMENTATION

If a state decides to supplement the basic federal payment, it would be required to provide benefit amounts that do not undermine the earnings disregard provision. A state could agree to have the federal government make the supplementary payments on behalf of the state. If a state agrees to have the federal government make its supplemental payments, the federal government would pay the full administrative costs of making such payments, but if it makes its own payments the state would pay all of such costs.

States could, but would not be required to, cover under Medicaid persons who are made newly eligible for cash benefits under the bill.

The federal government, in administering supplemental benefits on behalf of a state, would be required to recognize a duration of residency requirement if the state decided to impose such a requirement.

4. Procedural and General Provisions

PAYMENTS AND PROCEDURES

The secretary would be permitted to pay the benefits at such times as best carry out the purposes of the title and could make payments to a person other than a member of the family or to an agency where he finds inability to manage funds. The secretary's decision would be subject to hearing and review.

The family benefits could not be paid to an individual who failed to register, or take work, training or vocational rehabilitation.

Cash advances of $100 or less could be paid if a family appears to meet all the eligibility requirements and is faced with a financial emergency.

The secretary may arrange for adjustment and recovery in the event of overpayments or underpayments, with a view toward equity and avoiding penalizing people who were without fault.

People who are, or claim to be, eligible for assistance payments, and who disagree with determinations of the secretary, could obtain hearings if they request them within thirty days. Final determinations would be subject to judicial review in federal district courts, but the secretary's decisions as to any fact would be conclusive and not subject to review by the courts. The secretary would also be given authority to appoint qualified people to serve as hearing examiners without their having to meet the specific standards prescribed under the Administrative Procedure Act for hearing examiners.

The right of any person to any future benefit would not be transferable or assignable, and no money payable under this title would be subject to execution, levy, attachment, garnishment, or other legal process.

In addition, the secretary would establish necessary rules and regulations dealing with proofs and evidence, and the method of taking and furnishing the same, in order to establish the right to benefits.

Each family would be required to submit a report of income within thirty days after the end of a quarter and benefits would be stopped until the report was filed. If a family failed, without good cause, to report income or changes in circumstances as required by the secretary, it would be subject to a penalty of $25 the first time, $50 the second time, and $100 for later times.

The head of any federal agency would be required to provide such information as the Secretary of HEW needs to determine eligibility for benefits under this title.

PENALTIES FOR FRAUD

A penalty of $1000 or one year imprisonment, or both, would be provided in the case of fraud under the program.

. . . .

CHILD CARE

The Secretaries of Labor and Health, Education, and Welfare are each given the authority and responsibility for arranging day care for their respective recipients under the Opportunities for Families program and the Family Assistance Plan who need such day care in order to participate in training, employment, or vocational rehabilitation. Where such care can be obtained in facilities developed by the Secretary of Health, Education, and Welfare, these would be utilized.

Insofar as possible, arrangements would be made for after-school care with local educational agencies. All day care would be subject to standards developed by the Secretary of Health, Education, and Welfare, with the concurrence of the Secretary of Labor. Both secretaries would have authority to make grants and contracts for payment of up to 100 percent of the cost of care. The Secretary of Health, Education, and Welfare would have total responsibility for construction of facilities. $700 million would be authorized for the provision of child care services in the first fiscal year, and such sums as Congress may appropriate in subsequent years. In addition, $50 million would be authorized for construction and renovation of child care facilities for each fiscal year.

OBLIGATIONS OF PARENTS

A deserting parent would be obligated to the United States for the amount of any federal payments made to his family less any amount that he actually contributes by court order or otherwise to the family.

Any parent of a child receiving benefits who travels in interstate commerce to avoid supporting his child would be guilty of a misdemeanor and subject to a fine of $1000, imprisonment for one year, or both.

The secretary would report to appropriate officials cases of child neglect or abuse which came to his attention while administering the program.

LOCAL COMMITTEES TO EVALUATE PROGRAM

Local advisory committees would be set up throughout the country, with a minimum of one in each state, which would evaluate and report on the effectiveness of the elements of the program designed to help people become self-supporting. Each committee would be composed of representatives from labor, business, and the public, as well as public officials not directly involved in the administration of the programs.

E. Other Related Assistance Provisions

. . . .

PROHIBITION AGAINST PARTICIPATION IN FOOD STAMP PROGRAM BY RECIPIENTS OF PAYMENTS UNDER FAMILY AND ADULT ASSISTANCE PROGRAMS

The bill would amend the Food Stamp Act of 1964 by providing that families and adults eligible for benefits under the assistance programs in this bill would be excluded from participation in the Food Stamp program.

. . . .

DETERMINATION OF MEDICAL ELIGIBILITY

The secretary would be able to enter into agreements with states under which the secretary would determine eligibility for Medicaid both for those eligible for federal payments and the medically needy in cases where the state covered the medically needy. The state would pay half of the secretary's additional administrative costs arising from carrying out the agreement.

. . . .

LIMITATIONS ON INCREASES IN STATE WELFARE EXPENDITURES

States would be guaranteed that, if they make payments supplementary to the federal adult or family programs, it would cost them no more to do so than the amount of their total expenditures for cash public assistance payments during calendar year 1971, to the extent that the federal payments and the state supplementary payments to recipients do not exceed the payment levels in effect under the public assistance programs in the state for January 1971. The value of Food Stamps would be taken into account in computing whether the guarantee would go into effect if the state pays in cash the value of Food Stamps. Most states would save money under the provisions of the bill; this provision would guarantee that no state would lose money.

LIMITATION ON FEDERAL EXPENDITURES FOR SOCIAL SERVICES

The federal government would continue to provide 75 percent matching funds to the states for child care and family planning services on an open-end appropriation basis. Federal matching for other specified social services would be limited to the amounts appropriated by the Congress.

Subject Index